Gateway to Music

An Introduction to American Vernacular, Western Art, and World Musical Traditions

Jocelyn Nelson

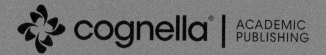

Bassim Hamadeh, CEO and Publisher
Amy Stone, Acquisitions Editor
Berenice Quirino, Associate Production Editor
Miguel Macias, Senior Graphic Designer
Trey Soto, Licensing Associate
Don Kesner, Interior Designer
Natalie Piccotti, Senior Marketing Manager
Kassie Graves, Director of Acquisitions and Sales
Jamie Giganti, Senior Managing Editor

"Appendix: Musical Elements" images courtesy of Bo Newsome and Paul Daniel.

Printed in the United States of America.

ISBN: 978-1-63487-945-3 (pbk) / 978-1-63487-946-0 (br)

Gateway to Music

An Introduction to American Vernacular, Western Art, and World Musical Traditions

CONTENTS

Acknowledgments

I thank my students at East Carolina University, who inspired this book with their curiosity about music. All of my hardworking graduate assistants and several former students deserve thanks, especially Sarah Hemminger, Colleen Hussion, Joseph Roenbeck, and Melody Steinbart for their comments and help in regard to this book.

I owe special thanks to my colleague Bo Newsome of East Carolina University, who has adopted preliminary editions of this book while teaching the same course as I do and, with the help of Paul Jason Daniel, has clarified important concepts in this text with his illustrations for the musical elements appendix in this first edition. His friendship, constructive comments, and collaborative presence continue to benefit this book and, thus, our students.

Additionally, the following peer reviewers and colleagues helped develop this book with information and insightful comments:

The late George Broussard, East Carolina University

Amy Carr-Richardson, East Carolina University

Mamadi Corra, East Carolina University

Felix Cox, Latham United Methodist Church

Harley Dartt, East Carolina University

Rai d'Honoré, Occitan Cultural Initiatives

Michael Dixon, University of Richmond

Miranda Fedock, The City University of New York

Michael Fink, University of Texas, San Antonio

Randy Gilland, East Carolina University

John Given, East Carolina University

John Griffiths, Monash University

Daniel Guberman, Purdue University

Gregory Hurley, East Carolina University

Bill C. Malone, Tulane University

The late Patrick O'Brien, Lute Society of America and New York Continuo Collective

Anna Ochs, Purdue University

Mario Rey, East Carolina University

Brenda Romero, University of Colorado, Boulder

Anthony Seeger, University of California, Los Angeles

Mort Stine, East Carolina University

Yale Strom, Founder of Hot Pstromi, klezmer scholar-performer

Caroline Usher, Duke University and Lute Society of America

Lori Wacker, East Carolina University

All of these scholars as well as my anonymous peer reviewers have been generous with their time, and I appreciate their expertise. Any mistakes that still exist in this edition are mine and not theirs.

I am indebted to several organizations. The Music Library at East Carolina University has offered me long-standing, almost daily help with research, in particular Head Music Librarian David Hursh and staff members Judy Barber and Kevin-Andrew Cronin. The Textbook and Academic Author's Association provides indispensable support to me as it does to all its members; the leaders and presenters of this organization are tireless and inspiring. Since I first joined the Lute Society of America as a graduate student, this organization has always reminded me of the significance of historically informed performance practices and musical style, and of any music's deep connections to all aspects of culture. These values are embodied especially in my good friend Caroline Usher and in the legacy of the late Patrick O'Brien. This textbook would not be possible without my publisher. I owe Cognella's founder and CEO Bassim Hamadeh, my project editor Jamie Giganti, and all others who have worked on my book through Cognella and University Readers a huge debt of thanks for their professionalism, their patience, and their belief in my project.

My extended family inspires me, especially my cousin Nancy Lynn Simmer: her curiosity, intelligence, and generous heart keeps the rest of us more closely connected. I am grateful to my parents, George Estep and Shirlee Estep Riley, a writer and a painter, respectively, for teaching me about the joys of a creative life and for my mother's continuing love and encouragement long after my father's passing. My husband and children—Dave, Beth with her husband Aaron, and James—have been a constant source of support, love, and thoughtful conversations about music and musicians. I am lucky to have had Dave's help and patience throughout this project: he's a sharp proofreader, a thoughtful advisor, and, most importantly, he's always ready to remind me that success is within reach.

Jocelyn Nelson

Greenville, NC
2017

Preface

Students have many ways of teaching their teachers. Much of their wisdom comes in hints over several semesters: the sudden wakeful attention with certain topics, the disappointment with others, and even the dutiful and diligent surrender to a task that plainly does not satisfy.

After several years of teaching the traditional music appreciation course—that is, the Western "canon" of art music, I began to consider alternatives. Any other approach is rare among music appreciation texts; most teach Western art music (albeit with supplemental material on vernacular and world music), and many of these are excellent books. But is this the best approach for the nonmajor? When students sign up for a course understood to be "music appreciation," is the generic quality of the title honest? Is the topic completely relevant to today's student?

This textbook, geared for the nonmajor undergraduate student, explores American vernacular music, Western art music, and musical traditions throughout the world beyond the US and Western Europe. The three units are arranged beginning with music most familiar to American students and radiate outward to the least familiar musical traditions.

The styles and musical languages represented here are as far apart as cultural expressions can possibly be, but the study of this wide range of listening demands certain skills in common. For each musical example, we explore musical elements, performance practices, and cultural contexts.

A combination of narrative, "playlist options" sections with listening guidance, and brief primary source quotations that caption images of important figures in music provide our foundation for this study of music throughout a wide-ranging span of time and geography. Vocabulary provides a language for listening as well as reading. Musical elements, genres, and other terms considered helpful to our study are included throughout the book and in the glossary. Appendices on musical elements and musical instruments are featured as well.

Finally, the purpose of this book is much like that of an usher at a concert: to settle the student in just the right place to let the music—with all its attendant sonic elements and cultural trappings—speak for itself.

Special Note to Students on Playlist Options

Throughout each chapter, note the "Playlist Options" sections: after you read about a musical genre, this is your chance to explore suggested examples for yourself. Instead of a fixed list of musical examples, as in most music appreciation texts, here, you can let your interests lead you while you take your own journey online.

Each Playlist Options includes "FIND," "OBSERVE," and "ASK" prompters in the following bullet point format:

PLAYLIST OPTIONS

FIND

- Unless otherwise noted, use exactly the same phrase in the bullet points for your search term.
- The quality of performance, sound, and video varies widely. Don't waste time on examples that show

problems from the very beginning; instead, look for good, clear performances that will help you learn.

- If you are not fluent in the language of a texted vocal music example, refer to the English translation provided or try to find translations online.

- For operas and other staged dramatic works, subtitled videos are recommended so you can understand the words, see the visual aspects of the production, watch the singers act, and listen to the music all at the same time, which is just how operas are meant to be experienced.

- Therefore, you might see one of the following reminders:
  - Search "[title of work] [lyrics] or [subtitles]"
  - Those not fluent in [language of example] can add "translation" or "subtitles" to search term
  - Translated librettos are available online

OBSERVE

- This is a short list of musical elements and styles, such as instrumentation and texture, which helps you focus on relevant aspects of the music.

ASK

- One or two reflective questions will help you explore the significance and historical context of the music.

An astonishing amount of music is available on some sites—especially YouTube—that don't even require a fee or any kind of membership. Nevertheless, listeners are encouraged to explore other legitimate online music databases that have large numbers of tracks legally available for streaming. Some, such as Spotify or Napster (formerly Rhapsody), provide exactly what is asked for from a vast library of musical examples. Others, such as Pandora, respond to search terms with *similar* music, instead, to help the listener create a customized "radio station." When considering membership in one of these online databases, take into account these important issues:

- What is your preference in regard to the "radio station" or exact musical works approaches of streaming databases?

- What is the cost for the type of membership that would best serve your needs? Be mindful that these services have different access and pricing levels. Some include membership and service levels that are free of charge.

- Is the database comprehensive, or does it seem to be strong in certain areas and weak in others? Test this with world music or art music examples.

- Does the database provide your most convenient mode of access, such as a smart phone app?

The goal here is to help you understand music but also to help you learn how to search for specific types of music online and how to notice qualities in the music you find. Even if your instructor has a set list of assigned musical examples (as most instructors must in order to teach and assess what you've learned), Playlist Options will help you understand any style you explore. So it will improve your grade and give you some great topics for in-class participation, which will impress your instructor. More importantly, you will be more likely to enjoy the music and connect with it when you are in the driver's seat.

WARNINGS

- **Stay on the right side of the law.** We have a moral imperative to honor intellectual property. If that's not enough for some, know that the entertainment industry has developed the ability to detect an online breach—exactly which site, which account, and which computer—and they follow up with consequences.

- "Options" means you pick **just one or two out of numerous examples** listed in each playlist section. Keep your explorations limited to avoid becoming bogged down; that and listening fatigue will be a turn-off. Stop *before* you're tired, and always remember that if you're still curious, you can go back and listen to more, later.

- You may find that the Playlist Options whet your appetite for live performances. Go ahead. That is the best possible outcome, in fact.

UNIT 1

American Vernacular Music

Introduction to
Unit One

This Unit's Story

We begin with the music most familiar to American students. The chapters in this unit will explore traditional sacred and secular musical styles. One would think that a unit on American music ought to begin with the music of Native Americans, but the European colonists did not assimilate Native American music or, for that matter, many other aspects of American indigenous cultures. Native musical traditions were virtually ignored, in fact, until the late twentieth century. The most familiar music to most people in this country has other influences instead. We will look at the rich American indigenous musical traditions in Chapter 11, Music in the Americas, later in the text.

Vernacular Music Versus Art Music

"Vernacular" refers to the common, everyday language that everyone in a particular region understands. **Vernacular music**, therefore, is the music that is most accessible to most people. One doesn't necessarily have to be trained in order to listen, enjoy, and participate. "Art" music (also known as "classical" music, which we cover in Unit 2, Western Art Music), on the other hand, is a term that implies cultivation and sophistication; musicians develop their craft through many years of training, and even listeners need some education to appreciate what they hear.

Western culture, especially in the United States, has developed a strong division between vernacular and art musics: the techniques and sounds, the audience members, and even the way audiences listen seem to be in complete opposition to each other. It's a contrast that is nice and clear; the problem is that it often is not true. Much of what listeners will hear from this first unit—especially mid-twentieth-century jazz—is highly cultivated art in all respects. Even the simplest folk song might use sublime poetry with subtle nuances of meaning or historical significance. A significant portion of what we now call classical music was popular with and quite easily understood by general audiences in another time, especially lute songs in Elizabethan England and eighteenth-century light operas throughout Europe (their lyrics were in *vernacular* languages, not coincidentally). Not only are "vernacular" and "art" somewhat artificial descriptors, but the dichotomy itself misleads. Some of the most complex art music is enriched and invigorated by its folk music roots—it would be sterile without them, in fact.

Nevertheless, we will use these terms in order to help us focus on our topics as they are commonly understood. I urge readers, however, to keep aware; find the many intersection points of these labels throughout this unit and the rest of the text. For instance, some of the "Western" music from Chapter 1, American Traditional Music, is really commercialized popular "Country and Western" that could just as easily fit in Chapter 4, Modern American Popular Music Part I: Up to 1970. Is Cajun music from Chapter 1 an American vernacular folk music or is it, rather, a "world music" style that ought to be placed in Chapter 11, Music in the Americas, alongside Native American and Latin American traditions? The close bond between Cajun and Creole with country and blues musics made their position in Chapter 1 seem appropriate, but they can just as easily fit in Unit 3, World Music. Let labels help you learn, at least up to a certain point, and then look beyond them.

Vernacular music
The music that is most accessible, or familiar, to most people in a given culture.

Unit 1, American Vernacular Music, offers a deep look into the music we hear every day. We'll find out the "back stories" of styles, songs, and artists. Students—including those without musical backgrounds—also have an opportunity to learn about musical elements through familiar musical examples. Be sure to consciously step out of "fan" mode (especially tempting for favorite styles) and become the scholar instead in order to get the most out of this unit—at least for the brief period of time we make our way through our survey of musical topics. That takes a bit of discipline, but afterward, you'll know something more than you did before about the characteristics and origins of the music you love.

CHAPTER

1

American Traditional Music

I

SACRED MUSIC

Europeans performed and taught their own musical traditions in North America from the time of their earliest settlements. Sacred music was an especially high priority since many of them were religious pilgrims and missionaries. Their influence was eventually widespread: in the sixteenth and seventeenth centuries, European missionaries brought Catholic liturgical music to the southern, northeastern, and mid-Atlantic regions of the United States. During the next two centuries, many Protestant groups developed distinctive styles of religious musical expression throughout North America. The European settlers almost universally ignored Native American music—sacred or otherwise—until much later (see Chapter 11, Music in the Americas). African American musical traditions, however, ultimately exerted a deep and lasting influence on music of all kinds in North America, including that of sacred music. Our examination of the most prevalent styles of sacred music in the US will include music-making by both Black and White Americans.

The author owes special thanks to Felix Cox, PhD, who guided the preparation of Chapter 1 in great detail.

Opposite: *The Banjo Lesson* by Henry Ossawa Tanner (1859–1937), 1893.

Psalmody in Eighteenth-Century New England

Religious freedom was what prompted the immigration of many European colonists and settlers to North America, so it is no surprise that published music in what was to become the United States began with religious songs. The *Bay Psalm Book*, first published in Cambridge, Massachusetts, in 1640, featured psalms meant to be sung; its 9th edition of 1698, which included musical notation, was the first published music in North America.

Psalmody most strictly means "the singing of psalms," but here we refer especially to seventeenth- through nineteenth-century Protestant vocal sacred music in North America. During colonial times and the early years of the United States, church music was generally the domain of everyone; the entire congregation was expected to sing. Most of the hymns were sung in **strophic form**, a type of song structure in which the music is repeated for each stanza of the text. This helped the congregation, most of whom could not read music, memorize the tune quickly so that they could devote their attention to the words.

A group of late-eighteenth-century musicians from Massachusetts and Connecticut—later referred to as the "First New England School"—wrote original sacred vocal music. The composers were self-taught musicians with "day jobs": **William Billings (1746–1800)** of Boston, for instance, was a tanner; others, such as Daniel Read, Oliver Holden, and Justin Morgan, were shopkeepers, carpenters, or farmers. Billings was also a choral teacher with a vested interest in the lively participation of each singer. Some of the sacred hymns he wrote were **fuging tunes** (pronounced "FEW-ging"), which featured imitative **part-singing**. Although these tunes usually begin with voices together, the songs feature sections with successive, imitative entrances of musical lines just as they are in musical rounds such as the familiar nursery song, "Row, Row, Row Your Boat." Unlike rounds (which continue in strict imitation throughout the entire **melody**), the musical lines of fuging tunes depart from strict imitation at some point before they end. This technique increases the listener's interest in the resulting "cascading" melody and, at the same time, demands more skill of the singers.

Billings had limited opportunity for musical education, and he faced financial and physical challenges throughout his life. His talent and sheer enthusiasm for music, however, transcended these difficulties. *The New-England Psalm-Singer* (Boston, 1770), a collection of his original religious

Psalmody The singing of psalms.

Strophic form Song structure in which the music is repeated with each stanza of the text; also see Musical Elements Appendix.

Fuging tunes Genre of early American imitative part-songs that feature sections with staggered entrances.

Part-song, Part-singing Choral music, or a way of singing choral music in which the vocal parts are divided into sections according to ranges. (Also see Chapter 9, Romantic Music.)

Melody A succession of musical tones or pitches that has identifiable shape and meaning; see Musical Elements Appendix.

tunes, is considered his most significant work. His themes sometimes include references to the struggle for independence that led to the Revolutionary War as in the song, "Chester." He often arbitrarily entitled his tunes with place names ("Africa" or "Asia") as was common in his day. He died over 200 years ago, but his talent and his passionate personality come alive as soon as we hear his music.

Figure 1-2 Frontpiece of *New England Psalm-Singer* (1770) by William Billings

PLAYLIST OPTIONS
18TH-CENTURY NEW ENGLAND PSALMODY

FIND

"Bay Psalm Book" music
Or a William Billings tune using his name plus a title
as your search term, such as

- "Africa"
- "Chester"
- "Creation"
- "O Praise the Lord of Heaven"

OBSERVE

- Melodic **range** and **contour**
- Strophic form

Melodic range   The distance between the lowest and highest notes of any given melody; see Musical Elements Appendix.

Melodic contour   The shape of a melody, such as ascending, descending, or wavelike; see Musical Elements Appendix.

- Texture: voices lined up together or staggered, imitating one another
- Many songs feature a "lined-up" section first, then an "imitative" section.

ASK

- Is your example a fuging tune, with a section that features successive entrances of the same melody?
- Where does the text come from, and what themes do you recognize?

African American Sacred Music

Sacred music of African American lineage is rich with influences from West Africa, Western Europe, and the Americas. Most of the harmonic language, text, musical structure, and musical instruments come from European and British traditions. African cultures bring a full-bodied emotional vocal style, rhythmic complexity and drive, and a propensity for improvisation and movement to the mix. America itself brings—as *its* most important contributing influence—the condition of slavery and oppression: the setting against which Black sacred music resonates.

West African Griot Tradition

Griot tradition
A hereditary class of oral historians who carry on the musical and literary traditions of the culture in Western Africa (Chapter 13, Music in Sub-Saharan Africa).

Oral tradition
Transmission of skills and information in spoken rather than written form.

West African bards, or oral historians, who carry on the musical and literary traditions of the culture, are known by a number of names, including **griots** and *jeli* (see Chapter 13, Music in Sub-Saharan Africa). Their songs and story recitations about history and the life of the spirit are passed along through **oral tradition** in which the transmission of knowledge and skills are passed down in spoken rather than written form, teacher to student. Many of these *griots* are also healers or ritual leaders for their communities. This vocation is hereditary: custom dictates that youths in *griot* families will follow in their ancestors' footsteps and devote themselves to their lives as bards. To this day, the tradition lives; in fact, many popular West African musicians are *griots*.

No one knows how many *griots* survived as slaves in North America, but evidence of their presence exists. For instance, the American scholar and founder of the NAACP, W. E. B. Du Bois (1868–1963), described the community "priest" who healed and comforted his community.

> *"... some traces were retained of the former group life, and the chief remaining institution was the priest or medicine man. He early appeared on the plantation and found his function as the healer of the sick, the interpreter of the unknown, the comforter of the sorrowing, the supernatural avenger of wrong and the one who rudely, but picturesquely, expressed the longing, disappointment and resentment of a stolen and oppressed people."*[1]

Performance practices, vocal styles, and musical techniques are among the many aspects of African musical culture that would have been—surely *were*—transferred by the enslaved West African bards.

Spirituals ("Negro Spirituals"; "African American Spirituals")

Enslaved African Americans gathered at meetings on plantations and elsewhere to worship and socialize. These gatherings represented variable fusions of African, European, and American religious elements. Their conversion to Christianity, especially before the nineteenth century, was subject to the inclination of the slave master, so religious services might be banned and, therefore, secret. Others were sanctioned, or even compelled, and would have proceeded on the terms of the slave owners or White religious leaders.

Musical styles common in West African cultures were used throughout the meetings. These styles included **call and response**, or alternation between leading and responding groups or individuals in music or speech. The **lining out** technique is one common type of call and response practice in which the leader shouts or sings each line in advance for the rest of the singers to imitate. Black singers used a wide range of vocal techniques: instead of the simple, somewhat nasal delivery with little or no vibrato especially common with European Americans, African Americans used emotional shouts, sighs, and moans to punctuate heavily ornamented melodies and rhythms. Furthermore, dance, or at least movement, was continuous and integral to the event for everyone present. Black congregations would often move in a circle as they worshipped, clapping their

Call and response
The alternation between leading and responding groups or individuals in music or speech (Chapter 1, American Traditional Music, and Chapter 13, Music in Sub-Saharan Africa).

Lining out Performance practice in which the leader shouts or sings each line of a song in advance for the rest of the singers to imitate.

hands and stomping or shuffling their feet in a practice known as the "ring shout."

European American observers were often scandalized by these vocal styles and accompanying movements; some undoubtedly expected Christian conversion to encourage a more "conventional" approach (in the European Americans' perspective) from the Black worshippers. Many White religious leaders redoubled their efforts to proselytize slaves during the Great Awakenings, a series of religious revivals that occurred in the United States in the eighteenth and nineteenth centuries. These rural festivals sprang up throughout the country; the meetings typically lasted a number of days spent in communal prayer and religious singing among charismatic leaders who sermonized, converted, and often baptized both White and Black Americans. The Second Great Awakening of the late eighteenth and early nineteenth centuries, in particular, powerfully influenced Black worshippers through conversion and the establishment of increasing numbers of Black churches. The Black performance practices noted above, however, didn't go away when they accepted Christianity: instead, the new Christians *transformed* Christian music.

Figure 1-3 *The Underground Railroad* by Charles T. Webber (1893). Note banjo in lower right.

Hymns of European lineage were altered by Black performances in almost every possible way: melodically, rhythmically, harmonically, and sometimes even textually. Other songs, however, did not emerge from European hymnody and may have been extemporaneously, and often communally (by more than one person), composed. A variety of songs from both groups seem to include coded language that might have directed listeners to secret meetings or, perhaps "underground railroad" tips for travelers along a trail to freedom in the North. Frederick Douglass (see below, under "Work Songs and Dance Music on the Plantation") and others have written about such songs, but the evidence of an underground railroad repertory is uncertain. Topics, however, undeniably focused on the experiences of journey, slavery, and deliverance. "Go Down, Moses," "Swing Low, Sweet Chariot," and "Michael, Row the Boat Ashore" are popular examples; see, for instance, the text of "Go Down, Moses" (on right).

Over time, performance practices were altered to match the circumstances, especially in the case of formal concert performances by choral groups and soloists influenced by traditional European art music education. Late-nineteenth-century touring choral groups who represented Black colleges incorporated part-songs with established European choral style performance practices. As a result, they enjoyed more success than they might have had with a more authentic presentation. They were able to raise money for their schools and, at the same time, disseminate what became known as the "Negro spiritual" worldwide. One of the most prominent concert style ensembles is the **Fisk Jubilee Singers**, who began in the late nineteenth century when they went on tour for Fisk University. (See Chapter 13, Music in Sub-Saharan Africa, "*Nkosi Sikelel' iAfrika*" ("Lord Bless Africa"), on how the Fisk Jubilee Singers may have influenced the current South African national anthem.) They are still popular today as a highly acclaimed performing ensemble (see Figures 1-4a and b).

Black Gospel Music

Black congregations in northern cities such as Chicago and Philadelphia sang some of the same hymns as the White congregations but imbued them with blues idioms like the heavier beats and **blue notes** from secular music. **Thomas A. Dorsey (1899–1993)** dominated the development of gospel throughout the early and middle twentieth century. Known as "Georgia Tom" during his days as a blues piano accompanist, Dorsey's

GO DOWN, MOSES

When Israel was in Egypt's Land,
Let my people go.
Oppressed so hard they could not stand,
Let my people go.

Go down, Moses, way down in Egypt land,
Tell ole Pharaoh, Let my people go.

No more shall they in bondage toil,
Let my people go.
Let them come out with Egypt's spoil,
Let my people go.

Go down, Moses, etc.

O let us all from bondage flee,
Let my people go.
And let us all in Christ be free,
Let my people go.

Go down, Moses, etc.

We need not always weep and moan,
Let my people go.
And wear these slavery chains forlorn,
Let my people go.

Go down, Moses, etc.

I do believe without a doubt,
Let my people go.
That a Christian has the right to shout,
Let my people go.

Go down, Moses, etc.[2]

Theodore F. Seward, "Go Down, Moses." 1872.

Blue notes   Slightly lowered pitches on certain scale degrees in blues and jazz melodies (Chapter 3, Jazz).

Figures 1-4a & 4b (a) An engraving of the Fisk Jubilee Singers on their second European tour during the 1870s. (From the 1873 issue of *The Illustrated London News*.) (b) The Fisk Jubilee Singers in 2012

gospel style includes a strong role for keyboard accompaniment that emphasizes a heavy beat conducive to motion, copious ornamentation of the melody, and the practice of lining out the hymn verses to bring all who are present into the song. Dorsey wrote many popular hymns, including "Precious Lord, Take My Hand." Thanks to his formal music education in Chicago, his business experience as a bandleader, a publisher, an agent for Paramount, and his close association with the renowned gospel singer **Mahalia Jackson (1911–1972)**, Dorsey was well equipped to compose, produce, and publicize his music. His amalgamation of sacred and secular idioms developed the Black gospel style of the twentieth century, and he is known as the "father of gospel music."

PLAYLIST OPTIONS
AFRICAN AMERICAN SACRED MUSIC

FIND

A spiritual or gospel song, such as

- "Go Down Moses"
- "Precious Lord, Take My Hand"
- "Swing Low, Sweet Chariot"
- "We Shall Overcome"

Suggested performers and ensembles:

- Marian Anderson (1897–1993)
- Boy's Choir of Harlem

- The Fisk Jubilee Singers
- Aretha Franklin (b. 1942)
- The Golden Gate Quartet
- Mahalia Jackson (1911–1972)
- Aaron Neville (b. 1941)
- Jessye Norman (b. 1945)
- Paul Robeson (1898–1976)

OBSERVE

- Vocal fluctuations in pitch, tone, dynamics, and tempo
- Accompaniment of the main melody
  - Instrumental or vocal
- Strophic form

ASK

- How does the topic transcend faith, and what references were particularly relevant for enslaved Black Americans?
- What is the performance context: A church service? A ticketed concert? A recording?

Further Developments in American Sacred Music

Figure 1-5 Four-shape system of the *The Sacred Harp*. C Major scale in shape notes.

Congregations throughout the eighteenth and nineteenth centuries in North America had little access to musical training, unlike their European counterparts. For those without music books, a leader could sing out each line just ahead of the music for the rest to imitate in lining out tradition. But others urged musical literacy, and by the early nineteenth

Shape-note tradition
Notation with variously shaped note heads to help hymn singers learn to read music.

Pitch The "highness" or "lowness" of a sound; see Musical Elements Appendix.

century, an American **shape-note tradition** had developed in which each note head had a specific shape. By associating the shape of the note head with a given **pitch**, singers could learn to read music more easily. The religious revivals of the "Great Awakenings" (see above) helped to spread this tradition throughout the American South and beyond.

The defining outcome of the shape-note tradition, *The Sacred Harp* (Philadelphia, 1844), is a compilation of favorite hymns by B. F. White and E. J. King. Editions of *The Sacred Harp* continue to be published, and the shape-note tradition continues to this day, especially in the American South. "Amazing Grace," one of the hymns included in *The Sacred Harp*, has a special significance. It was not an American who wrote the text, and the origin of the preexisting tune most associated with it, "New Britain," is unknown; however, this song is easily the most popular and familiar Christian melody in the United States. John Newton (1725–1807), author of the lyrics to "Amazing Grace," was an English clergyman who had been a sailor involved in the slave trade. His own writings relate his dramatic conversion, which began during a storm at sea on a slave ship. Christians first sang his inspiring message of redemption to several different melodies, but the "New Britain" tune has become indelibly associated with Newton's poem. This song has appeared in numerous hymnals, including shape-note hymnals, since the nineteenth century (see Figure 1-4), and it is also commonly lined out in performance. Throughout the past two centuries, "Amazing Grace" has been performed in a staggering number of different ways, making this song an ideal opportunity to explore a variety of vocal styles.

Figure 1-6 "Amazing Grace" tune under the title "New Britain," in the Southern Harmony shape-note hymnal, 1848.

Lowell Mason (1792–1872) took a different approach to the problem of musical illiteracy. Active in church music as a hymn writer and arranger, Mason also devoted himself to the musical education of children and adults both inside and outside of church. He promoted traditional European techniques of voice leading and harmony rather than the fuging tunes and shape note singing cultivated in the United States. His successful teaching methods and publications led to the establishment of music education in public schools and ensured his legacy as an extraordinarily influential figure in American music.

PLAYLIST OPTIONS
"AMAZING GRACE" COMPARISON OF
TRADITIONAL AND CONTRASTING STYLES

FIND

First: An "Amazing Grace" traditional performance with ensembles and search terms, such as

- Alabama Sacred Harp Singers (ensemble)
- The Harpeth Valley Sacred Harp Singers (ensemble)
- New Britain (search term)
- Sacred Harp (search term)

Then compare with: An "Amazing Grace" performance in a contrasting style, such as

- African American gospel: Mahalia Jackson or Aretha Franklin
- Country-Western: Willie Nelson or Randy Travis
- Folk music revival: Judy Collins
- Rhythm and blues: Aaron Neville
- Operatic: Jessye Norman
- In Cherokee language, pop music influence: Walela, with Rita Coolidge
- Instrumental: bagpipes, orchestra, or smaller ensembles

OBSERVE

- Melody
  - Either the familiar "New Britain" tune or a different tune

- Vocal style
  - Emotional or restrained
  - Ornamented or strictly faithful to the original tune

ASK

- What is the performance context in each of your two examples?
  - Untrained church congregation?
  - Highly trained and "polished" in operatic or commercial styles?
  - Recording studio?
  - Live, ticketed concert?

II

SECULAR MUSIC

F olk" or "traditional" music, used here to refer to music that reflects a common experience and worldview among its listeners, is relatively simple to understand and perform and even imparts a sense of ownership among participants and listeners that sophisticated art music and heavily marketed popular music cannot. In the United States, the wide range of cultures and origins from which these songs emerge create a kaleidoscopic array of styles and themes, yet they somehow serve to unify elements of American culture at the same time that they express its diversity. Generally accessible and typically taught through oral tradition from teacher to student, rather than through notated music, simple melodies with or without accompaniment are often constructed in predictable strophic forms. But these songs do not necessarily lack sophistication and importance.

Ballad Typically a narrative, strophic song. "Child ballads" refers to songs that nineteenth-century scholar Francis James Child found in his research.

Songs of the East: British Influences

Ballads, which are usually strophic, narrative songs, are the mainstay of Anglo-American folk music. Topics range from everyday hardships of working people to historical events. Local references, familiar regional melodies, and traditional vocal styles create a vivid "flavor" so that the songs can often bring us into their social and historical realities in ways that even the best textbooks would never be able to accomplish. Perhaps more than any other genre, folk songs have a "grassroots" origin with anyone moved to sing them. For this reason, the words, the accompaniment, and even the melodies for many songs have undergone continuous change among performances and singers. Instrumentation in traditional European American folk music tends to emphasize plucked and bowed stringed instruments, such as the **guitar**, **dulcimer**, and **fiddle** (see Musical Instruments Appendix). Scholarship in American folk music, which eventually became inextricably linked with its performance, has its own interesting story to tell.

Francis James Child (1825–1896) compiled songs in *The English and Scottish Popular Ballads* (1882–1898). Child studied folk music through the lens of philology, or the study of linguistics and literature, by comparing poetic texts; one might say he made his discoveries in libraries. The "**Child ballads**" described in concert programs and commentaries, such as "Barbara Allen" (Child no. 84), are references to the songs that Child found in his research. Other scholars such as Cecil Sharp (1859–1924), however, collected folk songs in "the field;" that is, he traveled to the music-makers and transcribed or recorded the songs as they were performed. He examined music in the Appalachian regions, especially western North Carolina. These songs were collected in his *Folk Songs of the Southern Appalachians* (1917). Child, Sharp, and other scholars identified strong links between British and American traditional songs: many musical elements and topics were similar and sometimes virtually the same between American and British traditions.

Guitar A plucked stringed chordophone with a fretted neck; see Musical Instruments Appendix.

Dulcimer A box zither chordophone family of instruments with various numbers of strings that are plucked, strummed, hammered, or bowed; see Musical Instruments Appendix.

Fiddle A bowed stringed chordophone. Structurally identical to a violin, the term "fiddle" implies a traditional folk or bluegrass style of repertory, technique, and performance practice; see Musical Instruments Appendix.

Child Ballads "Child ballads" refers to songs that nineteenth century scholar Francis James Child found in his research.

PLAYLIST OPTIONS
CHILD BALLAD COMPARISON

FIND

At least two versions of one Child ballad, such as

- "Barbara Allen" or "Barbry Allen" and other various spellings (Child no. 84)
- "Queen Eleanor's Confession" (Child no. 156)
- "Riddles Wisely Expounded" (Child no. 1)
- "The Unquiet Grave" (Child no. 78)

Look for traditional performances with singers, such as

- Shirley Collins, Custer LaRue, Ewan McColl, John Jacob Niles, Hermes Nye, Jean Ritchie, Pete Seeger, Lucy Stewart, Jean Thomass

Or recording labels, such as

- Rounder Records, Shanachee Entertainment, Smithsonian Folkways

OBSERVE

- Vocal style
  - Full-bodied or a thinner, more nasal delivery
- Instrumental accompaniment
  - What instrument, if any
- Strophic form

ASK

- Do the words or melodies vary in different versions of the same song?
- Do the vocalists in your examples seem to be formally trained musicians, or do you hear an untrained vocalist performing in a local, "grass-roots" style?
- Where does the story come from? Can you discern any reference to the British Isles in the story or word usage?

Songs of the South: African American and Creole Influences

While European—and especially British—music informs the harmonic language of traditional music from the southern United States as it does in points north, the concentration of African Americans in the South brought West African and Caribbean influences. The earliest themes necessarily include the hardships of slavery and relentless work; troubles with relationships, racism, law, and drugs emerge as topics in the twentieth century. Throughout all the sadness, however, we can still hear the spiritual strength (even in secular music) and ironic humor of the singers.

Work Songs and Dance Music on the Plantation

Work songs are common throughout the world, and they are especially popular in African cultures. They are typically spontaneously improvised or at least embellished by a group of singers who alternate with a leader in call and response. The rhythm suits the task and might even seem to propel the singers along in it, lightening their burden. This was a valuable tradition for enslaved African Americans who labored on the plantations of the American South. In fact, according to former slave **Frederick Douglass (1818–1895)**, the overseers found this to be a useful practice as well, for it apparently aided productivity (see Figure 1-7). Douglass was a prominent writer and reformer, who wrote about his life as a slave in *My Bondage and My Freedom* (1855). **Field hollers** are a type of work song associated with field and levee workers; they were often sung by individual workers as a way of communicating across a distance with other workers and passersby. They have been described as long shouts, or cries.

Drumming was forbidden on many slave plantations due to the owners' concerns over the possibility of communication among the slaves, but stringed instruments were allowed. The earliest and most popular instrument built by African Americans was the banjo-like instrument (See Chapter 13, Music in Sub-Saharan Africa, "Encounter I: Ancestor of the American Banjo?"), which originated from similar instruments in West Africa. The practice of handclapping and body-slapping with stomping and dancing, known as "juba," or "pattin' juba," served as a substitute for drums and could become quite rhythmically complex. Another type of secular dance was the cakewalk, a competition in which the participants strutted pompously in imitation of the plantation owners, accompanied by music that was later to influence ragtime (see Chapter 3, Jazz). Winners were awarded cakes and other prizes; thus, the origin of the phrase, "that takes the cake."

Work song Music to accompany work-related tasks.

Field Holler A type of work song associated with field and levee workers; long shouts, or cries.

Cajun and Creole Music

Cajun and **Creole** music developed from several distinct cultural groups in southwestern Louisiana. Cajuns (a corruption of "Acadians") are French-speaking descendants of colonists in Nova Scotia, Canada, who were expelled by the British in the eighteenth century. Many settled in Louisiana and developed their own cultural identity in dialect, music, cuisine, and other aspects of daily life. During the twentieth century, Cajun culture

Cajun French-speaking cultural group in southwestern Louisiana. Cajun music is drawn from a variety of cultures, and the music is traditionally sung in French, or French and English.

Creole A cultural group in Louisiana that includes people of European and/or Afro-Caribbean descent.

Frederick Douglass: "Slaves are generally expected to sing as well as to work. A silent slave is not liked by masters or overseers. 'Make a noise,' 'make a noise,' and 'bear a hand,' are the words usually addressed to the slaves when there is silence amongst them. This may account for the almost constant singing heard in the southern states. There was, generally, more or less singing among the teamsters, as it was one means of letting the overseer know where they were, and that they were moving on with the work."[3]

spread to other regions, including parts of Texas, continually absorbing new influences.

Cajun musical style is drawn from a variety of cultures from Europe, West Africa, and the Caribbean. **Syncopation**, **improvisation**, and complex rhythmic styles from Africa and the Caribbean, dances and folk tunes from European countries, can be heard in Cajun bands. Traditional French ballads and drinking songs were originally sung unaccompanied in Cajun music, but by the twentieth century, instrumental accompaniment was prevalent. Throughout the century, instruments and performance practices evolved: accordions as lead instruments gave way to fiddles backed by string bands in the 1930s, English lyrics began to appear along with French lyrics in the 1940s, and the rock 'n' roll–influenced "swamp pop" emerged in the 1950s. New developments, along with revivals of more traditional styles, continue to the present. Dewey Balfa (1927–1992), who formed a band with his brothers known as the Balfa Brothers, was an influential Cajun musician during the mid-twentieth century. More recently, BeauSoleil, a Cajun band founded by Michael Doucet (b. 1951) became prominent in the late twentieth century.

Although the term "Creole" can refer generically to a mixture of cultures and languages, in Louisiana this term usually refers to one cultural group, in particular, that includes a combination of European and Afro-Caribbean descent. Louisiana Creole music, known as **zydeco**, is a blend of African American, Caribbean, and Cajun styles. Common instrumentation includes fiddle, accordion, electric guitar, brass instruments, and washboard. The music is improvisatory and traditionally sung in French. Zydeco and Cajun musical styles are closely linked and often performed at the same events. Influential zydeco musicians include Clifton Chenier (1925–1987), also known as "the king of zydeco," who blended blues with traditional Creole music, and **Buckwheat Zydeco**, the stage name of accordionist and band leader Stanley Dural Jr. (1947–2016) and also the band title of his leading zydeco music ensemble.

Syncopation Shift of metric accent from the expected pattern to the unexpected; see Musical Elements Appendix.

Improvisation The creation of music during performance; common in many cultures and genres, it is a hallmark of American jazz. (Chapter 3, Jazz).

Zydeco music A blend of African-American, Caribbean, and Cajun styles.

PLAYLIST OPTIONS
CAJUN AND ZYDECO MUSIC

FIND

A prominent Cajun and Creole musician or ensemble, such as

* Dewey Balfa and His Balfa Brothers Band
* BeauSoleil
* Clifton Chenier
* Buckwheat Zydeco (Stanley Dural, Jr.)

OBSERVE

* Language and topic of text
    * Seek out translated lyrics, if needed
* Instrumental accompaniment
* Strophic form

ASK

* How does instrumentation and language in your example help place it in chronology in the twentieth century or beyond (remembering that instrumentation changed through time)?
* Do you hear influences, such as blues, European polka, or country music?

Figure 1-8 Buckwheat Zydeco at the Kitchener Blues Festival, 2010.

Songs of the West: Labor, Loneliness, and Adventure

Throughout the nineteenth and early twentieth centuries, cowboys and pioneers carried with them the musical traditions of the British Isles and Europe, absorbed local southwestern Latin American influences (see Chapter 11, Music in the Americas, "Latin American Music"), and developed a distinct genre of song. As with most folk songs, the western songs are usually simple, strophic melodies with minimal accompaniment. Guitar predominates in western songs, frequently supplemented by the harmonica. Since the mid-twentieth century, country instrumentations and musical styles are common in the music of the western United States. The topics in western songs throughout the nineteenth and twentieth centuries, however, often evoke an extra measure of nostalgia and loneliness, and nature is a common reference—often in the form of wide expanses of land or sky—such as in the following stanza from "Home on the Range."

> How often at night when the heavens are bright
> With the light from the glittering stars
> Have I stood here amazed and asked as I gazed
> If their glory exceeds that of ours.[4]

The western United States, so well known for its cowboys, was populated with many others, such as loggers, miners, railroad workers, and pioneer settlers. Adventure seekers from east of the Mississippi streamed westward, especially during gold rushes, when they risked their safety and everything they owned for the chance to find precious metals in the region's mines. John A. Stone's story of a couple's westward journey in "Sweet Betsy from Pike" emphasized the gold-seeking travelers' newfound freedom from the strict, Victorian lifestyles of those in the eastern part of the country as we can read in this excerpt of the ballad:

> Oh, don't you remember sweet Betsey from Pike,
> Who crossed the big mountains with her lover Ike,
> With two yoke of cattle, a large yellow dog,
> A tall shanghai rooster and one spotted hog.[5]

Excerpt from Brewster M. Higley, "Home on the Range." 1872.
Excerpt from John A. Stone, "Sweet Betsy from Pike," Put's Golden Songster, p. 50. 1858.

It was the cowboy, however, already a charismatic figure in popular literature by the late nineteenth century, that captured the imaginations of little boys (and everyone else) to mythic proportions by the mid-1930s when **Gene Autry (1907–1998)** began starring in cowboy movies. Nicknamed "the singing cowboy," Autry entertained in movies, recordings, radio shows, and TV shows for many years. Although his glamorous and happy portrayal of cowboy life was far from the truth, he used his fame with youngsters to good effect with his "Cowboy Code of Honor," a list of virtues boys could aspire to, reminiscent of the Boy Scout Oath. Roy Rogers (1911–1998) and his wife, Dale Evans (1912–2001), were also popular singers and entertainers throughout the mid-twentieth century.

Figure 1-9 Gene Autry, 1960.

Dale Evans wrote the theme song to the popular *Roy Rogers Show*, "Happy Trails." These newer, heavily marketed songs by Autry, Evans, and other professional entertainers have been categorized as "western" songs, along with the older, traditional songs from the frontier to form a hybrid genre of traditional and popular western music. We'll hear echoes of this style in the country music sections of Chapters 4 and 5, Modern American Popular Music I and II.

PLAYLIST OPTIONS
WESTERN SONG

FIND

A western song (either popular or less well known), such as

- "Don't Fence Me In"
- "Git Along, Little Dogies"
- "(Ghost) Riders in the Sky"
- "Home on the Range"
- "Little Joe, The Wrangler"
- "Red River Valley"
- "Streets of Laredo"
- "Sweet Betsy From Pike"
- "Zebra Dun"

Or a prominent performer or ensemble, such as

- Gene Autrey
- Dale Evans
- Martin Murphey
- Riders in the Sky
- Roy Rogers
- Sons of the Pioneers

LISTEN FOR

- Vocal style
- Instrumental accompaniment style
- Strophic form

ASK

◆ Do you hear themes that reference nature, regional history, or a personal story?

◆ Can you recognize structural, melodic, and textual influences from the British Isles reminiscent of the Child ballad playlist?

◆ Does the vocal style of your example feature the hoots and shouts that must have been used on the ranches?

The Lomax Family and The American Folk Music Revival

John Lomax (1867–1948) collected and archived traditional music in the United States and elsewhere. Publications include *Cowboy Songs and Other Frontier Ballads* (1910) and *American Ballads and Folksongs* (1934). He became curator of the Archive of American Folksong in the Library of Congress in 1933. His travels have become legendary; especially notable are his song-collecting tours of the American South with his son, **Alan Lomax (1915–2002)**, in the 1930s. These expeditions, which took the pair on visits to a variety of settings, including churches and prisons, yielded an abundance of music. Much of the music recorded by the Lomax collaboration was performed by African Americans and led to a wealth of cultural information on Blacks in the South, as well as "discoveries" of musicians such as Lead Belly and others.

Figure 1-10 Alan Lomax performing at the Mountain Music Festival, Asheville, North Carolina.

Alan Lomax, who began by working with his father, continued in his own inspired career, recording and studying folk music in many different regions of the world after his father's death. He was interested in the cultural contexts of folk music and, particularly, in the relationship between musical elements such as vocal style or song structure and sociological characteristics (See an explanation of Lomax's "cantometrics" theory on his Cultural Equity website.). Alan's sister, Bess Lomax Howes (1921–2009), studied and performed folk music and taught anthropology at California State College. Perhaps her greatest contribution, however, was her lifelong work in arts administration. As director

Woody Guthrie: "I never heard my guitar ring so loud and so long and so clear as It did there in them high-polished marble halls. Every note was ten times as loud, and so was my singing. I filled myself full of free air and sung as loud as the building would stand. I wanted the poodle dogs leading the ladies around to stick up their noses and wonder what in the hell had struck that joint. People had walked hushed up and too nice and quiet through these tile floors too long. I decided that for this minute, for this one snap of their lives, they'd see a human walking through that place, not singing because he was hired and told what to sing, but just walking through there thinking about the world and singing about it... heard a cop say, 'Cut it! Hey! Yez cain't pull dat stuff in here!' But before he could get at me, I'd whirled through a spinning door ..."[6]

of the Folk Arts Program of the National Endowment for the Arts, she was a powerful influence in the establishment of folk arts programs throughout the United States.

The Lomax family's foundational work in folk music was a strong impetus toward the American folk music revival of the mid-twentieth century. Alan Lomax circulated with many contemporary folk music performers in his work with the recording, radio, and television industries. He was especially drawn to the music of folksinger **Woody Guthrie (1912–1967)**, who wrote or arranged more than 1,000 songs. Guthrie's songs often focused on social activism and the hardships of the Great Depression. His most famous song, "This Land Is Your Land," was written as a response to Irving Berlin's popular "God Bless America," which Guthrie felt was too uncritically patriotic (see more about Berlin in Chapter 2, American Music for Stage and Screen, "The Composers: Roots in Tin Pan Alley.") Guthrie's leftist politics, which included protest against unrestrained capitalism, are reflected in this often omitted stanza from "This Land Is Your Land".[7]

> As I went walking I saw a sign there
> And on the sign it said "No Trespassing."
> But on the other side it didn't say nothing,
> That side was made for you and me.[8]

Lomax recorded Guthrie's repertory, which secured Guthrie's influence on later twentieth-century folk singers such as Bob Dylan (b. 1941) and Joan Baez (b. 1941). Another significant influence on the American folk music revival was the long and devoted folk-singing career of **Pete Seeger (1919–2014)**. In the 1930s and 40s, he collaborated with Woody Guthrie and Alan Lomax, and during the Civil Rights movement, he popularized the iconic song which he helped arrange, "We Shall Overcome." In recent years, he sang at President Obama's 2009 inauguration and joined the Occupy Wall Street protest one evening in 2011. A songwriter and banjo player, Seeger's song credits include "If I Had a Hammer," "Turn, Turn, Turn," "Where Have All the Flowers Gone?", and "Wimoweh" (see Chapter 13, Music in Sub-Saharan Africa, for the origin and story of this song in the section "Song As Expression and Dignity"). Social justice remained a quintessential theme in folk music, and by the late twentieth century the antiwar movement's protest of the Vietnam War instilled many of the songs with a passionate message.

Figure 1-12 Pete Seeger, 1986.

PLAYLIST OPTIONS: AMERICAN FOLK MUSIC REVIVAL SONGS

FIND

A folk song with a title as your search term, such as

- "Charlie on the MTA"
- "Goodnight, Irene"
- "So Long, It's Been Good to Know You"
- "Sweet Sir Galahad"
- "This Land Is Your Land"
- "Waist Deep in the Big Muddy"
- "We Shall Overcome"

Or with a prominent performer or ensemble as your search term, such as

- Joan Baez

- Arlo Guthrie
- Woody Guthrie
- Kingston Trio
- The New Lost City Ramblers
- Tom Paxton
- Pete Seeger

OBSERVE

- Instrumental accompaniment
  - Single instrument played by the singer or an ensemble
- Strophic form
- The presence or absence of vocal harmonies

ASK

- What is the topic; is it about love or work as is typical of many genres? Or do you hear themes that reference political and socioeconomic struggle, with a populist or leftist perspective?
- What is the context of your example's performance?
  - A large, inclusive performance venue with audience participation, a recording studio, a TV performance?

CHAPTER 1 VOCABULARY & IMPORTANT FIGURES

Vocabulary

Ballad

Cajun

Call and response

Child Ballads

Creole

Dulcimer

Fiddle

Field Holler

Fuging tunes

Guitar

Lining out

Melodic contour

Melodic range

Melody

Oral tradition

Part-song, Part-singing

Pitch

Psalmody

Shape note tradition

Strophic form

Work song

Zydeco music

Important Figures

Gene Autry (1907–1998)

William Billings (1746–1800)

Buckwheat Zydeco (1947–2016)

Francis James Child (1825–1896)

Thomas A. Dorsey (1899–1993)

Frederick Douglass (1818–1895)

Fisk Jubilee Singers (active since 1871)

Woody Guthrie (1912–1967)

Mahalia Jackson (1911–1972)

Alan Lomax (1915–2002)

Lowell Mason (1792–1872)

Pete Seeger (1919–2014)

ENDNOTES

[1] W. E. B. Dubois, "The Religion of the Common Negro," *New World IX* (December 1900), 618, as quoted in Blassingame 1972, 32–33.

[2] Selected lyrics to the 1872 Theodore F. Seward's arrangement of "Go Down, Moses," a traditional spiritual, as reprinted in Crawford's *An Introduction to American Music*, W. W. Norton, 2001, pages 253–255.

[3] Frederick Douglass, from *My Bondage and My Freedom*, pp. 1258–1260. Copyright in the public domain.

[4] [Music by Dan Kelley Words by Brewster Higley As posted in Jim Hoy and Tom Isern, "Tales Out of School October 2003 Home on the Range—A Lesson on our State Song." Emporia State University: http://www.emporia.edu/cgps/tales/nov2003.html , accessed 12/5/16.]

[5] (As printed in John A. Stone, Put's Golden Songster, San Francisco: D. E. Appleton & Co., 1858, pp. 50–52.)

[6] from Bound For Glory by Woody Guthrie, Dutton, 1943/1968, pp. 395–6.

[7] Special thanks to my colleague Dr. Felix Cox for his help with this passage.

[8] Lyrics from the Official Woody Guthrie Website, http://woodyguthrie.org/Lyrics/This_Land.htm accessed 6/4/2013.

Image Credits

- Figure 1-6: William Walker / Copyright in the Public Domain.

- Figure 1-7: Source: https://en.wikipedia.org/wiki/File:Frederick_Douglass_portrait.jpg

- Figure 1-8: Copyright © 2010 by Tabercil, (CC BY-SA 2.0) at https://commons.wikimedia.org/wiki/File:BuckwheatZydeco-KitchenerBlues-2010a.jpg.

- Figure 1-9: Seattle Packing Company-Bar-S Brand / Copyright in the Public Domain.

- Figure 1-10: Source: https://commons.wikimedia.org/wiki/File:Alan_Lomax.jpg.

- Figure 1-11: Al Aumuller / Copyright in the Public Domain.

- Figure 1-12: Copyright © 1986 by Josef Schwarz, (CC BY-SA 3.0) at https://commons.wikimedia.org/wiki/File:Pete_Seeger_1986.jpg.

2 American Music for Stage and Screen

I

AMERICAN THEATER: NINETEENTH AND EARLY TWENTIETH CENTURIES

Influence from Abroad: Operetta and Melodrama

Popular light, comic operas known as operettas laid a foundation for future styles in American theater during the nineteenth-century. British and European productions heavily influenced the American stage. *H.M.S. Pinafore*, for instance, by the English collaborators Gilbert and Sullivan, opened on Broadway in 1878 to great acclaim with its irresistible melodies and hilarious lyrics.

The melodrama was another stage genre mostly imported from Great Britain and Europe. These dramas boiled morality down to simple good versus evil messages with stock characters, formulaic plots, and

Opposite: The Cathedrals of Broadway by Florine Stettheimer, 1929.

an exaggerated, emotional delivery. Many melodramas did not include music. One of the most popular songs of the nineteenth-century, however, came from a poignant moment in the melodrama *Clari, the Maid of Milan* by Payne and Bishop: the heroine proves her virtue by thinking only of home when she's offered every possible luxury to live as a "kept" woman. Her song, "Home, Sweet Home," is still widely recognized (see Chapter 9, Romantic Era Music, "The Parlor Song").

Figure 2-2 Cover of sheet music for "Home, Sweet Home!," c1914. Originally written for an 1823 melodrama, this song became widely popular on its own.

Influence from Home: Minstrelsy

American minstrelsy (blackface minstrelsy) Popular nineteenth-century musical variety shows that portrayed Black plantation life with actors in blackface playing stereotyped characters.

The most popular American nineteenth-century musical entertainment, however, was born at home. Musical variety performances, known as **American minstrelsy** (also known as "blackface minstrelsy"), featured actors in blackface who portrayed Black plantation life. Stereotyped characters such as "Jim Crow" were depicted as rowdy, comical, uneducated people without a care in the world.[1] Above all, these characters were always ready to make music.

The songs were typically in simple, **strophic** form, with **verse** and **chorus** structure, and danceable (see Musical Elements Appendix). Banjos generally dominated, accompanied by other instruments such as **fiddle**, **tambourine**, and **bones**. Minstrel shows became a vehicle, to some extent, for the dissemination of Black culture in the form of songs, dance, and, in particular, the **banjo**, an instrument which likely originated in Africa. Some minstrel show writers and composers took pains to include idiomatic musical traditions once they knew audiences were interested. Their representation of Black culture, however, was hardly systematic or authentic. Mingled with western idioms and tied to ticket sales, the resulting pastiche of traditional and commercial musical styles was transmitted throughout the US, Europe, and other parts of the world by touring minstrel productions.

Why was minstrelsy so popular? Perhaps nineteenth-century White audiences, obligated to conduct themselves according to a strict moral code throughout their own daily lives, found in minstrelsy an opportunity to cast off their Victorian restraints and vicariously enjoy the "carefree" lifestyle and music of a different culture. Furthermore, minstrelsy's portrayal of Black people as happy plantation slaves—as well as entertainingly musical and funny—would have been reassuring to White audiences who accepted the institution of slavery. Whatever their reasons, and despite the mostly shallow and inherently bigoted portrayal of the characters, this was the lens through which nineteenth-century minstrel show audiences saw Black Americans.

The Virginia Minstrels, led by **Dan Emmett (1815–1904)**, was one of the most successful troupes of the mid-nineteenth century. Emmet developed the "walk-around," a grand march on the minstrel show stage. Perhaps a parody of the "juba" and the "ring shout" (see Chapter 1, American Traditional Music, "Work Songs and Dance on the Plantation" and "Spirituals," respectively), the walk-around was performed with exaggerated gestures. One of Emmett's walk-around songs was the now famous "I Wish I Was In Dixie's Land" (1860), the same song that is now known simply as "Dixie."

Songwriter **Stephen Foster (1826–1864)**, who called himself a "tunesmith," contributed many songs to minstrel shows. His styles and topics covered a wide range, from nonsense to nostalgia, and included moving testimonies of tragedy from the mouths of African American characters. "Oh! Susanna" (1848) and "Camptown Races" (1850) are upbeat songs with nonsense verses; his nostalgic "My Old Kentucky Home, Good Night!" (1853), inspired by Harriet Beecher Stowe's *Uncle Tom's Cabin*, has been the Kentucky state song since 1928; and in the poignant "Nelly

Strophic form   Song structure in which the music is repeated for each stanza of text; see Musical Elements Appendix.

Verse   A group of lines that form a unit within a poem. In American vernacular music, the verse text does not usually repeat; see Musical Elements Appendix.

Fiddle   A bowed stringed chordophone. Structurally identical to a violin, the term "fiddle" implies a traditional folk or bluegrass style of repertory, technique, and performance practice; see Musical Instruments Appendix.

Chorus (refrain)   In American vernacular music, a line or group of lines in a poem or song that repeats both text and music; see Musical Elements Appendix.

Tambourine   Small-frame drum membranophone, which can also be an idiophone when the frame includes metal cymbals; see Musical Instruments Appendix.

Bones   A pair of stick idiophones made of bones or wood that are rhythmically struck together; see Musical Instruments Appendix.

Banjo   A plucked stringed chordophone with a fretted neck; see Musical Instruments Appendix.

Figure 2-3 Stephen Foster, c1860.

was a Lady" (1849), the singer mourns the death of his "dark Virginia bride." Some of Foster's lyrics expressed respect and sympathy for his African American subjects, unlike many other minstrel show songs.

Black musicians also participated in minstrelsy shows as performers, composers, directors, and producers, especially in the years after the Civil War. **James Bland (1854–1911)** was a celebrated Black songwriter, singer, banjo player, and comedic performer who toured Europe as well as the US and wrote hundreds of songs. His new lyrics to the older tune, "Carry Me Back to Old Virginny" reflect the poignant homesickness of a former slave who struggles in his new life. It was the Virginia state song for many years before it was retired in 1997 due to controversy over its sensitive topic.

Figure 2-4 Sheet music cover for "James Bland's 3 Great Songs," 1879.

PLAYLIST OPTIONS
MINSTREL SHOW SONG

FIND

One or two examples of a minstrel song, such as

- "Carry Me Back to Old Virginny" by James Bland
- "Dixie" attributed to Dan Emmett
- "My Old Kentucky Home" by Stephen Foster
- "Nelly Was A Lady" by Stephen Foster
- "O, Dem Golden Slippers" by James Bland
- "Oh! Susanna" by Stephen Foster
- "Old Dan Tucker" by Dan Emmett
- "Turkey In The Straw" by Dan Emmett

Special note: The original lyrics of many minstrel songs would be considered offensive today. Most, but not all, modern arrangements have substituted or deleted the offending words.

OBSERVE

- Topic or theme: can either be realistic or nonsensical with comical or caricatured subjects.
- Instrumentation: vocalists may or may not have instrumental accompaniment.

ASK

- A wide range of styles is possible in a modern arrangement: does your example resemble a specific musical style, such as folk, country, or blues?
- Do you believe your example has lasting value and should still be performed even if some words need to be changed?

Vaudeville

Variety shows, long popular with predominantly male audiences in dance halls and saloons, achieved a more family-friendly status in the late nineteenth-century with the adoption of **vaudeville** (Fr., "city voices") by impresario Antonio (Tony) Pastor (1837–1908). A former minstrel show

Vaudeville (Fr. "city voices") Light variety show that can include music, dance, comedic skits, and acrobatics.

Figure 2-5 Al Jolson, c1925.

and circus performer, Pastor forged a new type of American theatrical entertainment that attracted middle-class audiences with light-hearted comedy, acrobatics, circus stunts, and music. Vestiges of minstrelsy survived in occasional blackface skits, but most of the themes had changed.

Vaudeville was popular from the 1880s through the 1930s. These were true variety shows with a series of about eight to twelve "turns," or acts, each no longer than around twenty minutes. The genre, which flourished first in New York City, offered a diverse roster of performers who toured around the country. Shows often featured African American, Irish, and Jewish comedy teams and dancers.

The vaudeville genre jump-started the careers of a large number of performers, many of whom later appeared on Broadway and in film. Two in particular stand out. The great Black tap dancer Bill "Bojangles" Robinson (1878–1949) was noted for his consummate technique and brilliance. He had performed since he was a child, and after a long career in vaudeville, he was able to branch out to Broadway and film in the 1930s when he often danced alongside the young Shirley Temple. **Al Jolson (1886–1950),** the son of a rabbi, emigrated with his family to the US from eastern Europe. His trademark blackface character came from a minstrel show performance that predates his career in vaudeville. Jolson was known for his expressive vocal style for which he used both operatic and blues techniques. Perhaps the most celebrated performer of his day, he reached the pinnacle of his career when he starred in the first feature-length film with talking sequences, *The Jazz Singer,* released by Warner Brothers in 1927 (see this chapter's section on film music, below).

Extravagant vaudeville shows with glamorous chorus lines, known as "revues," were best exemplified by the famous *Ziegfeld Follies,* produced by impresario Florenz Ziegfeld Jr. (1867–1932). Ziegfeld produced a number of Broadway shows, including the celebrated *Show Boat* (see this chapter's section on musical theater, below), and he built the "Ziegfeld" theater in New York City in 1927. **Fanny Brice (1891–1951)** starred as a comedian and singer in many *Follies* shows for several years after a show-stopping appearance in a 1910 *Follies* production. Her famous *shtick* (comedic routine or theme) as the bratty child "Baby Snooks," which she first performed in a *Follies* show, earned her success with a long-running radio show devoted to the character.

Burlesque, which originally referred to staged comedic satire, gradually became the term for "girlie shows" that featured striptease in the context of costumed spectacle, dance, and vocal performance during the early twentieth century. **Josephine Baker (1906–1975)** was a Black dancer, singer, and actor who began as a chorus line dancer in vaudeville revues. She moved to France in 1925, where she achieved world fame as an entertainer whose acts included erotic dance. Her involvement in the French Resistance during World War II and her outspoken support of the American Civil Rights Movement made her a hero to many on both sides of the Atlantic.

Vaudeville gave us many well-known and influential performers, such as the Marx Brothers, Jack Benny, and Bob Hope, most of whom included music in their comedic *shticks* as they went on to star in radio, film, and television after vaudeville was no longer a popular genre. Latter-day television comedy variety shows that owe much to vaudeville's legacy include *The Ed Sullivan Show* (1948–1971), *The Tonight Show* (1954–present), and *Saturday Night Live* (1975–present).

PLAYLIST OPTIONS
VAUDEVILLE

FIND

A musical video of a prominent performer or ensemble whose careers included vaudeville, such as

- Fred Astaire and Ginger Rogers
- Pearl Bailey
- Josephine Baker
- Fanny Brice
- George Burns and Gracie Allen
- Al Jolson
- Gypsy Rose Lee
- The Marx Brothers
- Bill "Bojangles" Robinson

OBSERVE

- The role of music in your example's "act." The skit might be comedic, dramatic, or even athletic in the case of many dancers.
- Whether sexuality plays a role in your example's performance in either dance or topic. This might be an example of burlesque theater.

ASK

- Is your example still as impressive or funny as it must have been originally, or is it outdated?
- Does your example satirize or otherwise reference a particular ethnic group, either openly or subtly (with appearance, costume, or spoken idioms)?

II
BROADWAY DOMINATES MUSICAL THEATER

The Composers: Roots in Tin Pan Alley

Tin Pan Alley Early twentieth-century song-writing and sheet-music industry; industry district in New York City; style of songwriting that developed what became known as the "standard" form: AABA.

Sheet music Unbound sheets of printed music, usually of individual songs or brief instrumental works.

Much of the music for Broadway musical theater was born in **Tin Pan Alley**: a term that describes an industry, a place, and a style. When several music publishers set up shop close to each other in the late 1890s on West 28th Street between Fifth and Sixth Avenues in Manhattan, this became known as the Tin Pan Alley district after the noisy sound of the songwriters' pianos emanating from the publisher's offices.

A popular song structure emerged and became the dominant Tin Pan Alley formula, known as the "standard" form, expressed as AABA: repeated choruses with a contrasting bridge section between the last two choruses (see the Musical Elements Appendix.) Songs were marketed with "song pluggers," singers and piano players who performed songs in public. They hoped to encourage consumers to buy the **sheet music—**

Figure 2-6 Tin Pan alley on West 28th Street in New York City, late 19th or early 20th century.

Figure 2-7 Sheet music cover for "The Sidewalks of New York," 1914.

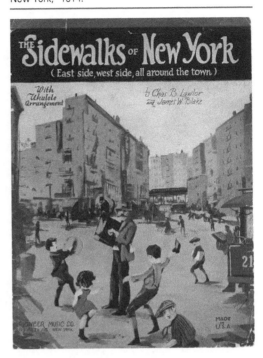

the published notated versions of the songs, usually in piano score. Sheet music title pages often used captivating images to evoke the themes of the songs and attract buyers. Famous early Tin Pan Alley songs include "After the Ball" by Charles K. Harris (1891), "The Sidewalks of New York" by Black and Lawlor (1894), and "Take Me Out to the Ball Game" by Norworth and Von Tilzer (1908). Some of the most prominent Broadway composers described below began their careers as songwriters and song pluggers in Tin Pan Alley.

George M. Cohan (1878–1942) began as a child vaudeville performer with his family and grew up to become a prominent composer in Tin Pan Alley, as well as a Broadway playwright and performer. He is most well known for his patriotic songs such as "You're a Grand Old Flag" and "Yankee Doodle Boy." Although his songs are relatively simple, Cohan is considered by many to be the father of American musical theater for the unabashedly American vernacular style of his contributions. A bronze statue of Cohan, who composed "Give My Regards to Broadway," stands in Times Square on Broadway and 46th Street.

Irving Berlin (1888–1989) was a self-taught musician who became known for his simple and appealing melodies. "Alexander's Ragtime Band" (1911) was his first successful song, and many hits followed.

Figure 2-8 George Gershwin, 1937.

He was awarded a Congressional Medal of Honor for his "God Bless America" (1938). After building a reputation as a songwriter, he went on to write Broadway musicals, including *Annie Get Your Gun* (1946). He also contributed to Hollywood films, such as *White Christmas* (1954).

The wealthy and well-educated **Cole Porter (1891–1964)** was not associated with Tin Pan Alley but, nevertheless, deserves mention in this list of prominent contributors to American song and Broadway musicals. Originally from Indiana, he wrote hundreds of songs while taking music classes at both Yale and Harvard. He moved to Paris in 1917 where he continued his musical studies. There, he married a socialite and together they gave fashionable parties at which he performed his own songs. By the late 1920s, his music was an important force on Broadway. *Anything Goes* (1934) was one of his most successful hits. One of the few songwriters who wrote the lyrics as well as the music, Porter was brilliant at both. His witty lyrics included surprising rhymes and daring double entendres with references that can still shock audiences. The music of this thoroughly educated composer was no less sophisticated: unusual melodies, harmonies, and rhythms challenge performers, surprise listeners, and powerfully convey the layers of meaning in each song.

George Gershwin (1898–1937) dropped out of high school to work as a song plugger on Tin Pan Alley. He played and sang for hours to advertise new songs written by others, and before long, he began composing his own. Al Jolson recorded Gershwin's first hit song, "Swanee," in 1920. Throughout his successful career as a songwriter, Gershwin continued his classical music studies, and in 1924, he performed the piano part in the premiere of his *Rhapsody in Blue* for piano and orchestra. This was a landmark work, which blended art and popular music with the new style, jazz. Western art and African American influences remain strong in his future crossover works, such as in the orchestral tone poem, *An American in Paris*. Gershwin's Broadway musical career also flourished. He collaborated with his brother, lyricist Ira Gershwin (1896–1983). "I Got Rhythm" became an especially popular song, and has become a jazz standard throughout the twentieth century. Gershwin's "American folk opera" *Porgy and Bess* (1935) from the novel *Porgy* by DuBose Heyward is about life in a Charleston, South Carolina, Black community. It includes the famous song, "Summertime."

The Shows: Song, Book, and Concept

Many shows in musical theater can be roughly categorized according to their focus: song, story, or theme. Musicals that emphasize song feature just enough plot to justify a string of songs, each plugged in wherever the opportunity allows throughout the show. The songs are the focus, and the drama serves only as their framework. These shows were especially popular in the early twentieth century with Cohan and others (see *Little Johnny Jones* and *Shuffle Along*, below; also see Cohan's comment in the caption to Figure 2-4). Their popularity continues today. "Jukebox musicals," for instance, use preexisting songs by beloved performers and often very little plot. *Ain't Misbehavin'* (1978), a tribute to Harlem Renaissance musicians, and *Come, Fly Away* (2010), which features Frank Sinatra songs, are two examples.

The story, rather than the song, is most important in a **book musical**. "Book," in Broadway jargon, means the same thing as opera's term **"libretto"** (It., "little book"): the dramatic script. Dramatic narrative is the focus, and everything else serves the drama. Songs happen—and plot is arrested—at emotional or reflective moments, but they are carefully interwoven in a way that supports the dramatic scheme. Book musicals are often based on preexisting literary works, such as *Showboat* or *South Pacific* (see descriptions below).

Certain late-twentieth-century musicals without traditional, linear story lines, but which featured innovative themes, settings, and music, began to be called **concept musicals**. Some of these musicals seem to make statements on culture, politics, religion, or some other aspect of the human condition. *Hair* (1967), *Jesus Christ, Superstar* (1971, see description below), and more recently *Hamilton* (2015), for instance, each address aspects of the late-twentieth- and early-twenty-first-century sociopolitical viewpoints.

Whether we should think in terms of "song musicals," "book musicals," or "concept musicals" is arguable. Many musicals draw from all three spheres; in fact, don't all musicals have songs, a story line, and a governing concept to unify them? We use these terms here to help us explore the differences between musicals and to understand the way musicals

Book musical Musical theater in which the drama, rather than song, is most important; usually adapted from a book.

Libretto: (It. "little book") The text, or dramatic script, of a musical work. A librettist is the author of the text (also see Chapter 7, Baroque Music).

Concept musical Musical theater that emphasizes innovative themes, settings, and music rather than traditional, linear story lines.

are talked about; but the usefulness of these labels is limited. After this introduction to the genre, listeners are encouraged to experience each show as a unique entity and to value each on its own merits. We should also remember that the term "Broadway musical" often denotes genre rather than the origin of a particular musical. Many well-known musicals, some of which end up on Broadway, begin as shows in other parts of the country or in other countries. *Cats* (1981) and *The Phantom of the Opera* (1986), for instance, both began in the West End of London.

Little Johnny Jones (1904)
George M. Cohan (1878–1942)
Songs include "Yankee Doodle Boy" and "Give My Regards to Broadway."

Cohan wrote the book, lyrics, and music and directed and starred in this show about an American jockey who visits England and is tempted by corruption but stays true to his all-American principles. Although this musical originates from Cohan's book, story is not the focus (see Figure 2-4 caption); the plot is a simple morality tale in the style of a melodrama. Musical and thematic aspects, however, break new ground. During a time when European operettas and melodramas were still popular on American stages, Cohan assertively threw off the yoke of foreign artistic sensibilities with a patriotic testimony to everything American. His future contributions would continue in this vein.

Shuffle Along (1921)
Noble Sissle (1889–1975) and Eubie Blake (1883–1983), music and lyrics; based on the book by Flournoy Miller and Aubrey Lyles.
Songs include "Love Will Find a Way" and "I'm Just Wild About Harry."

Shuffle Along was a breakthrough Black musical, which paved the way for eight more to follow on Broadway by 1924. The simple plot about a mayoral campaign is used as an excuse to hang together a "musical *mélange*" of skits that includes old minstrel show stereotypes in blackface humor. The show's energetic **choreography** featured jazz-inspired moves and was particularly influential. In fact, Ziegfeld hired the show's chorus girls to coach his *Ziegfeld Follies* dancers. The music and dancing made *Shuffle Along* an unexpected hit: the troupe went on national tour after hundreds of performances on Broadway. The show's success helped launch the careers of a significant number of musicians associated with the Harlem

Choreography The sequence of dance movements or the notated version of dance movements.

George M. Cohan: "As for the plot, the masses don't want it. At least, that's my dope on the matter. It's like coating bitter medicine with sugar—this business of feeding plot to an audience. And it must slide down without too much irritation. I try to unweave my plot without letting the audience know they're getting plot. It's sort of slipped in, unknown to them. Hand plot to an audience in brazen fashion, and it rankles. I merely suggest, and let the audience write out the history to suit themselves."[2]

Renaissance, including Josephine Baker (see above), **Paul Robeson (1898–1976),** and the show's writers. Robeson played football at Rutgers and then studied law at Columbia before achieving worldwide fame as a singer and actor. He was blacklisted during the McCarthy era in the 1950s when Senator Joseph McCarthy accused hundreds of Americans—especially in the entertainment industry—of treasonous Communist ties.

Figure 2-10 Sheet music cover for "I'm Just Wild About Harry" from *Shuffle Along*, 1921.

Figure 2-11 Paul Robeson, 1942.

Show Boat (1927)
Jerome Kern (1885–1945), music; Oscar Hammerstein II (1895–1960), lyricist; Ziegfeld, producer
Songs include "Can't Help Lovin' Dat Man" and "Ol' Man River."

This story, based on the Edna Ferber novel of the same name, describes a racially mixed marriage and the devastating impact of racism. The melodic and rhythmic sophistication of Kern's music betrays his strong musical education and his experience as a prolific songwriter and composer of Broadway musicals. The music for *Show Boat* was artfully interwoven into the drama more than most other musicals of its day, which often simply "plugged in" Tin Pan Alley songs throughout the show. This made *Show Boat*, arguably, the first "book" musical: a watershed moment in American musical theater. Paul Robeson's performance of "Ol' Man River" in several productions and in the 1936 film version was especially acclaimed. *Show Boat* remains an important—many would say the most significant—musical in the repertory of American musical theater.

South Pacific (1949)

Richard Rogers (1902–1979), music; Oscar Hammerstein II (1895–1960), lyricist.
Songs include "Some Enchanted Evening," "There Is Nothing Like a Dame," and "You've Got to Be Carefully Taught."

The long-running **Rogers and Hammerstein** collaboration created this show as one among their string of Broadway hits, which included *Oklahoma* (1943), *The King and I* (1951), and *The Sound of Music* (1959). Based on stories from James Michener's *Tales of the South Pacific* (1947), the plot of *South Pacific* addresses racism. The story takes place in the South Pacific during World War II where an American nurse falls for an older Frenchman. She's disturbed, however, when she finds that his children from his late wife are Polynesian. Meanwhile, a US Navy Lieutenant loves a Polynesian girl but doesn't want to make a commitment to her; he faces his own prejudices when he sings, "You've Got To Be Carefully Taught." This musical and others by Rogers and Hammerstein feature stories that examine culture, gender, and class roles and include strong female characters. Many of their musicals later evolved into popular film versions.

Figure 2-12 Richard Rogers (left) and Oscar Hammerstein II, sometime before 1960.

Figure 2-13 Final scene from the original production of *South Pacific*, 1949. From left, Ezio Pinza, Barbara Luna, Michael or noel De Leon, and Mary Martin.

West Side Story (1957)
Jerome Robbins, choreographer and director; Leonard Bernstein, music; Stephen Sondheim, lyrics; Arthur Laurents, libretto. Songs include "Maria," "Somewhere," and "Tonight."

In *West Side Story,* urban gangs, violence, racism, and taboo romance in mid-twentieth-century New York City provide an updated setting for Shakespeare's tragedy, *Romeo and Juliet.* This challenging topic inspired innovative expressions in dance and music. The show's collaboration included several of the most creative professionals on Broadway at the time, which helped secure its critical and popular success: Jerome Robbins (1918–1998) was a versatile dancer, choreographer, and director and **Stephen Sondheim (b. 1930)** would go on to become the most respected lyricist and composer on Broadway in his generation. **Leonard Bernstein (1918–1990)**, a composer and conductor who was well educated in art music at Harvard, nevertheless maintained strong ties to art, music, and musical theater at the same time. His legacy as an educator was built both in academia and in the public sector in which he described and demonstrated the inner workings of art music to nonmusicians and children in national television broadcasts that included "Young People's Concerts" (1958–1972), influencing many in that generation, including this writer.

Figure 2-14 Leonard Bernstein, 1971.

Jesus Christ, Superstar (LP, 1970; Broadway production, 1971)

Andrew Lloyd Webber, music;
Tim Rice, lyrics; based on New Testament accounts of the Passion.
Songs include "I Don't Know How to Love Him," and "Jesus Christ, Superstar."

First a best-selling **concept album**, then, in the following year, a Broadway show, this portrayal of Christ's last week explores the inner—and very human—feelings of Jesus and of those closest to him. This controversial "rock opera" unveiled a radically different musical sensibility from the established Tin Pan Alley lyrical ballad, with more up-to-date popular musical idioms complete with prominent electric guitars and rebellious irony in the lyrics. **Andrew Lloyd Webber (b. 1948)**, a well-educated English musician, combines popular and art idioms in his music and has since achieved unprecedented international success. His longtime collaboration with lyricist Tim Rice also produced *Joseph & the Amazing Technicolor Dreamcoat* (1967), *Cats* (1981), and *Phantom of the Opera* (1986).

Concept album
An album that provides thematic unity with ambitious virtuosity, depth, and often experimentation in the music, lyrics, and cover art (Chapter 4, Modern American Popular Music Part I: Up to 1970).

Figure 2-15 Andrew Lloyd Webber, 2007.

A Chorus Line (1985)
**Michael Bennett (1943–1987), choreographer
and director, in collaboration with Bob Avian;
Marvin Hamlisch (1944–2012), music;
James Kirkwood Jr. and Nicholas Dante, book.
Songs include "I Hope I Get It," and "What I Did For Love."**

In this concept musical, the audience watches a show about an audition for a show. The chorus line applicants, or "Broadway gypsies," share their backgrounds, dreams, and talents while the director's voice occasionally interjects from the back of the theater. This can give the impression that the choristers are auditioning for the audience as well. We know that this portrayal of the sometimes unmercifully demanding world of chorus line work becomes a metaphor for any job search when we hear these lyrics in "I Hope I Get It":

> Who am I, anyway?
> Am I my resume?
> That is a picture of a person I don't know.

Bennett, who considered dance the essence of Broadway theater, was already a prominent choreographer when he developed this innovative idea. The creation of the show began as a workshop with several dancers, and the book and score followed. *A Chorus Line* opened off-Broadway at the New York Shakespeare Festival and moved to Broadway shortly afterward. The show was a great success for hundreds of performances before its first Broadway run was over in 1990.

The Lion King (1994 film/1997 stage show)
**Julie Taymor, director; Elton John, Lebo M., and Hans Zimmer,
music; Tim Rice, lyrics; Garth Fagin, choreographer;
Roger Allers and Irene Mecchi, book;
based on the Disney 1994 feature length animated film.
Songs include "Circle of Life," "Hakuna Matata," and
"Can You Feel the Love Tonight."**

Disney's *The Lion King* began as a feature length animated film in 1994 and became a Broadway stage show in 1997. In between those dates, however, Walt Disney Records released an album based on the film soundtrack, *Rhythm Of The Pride Lands,* in 1995. All three productions include Zulu lyrics, but the 1995 album's music goes further than the film soundtrack to evoke African musical styles, and the stage show travels further still into African territory with additional music and intentionally visible percussionists on African drums during performances. Other parts of the world inform the stage show as well: both African and Indonesian dance inspired the choreography, and director and costume designer Julie Taymor's (b. 1952) large, colorful puppets, masks, and costumes—which make a point of showing the human performers—draw on Japanese puppetry and Balinese mask-making in addition to African styles.

The film, album, and stage show music was created by a variety of composers and lyricists, most notably Hans Zimmer, Elton John, and South African composer and singer Lebohang "Lebo M." Morake (b. 1964), whose Zulu chant opens the film (see more about Zimmer and John in this chapter's section on film music, below, and in Chapter 5, Modern American Popular Music Part II: After 1970, respectively). Lebo M., who left South Africa as a youth during apartheid, brought African music and a deeper meaning to the production: he took the project very personally. A tale of a rightful king's return to his homeland after unjust treatment resonated with the South African expatriate musician during the dismantling of apartheid and Nelson Mandela's election to the presidency after 27 years as a political prisoner. Remarkably, Mandela's release and election happened during the same year as the release of the film.

This show's most important legacy would not be about the conversion of an animated feature film into a stage show; *Beauty and the Beast* had already done that in 1994. The staged version of *The Lion King* inspired innovative ways to portray nonhuman animals as characters and, at the same time, pioneered new territory in blending world cultural influences in American musical theater.

PLAYLIST OPTIONS
MUSICAL THEATER

FIND

- A filmed version of a musical to view either as an excerpt or in its entirety. (Most shows discussed above, and many more, are generally available as films.)

OBSERVE

- Theme and plot: whether the story takes on a controversial or otherwise difficult topic.

- Visual "feast": Note choreography, setting, and costumes.
- Song structure: whether the structure is the Tin Pan Alley standard "AABA" or something different.
- Instrumentation: Piano, orchestra, late-20th-century popular and rock, or non-Western musical instruments and idioms.

ASK

- What is the most important aspect of your musical; does your example fit into a "song," "book," or "concept" category of musical? Or does it draw from more than one of those types?
- Does the musical style reflect the cultural setting of the musical?

III
FILM MUSIC

History of Film Music

An important new medium emerged just before the twentieth century. Dramatic visual techniques not feasible in live theater were suddenly viable in film, and the same can be said for musical techniques. Film has provided much more than simply another venue for musical accompaniment: the medium is a platform for a wide variety of functions and techniques in dramatic music, some of which put the importance of music on an equal footing with image.

Music was involved from the start. In the earliest years, from the 1890s to the late 1920s before sound was successfully incorporated into film, musicians (often keyboardists or orchestras) accompanied viewings in movie theaters. Of course, the goal was to enhance the drama, but music was also needed to drown out the mechanical projector sounds. Musical accompaniment included preexisting art and popular music, originally composed prepared music, and improvised music with cue sheets. Musicians, often drawing on techniques from melodrama, used formulaic phrases and harmonies to describe stereotyped characters and situations.

Advances in film sound technology came in spurts, with major milestones in the 1920s. In 1926, Warner Brothers debuted a technology that synchronized recorded music and sound effects—but no audible dialogue—in the film, *Don Juan*. *The Jazz Singer* (1927) with Al Jolson was another important step in the process with recorded music, sound effects, and a few talking sequences; the rest of the dialogue was titled in silent-film style. The plot, concerning a young singer's struggle between tradition and modernity, is especially significant here, at a turning point in film history. The first complete sound film in which all dialogue, as well as music and sound effects, was incorporated into the film, came in 1928 with the crime drama, *Lights of New York*.

Figure 2-16 Poster for the film, *The Jazz Singer*.

Major Film Music Composers

The style of early-twentieth-century film music was mostly rooted in nineteenth-century European romantic orchestral music. Show tunes, popular songs, and the Tin Pan Alley formulas naturally became part of the mix when a number of Broadway composers migrated to Hollywood during the Depression. Austrian born **Max Steiner (1888–1971)** worked on Broadway when he first came to the US before moving to Hollywood in 1929 where he scored the music to hundreds of films. His style was based on Western art music traditions, but he incorporated popular, folk, and show tunes when called upon by dramatic necessity as in *Gone with the Wind* (1939) and *Casablanca* (1942). American musician **Alfred Newman (1901–1970)** made his move from Broadway to Hollywood in 1930. He arranged popular songs and Broadway music for film in *Tin Pan Alley* (1940), *South Pacific* (1958), *Camelot* (1967), and many others. He wrote original film scores to *Wuthering Heights* (1939) and *How the West Was Won* (1962). Newman also composed the iconic 20th Century Fox fanfare, which still opens that company's films. Both Steiner and Newman were among the most influential film musicians of their day. The Newman influence did not stop with Alfred: other members of his family, most notably his nephew Randy Newman (b. 1943), also rose to prominence in film music.

Figure 2-17 James Horner.

Later generations of film composers continue to carry the romantic orchestral tradition forward. We hear this in the richly textured symphonic film scores of **John Williams (b. 1932)** such as *Jaws* (1975), *Close Encounters of the Third Kind* (1977), all of the *Star Wars* movies (from 1977, ongoing at the time of this writing), *Raiders of the Lost Ark* (1981), and *Jurassic Park* (1993). **James Horner (1953–2015)**, who wrote the scores for *Titanic* (1997), *A Beautiful Mind* (2001), *Avatar* (2009), *The Magnificent Seven* (2016; posthumous release), and many other films, adds electronic elements and cultural references to his music. German composer **Hans Zimmer (b. 1957)** pushes electronic music much further and also brings in rock elements to create a hybrid style. Zimmer's film work includes *Rain Man* (1988), *The Lion King* (1994),

Hans Zimmer: "When all is said and done, and we've built the highest high-rises and we've built the fastest machines, there's still gonna be room for somebody to tell you a story or somebody to write you a piece of music."[3]

Inception (2010), *12 Years a Slave* (2013), and *Interstellar* (2014). Zimmer also began composing video game music in 2010 with *Call of Duty: Modern Warfare 2.*

What Is Film Music?

Soundtrack (sound track, film score) All the sound in a film, including special effects, dialogue, and music; specifically, the music in a film.

The "sound track" includes all the sound in a film, including special effects, dialogue, and music. When the music became commercially successful as a packaged entity on its own, however, the term **soundtrack** (or **sound track**) can refer specifically to the music in a film and, even more specifically, those excerpts that are collected and published as albums. A film's music may also be described as the "film score." Soundtracks are usually composed after filming. Modern composers view the film on a video console with a time counter and software to aid synchronization as they work on the music. Orchestrators, music copyists, synthesizer programmers, and others are involved in the process of developing film music.

Film Music's Function

The function of music in a film is often more layered and changeable than we realize. While we watch the story, we assume that the music tells the truth about the setting, characters, and impending events, and it usually does. But sometimes the music deceives or scares us; other times it confuses us, or it can simply fall silent. Everything about music in film is meaningful in its presence or absence, its source, and its commentary on—or disregard of—what we see.

Diegetic music (source music) In film, music that the characters experience from inside the story; the characters hear, or might even produce, the music.

We can begin with the important distinction between music that is part of the characters' world or music intended only for the audience. Music that the characters experience is known as **diegetic**, or **source music**. The characters hear, or might even produce, the music, which could be a band playing at a wedding reception or a main character's rehearsal for a concert. Diegetic music can help set a realistic scene with TV or radio music playing in the background of a dialogue, and it can even add spatial depth to the film's fictional world with faintly heard music from another room. The nightclub setting for *Casablanca,* directed by Michael Curtiz with film score by Max Steiner (1942), provides plenty of opportunity for diegetic music with Sam's character, the cabaret performer who sings for the patrons. His repertory includes the iconic theme song of the movie, "As Time Goes By," upon which Steiner based much of his film score.

But only the film's audience can hear **nondiegetic music**, also known as **underscoring**, which is meant to heighten the narrative and symbolically express emotions and meanings the filmmakers want the audience to experience. When a couple's first kiss is amplified by a full orchestra, it doesn't matter that a 100-piece orchestra would never fit in the tiny apartment or hallway where it happens because we know it is a special effect to make us feel the significance of the kiss.

In *A Beautiful Mind,* directed by Ron Howard (2001), James Horner's film score shifts back and forth between diegetic and nondiegetic music. This story is based on the life of the Nobel Prize–winning mathematician John Nash; the film describes his discoveries as well as his mental illness. When he makes a theoretical breakthrough as a Princeton student, the audience needs musical help to create the illusion that we can comprehend his abstract thought. His first glimmer of the idea takes place in a tavern with music diegetically emanating from a jukebox. When the idea dawns on Nash, the jukebox sound shifts to nondiegetic music that represents Nash's abstract thought process with a rich, complex, texture; a hypnotic blend of voice and instruments seems to imply a thought process in patterns. Moments later, the nondiegetic music is gone: we're back in the tavern soundscape with the diegetic jukebox music, and Nash is explaining his idea to his companions. The nondiegetic film score helped to bridge the gap between a mathematician's most advanced idea and the audience's comprehension of it.

Music in a film can move with the action in synchronization. Close physical synchronization to the point of cartoon-like mimicry is known as "mickey-mousing" and can have a humorous effect … or not, as in Alfred Hitchcock's *Psycho*, scored by Bernard Herrmann (1960). In the famous shower scene, the music mimics the murderer's stabbing motions as well as the victim's screams. The music is emotionally synchronized with the horrifying event, as well, with sharp, jabbing, dissonant (clashing) chords. The music doesn't always match what we see, however. In Martin Scorsese's *Goodfellas* (1990), Donovan's lyrical utopian song "Atlantis" (Donovan, 1968) is set against another savagely violent murder scene. This use of irony—an opposition between visual drama and music—heightens both intellectual and emotional tension when it shows the incongruity between what is expected or wished for with what actually happens.

The film score can indicate dramatic structure when it punctuates a turn of events or a character's emotions with changes in theme and instrumentation. Musical silence is particularly effective: the sudden

Nondiegetic music (underscoring) In film, music from outside of the story that only the film's audience can hear, which is meant to heighten the narrative and symbolically express emotions and meanings the filmmakers want the audience to experience.

absence of music is a powerful statement that forces the audience to refocus. *A Beautiful Mind* uses the absence of music as an after-effect: when Nash is ushered into the Pentagon in order to decode a Soviet communication, we hear a majestic theme suitable for the impressive halls of the country's military nucleus and for the service he is about to perform. Once he's presented with the problem, the film score expands on the theme from the earlier tavern scene's birth of an idea, taking another opportunity for nondiegetic music to bridge the gap between his realization of a complex, abstract problem and the audience's comprehension of it. After he ingeniously solves their problem, however, the generals are no longer interested in him, the thank you and handshake seem perfunctory, and the noticeable absence of music as he leaves expresses his disappointment.

PLAYLIST OPTIONS
FILM MUSIC

FIND

- Scenes that include music from one or two of your favorite films.

OBSERVE

- The points at which music is present or absent.
- Examples of diegetic or nondiegetic music.
- Examples of synchronization or irony between what you see and what you hear.
- The name/s of the film score composer/s if the film has one.

ASK

- How effective are your examples in helping you to experience the drama?
- What would the scene be like without the music or with different music? Try your scenes without sound, with subtitles for dialogue, and imagine what your soundtrack would be like.

Some directors decide to use only preexisting music, such as popular songs, in films such as George Lucas's *American Graffiti* (1973), Martin Scorsese's *Goodfellas* (1990), and Quentin Tarantino's *Pulp Fiction* (1994).

Fully orchestrated scores, however, dominate other films. Composer John Williams uses **leitmotifs**, or musical motives that represent characters, places, objects, or ideas, throughout the *Star Wars* cycle (1977–2005) much as they are used in Wagnerian opera (see Chapter 9, Romantic Era Music). Many film scores quote preexisting music; Max Steiner does this in his score for *Gone With The Wind* (1939), which incorporates well-known tunes to heighten nostalgic or patriotic emotions, the minstrel tune "Dixie" among them.

Much of the music we hear in film is fluid in its functions and meanings, constantly shifting between presence and absence, diegesis and nondiegesis, synchronization and irony. The blurred functions and implications of the soundtrack are intentional, meant to intensify the audience's experience of the drama. But film music can be more than accompaniment: it often defines the meaning of the images we see.

Leitmotif (**Ger. "leading motif"**)   A musical motive that represents a person, place, object, or idea. The term is associated with Wagner, and is similar to *idée fixe* (Chapter 9, Romantic Era Music).

CHAPTER 2 VOCABULARY & IMPORTANT FIGURES

Vocabulary

American minstrelsy (blackface minstrelsy)

Banjo

Bones

Book musical

Choreography

Chorus (refrain)

Concept musical

Diegetic music (source music)

Libretto: (It. "little book")

Musical Form

Nondiegetic music (underscoring)

Sheet music

Soundtrack (sound track, film score)

Tambourine

Tin Pan Alley

Vaudeville (Fr. "city voices")

Verse

Important Figures

Josephine Baker (1906–1975)

Irving Berlin (1888-1989)

Leonard Bernstein (1918–1990)

James Bland (1854–1911)

Fanny Brice (1891–1951)

George M. Cohan (1878–1942)

Dan Emmett (1815–1904)

Stephen Foster (1826–1864)

George Gershwin (1898–1937)

James Horner (1953–2015)

Al Jolson (1886–1950)

Alfred Newman (1901–1970)

Cole Porter (1891-1964)

Paul Robeson (1898–1976)

Rogers and Hammerstein: Richard Rogers (1902–1979), composer, and Oscar Hammerstein II (1895–1960), lyricist

Stephen Sondheim (b. 1930)

Max Steiner (1888–1971)

Andrew Lloyd Webber (b. 1948)

John Williams (b. 1932)

Hans Zimmer (b. 1957)

ENDNOTES

[1] The racial segregation laws throughout the American South in the late nineteenth through the first half of the twentieth century were nicknamed "Jim Crow" laws after the minstrel show character.

[2] As printed in The Greatest of These… by Laurette Taylor, Published by George H. Doran Company, 1918, housed in the Library of Congress.

[3] (From the official trailer to "Hans Zimmer Teaches Film Scoring," masterclass.com: https://www.masterclass.com/classes/hans-zimmer-teaches-film-scoring?utm_source=Paid&utm_medium=Bing&utm_term=Aq-Prospecting&utm_content=Search&utm_campaign=HZ accessed 5/25/17.)

Image Credits

- Figure 2-1: Florine Stettheimer / Copyright in the Public Domain.
- Figure 2-2: H.R. Bishop and John Howard Payne / Copyright in the Public Domain.
- Figure 2-3: Source: https://commons.wikimedia.org/wiki/File:Stephen_Foster.jpg.
- Figure 2-4: Robert Toll / Copyright in the Public Domain.
- Figure 2-5: Source: https://commons.wikimedia.org/wiki/File:Al_Jolson_-_publicity.JPG.
- Figure 2-6: Source: https://commons.wikimedia.org/wiki/File:Tinpanalley.jpg.
- Figure 2-7: Source: https://commons.wikimedia.org/wiki/File:Sidewalks_of_New_York_cover.jpg.
- Figure 2-8: Carl Van Vechten / Copyright in the Public Domain.
- Figure 2-9: Carl Van Vechten / Copyright in the Public Domain.
- Figure 2-10: Noble Sissle and Eubie Blake / Copyright in the Public Domain.
- Figure 2-11: Gordon Parks / Copyright in the Public Domain.
- Figure 2-12: Source: https://commons.wikimedia.org/wiki/File:R_and_H.jpg.

The King & Carter Jazzing Orchestra, 1921.

CHAPTER

3 Jazz

I
PRECURSORS TO JAZZ

Jazz emerged out of an abundant assortment of cultural influences from at least three continents. Sub-Saharan African cultures contributed the expressive vocal styles and the call and response techniques we learned about in Chapter 1, American Traditional Music. The slightly lowered pitches on certain scale degrees in jazz melodies mark a blend of African and Western musical scales, later known as **blue notes**. African cultures also influenced the music's lively accents and complex layers of rhythms. **Improvisation**, the creation of music during performance, is a hallmark of both African musical styles and American jazz.

Creole musicians, with mixed European, Caribbean, and African heritages and a tradition of music education, added a strong element of cultivated musicianship. Their technical prowess in performance and in written notation added power of expression in ensemble and in solo music. Many non-Creole Black performers were well-trained musicians, too, but the high value placed on musical education by the Creoles of New

Blue notes Slightly lowered pitches on certain scale degrees in blues and jazz melodies.

Improvisation The creation of music during performance; common in many cultures and genres, it is a hallmark of American jazz.

The author owes special thanks and fond memories to George Broussard (1943–2017), who guided the content of Chapter 3 in great detail.

Orleans, in particular, injected strong elements of Western harmonies and Caribbean dance music into the blend. White musicians also played an important role in the birth of jazz, not only as a talented backdrop to a genre created by Americans of color but as musical innovators in their own right. European art music, to be studied in Unit 2, influenced structural and harmonic elements of jazz.

If cultural groups were important in the making of jazz, so were genres of music, each of which had a particular function for the listeners. The work songs, field hollers, spirituals, cakewalks, and other types of traditional African American music described in Chapter 1, American Traditional Music, played a key role in establishing the basic voice of jazz. The cakewalk was taken up by the minstrel shows, vaudeville, and musical theater and, in the process, became a popular dance for both Blacks and Whites in the late nineteenth and early twentieth centuries in the US and parts of Europe. Marching bands were also popular throughout the US, but they were especially prevalent in New Orleans where they performed for weddings, funerals, community festivals, and other events, as they still do. That city's love of parades crossed color barriers: Whites, Blacks, and Creoles all cultivated marching bands that played a wide variety of popular, sacred, and patriotic music.

Ragtime Syncopated musical genre popular in the late nineteenth and early twentieth centuries.

Figure 3-2 Scott Joplin, 1903.

Ragtime

The cakewalk's accented, "ragged" rhythms influenced—some say developed into—**ragtime**, a popular dance, vocal, and instrumental style. The distinctive accented rhythms of banjo strumming can be heard in ragtime's piano solos, and marching band music must have contributed to its repeating sections and march-like pulse. Ragtime was originally improvisatory music that later developed into a cultivated, written art form. St. Louis saloon owner Tom Turpin (1871–1922) was one of the first to publish instrumental ragtime music, and he developed a "school" of St. Louis ragtime when he hosted regional ragtime musicians at his establishment. The genre's most renowned composer, **Scott Joplin (c. 1867–1917)**, considered ragtime an art. He was a pianist and bandleader whose performance venues included minstrel shows and clubs. His published ragtime compositions earned him fame and some royalties, but he struggled in vain to find acceptance for his dramatic works. Despite a good review for his opera *Treemonisha* (see Chapter 10, "Nationalist Perspectives" section for more on Joplin's *Treemonisha*), he had no support for its production, and it wasn't until the late twentieth century, long after his death, that the opera was fully staged for the public. He wrote other operas, many of which were lost. He was awarded a posthumous Pulitzer Prize in 1976 for his contributions to American music.

Figure 3-3 Sheet music cover for "Maple Leaf Rag" by Scott Joplin, 1899 edition.

**PLAYLIST OPTIONS
RAGTIME**

FIND

An early ragtime title, such as

- "Harlem Rag" by Tom Turpin
- "Maple Leaf Rag" by Scott Joplin

Or a prominent ragtime performer, such as

- Eubie Blake
- Max Morath
- Joshua Rifkin

OBSERVE

- Distinctive accents
- March-like rhythms
- AABBCCDD or similar musical structure

ASK

- Do you hear more than one melody at a time in your example?

Blues

Early-twentieth-century musicians sang a variety of ballads and dance songs. Some played banjo or guitar while they sang, and others left the accompaniment to nonsinging players on banjo, guitar, fiddle, or other instruments. Their music included traditional Anglo-American style ballads, popular songs of minstrelsy (see Chapter 2, American Music for Stage and Screen), Black work songs such as field hollers, and the earliest blues songs. The large repertories of singers such as **Huddie "Lead Belly" Ledbetter (1889–1949)** encompass these genres; thus, these musicians provide a link to the blues. Lead Belly, "discovered" by John Lomax (see "The Lomax Family and the American Folk Music Revival" in Chapter 1, American Traditional Music), was a talented singer and songwriter who played various instruments, including the 12-string guitar, mandolin, and accordion. Lead Belly wrote songs on wide-ranging topics, including racism, religion, and even Hitler.

Figure 3-4 Huddie "Lead Belly" Ledbetter, c1942.

The most familiar aspect of the **blues** is its common theme of hardship and sorrow. Topics include love and eroticism, loss, crime, imprisonment, addiction, oppression, and the wish for a better life. By the first blues recordings in the 1920s, guitar or piano were the favorite accompanying instruments. The melodic structure usually follows the most typical poetic AAB structure such as in this first stanza of Robert Johnson's (1911–1938) "Cross Road Blues":

> I went to the crossroad, fell down on my knees
> I went to the crossroad, fell down on my knees
> Asked the Lord above "Have mercy, now save poor
> Bob, if you please."

In the lines above, and in each ensuing stanza, the accompanying melody stays nearly the same for each of the two first lines and then changes to accommodate a different, and longer, third line. In many blues songs, the repeating musical pattern is essentially strophic *as written*, but we *hear* plenty of variation in the sung performance practice of the melody when the singer offers extra emphasis and ornamentation in order to express

Blues Popular musical style with distinctive, recognizable harmonic and melodic patterns, which originated with American Black musicians.

Excerpt from Robert Johnson, "Cross Road Blues." 1936.

nuances of meaning in each stanza; in fact, improvisation permeates the music of blues singers and instrumentalists.

PLAYLIST OPTIONS
BLUES

FIND

An early-twentieth-century blues song, such as

- "Crossroad Blues"
- "Death Letter Blues"
- "Down Hearted Blues"
- "Hellhound on My Trail"
- "Kind Hearted Woman"
- "Memphis Blues"
- "St. Louis Blues"

Or a prominent early blues singer, such as

- Son House
- Robert Johnson
- Muddy Waters
- Huddie "Lead Belly" Ledbetter (also try "Leadbelly")
- Bessie Smith
- Mamie Smith (no relation to Bessie; another "classic" blues singer)

OBSERVE

- The topic
- AAB (or similar) poetic and musical structure
- Instrumental accompaniment
  - Single instrument played by the singer or an ensemble
- Twelve-bar blues chord progression

ASK

- Do you notice expressive ornamentation and improvisation from the vocal or instrumental line?
- What is the context of the performance? A crowded urban club; a professional recording studio; a rural setting?

Figure 3-5 W. C. Handy, 1941.

Figure 3-6 Blues singer Bessie Smith, 1936.

A distinctive blues harmonic sequence had been informally performed for years before **William Christopher ("W. C.") Handy (1873–1958)** captured it in written notation. Handy was a well-trained musician who composed his own music and also arranged others' blues songs. He standardized the **twelve-bar blues form**, a **chord progression** over which a melody is varied. The types of chords as well as the number of chords in a blues progression can vary, but the basic twelve-bar blues chord progression he popularized has become iconic in many musical genres.

A variety of styles developed among blues singers throughout the twentieth century. The earliest recorded blues songs were primarily sung by Black female singers in a style known as "classic" blues, accompanied by piano and sometimes a small band as well; their vocal approach was generally full-bodied and expressive. These performers were familiar with city life; Bessie Smith (1894–1937), for example, who made the some of the earliest blues recordings in the 1920s, sang in cabarets and on vaudeville stages in cities throughout the South and in northern cities such as St. Louis and New York City. Another distinctive early blues genre (often called "Delta blues") consisted of mostly Black male singers such as Son House (1902–1988), who accompanied themselves on guitar or similar instruments in rural settings, especially in the Mississippi Delta

Twelve-bar blues form In the context of American blues music, a chord progression over which a melody is varied; see Musical Elements Appendix.

Chord progression A series of chords; see Musical Elements Appendix.

Chord Two or more different pitches sounded together; see Musical Elements Appendix.

region. Compared to Bessie Smith, their vocal styles were rougher and their performances less commercial. As a genre, the blues has been and continues to be a pervasive and powerful influence on music throughout the world since the early twentieth century.

II
NEW ORLEANS, DIASPORA, AND THE JAZZ AGE

Naming New Orleans "the birthplace of jazz" would be an exaggeration: worksongs, blues, ragtime, and all the other precursors to jazz mentioned above came from wide regional areas in the United States throughout the South and even parts of the Midwest and Northeast. But New Orleans can be considered the first center of what later comes to be called "jazz," the place where much of the synthesis happened. This city was fertile ground for several reasons.

Antebellum New Orleans was unusual in that enslaved African Americans were given Sundays off and had permission to congregate. They gathered in what was then known as Congo Square (now a corner of Louis Armstrong Park). The cultural melting pot here was rich; congregants included not only Africans of many different ethnicities and their descendants but Caribbeans as well. Hundreds of people performed music and dance, spoke a variety of native languages and foods, and traded wares.

The passage of strict segregation laws in 1894 forced another synthesis after the Civil War. Up to this time, the Creoles in New Orleans lived and made music in an entirely different social sphere from Blacks. With segregation, the Creoles' technical prowess and cultivated musicianship were thrown together with the improvisatory and expressive styles of the Blacks. Dance band music from the rough clubs in the red-light district began to influence the music of the marching bands. Caribbean rhythms recalled by the Creoles found their way into ragtime, which mingled together with the blues, and a diverse but cohesive style began to develop. In the early twentieth century, these oppressive segregation laws spawned the poverty and racial tensions that fueled the first wave of the great migration of Blacks to northern cities in search of jobs. Many

New Orleans musicians, including two key figures in particular, moved North soon after they began their musical careers.

Figure 3-7 Depiction of late 18th century dancing in "Congo Square," later named "Louis Armstrong Park," in New Orleans, by E. W. Kemble in 1886.

The Creole musician **Ferdinand DeMenthe "Jelly Roll" Morton (1890–1941)** began playing piano in a New Orleans bordello as a teenager. He soon left to travel with minstrel shows, performing many styles of music: ragtime, blues, minstrel show songs, spirituals, and popular songs. As a bandleader and a soloist, he became one of the earliest recording artists in jazz. He was a consummate professional who stressed preparation and rehearsal. Ragtime was his foundation, but improvisation and the rich variety of textures in his music led his style into another sphere: jazz. He was celebrated for his structured ensemble music and for his sophisticated solo piano compositions. In 1938, folksong scholar Alan Lomax recorded a series of interviews with him at the Library of Congress, which includes performances by Morton as well as his comments on early jazz styles and musicians.

Figure 3-8 Ferdinand DeMenthe "Jelly Roll" Morton, c1917.

If ragtime was Morton's foundation, blues was Armstrong's. **Louis Armstrong (1901–1971)** had a difficult start in life: his odd jobs as a child included coal delivery; and after an arrest in 1912 at 11 years old, he was sent to the Colored Waif's Home for Boys in New Orleans where he received his first musical training and played cornet in a band. Later, he played professionally in clubs and on riverboat bands. He moved to Chicago in 1922 and built a national and international career as what many call the greatest jazz virtuoso of his generation and, perhaps, the most important

---

Scat Improvised jazz vocalizations of nonsense syllables that are improvised, often in imitation of musical instruments.

figure in jazz history. Listeners marveled at his lyrical improvisational style, which crossed rhythmic and harmonic boundaries. He did this with his voice, too, for Armstrong was a singer as well as a trumpeter, composer, and bandleader. He was one of the first to popularize **scat** singing, in which nonsense sounds are improvised, often in imitation of musical instruments. He also helped to standardize the solo chorus structure of jazz performances: the whole ensemble states the melody in beginning and ending choruses, but members each solo for a chorus in between. Armstrong, along with other jazz brass instrument players, used mutes in the bell of his trumpet in order to change the tone color. He helped to develop and popularize this practice, which led to a distinctive sound in jazz band music.

Figure 3-9 Louis Armstrong, 1955.

Harlem Renaissance An interdisciplinary cultural movement that celebrated and fostered African American achievements in scholarship and the arts, which reached its height in the 1920s.

Although what we now call jazz seemed to first coalesce in New Orleans before the 1920s, it wasn't known by that term until these musicians and many others moved to places like New York, Chicago, St. Louis, and Washington, DC. Harlem in New York City was the largest terminal of the Great Migration and the locus of the "New Negro Movement," later known as the **Harlem Renaissance**, which reached its height in the 1920s. This was an interdisciplinary cultural movement that celebrated and fostered African American achievements in scholarship and the arts. Philosopher Alain Locke, sociologist and co-founder of the NAACP W. E. B.

Du Bois, and poet Langston Hughes were a few of this movement's leaders. Musicians associated with the Harlem Renaissance include Louis Armstrong, Duke Ellington, W. C. Handy, Jelly Roll Morton, William Grant Still (to be discussed in Chapter 10, Modern Art Music), and many others.

The popularity of legendary clubs such as the Apollo Theater, the Cotton Club, and the Savoy Ballroom ensured good salaries for their dance band entertainers. Many speakeasies and private rent parties, which secretly served alcoholic beverages despite prohibition laws forbidding their sale, featured live entertainment as well. A distinctive characteristic of the piano music in these venues was the "stride" piano style, which features the left-hand alternation of low bass notes and treble chords (a repeating "boom-chick, boom-chick" rhythm) while the right hand plays the melody. This style features a strong rhythmic drive that makes listeners want to move and tap their feet.

But Harlem wasn't the only hotbed of jazz: other cities around the country cultivated jazz as well; Kansas City, Chicago, and St. Louis, among others, each developed their own "schools" of jazz. Thanks to radio broadcasts and concert tours featuring the most notable performers, many Americans and Europeans fell in love with the music, giving the name "the jazz age" to the 1920s.

PLAYLIST OPTIONS
JAZZ AGE PERFORMANCE

FIND

A 1920s performance by a prominent early jazz musician, such as

- early Louis Armstrong (keep in mind his career lasted well into the 1960s)
- King Oliver
- Jelly Roll Morton
- Fats Waller

Or a performance of a famous title, such as

- "Ain't Misbehavin'" by Fats Waller, Harry Brooks, and Andy Razaf
- "Black and Blue" by Fats Waller
- "St. Louis Blues" by W. C. Handy

- "West End Blues" by King Oliver (Louis Armstrong performance recommended)

OBSERVE

- Topic
- Instrumentation, such as piano or trumpet
- The role of each player in ensembles

ASK

- Do you notice influence from older styles, such as blues or ragtime?
- Do you notice newer styles, such as stride piano, scat singing, or the use of mutes with brass instruments?

III
SWING: BIG BANDS OF THE 1930S AND 40S

Tin Pan Alley Early twentieth century song-writing and sheet-music industry; industry district in New York City; style of songwriting that developed what became known as the "standard" form: AABA (Chapter 2, Music for Stage and Screen).

Swing The characteristic lilting rhythm of jazz; an improvisational expression of music that engages listeners. Swing dance music ranges from **sweet** (simple, danceable) to **hot** (sophisticated, sometimes complex) styles.

The popularity and influence of 1920s jazz helped lay the groundwork for the success of jazz dance bands during—and despite—the Great Depression of the 1930s. These large ensembles of 10–15 or more band members included brass, reeds, rhythm instruments, and often a vocalist. While many in the entertainment industry suffered, the big bands thrived by performing dance music based on popular **Tin Pan Alley** tunes, which they called "standards." It helped that after the 1933 repeal of Prohibition, the dance clubs were once more allowed to sell alcoholic beverages, which created more demand for live entertainment.

Performances sprang from a combination of notated compositions and arrangements, intense rehearsal, and improvisation. The music ranged from **sweet** (simple, danceable) to **hot** (sophisticated, sometimes complex) styles. Most importantly, the music was guided by a charismatic "swing" style, infectious but difficult to define. **Swing** refers to the characteristic lilting rhythm of jazz, but it carries a much deeper and more subjective meaning, as well: an improvisational melodic and rhythmic expression of music that, at its best, engages listeners physically, emotionally, and intellectually.

By the start of the big band era, **Duke Ellington (1899–1974)** was already a prominent bandleader in Harlem, performing regularly at the Cotton Club. He was a pianist from Washington, DC, whose earliest influences stemmed from ragtime. Professionally, his music needed to suit the situation: sometimes his band, for instance, accompanied burlesque style dancers during their years at the Cotton Club. But his most signature band music was "hot": sophisticated and elegant, with harmonic and rhythmic complexity. He was prolific; he wrote around 2,000 works, including songs, larger scale works, film scores, and an unfinished opera. Many consider him to be the most important composer in jazz history and among the best American composers of any style.

Clarinetist **Benny Goodman (1909–1986)** had some formal training at his family's synagogue in Chicago, but New Orleans blues musicians were his inspiration. He became a touring bandleader renowned for his high standards, which earned him the nickname, "the professor." The unprecedented success of his nationally broadcast 1935 Los Angeles performance launched the big band era. Enthusiastic teenagers began showing up at his performances, making him a teen idol despite his somewhat cool, intellectual persona.

Up to the late 1930s, Blacks and Whites seldom, if ever, performed together publicly; the US was a segregated nation. Blacks were prohibited from attending White establishments as customers even when they were employed as servers or performers (as in the Cotton Club). It was generally understood that the bands onstage were to be either all White or all Black. Most jazz musicians of any color, however, were frustrated and obstructed by the institutionalized racism. Musicians who appreciated each other's talents "jammed" (rehearsed and improvised) together privately or after closing hours, but it wasn't until well into the big band era that they began to come together on stage. Goodman, who was White, had always sought out his most talented colleagues, White and Black; for instance, he employed Black bandleader Fletcher Henderson to compose and arrange music for his band. In the late 1930s, Goodman helped pioneer integration onstage when he invited premier Black performers to his smaller ensembles, such as pianist Teddy Wilson, vibraphonist Lionel Hampton, and guitarist Charlie Christian to perform alongside himself and drummer Gene Krupa. His 1938 Carnegie Hall concert, which included Hampton and many other Black performers, was a racially integrated landmark public performance as well as an important debut for jazz in a venue renowned for its art music concerts.

Duke Ellington on playing piano: "When your pulse and my pulse are together we are swinging, with ears, eyes, and every member of the body tuned into driving a wave emotionally, compellingly, to and from the subconscious."[1]

Figure 3-11 Benny Goodman, c1970.

PLAYLIST OPTIONS
BIG BAND PERFORMANCE

FIND

A big band performance by a prominent bandleader or soloist, such as

- ◆ Count Basie
- ◆ Duke Ellington

- ◆ Ella Fitzgerald
- ◆ Benny Goodman

- Billie Holiday
- Glenn Miller

Or a performance of a famous title, such as

- "All of Me" as performed by Billie Holiday
- "A Tisket, A Tasket" as performed by Ella Fitzgerald
- "Begin the Beguine" as performed by Artie Shaw and His Orchestra
- "In the Mood" as performed by Glenn Miller and His Orchestra
- "It Don't Mean a Thing (If It Ain't Got That Swing)" as performed by Duke Ellington and His Orchestra with soloist Ivy Anderson
- "Satin Doll" as performed by Duke Ellington and His Orchestra
- "Sing, Sing, Sing" as performed by Benny Goodman and His Orchestra
- "Take the A-Train" as performed by Duke Ellington and His Orchestra

OBSERVE

- Instrumentation, and the presence or absence of a vocalist.
- Whether brass players are using mutes.

ASK

- Is your example "sweet" or "hot" swing?
- Why is this music "popular" rather than "art" (or is it)?

Vocal soloists added another dimension to the big bands. They cultivated their technical, improvisatory, and interpretive abilities just as the instrumentalists did. The best singers imbued their musical phrases with a depth of meaning and emotional expression that deeply affected their listeners. Some of them developed the fine art of scat improvisation.

Billie Holiday (1915–1959) grew up listening to Bessie Smith and Louis Armstrong. She was born in Baltimore but moved to New York City in the late 1920s where she sang to club patrons in Harlem jazz clubs and speakeasies. In 1935, she debuted at the Apollo and appeared in Duke Ellington's short film, *Symphony in Black*, as the blues singer. Despite a rather narrow vocal range, her powerful interpretive style and unusual vocal timbre inspired a loyal following who called her "Lady Day." Her melodic and rhythmic flexibility, which she used to imbue lyrics with meaning, achieved great emotional effect. She was courageous enough to perform Abel Meeropol's song, "Strange Fruit" (1939). The lyrics, which graphically paint a picture of a lynching, combined with her unique style of expression, are unforgettable. She was a soloist for several prominent bands, but she gravitated toward a solo career by the late 1930s after suffering through the racism she encountered on concert tours, especially when traveling with Artie Shaw's White band. Much of her short life was beset by stormy relationships, substance abuse, and legal problems, but she left behind dozens of recordings and a legacy as one of the most beloved jazz singers.

Figure 3-12 Billie Holiday, c1947

Ella Fitzgerald: "I know I'm no glamour girl, and it's not easy for me to get up in front of a crowd of people. It used to bother me a lot, but now I've got it figured out that God gave me this talent to use, so I just stand there and sing."[2]

When **Ella Fitzgerald (1917–1996)** won an Apollo Theater talent contest in 1934, she was a homeless runaway from an orphanage. She was soon a regular performer with drummer Chick Webb's band at the Savoy Ballroom, and when Webb died in 1939, she became leader of the band and renamed it "Ella Fitzgerald and her Famous Orchestra." She recorded and performed the rest of her long and distinguished career, often with other prominent musicians, including Louis Armstrong, Count Basie, Duke Ellington, and Benny Goodman. Her extremely wide vocal range and brilliantly executed scat improvisations earned the respect of instrumentalists and singers, as well as a devoted audience worldwide.

IV
ART: BEBOP, COOL, AND AVANT-GARDE (FREE) JAZZ

A new jazz style emerged during the 1940s, partly as a response to World War II era conditions. Big bands were no longer sustainable; these were hard times when most of the country's available resources went toward the war effort. Restaurants and clubs were not able to pay such large ensembles, and many of the bands' personnel and audience had enlisted in the military. The ensembles became much smaller: combos usually consisted of only four to six musicians. Trumpet, saxophone, piano, and drums dominated the new music, but others such as guitar and voice would often be included. This new music, called **bebop** (or "bop"), was also a reaction to the regimented big band practices of strict uniformity. Bandleaders had dictated everything from melody and rhythm to clothing and choreographed movement. Bebop (the name might have come from the sound of an improvised phrase) is creative, highly improvisatory music, which encouraged individualism among performers. The music is complex: its irregular phrasing, unexpected accents, and fast pace raises the level of this genre to high art, but it is not dance music. When musicians based their improvisations on familiar songs, listeners could hardly recognize the fragments of their beloved tunes, which the performers would leave in the dust after brief moments of clarity.

Bebop (or bop)
Creative, highly improvisatory, complex jazz genre, which encouraged individualism among performers in small combos that usually consisted of only four to six musicians.

Charlie Parker: "The beat in a bop band is with the music, against it, behind it, ... It pushes it. It helps it. Help is the big thing. It has no continuity of beat, no steady chugging. Jazz has, and that's why bop is more flexible."[3]

Numerous talented musicians are associated with the style, but two in particular are central to its development: trumpet player **John Birks "Dizzy" Gillespie (1917–1993)** and saxophonist **Charles "Charlie" Parker Jr. (1920–1955)**, also known as "Bird." Gillespie moved from his native South Carolina to New York in 1937 and developed an interest in Afro-Cuban idioms, which he incorporated into his jazz music. A picturesque stage presence with his signature beret, sunglasses, and puffed-out cheeks when he played his trumpet, Gillespie was an important influence on the "beat" movement (which included literature, art, and fashion) as well as the founder of bebop. Parker was a brilliant improviser with a wide range of musical interests that included country music and symphonic music, which he sometimes quoted in his improvisations. He grew up in Kansas City, Missouri, where he met Gillespie when the trumpet player was on tour in 1940. This began a collaboration that included after-hours jam sessions, live performances, and recordings. But Parker had been a heroin addict since his teens. Emotional and physical breakdowns related to his drug abuse repeatedly interrupted his career and his family life, and he died when he was only 35. By then, many other musicians had taken up the style. The extreme **dissonance** and wide, jagged intervals of bebop were not friendly to vocalists; nevertheless, several singers participated to great acclaim. Sarah Vaughan (1924–1990) and Ella Fitzgerald (see above, under "Big Bands") became renowned specialists in bebop scat improvisation.

Figure 3-15 John Birks "Dizzy" Gillespie, 1955.

Dissonance A combination of pitches that clash or sound unstable; see Musical Elements Appendix.

PLAYLIST OPTIONS
BEBOP, COOL, AND AVANT-GARDE (FREE) JAZZ

FIND

A post-WWII bebop, cool, or avant-garde jazz performance by one of the following performers:

- Dave Brubeck

- Miles Davis
- Ornette Coleman
- John Coltrane
- Ella Fitzgerald
- Modern Jazz Quartet
- Charles Mingus
- Thelonious Monk
- Gunther Schuller
- Cecil Taylor
- Sarah Vaughan

OBSERVE

- Whether the performance is based on a recognizable "standard" popular tune.
- The balance between familiar traditions and experimentation.

ASK

- Does your example fit one or more of the categories for this section (bebop, cool, or avant-garde)?

Cool jazz Sophisticated jazz genre after bebop with a more relaxed and less frenetic style.

Tonality (key) The organization of pitches and harmonies in hierarchical systems. Major and minor tonalities are the most common types in Western music; see Musical Elements Appendix.

Figure 3-16 Miles Davis, 1971.

Bebop inspired its own reaction: **cool jazz**. Still sophisticated—the rhythms and the **tonality** are not simple—but far less frenetic than bebop; cool is more relaxed, with narrower ranges and more emphasis on small ensembles than on individuals. Cool's combination of improvisation with carefully crafted composition, often performed in formal concert venues, place this style closer to classical "art" music than other jazz styles. An album called *Birth of the Cool* (1957) launched the style under bandleader **Miles Davis (1926–1991)**. A trumpet player, bandleader, and composer from Illinois, Davis moved to New York in 1944 and played with Charlie Parker before innovating his own style in experimental jam sessions with his talented colleagues.

After World War II, jazz developed in a variety of ways. Popular music influenced some of the jazz styles (see "Latin and Popular Influences," below), but for others, the music became ever more creative and complex. The new free (avant-garde) jazz style flourished along with the Civil Rights

Movement of the 1960s. Indeed, the music freed itself from musical rules of the past, creating an intellectual climate that hearkened back to the Harlem Renaissance or, as some would say, revived it. Pioneers in this style include pianist Dave Brubeck (1920–2012), saxophonists John Coltrane (1926–1967) and Ornette Coleman (1930–2015), pianist Theolonius Monk (1917–1982), horn player and jazz critic Gunther Schuller (1925–2015), and classically trained pianist Cecil Taylor (b. 1929). Political, social, and spiritual topics permeate much of this primarily instrumental style. World music and even historical "classical" music (in "third stream" jazz) are strong influences. Improvisation returned to the forefront, but conventional structures, such as the twelve- or sixteen-bar blues chorus, were gone and so were the characteristic swing rhythms and familiar harmonies. Was it still jazz?

V
POPULAR AND LATIN
INFLUENCES

While the esoteric, experimental free jazz styles further alienated casual listeners, some musicians took jazz in another direction toward popular music. "Hard bop," which grew out of bebop in the 1950s, emphasized Black musical roots with the strong bass lines and repetitive, syncopated rhythms characteristic of blues, gospel, and R & B. This style often drew on social justice and spiritual themes. Hard bop is exemplified by the music of Art Blakey (1919–1990) with his band The Jazz Messengers. **Wynton Marsalis (b. 1961)** advocates an appreciation of the roots and earlier styles of jazz. He is a renowned trumpet player, composer, director, and educator and is arguably the most high-profile jazz musician of his generation.

Rock music suddenly dominated the airwaves in the 1960s, leaving other styles to struggle in its shadow. Early in the decade, much of the music was rather simple compared to jazz, but some brilliant musicians, such as Jimi Hendrix, developed rock's musical language to a level that inspired jazz musicians. Miles Davis radically veered jazz toward rock with his 1969 album, *Bitches Brew*, a psychedelic blend of rock's electrified instruments with jazz improvisational idioms. His album created controversy among jazz listeners, but it undeniably boosted the profile of jazz

Figure 3-17 Wynton Marsalis, 2009.

Fusion A blend of jazz and rock musical styles.

while influencing both jazz and rock musicians. The new style became known as **fusion**. What has followed since is a stream of blended popular and jazz styles that includes offshoots of soul, disco, funk, and gospel music. Even hip-hop "swing jazz" includes sampling and scratching with jazz improvisation. Other fusion pioneers besides Davis include performer, composer, and producer Quincy Jones (b. 1933) and keyboardist and composer Herbie Hancock (b. 1940).

Latin musical idioms were already present in jazz as early as the first two decades of the twentieth century when Creole musician Jelly Roll Morton used what he called "the Latin tinge" in his rhythms. A rich, lively, and complex rhythmic texture that emphasized dance dominated Latin music. Latin big band leaders such as Xavier Cugat (1900–1990) and Tito Puente (see "Salsa," Chapter 11, Music in the Americas, "Bossa Nova") helped popularize Latin dances such as the merengue and the cha cha cha in the 1920s and 30s. During the 1940s, bebop musicians Dizzy Gillespie and others developed a style some call "cubop" when they absorbed Afro-Cuban idioms from Cuban musicians Mario Bauzá, Chano Pozo, and others. In the 1960s, Stan Getz worked with João Gilberto in one of several examples of North American jazz collaborations with Brazilian Bossa Nova musicians (see Chapter 11, Music in the Americas). The resulting hybrids of jazz with popular and Latin idioms continually enrich jazz and amplify its popularity.

PLAYLIST OPTIONS
POPULAR AND LATIN INFLUENCES

FIND

A hard bop, fusion, or Latin jazz performance by one of the following performers:

- Art Blakey and The Jazz Messengers
- Xavier Cugat
- Miles Davis music from his *Bitches Brew* (1969) album
- Stan Getz and João Gilberto Bossa Nova music
- Dizzie Gillespie Cubop music
- Herbie Hancock
- Quincy Jones
- Wynton Marsalis
- Tito Puente

OBSERVE

- Instrumentation, such as electrified instruments in rock-influenced music, or Latin percussion in Latin-influenced music.
- Vocal style.

ASK

- What are the most important influences in your example: Jazz roots? Rock? Latin music?

CHAPTER 3 VOCABULARY & IMPORTANT FIGURES

Vocabulary

Bebop (or bop)

Blue notes

Blues

Chord

Chord progression

Cool jazz

Dissonance

Fusion

Harlem Renaissance

Improvisation

Ragtime

Scat

Swing

Tonality (key)

Twelve-bar blues form

Important Figures

Louis Armstrong (1901–1971)

Miles Davis (1926–1991)

Duke Ellington (1899–1974)

Ella Fitzgerald (1917–1996)

John Birks "Dizzy" Gillespie (1917–1993)

Benny Goodman (1909–1986)

William Christopher ("W. C.") Handy (1873–1958)

Billie Holiday (1915–1959)

Scott Joplin (c. 1867–1917)

Huddie "Lead Belly" Ledbetter (1889–1949)

Wynton Marsalis (b. 1961)

Ferdinand DeMenthe "Jelly Roll" Morton (1890–1941)

Charles "Charlie" Parker Jr. (1920–1955)

ENDNOTES

[1] (As quoted in Richard Crawford, An Introduction to America's Music, W. W. Norton, 2001, p. 396.)

[2] (From Ella Fitzgerald official site: http://www.ellafitzgerald.com/about/quotes, accessed 5/25/17.)

[3] (From "The Chili Parlor Interview," Down Beat, March 11, 1965, p. 13, revised from the original article published in Down Beat. September 9, 1949; as quoted in J. Heywood Alexander, To Stretch Our Ears: A Documentary History of America's Music, New York: W. W. Norton, 2002, p. 452.)

Image Credits

- Figure 3-1: Robert Runyon / Copyright in the Public Domain.
- Figure 3-2: Source: https://commons.wikimedia.org/wiki/File:Scott_Joplin_19072.jpg
- Figure 3-3: Scott Joplin / Copyright in the Public Domain.
- Figure 3-4: Source: https://commons.wikimedia.org/wiki/File:Leadbelly_with_Accordeon.jpg
- Figure 3-5: Carl Van Vechten / Copyright in the Public Domain.
- Figure 3-6: Carl Van Vechten / Copyright in the Public Domain.
- Figure 3-7: E. W. Kemble / Copyright in the Public Domain.
- Figure 3-8: Source: https://commons.wikimedia.org/wiki/File:MortonBricktopRow.jpg.
- Figure 3-9: Copyright © 1955 by Herbert Behrens, (CC BY-SA 3.0) at https://commons.wikimedia.org/wiki/File:Louis_Armstrong_(1955).jpg.
- Figure 3-10: Source: https://en.wikipedia.org/wiki/Duke_Ellington#/media/File:Duke_Ellington_-_publicity.JPG.
- Figure 3-11: Source: https://commons.wikimedia.org/wiki/File:Benny_Goodman_-_c1970.jpg.
- Figure 3-12: William P. Gottlieb / Copyright in the Public Domain.
- Figure 3-13: Carl Van Vechten / Copyright in the Public Domain.
- Figure 3-14: William P. Gottlieb / Copyright in the Public Domain.

The Bog Trotters Band, Galax Virginia, 1937. From left, Doc Davis on autoharp, Alex Dunford and Crockett Ward on fiddles, Wade Ward on banjo, and Fields Ward in back with guitar.

CHAPTER 4

Modern American Popular Music Part I: Up to 1970

P opular music in the twentieth century has emerged in the context of two important technological developments: radio and recording. Both innovations became widespread early in the century and, thus, profoundly influenced what Americans listened to and how they listened to it. Suddenly, people didn't have to play the music themselves in order to hear it: all they had to do was turn a dial or push a button. With the exception of mechanical devices from earlier centuries such as music boxes, this was the first time in human history that music could be performed without the performers. After tens of thousands of years of human development, the ability to *recreate* musical performance has only happened within the past 150 years.

How did such extraordinarily convenient technologies affect our listening habits? The preservation and dissemination of musical style are the most transformative aspects of radio and recording. Treasures of a single culture can be distributed throughout the world, with the simple act of turning on the radio. Traditional songs that could easily have disappeared in twenty years' time are now literally engraved and will last as long as the recordings are archived. Performers who might never have been known outside of their own neighborhood can become world celebrities. Special interest styles of the early twentieth century were suddenly available to everyone and would help shape future styles. This chapter will look at the array of popular styles and their problematic labels, a new youth market that emerges, and the powerful music industry that grows up around it through 1970. Chapter 5, Modern American Popular Music Part II, will explore popular music's development after 1970 to the present.

I
BEFORE 1950: COUNTRY AND THE ROOTS OF POPULAR MUSIC

The foundations of popular music come from an amalgamation of much of the music covered in Chapters 1–3 (American Traditional Music, American Music for Stage and Screen, and Jazz, respectively): traditional ballads from Scotch-Irish immigrants; theater songs from minstrelsy, vaudeville, and Broadway; songs from the American West; big band swing; and, exerting a widespread and abiding influence throughout the rest of the styles, blues, gospel, and jazz music of Black Americans.

Southern String Bands, Close Vocal Harmony: "Country ..."

Bluegrass music
Improvisatory dance music style rooted in rural American string bands. Banjo, guitar, and fiddle are the most dominant musical instruments.

One of the most influential and deeply rooted foundations of popular music in the US comes from songs and string bands of the southern US. String bands are generally comprised of vocalists with accompanying fiddle, guitar, banjo, mandolin, and bass. Instrumentalists display their skill in popular competitions with rapid, syncopated musical passages. Although the melodies are predominantly sung by solo vocalists, chorus sections often feature added singers in close vocal harmony. Love laments, poverty, coal mining, railroads, and spiritual redemption are typical song themes. Ballads and dances, such as jigs and reels of the British Isles, are the musical ancestors of much of this music, which continues to develop and gain newly composed songs and dances. **Bluegrass** as a genre was named after a popular band from the 1940s: **Bill Monroe and the Bluegrass Boys (founded late 1930s)** included mandolinist and director Bill Monroe, banjoist Earl Scruggs, vocalist and guitarist Lester Flatt, and others over the years who developed the iconic bluegrass string band style.

Figure 4-2 Bill Monroe (left), with his brother Charlie, c1936.

"... And Western"

In the meantime, the older western cowboy songs (see Chapter 1, American Traditional Music) continued to develop. These songs still had plenty of references to nature and the West, but as we go forward into the twentieth century, western music incorporates big band jazz. During the 1930s and into the 1940s, "western swing," based in Texas, used traditional instrumentation—especially the fiddle and guitar—but added amplification, drums, and other big band instruments such as brass sections. Dance was the focus, but these bands performed with a flexible approach that included improvisation with larger instrumental forces blended with country style steel guitars (see Musical Instruments Appendix) and **mariachi** influences in vocal and instrumental parts. Bob Wills and His Texas Playboys was a popular western swing style band in the early twentieth century.

Mariachi Traditional Mexican folk music that includes vocalist with trumpet or violin on melody, guitar or harp as harmonic accompaniment, and *guitarrón* on the bass line; (Chapter 11, Music in the Americas).

At about the same time, "honky-tonk" music was associated with bars and other public establishments that presented live music and alcohol (often referred to as "honky-tonks" or "beer joints"), especially in the American Southwest. Lyrics often describe marital strife or drinking. This music, too, often functions as dance music: it delivers a loud, strong beat with percussion, bass, and electrified instruments. Piano is more common in honky-tonk than in other country styles, and the emphasis on **rhythm** betrays a likely connection with ragtime. Song structures are often based on blues chord progressions. Honky-tonk singer and songwriter **Hank Williams (1923–1953)** was one of the most significant country music performers of all. Songs such as "Honky-tonk Blues," "I Saw the Light," and "Your Cheatin' Heart" show how strongly he was influenced by blues and gospel music.

Rhythm The duration of individual notes and pauses; see Musical Elements Appendix.

Figure 4-3 Hank Williams at WSM, 1951.

Black Mentors and Performers in Country Music

Black musical styles profoundly influenced early country music through the significant but generally unacknowledged contributions of performers and mentors. Rufus "Tee Tot" Payne mentored Hank Williams Sr. during the Great Depression: "The Tee Tot Song" by Hank Williams Jr. refers to the powerful influence of Tee Tot's blues music on Hiram (Hank Williams), their love for each other, and the tragedy that their time together was too brief. Guitarist and fiddler Arnold Shultz (1886–1931) was a significant influence on bluegrass music through his mentorship of Bill Monroe, the director of the group after which bluegrass was named. Guitarist and singer Leslie Riddle is said to have taught several of his own songs, including "The Cannon Ball," to the Carters, arguably the most important family in early country music.

Black musicians were also early country music performers in their own right. Father and son duo Andrew and Jim Baxter, who played fiddle and guitar, respectively, recorded in late 1920s Georgia; they were African Americans said to have Cherokee ancestry, as well. The "string band" style of their music, a syncopated, strident fiddle melody with a simple guitar accompaniment, has much in common with later bluegrass music. That melodic fiddle style replete with blue notes can also be heard in the brilliant harmonica performances of **DeFord Bailey (1899–1982)**, the first solo performer—of any color—in the Grand Ole Opry (see below) and one of only three African American Country Music Hall of Fame inductees. Joe and Odell Thompson were cousins from North Carolina who played string band music, with Joe on fiddle and Odell on banjo and guitar. Both of their fathers had been in demand as square dance accompanists. People of color in the early twentieth century, however, had scarce support or opportunity to perform, record, and publish; one can only guess at the identity and number of other performers and teachers who inspired and influenced early country music.

Figure 4-4 DeFord Bailey, 1970s.

On Stage Together at the Grand Ole Opry

Hillbilly music Term used in the early twentieth century to denote southern popular music; the music industry replaced this term with "country" and later "country and western" in the mid-twentieth century.

Grand Ole Opry Radio show broadcasting from WSM in Nashville, 1925 to present, which specializes in country music performance.

The young music industry used the terms **hillbilly** and "old-time" or "old-timey" music for rural southern popular music up to World War II, and then during the war years, supplanted the earlier terms with "country" and later "country and western." Popular radio shows of the early twentieth century—especially Nashville's **Grand Ole Opry**—gathered performers from different regions to broadcast variety shows. On stage together, the musicians met and learned from one another. The music we now call "country" accumulated their styles without completely blending them so that one can still distinguish songs or elements of the rural South, Texas and the Southwest, urban honky-tonk bars, and the blues.

The most common themes in this coalition of country styles include family; hardship with love, poverty, alcohol, and the law; regional references such as Texas or the mountains; vocational references such as coal mining or railway work; and spiritual redemption. Songs about faith are especially common ("I Saw the Light" by Hank Williams), but even in many "secular" songs about love, references to faith abound (Roy Acuff's "The Precious Jewel").

Figure 4-5 Jimmie Rodgers, unknown date.

The vocal style of traditional country music uses the yodel and derivations of yodeling techniques. The falsetto, or "head" voice (as opposed to the lower "chest" voice) is used in country music to ornament phrases: split-second transitions occur between the lower and higher voice to take this music into its characteristic falsetto wail. Where did the country music yodel come from? The traditional Swiss yodel came to the US from European immigrants, but other traditions likely played a part. **Jimmie Rodgers (1897–1933)**, one of the earliest and most influential singers in country music, who often added yodels in his songs, worked on railroad lines where he heard African Americans sing blues and field hollers. He spent time in the American West, so he might have also been familiar with the sound of cowboys and Latin Americans shouting in falsetto to round up livestock and, perhaps, with Mexican mariachi music, which includes plenty of falsetto hooting (see Chapter 11, Music in the Americas).

PLAYLIST OPTIONS
COUNTRY AND THE ROOTS OF POPULAR MUSIC

FIND

- An example of a pre-1950 country song or instrumental performance by one of the following performers or ensembles:

  - Bill Monroe and the Bluegrass Boys
  - The Carter Family
  - Bob Wills and His Texas Playboys
  - Hank Williams
  - DeFord Bailey
  - Jimmie Rodgers

OBSERVE

- Instrumentation and vocal style that point to influences from ragtime, big band jazz, string bands, or the blues.
- Topics such as faith or hardship.

ASK

- Do you hear the signature country steel guitar or yodeling?
- Do any of the instrumentalists in your example seem to be improvising or is the music highly prepared?

Traditional country music mostly kept the acoustic instruments of bluegrass but added the steel guitar (see Musical Instruments Appendix), which had been developing in Hawaii since the nineteenth century. Hawaiian music enjoyed immense popularity throughout the United States in the early twentieth century, and the Hawaiian steel guitar was embraced by country music (see Chapter 12, Music in Oceania). Amplification may have been introduced into country music through the steel guitar: the very first commercially produced electric guitars, in fact, were steel guitars from the 1930s.

During the twentieth century, country music proved itself strong and adaptable enough to build a loyal audience throughout the US and beyond as we will explore in this chapter and in Chapter 5, Modern American Popular Music Part II: After 1970. Today the Grand Ole Opry still broadcasts live over the same radio station as in its first 1925 barn dance: WSM, Nashville.

II
THE DAWN OF ROCK AND ROLL

Early Rhythm and Blues Inspires Rock 'n' Roll

Rhythm and blues in the 1950s was a fusion of blues and swing jazz music with Black sacred music vocal styles. Dance music often used the "boogie woogie" piano style, which outlines chords in the left hand with a strong walking (stepwise) bass line while the right hand plays syncopated melodies in a higher register. Vocal harmony groups that performed without musical instruments ("a cappella") used some of their own voices to supply the rhythm section with nonsense syllables such as "doo wop," which gives the name to its own subgenre of rhythm and blues. The topics are secular, but the vocal style reveals strong ties with the all-vocal gospel quartets known as "jubilee quartets" from earlier in the century. Rhythm and blues music usually used a blues chorus form with verse chorus song structures in **quadruple meter**. The topics—mostly about unrequited love—were geared for teens.

Rhythm and blues songs were performed by Black musicians, and, at least in the beginning, meant for Black listeners. But radio broadcasts and recordings were available to everyone, and this music's popularity sailed far beyond its intended market. White teens loved rhythm and blues, which included singers such as Little Richard and **Chuck Berry 1926-2017**. Teenage fans bought the records, listened to the broadcasts, and, in an era that was still very segregated, showed up at concert events, sitting right alongside the Black teens. The American teenage market established its own powerful identity as a culture and as a consumer. The power struggle between young adults and their parents is age-old, but this particular generation's youth market was so strong that it seemed to exert its own gravitational pull. The music industry that catered to this youth market experienced unprecedented success with new performers, recording labels, radio stations, and the radio disc jockeys (DJs) that introduced the music and sometimes became stars themselves.

Quadruple meter
A metric pattern in which every 4 beats is accented, typically with the first beat accented and the third beat secondarily accented, as in *strongest*, **weak**, *strong*, **weak**; see Musical Elements Appendix.

Figure 4-6 Chuck Berry, c1957.

A new genre was born from this crossover success. "Rock and roll," a term that originally signified sexual intercourse, came to denote a popular hybrid musical style from the 1950s and 60s that was rooted in rhythm and blues, country, and mainstream popular American styles such as Tin Pan Alley songs and big band jazz. Major record labels, which had not showed much interest in rhythm and blues music before, became involved once the genre was successful. Artists with the major labels made "covers," or rerecordings of the songs with changes: the earthy, sometimes sexually explicit lyrics were softened, the gritty blues vocal style was replaced with a smoother delivery reminiscent of Tin Pan Alley songs, and most of the performers with the major labels, such as Elvis Presley (see below) and Pat Boone, were White.

From the start, rock and roll's controversy simmered from within and without. The success of the covers, which enjoyed support from the overpowering marketing resources of the major labels, brought resentment and hardship to many of the all-but-forgotten original artists and their smaller, independent labels. Although some fans and DJs maintained a preference for the original rhythm and blues versions, big money—thus, fame and success—was on the side of the covers. The view from the outside, meanwhile, saw a racially diverse musical style and audience that threatened the status quo. Civil rights protests and court-mandated integration, which intensified during the 1950s, inspired Black artists while it increased White teens' awareness of racism and encouraged their acceptance of Black music. A cult of rebellious youth emerged with matinee idols such as James Dean in *Rebel Without A Cause* (1955). The youth culture's association with race, sex, and rebellion—manifested in rock and roll—was a dangerous cocktail that alarmed the older generation.

Teen idol A charismatic vocalist with a nonthreatening image who sings highly marketable music usually written by others. Teen idols are usually young, and their performances are marketed to teens and preteens.

The entertainment industry tempered that danger, however, by offering the **teen idol**: a charismatic vocalist with a nonthreatening image who sings highly marketable music usually written by others. Teen idols often began in television; for example, child actor Ricky Nelson from *The Adventures of Ozzie and Harriet* (1952–1966) recorded his first hit song when he was 17. The teen idol's image and music was—as it still is—heavily crafted by industry marketing aimed with laser focus at teens and preteens.

Figure 4-7 Alan Freed, c1956.

In the meantime, the crossover audience in radio and recording inspired a major industry. The two technologies worked together, hand-in-hand: radio advertised recordings by playing them repeatedly, which increased their mutual success and their interdependence. The amount of time any particular music or performer is broadcast on radio is known as "airplay." "Rotation" refers to the list of songs that are repeatedly played on radio. The most popular songs are repeated most often in "heavy rotation." Naturally, listeners want to hear their favorite songs played more often, which encourages a heavy rotation, but the influence flows in the other direction as well: songs that wouldn't necessarily become popular with the usual airplay might become hits once they are played in heavy rotation. This is a temptation that has sometimes encouraged

payola (from the terms, "pay" and "Victrola"), which refers to the use of money or other forms of bribery in the music industry to increase airplay for a song in order to make it more popular. Alan Freed, a DJ who popularized the term "rock 'n' roll" (but didn't invent it as he claimed), enjoyed spectacular success among his youthful listeners with his wild reputation and his edgy, racially integrated tastes in music. His career ended, however, when he was convicted of payola practices.

Payola From the terms, "pay" and "Victrola," the illegal use of money or other forms of bribery in the music industry to increase airplay for a song in order to make it more popular.

Country Music's Contribution: Rockabilly

Post-1950s popular music emerged from the now-colossal recording industry, aided by concert, theater, radio, and television performances. Country music at mid-twentieth century had already found some success in its biggest stars, but more popular styles, especially rock and roll, quickly dominated the market. The phenomenal success of rock and roll inspired the country music world—both artistically and financially—to incorporate elements of rock and other popular idioms into its own music. The result ensured country music's prominent place in present-day popular music.

Rockabilly, a name that reflects the combination of rock and hillbilly music, became popular in the mid-1950s. Topics about love were delivered through emotional lyrics with added vocal expressions such as gasps, trembling, hiccupping sounds, and moaning—strange and sometimes scandalous sounds to traditional listeners. The "corny" acoustic string band instruments (fiddle, banjo, mandolin, and acoustic guitar) were left behind for electric guitars, electric bass, and percussion. **Elvis Presley (1935–1977)** displayed a wide variety of influences in his performances, including a bluesy vocal style that made his listeners wonder whether he was White or Black. This ambiguity, combined with his charismatic and sexually provocative performance style, encouraged a quick rise to fame with a crossover audience in the mid-1950s for Presley, who was born in poverty in the deep South. Texan songwriter **Buddy Holly (1936–1959)** enjoyed only a brief career before his fatal plane crash in 1959, but he posthumously became one of rock and roll's most influential songwriters throughout the 1960s. The name of his band (the Crickets), as well as many of his songs, inspired the Beatles in England (see below, "British Invasion"). Led by Elvis Presley's unprecedented success and Buddy Holly's songwriting influence, rockabilly's appeal swept popular music and became a cornerstone of rock music.

Rockabilly Early rock and roll style heavily influenced by country and blues, characterized by expressive vocal sounds and electrified instrumental accompaniment.

Figure 4-8 Elvis Presley in Jailhouse Rock, 1957.

Figure 4-9 Buddy Holly and the Crickets publicity photo, c1957. From top to bottom: Jerry Allison, Buddy Holly, Joe Mauldin Jr.

PLAYLIST OPTIONS
THE DAWN OF ROCK AND ROLL

FIND

Two versions of an early rhythm and blues song that was covered by mainstream popular or rockabilly singers, such as

- "Hound Dog" (Lieber and Stoller, 1952)
  - originally performed by Big Mama Thornton; Elvis Presley cover
- "I Got a Woman" (Charles and Richard, 1954)
  - originally performed by Ray Charles; Elvis Presley cover
- "Maybellene" (Berry, 1955)
  - originally performed by Chuck Berry; Marty Robbins cover
- "Long Tall Sally" (Johnson, Blackwell, and Penneman, 1956)
  - originally performed by Little Richard; Pat Boone cover

- ◆ "Tutti Frutti" (Little Richard, LaBostrie, 1955)
  - ◆ originally performed by Little Richard; Boone or Presley cover
- ◆ "Whole Lotta Shakin' Goin' On" (Williams, 1955)
  - ◆ originally performed by Big Maybelle; Jerry Lee Lewis or Ricky Nelson cover)

OBSERVE

- ◆ Contrasting vocal and instrumental styles.
- ◆ Whether lyrics are different between the two versions.
- ◆ Whether original performer was also a writer (songwriters in parentheses).

ASK

- ◆ Do the contrasting versions of your song choice exemplify the free market in action? Theft? Something more complicated?

III
PRODUCERS SHAPE STYLE

Country Music's Reaction: The Nashville Sound

The Nashville sound was an updated approach to bring country music to popular music fans. From the late 1950s through the 1960s, the country music industry in Nashville produced recordings of country songs with heavy studio accompaniment forces: orchestras and full choruses were used as backups instead of the old string bands with three or four harmonizing singers as in earlier days. The emphasis on traditional songs was replaced by melodious ballads with more commercial appeal to urban audiences. This style promoted a fuller, less nasal vocal tone than earlier country singing styles. These were drastic changes that alienated some of its own, but the industry desperately wanted to broaden its audience and take its share of the growing market for popular music. **Patsy Cline (1932–1963)**, who specialized in heavily accompanied torch songs (heartbreaking songs about unrequited love), was an important talent representative of the Nashville sound. Many years after her untimely death in a plane crash, listeners are still transfixed by Cline's heartrending performances, and singers continue to emulate her.

Figure 4-10 Patsy Cline, c1961.

The Nashville sound emerged from recording studios that emphasized a specific style. But Nashville wasn't the only center of a musical style; throughout the country, pop music industry producers with strong ideas about how the music should sound headed recording studios with their own signature styles. Producers used the same team of songwriters and arrangers, instrumentalists, and backup vocalists for most of their recordings. Thus, a distinctive "sound" for that particular studio developed which, if the songs rose high on the charts, would influence new artists. Two examples in particular are important to describe here.

Berry Gordy: "I worked in the Ford factory before I came in the [record] business, and I saw how each person did a different thing, and I said, 'Why can't we do that with the creative process?'"[1]

Motown's "Sound of Young America"

One of the youngest siblings in his large, tight-knit family, **Berry Gordy Jr. (b. 1929)** practiced on the upright piano of his home in Detroit, Michigan. This formed the basis of his musical and songwriting skills. Later, he founded his independent recording studio, Motown (named after Detroit's nickname, "motor town"), in 1959. Having worked at an auto factory for a couple of years, Gordy used the assembly line business model in Motown: Gordy's Black employees and songwriters—each with specific tasks—worked together and in succession to make stars out of unknown musicians. Along with his studio's stylistic roots in gospel performance, he promoted a variety of repertoire and sought a crossover audience with his advertising slogan, "The Sound of Young America." Gordy consciously trained his young African American musicians—many from extremely humble circumstances—to be ready to perform for anyone: even royalty. Motown's artist development staff included specialists in etiquette and fashion, and performances were polished with choreographed stage routines. Gordy was able to negotiate his way through the entertainment industry's racial prejudice and achieve an unprecedented success by developing ties with prominent music industry personalities. Motown moved to Los Angeles to pursue its expansion into films in 1971, and Gordy sold Motown to MCA in 1988. Examples of artists who began their careers with Motown include Stevie Wonder, Diana Ross and the Supremes, and the Jackson 5, which included the very young Michael Jackson.

Spector's "Wall of Sound"

Phil Spector (b. 1940) founded Philles Records in 1962 with Lester Sill in Los Angeles, California. They used a large group of studio musicians known as "The Wrecking Crew" to provide accompaniment to the artists who signed with the studio, which specialized in female ensembles. Spector, a fan of the late-nineteenth-century German composer Richard Wagner's massive symphonic and operatic style, developed production techniques that made the large background ensemble blend together into the famous **wall of sound**, which Spector called a "Wagnerian approach to rock-and-roll" (see Chapter 9, Romantic Era Music, "Opera"). Examples include "Be My Baby" by the

Wall of sound Phil Spector's influential production technique in popular music of the 1960s, characterized by large background ensembles blended together to accompany vocal soloists and groups.

Ronettes and "Da Doo Ron Ron (When He Walked Me Home)" by the Crystals, both from 1963. Spector went on to work with the Beatles and other celebrated artists. He eventually became a recluse, and in 2009, he was convicted of second-degree murder for which he is currently serving a prison term. Although his signature style is not truly "Wagnerian," his influence on the sound of late-twentieth-century popular music continues to be attested to by many in the recording industry.

Figure 4-12 The Ronettes, 1966. From left: Nedra Talley, Veronica Bennett (Ronnie Spector), and Estelle Bennett.

British Invasion

In the meantime, teens on the other side of the ocean were listening and chiming in. British baby boomers grew up with much of the same popular music that Americans did. They heard country, rhythm and blues, early rock and roll, and the aesthetic foundations behind most of that music: Tin Pan Alley verse-chorus songs or the blues—sometimes a combination of both. The music of American musicians such as Lead Belly and Buddy Holly inspired an international "skiffle" revival. A hybrid folk blues style performed on traditional and found instruments such as acoustic guitar, harmonica, and washboard, skiffle originated in the 1930s with African American musicians. The 1950s skiffle revival was especially strong in England before it gave way to "beat," a British form of the more commercially viable rock and roll. British bands performed covers of American songs, and some, like the Beatles, began to write their own music as well.

Founded in 1960, **The Beatles** name referenced "beat" music and was also a nod to Buddy Holly and the Crickets. All four band members came from humble beginnings in the port town of Liverpool. A rowdy, streetwise quartet who wore black leather onstage, they performed at

Figure 4-13 The Beatles wave to fans after arriving at Kennedy Airport, 1964. From left, John Lennon, Paul McCartney, George Harrison, and Ringo Starr.

Liverpool's "The Cavern" in between gigs abroad. After discovering the Beatles in 1961, their new manager Brian Epstein reformed their image (à la Berry Gordy's mentorship of his Motown artists) with his push for more professional—and less threatening—clothes, haircuts, and behavior. Once they signed with a major studio, they began their association with producer and composer George Martin, who contributed heavily to their music throughout the 1960s. Their songs sold well, and their 1963 international tours generated unprecedented popularity and success. "Beatlemania" ensued, with massive crowds of screaming fans at concert venues and a stream of hit songs and albums.

PLAYLIST OPTIONS
PRODUCERS SHAPE STYLE

FIND

- A video performance of a song by one of the following performers:
  - The Beatles (early 1960s, Brian Epstein, producer)
  - Patsy Cline (Nashville sound)
  - The Crystals (Phil Spector)
  - Diana Ross and the Supremes (Motown's Berry Gordy, producer)
  - Jackson 5 (Motown's Berry Gordy, producer)
  - The Ronettes (Phil Spector, producer)
  - Stevie Wonder (Motown's Berry Gordy, producer)

OBSERVE

- Vocal style and instrumentation.
- Production style, especially of the background accompaniment.
- Stage presence: costumes and choreography.

ASK

- Does the production style enhance or overwhelm the performers' musical tradition?
- Is the performer in your example is trying to project a particular image?

In the early 1960s, their music, mostly written by band members John Lennon and Paul McCartney, was in the standard verse-chorus form used in Tin Pan Alley songs, which they sang in close harmony. Although the structure was formulaic and the lyrics had little substance, the success of these early songs such as "She Loves You" and "I Wanna Hold Your Hand" made industry history. But by the late 1960s, influences from antiwar and social justice movements, along with the psychedelic culture of recreational drug use, had changed their music indelibly. Songs such as "Revolution" had something important to say, and the music was often emancipated from formula and finite style expectations, borrowing from other idioms with, for instance, classical string quartet or Indian sitar accompaniments (see Chapter 15, Music in India and Japan, "Ravi Shankar").

In 1967, the Beatles released their **concept album**, *Sgt. Pepper's Lonely Heart's Club Band*. Thematic unity with ambitious virtuosity, depth, and often experimentation in the music, lyrics, and cover art characterize popular music's concept album, which strives toward—and sometimes achieves—cultivated art. Although this was certainly not the very first concept album, it was the one that put the name to the category. Experimental music drawn from many styles expresses the character of the Beatles' alter-ego marching band players throughout the album. The dawn of the 1970s brought the end of the Beatles as a band, and they each went their separate ways.

The Beatles paved the way for more British performers but with differences in musical style and image. The Rolling Stones, who first toured the US close on the heels of the Beatles, are a London-based band whose music is far more steeped in blues than the Tin Pan Alley formula songs of the early Beatles style. Furthermore, the Stones cultivated a "bad boy" reputation that contrasted with the Beatles image. Mick Jagger and Keith Richards are the main writers for the Stones, who continue to record and tour in the early twenty-first century. Other British performers who became successful in the US include bands such as Pink Floyd and The Who as well as popular solo singers such as Petula Clark and Tom Jones. The **British Invasion** as a term signifies not only a physical presence of touring performers: their music invaded the US charts and grabbed much of the market, forcing the domestic US music industry to struggle harder for their spots on the charts. The British "brand" ascended in film and fashion as well: for instance, James Bond movies began in 1962, and supermodel Twiggy's slender, leggy look became the point of reference for women's fashion by the late 1960s.

Concept album An album that provides thematic unity with ambitious virtuosity, depth, and often experimentation in the music, lyrics, and cover art.

British Invasion Extraordinary popularity of touring British performers in the US, beginning with the Beatles in 1963.

IV
SINCERITY BECOMES MARKETABLE

The Songwriter

By the middle twentieth century, New York City's Brill Building at 1619 Broadway had become the new Tin Pan Alley. Composers and lyricists inside Brill Building cubicles churned out song after song for the popular music industry, this time with a heavy dose of blues to go along with the verse-chorus formula. The writers included the Goffin and King team, who wrote hits for others to sing such as "Will You Love Me Tomorrow" (1961, performed by the Shirelles), and "(You Make Me Feel Like) A Natural Woman" (1967, performed by Aretha Franklin). Part of that songwriting team—**Carole King (b. 1942)**—later branched out to develop her own solo performing career with albums such as *Tapestry* (1970), which includes her own performances of the above named songs she originally wrote for others to sing.

King was responding to the rising popularity of the **singer-songwriter**. Influenced largely by the twentieth-century American folk music revival (see Chapter 1, American Traditional Music), many of these singers showed strong roots in country, blues, and rock music, as well. Singer-songwriters write their own lyrics and music by definition, but the depth and sincerity of their songs is what sets this genre apart. Instead of the polished, choreographed glamour of the teen idols and pop ensembles, singer-songwriters reach for personal wisdom and insight. Most play their own accompaniment and avoid the heavy production methods of other popular music styles. **Bob Dylan (b. 1941)** is the quintessential singer-songwriter of the late twentieth century. His early 1960s folk music soon spread to a repertoire that spans blues, gospel, and electrified rock idioms. Dylan's music and poetry profoundly influenced popular music, and he is one of the most important American musicians of his generation. For his lyrics, Dylan was awarded the 2016 Nobel Prize in Literature.

Singer-songwriter
Generally, performers who write their own music and lyrics. More specifically, singer-songwriters typically play their own accompaniment on acoustic instruments and whose themes offer depth and sincerity.

Carole King: "It takes a lot more people to deliver a song than most people are aware of, but you, the listener, are the most important person in the process. You complete the circle. You inspire us to write, sing, arrange, record, and promote songs that move us because we hope they will move you, too. There might still be an "us" without you, but you make us matter, and you make us better."[2]

Figure 4-15 Folksingers Joan Baez and Bob Dylan the Civil Rights March on Washington, D.C., 1963.

The Counterculture and Psychedelia

While the music industry responded to the youth market boom with commercialized production techniques, the youths themselves built a new culture—a counterculture—and developed their own ideas about what they wanted to hear. The Civil Rights Movement from the 1950s had burgeoned into a full-scale liberation movement that encompassed migrant workers, women, gays, the disabled, and other marginalized groups. As the Vietnam War escalated, college students and others protested the war. Important antiwar songs from this era include "Blowing in the Wind" (Bob Dylan, 1963), "War (What is It Good For?)" (Whitfield and Strong for Motown singer Edwin Starr, 1969), and "Imagine" (1971, John Lennon).

The popularity of recreational drugs—particularly LSD—inspired **psychedelia**: an artistic and musical style that evoked mind-altering drug use. Bright colors and surreal images prevailed in the visual arts and fashion. Music's sonic landscape was expanded by experimentation with electronic sounds and eclectic styles (see the Beatles concept album, *Sgt. Pepper's Lonely Heart's Club Band*, above). Peace, love, and social justice dominated themes in literature and song lyrics. The counterculture embraced ideas, belief systems, art, and music from other

Psychedelia An artistic and musical style of the mid-1960s that evoked mind-altering drug use. Music's sonic landscape was expanded by experimentation with electronic sounds and eclectic styles.

parts of the world. Ravi Shankar, the great Indian sitarist, was an especially influential figure after Beatles guitarist George Harrison studied with him. American roots music provided foundations to build upon and many influential idioms for new musicians. They revered and emulated aging or deceased folk, blues, and jazz musicians such as Woody Guthrie, Lead Belly, and Miles Davis.

Certain locales achieved symbolic status for the counterculture. Many of the country's talented folk singers and poets haunted the coffee houses and clubs of New York City's Greenwich Village in the early 1960s, most notably Bob Dylan. San Francisco's Haight-Ashbury district was the setting for the 1966 "summer of love," which many see as the birth of the hippie subculture and psychedelia. Tens of thousands of young people arrived to create a radically different lifestyle and to express themselves through psychedelic music and art. Two significant events took place, both popular music festivals, one on each side of the country. For three days in June 1967, 75,000 people attended the Monterey Pop Festival in California. And for three days in August 1969, hundreds of thousands attended the Woodstock Festival in upstate New York, making history and thereafter calling themselves "the Woodstock generation." Most of the performers described in the section below performed in both festivals. This environment of experimentation and psychedelia kindled a golden age in popular music. The 1960s saw the formation and transformation of bands and soloists who used wide varieties of styles and techniques, drawing not only from other American vernacular styles but on Western art and world music as well. Many of the musicians themselves attained artistic and even legendary status by the end of the 1960s.

In the early 1960s, the "surf music" songs of the **Beach Boys (founded 1961)** expressed the carefree life of summer on the beach with vocal harmony and production techniques inspired by doo-wop, early rock and roll, and Phil Spector. But with the critically acclaimed 1966 album *Pet Sounds* and the hit single "Good Vibrations," Beach Boys member Brian Wilson's creativity showed psychedelia's influence. "Good Vibrations" uses unusual structures,

Figure 4-16 Brian Wilson of the Beach Boys, behind a mixing board.

musical textures, and musical instruments, including the theremin, the eerie electronic instrument that the player does not have to touch in order to play (see Musical Instruments Appendix).

Led by songwriter Jerry Garcia, the **Grateful Dead (founded 1965)** used American roots music as its foundation in a heavily experimental, eclectic style that included non-Western and electronic music. Unlike most other bands, they specialized in live performances of their extended improvisations rather than recording, ensuring that no performance would be exactly like another. They developed a large and long-lived cult following of "deadhead" fans who famously traveled long distances to follow and attend their concerts. The album *Live/Dead* (1969) includes live performances of their extended improvisations.

The iconic psychedelic (or "acid" after LSD) rock band **Jefferson Airplane (founded 1965)** recorded "White Rabbit" in 1967 by Grace Slick (b. 1939), which describes hallucinogenic drug use in the context of Lewis Carroll's classic children's novel *Alice in Wonderland* (1865). The song's

Figure 4-17 Jefferson Airplane at The Matrix club, San Francisco, 1966. Top row from left: Jack Casady, Grace Slick, Marty Balin; bottom row from left: Jorma Kaukonen, Paul Kantner, and Spencer Dryden.

AABA structure, recalling Tin Pan Alley, is masked by the single continuing crescendo (gradual build in volume) from beginning to end and by Slick's powerful, riveting voice. Listeners are encouraged to compare this song to the symphonic ballet that may well have inspired Slick: French composer Maurice Ravel's *Bolero* (1928), which features a similar dance rhythm and another start-to-finish crescendo.

Figure 4-18 Janis Joplin, 1970.

Although both **Jimi Hendrix (1942–1970)** and **Janis Joplin (1943–1970)** performed with bands, they are most well known for their innovative, passionate, show-stopping performances as solo artists. Hendrix was a virtuoso guitarist who displayed a wealth of influences

Jimi Hendrix: "My own thing is in my head...I hear sounds and if I don't get them together nobody else will."[3]

in blues, jazz, rock, and even folk music from his days in New York City's Greenwich Village, where he performed covers of Bob Dylan songs. When Hendrix explored the sounds of his amplified audio equipment, including the newly introduced electric guitar wah-wah pedal, he learned to control the sounds: feedback and other types of electronic distortion became musical elements in his music. This gave his instrumental style a shockingly aggressive yet lyrical quality that can be heard to its fullest in his performance of the "Star Spangled Banner" at Woodstock in 1969 in which electronic sounds mimicked the "bombs bursting in air" from the lyrics. Was this patriotism or a form of satire? Hendrix ignited a controversy about such an unusual way to interpret the national anthem to a nation at war. Janis Joplin cultivated a stage image of uncontrolled passionate frenzy that belied her musical awareness and talent. Strongly influenced by Black blues singers such as Bessie Smith, Joplin developed her own hybrid blues and rock style (see Chapter 3, Jazz, "Blues"). Her performances were more expressive and assertive than audiences had ever heard from a woman.

Tragically, both Hendrix and Joplin died in 1970 in separate instances of drug overdoses. Joplin's album *Pearl* (1971) was released posthumously several months after her death; the ballad "Me and Bobby McGee" (Kristofferson and Foster, 1969) from the album was a bittersweet hit. Other women in popular music, such as Stevie Nicks and Pink, claim Joplin as an important influence. Hendrix's legacy as a musician would be hard to quantify. His pioneering electronic sounds led the way for the many guitar-dominated heavy metal rock bands that came later. But in a larger sense, Hendrix influenced popular music through his deft amalgamation of styles and his fearless rejection of the categories that would have limited him. The stage was set for the rest of the twentieth century: popular music was a kaleidoscope of styles with many roots.

PLAYLIST OPTIONS
SINGER-SONGWRITER, PSYCHEDELIA

FIND

- An example from a singer-songwriter or psychedelia band, such as
  - The Beach Boys (mid-late 1960s)
  - The Beatles (late 1960s)
  - Bob Dylan
  - The Grateful Dead
  - Jimi Hendrix
  - Jefferson Airplane
  - Janis Joplin
  - Carole King

OBSERVE

- Topic or theme, which might be introspective, surreal, a statement of protest, or something else.
- Whether instrumentation is simple, sophisticated, futuristic, or eclectic, drawing on classical and world traditions.

ASK

- Does your example have a message? If so, is it convincing?

CHAPTER 4 VOCABULARY & IMPORTANT FIGURES

Vocabulary

Bluegrass music

British Invasion

Concept album

Grand Ole Opry

Hillbilly music

Payola

Psychedelia

Quadruple meter

Rhythm

Rockabilly

Singer-songwriter

Teen idol

Wall of sound

Important Figures

DeFord Bailey (1899–1982)

Chuck Berry 1926-2017

Beach Boys (founded 1961)

The Beatles (founded 1960)

Patsy Cline (1932–1963)

Bob Dylan (b. 1941)

Berry Gordy Jr. (b. 1929)

Grateful Dead (founded 1965)

Jimi Hendrix (1942–1970)

Buddy Holly (1936–1959)

Jefferson Airplane (founded 1965)

Janis Joplin (1943–1970)

Carole King (b. 1942)

Bill Monroe and the Bluegrass Boys (founded late 1930s)

Elvis Presley (1935–1977)

Jimmie Rodgers (1897–1933)

Phil Spector (b. 1940)

Hank Williams (1923–1953)

ENDNOTES

[1] (As quoted in David P. Szatmary, Rockin' In Time: A Social History of Rock-and-Roll, 8th ed., Pearson, 2014, p. 142.)

[2] (From A Natural Woman: A Memoire, published by Grand Central Publishing, 2012, page 124–125.)

[3] As quoted in David P. Szatmary, Rockin' In Time: A Social History of Rock-and-Roll, 8th ed., Person, 2014, p. 193.

Image Credits

- Figure 4-9: Coral Records / Copyright in the Public Domain.

- Figure 4-10: Decca Records / Copyright in the Public Domain.

- Figure 4-11: Copyright © 2010 by Angela George, (CC BY-SA 3.0) at https://en.wikipedia.org/wiki/Berry_Gordy#/media/File:BerryGordyDec10.jpg.

- Figure 4-12: James Kriegsmann, General Artists Corporation-GAC / Copyright in the Public Domain.

- Figure 4-13: United Press International / Copyright in the Public Domain.

- Figure 4-14: Copyright © 2012 by Angela George, (CC BY-SA 3.0) at https://commons.wikimedia.org/wiki/File:CaroleKingHWOFDec2012.jpg.

- Figure 4-15: Rowland Scherman / Copyright in the Public Domain.

- Figure 4-16: Brother Records / Copyright in the Public Domain.

- Figure 4-17: RCA Victor / Copyright in the Public Domain.

- Figure 4-18: Grossman Glotzer Management Corporation / Copyright in the Public Domain.

- Figure 4-19: Source: https://commons.wikimedia.org/wiki/File:Jimi_Hendrix_1967_uncropped.jpg.

Two DJs creating new music by mixing tracks, 2007. DJ Hypnotize (left), and Baby Cee (right).

5 Modern American Popular Music Part II: After 1970

A merican popular music after 1970 and into the new millennium continues, transforms, and reinvents itself in its myriad identities. Labels—especially for music by African Americans—continue to be problematic reminders of discrimination between people as well as between styles. The UK "brand" that conquered the US in the 1960s still shines brightly on popular music charts in the years since 1970 with British rock bands and popular soloists such as Elton John and Sting (Gordon Sumner, b. 1951). The impact of the music video exerts profound influence on the performances and careers of musicians and on the audience's experience of music. Above all, the styles discussed (and, yes, labeled) throughout this chapter are not really such neat and simple fits: musical style in late-twentieth-century popular music is fluid, with blues moving through almost all of it. Although these styles intersect in many ways, this chapter is roughly segmented into four sections: "Song" looks at country and R & B; "The Band" explores rock, punk, new wave, and alternative; "Dance" focuses on disco and electronic dance music; and "A Dangerous Poetry" covers hip-hop culture and rap.

I
SONG

We Like Both Kinds of Music: Country and Western

Outlaw country
Country music style based in Texas that rejects established production conventions such as heavy studio accompaniment in favor of a more individualistic, authentic, and improvisatory approach.

Figure 5-2 Dolly Parton at the Grand Ole Opry in Nashville, 2005.

Country's stylistic continuum in recent decades spans bluegrass or honky-tonk roots to country pop and rock. Topics include family relationships, simple living, faith, political commentary, social justice, imprisonment, and nostalgia. The mid-twentieth century Nashville sound helped to establish country music's robust presence in popular music, and modern country music has continued to develop on the Nashville sound foundation ever since with elements of other popular music styles. The oldest generation of late-twentieth and early-twenty-first-century performers include icons such as Johnny Cash and Dolly Parton, who have used a variety of popular and traditional styles throughout their careers.

But reactions to mainstream production-heavy techniques gained momentum in the 1970s with revivals of past styles closer to country's roots. **Outlaw country**, based in Texas, rejected established production conventions such as heavy studio accompaniment in favor of a more independent and authentic approach inspired by earlier honky-tonk and western swing musical styles. Waylon Jennings, Willie Nelson, and others avoid the heavy-handed accompaniment style of Nashville sound and opt for more individualistic and improvisatory backup to their songs, instead. Bluegrass music, with its traditional string bands and close vocal harmonies, gained momentum in the late twentieth century and has recently enjoyed an especially strong revival fueled by the 2001 film, *O Brother, Where Art Thou*.

Figure 5-3 Singer-songwriter Willie Nelson and his guitar "Trigger," 2007.

Younger generations include bluegrass revivalists Alison Krauss and Ricky Skaggs and honky-tonk revivalist Dwight Yoakam. Mainstream country singers such as Garth Brooks are among the most successful country music performers of the late twentieth century. The youngest generation of prominent performers—including the Dixie Chicks, Lady Antebellum, Taylor Swift, and Gretchen Wilson—demonstrates strong popular and rock influence with country roots. Despite the often dominant mainstream influences, however, southern country identity is proudly announced in many songs, such as in Wilson's "Redneck Woman" (Rich and Wilson, 2004). The song title, repeated in each chorus, alternates with verses filled with emblems of southern individualism:

> Well, I ain't never been the Barbie doll type
> No, I can't swig that sweet champagne, I'd rather drink beer all night
> In a tavern or in a honky tonk or on a four-wheel drive tailgate
> I've got posters on my wall of Skynyrd, Kid and Strait...

Excerpts from John Rich and Gretchen Wilson, "Redneck Woman," Here for the Party. Copyright © 2004 by Epic Records.

Wilson honors Lynyrd Skynyrd (see below), Kid Rock, and George Strait, but she does much more to establish the function of this song as a country "anthem." Wilson rejects conventional definitions of womanhood in her lyrics throughout the song, such as in her dismissal of Barbie here. Most of all, she turns mainstream America's disdain of the South back on itself with her embrace of the derogatory term, "redneck."

Figure 5-4 Singer-songwriter Gretchen Wilson at Little Creek Amphibious Base, 2008.

k. d. lang: "My voice sounds a certain way; it sounds sort of the classic crooning style from the 40s or the 50s. But my mind and my instincts are much more alternative; much more contemporary. My taste is much more contemporary. So it's hard to find songs that really express all things to me. And so it's easier for me sometimes to write them."[1]

Alternative country integrates even more influences, such as folk, jazz, rock, and punk music, as well as country music that carries unusual or intensely political messages. The band Uncle Tupelo shows roots both of "hillbilly" and punk influences in songs such as "No Depression," a cover of a Carter family song. Lyle Lovett's music is a broad mix of Texas-based country, jazz, pop, and folk: one can hear the big band jazz in his "She's No Lady." **k. d. lang (b. 1961)**, an activist with a wide range of topics and musical influences, is celebrated for her covers including "Halleluja" (Cohen, 1984), her original songs such as "Constant Craving," and her rich, versatile voice; listeners will have no trouble hearing lang's idol, Patsy Cline, in lang's torch songs.

Performers of color maintain a small but significant presence in country music. **Charlie Pride (b. 1934)** achieved success as a Black country music singer in the late 1960s. His "Crystal Chandeliers" (Ted Harris, 1965) highlights the contrast between the narrator and his beloved's socioeconomic classes. More recent Black country music

Figure 5-6 The Carolina Chocolate Drops in Birmington, Alabama, 2008. From left, Dom Flemons on jug, Rhiannon Giddens on 5-string banjo, and Justin Robinson on fiddle.

artists include Darius Rucker, the traditional string band ensemble Carolina Chocolate Drops (founded 2005), and singer-songwriter and bassist Laura Love, who mixes a variety of genres in her music, including bluegrass, zydeco, and blues.

Many present-day country stars have cycled through Nashville sound and subsequent developments in popular music, as well as the various revivals of bluegrass, honky-tonk, and swing. This ability to adapt, collaborate, and transform has given the genre great strength. Most radio shows dedicated to mainstream popular music include country songs in their rotations because modern country music has so much crossover appeal. Love, faith, and hard times continue to be the topics of choice, with an influx of patriotic and political songs in the wake of the September 11, 2001 terrorist attacks and ensuing wars.

R & B: What's in a Name?

Labels for music written and performed by Black artists continued to evolve throughout the twentieth century and into the next millennium. The choices have been particularly important because specific musical characteristics are not the only issues here. The destructive history of racism in the US causes both industry and audience to tend to divide music according to race as well as, and sometimes despite, musical genre. History shows us that carefully chosen labels don't solve this problem, but since the words we choose are important, it's a worthy first step. *Billboard*, the industry periodical that has charted the popularity of songs and albums throughout the life of the music industry, played a major role in the choices.

In the early days of the recording industry from the 1920s through World War II, music created by Black artists for Black listeners was known as **race records**. (These were the same years that rural country music was labeled "hillbilly music.") In 1949, *Billboard* changed "race records" to "rhythm and blues," which also meant to encompass all types of music by African Americans. *Billboard* supplanted that term with "soul" in 1969 and then "Black music" in 1982 on the recommendation of the Black Music Association. *Billboard* adopted the present designation "R&B" in 1990, which references the earlier "rhythm and blues" without spelling out the words. In the meantime, musical genre terms that denote specific musical characteristics, for instance, "blues," "jazz," "funk," and "rap," have proliferated

Race records (or race music) Term used in the early twentieth century to denote music recorded by Black artists for Black listeners; after World War II this term was replaced with "rhythm and blues."

somewhat independently of industry terms for Black music, in general. This section will focus on the song-based post-1970 Black popular music, and hip-hop culture and rap will be discussed later in the chapter.

While the labels changed, African American music since the late twentieth century continued to evolve. The music was influenced by civil rights era changes, a cultural environment that spawned "blaxploitation" films such as *Shaft* (1971, featuring music by Isaac Hayes), and other musical styles including rock and disco. Music in the "soul" years is characterized by gospel idioms with secular, sometimes sociopolitical topics. Vocal delivery is extremely expressive, sometimes accompanied by shouts, grunts, and screams. **James Brown (1928–2006)** and **Aretha Franklin (b. 1942)** are two iconic performers popular throughout the late twentieth century who exemplify this style.

Figure 5-7 James Brown, 1973.

Figure 5-8 Aretha Franklin singing "My Country 'Tis Of Thee" at the U.S. Capitol during President Obama's inaguration, 2009.

Funk is dance music that uses soul, blues, jazz, and rock idioms. Its defining characteristic is a bass-heavy, **polyrhythmic**, **syncopated** dance rhythm, often referred to as a groove. Electrified band instruments are used along with synthesizers and wind instruments as funk matured in the disco era. Although the topic often mirrors its function as dance music with party and love themes, social justice themes are common as well. James Brown and others can be considered precursors to funk, but the style is most fully demonstrated in the music of Sly and the Family Stone and George Clinton. **Prince (1958–2016)** released dance-oriented albums, such as *1999* (released in 1982), that are considered funk although his eclecticism eventually crossed over into other styles as well.

R & B continues with many of the gospel and blues idioms of the past but with the influence of recent popular music technologies and continuing developments in other styles such as rock and hip-hop/rap. Ballads about love dominate song topics. Performers popular in the 1980s

Funk Dance music that uses soul, blues, jazz, and rock idioms. Its defining characteristic is a bass-heavy, polyrhythmic, syncopated dance rhythm, often referred to as a "groove."

Polyrhythm Different rhythms or meters performed simultaneously; see Musical Elements Appendix.

Syncopation Shift of metric accent from the expected pattern to the unexpected; see Musical Elements Appendix.

and 90s include Lionel Ritchie, **Michael Jackson (1958–2009)**, **Whitney Houston (1963–2012)** and the group Boyz II Men. A more recent generation that emerged during and after the 1990s features **Mariah Carey (b. 1970)**, Alicia Keys, and the English singer **Amy Winehouse (1983–2011)**.

Figure 5-9 Prince, 2006.

Figure 5-10 Whitney Houston, 2011.

Figure 5-11 Amy Winehouse, 2007.

PLAYLIST OPTIONS
COUNTRY AND R & B

FIND

- A late-twentieth- to early-twenty-first-century popular song performance by one of the following country or R & B singers, such as
  - Beyoncé
  - Garth Brooks
  - James Brown
  - Aretha Franklin
  - Whitney Houston
  - Michael Jackson
  - k. d. lang
  - Willie Nelson
  - Dolly Parton
  - Prince
  - Gretchen Wilson

OBSERVE

- Topic.
- Vocal and accompaniment style.
- Visual story or dance if your example is a video.

ASK

- What array of talents does the singer in your example project with this performance?
- Do the song and your singer's performance of it appear to convey the inner feelings or beliefs of the performer? Or is it a highly produced, choreographed "film" that projects a fictional character or a public image?

The rise of music videos since the 1980s has played a particularly important role in launching careers, emphasizing visual aspects of performances, and encouraging dance to be part of the show for all types of popular music. When MTV was launched in 1981, the network perceived its audience as White middle-class teens, so its programming mainly featured White performers' videos. Michael Jackson, who had recently launched his solo career after performing with his family members in

Figure 5-12 Michael Jackson, 1988.

Figure 5-13 Beyoncé, 2016.

The Jackson 5, was not only a talented singer-songwriter; he was also a riveting dancer with innovative ideas for video dance narratives. Jackson and his producers at CBS had to fight for Jackson's *Billie Jean* video to air on MTV, but once it was on, the video was a tremendous success for both Jackson and for MTV. Jackson's videos for *Billie Jean*, *Beat It*, and *Thriller* all aired in 1983 and established Jackson's stature as a major singer, songwriter, and dancer. With music video's influence, other stars, such as Michael Jackson's own sister, Janet Jackson, included dance as an important feature of their performances. A younger generation of performers with this focus includes **Beyoncé (b. 1981)** and Rihanna (b. 1988).

II
THE BAND

Rock

Reversing the eclectic 1960s trend to collect idioms and styles, rock bands splintered off into specialties during the 1970s. British talent remained an influential presence. British bands that based their music on the blues included Led Zeppelin, whose "Stairway to Heaven" became a rock anthem. British "progressive" rock, also known as "art" or "classical" rock, bands feature poetic depth, artistic musical idioms, and an emphasis on concept albums. *Tommy* by The Who (1969) and Pink Floyd's *The Wall* (1979) are two prominent examples of progressive rock concept albums both of which explore themes of isolation and imprisonment.

Heavy metal bands feature aggressive and virtuosic electric guitar performances, vocal screams, dramatic staging with light shows, outrageous costumes, "big" hair, and heavy makeup. Heavy metal can arguably be used as an umbrella term for several widely disparate styles among both US and UK bands, including "hard" rock, "glam" (short for glamour) metal, "thrash metal," and others. True to its name, the British band Black Sabbath with lead singer Ozzy Osbourne emphasized horror themes and

Heavy metal Rock music that emphasizes aggressive and virtuosic electric guitar performances, vocal screams, dramatic staging with light shows, and sometimes outrageous costumes, "big" hair, and heavy makeup.

gothic fashions. The British glam rock band **Queen (founded 1970)** released the celebrated, nearly six-minute long "Bohemian Rhapsody" (Freddie Mercury) song and video in 1975. In the US, **Aerosmith (founded 1970)**, Van Halen, Kiss, Mötley Crüe, and others kept heavy metal and similar styles popular. Aerosmith's "Walk This Way" (Tyler and Perry, 1975) would be covered by a hip-hop group a decade later, leading to an interesting encounter between metal and rap music (see this chapter's section on "Hip-Hop Culture and Rap," below).

Figure 5-14 Queen, c1976. From left, John Deacon, Freddie Mercury, Brian May, and Roger Taylor.

In contrast, American blues-based southern rock, country rock, and, by the 1980s, "classic" rock bands stressed an unpretentious authenticity in music, dress, and topics that express mostly country or heartland values and that often go beyond simple love stories. Lynyrd Skynyrd and the Eagles are examples of the southern or country rock genre. **Lynyrd Skynyrd's (founded 1964)** "Sweet Home Alabama" is notable for its reply to lyrics by singer-songwriter Neil Young (b. 1945) that comment on the American South's history of slavery:

Young's "Southern Man" (1970):

> Southern man, when will you pay them back?

Excerpt from Neil Young, "Southern Man," After the Gold Rush. Copyright © 1970 by Reprise Records.

Lynyrd Skynyrd's "Sweet Home ..." (King, Rossington, and Van Zant, 1973)

> Well I heard mister Young sing about her
> Well, I heard ole Neil put her down
> Well, I hope Neil Young will remember
> A Southern man don't need him around anyhow.

The Eagles' "Hotel California" (Felder, Frey, and Henley, 1976-77, from the album of the same name) uses metaphor to describe the insidious effects of music industry wealth and power. Wondering whether he is in heaven or hell, the singer steps in and seems to become trapped by celebrity and decadence:

> Welcome to the Hotel California...
> Mirrors on the ceiling,
> The pink champagne on ice
> And she said "We are all just prisoners here, of our own device..."

An extended instrumental guitar duet by Don Felder and Joe Walsh ends the song, helping to ensure the remarkable success of both the album and its title track.

John Cougar Mellencamp (b. 1951) and **Bruce Springsteen (b. 1949)** are singer-songwriters that lead classic rock bands. Mellencamp's "Small Town" (1975) lyrics declare his ideal of authentic, small town America. Both have become iconic figures for the American regions they represent: the Midwest heartland for Mellencamp, blue-collar New Jersey and the East Coast for Springsteen.

More soloistic singer-songwriters, who often cover wide-ranging topics and musical styles, also excel with simple, mainstream popular love ballads, typically based on a combination of blues harmonies and standard verse-chorus structure. British born **Elton John (b. 1947),** who collaborates with lyricist Bernie Taupin, has enjoyed unprecedented success with many hit songs over the past half century. "I Guess That's Why They Call It the Blues" (John, Taupin, and Johnstone, 1983) features Stevie Wonder on harmonica and is one of John's many love songs that endures.

Latin, jazz, and fusion rock bring in talent and influences from these respective genres and from other parts of the world. Guitarist and bandleader Carlos Santana has fused Latin and rock music during his long career since the 1960s. Miles Davis, the jazz trumpet player who launched the cool jazz movement (see Chapter 3, Jazz), became interested in rock music and, in collaboration with guitarist John McLaughlin and others, blended rock with jazz in albums such as *Bitches Brew*. Rock bands with large brass sections, such as Blood Sweat & Tears and Chicago, evoked the big band sound from the swing era. Rock and popular music has also embraced world idioms. McLaughlin formed the Mahavishnu Orchestra in 1971, which fused rock, jazz, and Indian classical music. Singer-songwriter **Paul Simon (b. 1941)**, from the Simon and Garfunkel folk duo popular in earlier years, visited South Africa during apartheid to collaborate with Zulu *mbaqanga* musicians for his album, *Graceland,* in 1986. His visit during the UNESCO cultural boycott, when many artists refused to perform there in protest of apartheid, sparked a controversy, but *Graceland* was critically acclaimed and

Figure 5-15 Bruce Springsteen, 2012.

Figure 5-16 Elton John with lyricist Bernie Taupin, c1971.

has sold well (see Chapter 13, Music in Sub-Saharan Africa, "Song as Expression and Dignity").

Punk, New Wave, and Alternative

Punk Experimental and provocative rock music that furiously challenges the status quo. Song lyrics protest the establishment with irony and, at times, intense bitterness.

Punk music furiously challenged the status quo. Musicians and poets found targets in government, social mores, and even—or especially—the successful music industry, with its polished production machine. Roots of this movement began in the 1960s with experimental bands such as the Velvet Underground, which was associated with avant-garde artist Andy Warhol. A performer from Michigan, Iggy Pop often wounded himself on stage as part of his outrageous performances in the late 1960s and early 1970s. Singer-songwriter, poet, and artist **Patti Smith (b. 1946)** was among the many performers who made New York City's CBGB & OMFUG club a legendary cradle of punk. (The acronym stands for "Country, Bluegrass, Blues, and Other Music for Uplifting Gourmandizers.")

Figure 5-17 Patti Smith, 2007.

Punk came to England with the founding of **The Sex Pistols** in 1975, who generated extreme controversy two years later when the band released its version of "God Save the Queen" (Sex Pistols, 1977) during Queen Elizabeth II's silver jubilee. The song, which compared the English monarchy to a "fascist regime," was banned, but that only ensured its success. Punk rock was now an international style with a fierce reputation.

Allied with the avant-garde art world from the beginning, punk is inherently experimental and provocative. The music is self-consciously simple and emphasizes aggressive guitar strumming with an often confrontational, loud, and strained vocal delivery. Song lyrics protest the establishment with irony and, at times, intense bitterness. Throughout the 1970s, punk's music and message opposed disco's smooth dance tracks and seductive lyrics. At the same time, punk opposed the hippie culture's idealistic themes of peace, love, and mind-expanding psychedelia.

Figure 5-18 The Sex Pistols, 1977. From left, Sid Vicious, Steve Jones, and Johnny Rotten.

Figure 5-19 Sting, 2007.

As the 1970s progressed, much of the music became more accessible, commercial, and accommodating to the music industry. **New wave**, as the post-punk style came to be called, still expressed alienation and independence from the establishment but with less scandal and more humor and artistry. Devo and Talking Heads from the US, and from the UK, Elvis Costello and The Police, all began with styles that can be considered new wave. Devo is especially well known for its quirky cover of the Rolling Stones song, "(I Can't Get No) Satisfaction" (Jagger and Richards, 1965; Devo cover, 1977). **Sting (Gordon Sumner, b. 1951)** from The Police is an especially versatile singer-songwriter and multi-instrumentalist who transcended the "new wave" label and went on to distinguish himself in many styles of music.

The term **alternative or "indie" rock** connotes underground or experimental rock music from "indie" (short for independent) rather than major record pro-

New wave A "post-punk" style that still expressed alienation and independence from the establishment but with less scandal than punk and more humor and artistry.

Alternative rock Originally, underground or experimental rock music from "indie" rather than major record producers.

ducers. The roots of many alternative bands are in punk rock music, and college students have been a particularly strong fan base since the 1980s. But despite the term's connotation of nonconformity, this music currently enjoys wide commercial success among mainstream audiences. Radiohead and R.E.M. are both examples of popular alternative rock bands. Originally from Seattle, "grunge" features aggressive metal guitar idioms and the disaffected, cynical point of view of punk. Nirvana was one of the most celebrated grunge bands until its lead singer and songwriter Kurt Cobain's 1994 suicide.

PLAYLIST OPTIONS
ROCK, PUNK, NEW WAVE, AND ALTERNATIVE

FIND

- A performance of a song by one of the following performers:
    - Aerosmith
    - Devo
    - Elton John
    - Nirvana
    - The Police
    - R.E.M.
    - The Sex Pistols
    - Lynyrd Skynyrd
    - Bruce Springsteen
    - Queen

OBSERVE

- Vocal style.
- Instrumentation and accompaniment.
- Stage presence and visual impression if your example is a video.

ASK

- What is the performers' message?
- Does your example neatly "place" the performer in one particular style or geographical region? Or is the essence of the performance more eclectic, and harder to pin down?

III
DANCE

Disco

Disco Dance club or dance music especially successful during the 1970s. Disco featured highly produced with electronic beats based on funk rhythms, typically in quadruple meter.

Beat Basic unit of musical time; see Musical Elements Appendix.

Quadruple meter
A metric pattern of 4 beats, typically with the first beat accented and the third beat secondarily accented, as in *strongest*, weak, *strong*, weak; see Musical Elements Appendix.

Short for "discothèque" (a nightclub in which patrons dance), **disco** refers to the type of club or to the dance music. During the 1970s, disco became phenomenally successful: many flocked to night-clubs to dance for hours. The music was highly produced with electronic **beats** based on funk rhythms, typically in **quadruple meter.** Since the music was usually electronically generated, DJs (disc jockeys) became the key personnel and, sometimes, cult figures.

Many of the most devoted patrons were from marginalized groups such as Black, Latino, and gay: disco was a social, as well as musical, phenomenon. Recreational drugs, erotic music, and the opportunity for promiscuity were plentiful. Much of the same can be said of the hippie lifestyle from the late 1960s, but the aesthetic and social goals were very different. In disco, fashion and pure escapism were valued, and ropes at high-end club entrances kept out enough people every night to maintain the clubs' elite image. Any lofty ideal of "liberation" was usually centered on sexuality.

Disco entered the mainstream with the 1977 release of the film *Saturday Night Fever*, starring John Travolta and featuring the music of the Australian group, the Bee Gees (founded 1958). It was a smashing success with both critics and audiences, hurtling disco music into the radio airwaves and the recording industry. The Bee Gees and solo singer Donna Summer flourished with disco music. **The Village People**, founded in 1977 by French producer Jacques Morali, created a sensation that lasted beyond disco's lifespan in the US. Their songs and videos, such as "YMCA" (1978) and "In the Navy" (1979), both written by Belolo, Morali, and Willis, were filled with double entendres hinting at a gay sexual orientation. Some performers, such as the superstar singer-songwriter and dancer Madonna, began in disco. Artists who were based in other styles, such as Prince, Michael Jackson, and even the heavy metal band, KISS, capitalized on disco music's popularity.

Figure 5-20 The Village People, 1978. From left, Randy Jones, Glenn Hughes, Felipe Rose, Victor Willis, David Hodo, and Alex Briley.

Disco music so effectively flooded the market that many radio stations and clubs switched their programming to disco, leaving a number of rock musicians and rock DJs out of work and some of the most loyal rock fans without their favorite stations and venues. A full-fledged backlash, which some believe was fueled by racist and homophobic attitudes, culminated in an antidisco rally during the intermission between two baseball games at Chicago's Comiskey Park in 1979. A large pile of disco records was burned at the "Disco Demolition Night" as it was called in the radio promotions leading up to the event. Once the fire was lit, thousands of rock fans stormed the field, chanting "disco sucks!" The ensuing riot forced a cancellation of the second baseball game, and some remember the event as "the day disco died." Disco's top position in the US charts would soon be replaced by other styles, but disco maintained its popularity in Europe. In the US and in Europe, it continued to develop into what is now known as "electronic dance music."

Electronic Dance Music (EDM)

EDM Electronic dance music after the disco era. Popular genres of EDM include "house," "techno," "trance," and "dubstep."

Remix A new, electronically edited version of a preexisting work (see "mashup).

Mashup A new electronically edited version of two or more preexisting musical works that are combined (see "remix").

The DJ techniques used in 1970s disco and hip-hop music emerged in the early 1980s as electronic dance music, now known as **EDM**, and have continued to develop into the twenty-first century. EDM's methods are taken directly from the Jamaican, hip-hop, and disco DJs who pioneered mixing and sampling methods using turntables with mixers, synthesizers, and, later, a variety of electronic music software (see this chapter's section on 'Hip-Hop Culture and Rap," below). Two techniques became particularly important in dance music: a **remix** is a new, electronically edited version of a preexisting work, and a **mashup** is a new, electronically edited version of two or more preexisting musical works that are combined. Just as in disco or hip-hop music, an EDM performance is typically based on a DJ's manipulation of electronically generated music (although the recordings can be from live performers), with two turntables and a mixer. EDM, however, uses lengthy remixes with gradually and seamlessly changing tempos and dynamics meant to support the dancers' experience.

The German group Kraftwerk (founded 1970) emphasized a futuristic sound that would influence hip-hop: bits of their "Trans Europe Express" (Hütter and Schult, 1976) were sampled by hip-hop DJ Afrika Bambaataa on his album *Planet Rock* (1982) (see more on Bambaataa below in "Dangerous Poetry"). Italian disco DJ and producer Giorgio Moroder (b. 1940) popularized electronic music with his futuristic, "techno" sound that can be heard in Donna Summer's "I Feel Love" (Summer, Moroder, and Bellotte, 1977) or in the hit film *Flashdance* (1983) for which he wrote the music. The British band Depeche Mode experimented with a wide variety of electronic styles.

Disco DJ **Frankie Knuckles (1955–2014)** left New York to make music at Chicago's Warehouse dance club in 1977. His eclectic disco remixes with added vocals coalesced into a style that became known as "house" music after the name of his club. In Detroit, a trio of DJs nicknamed "The Bellville Three" (Juan Atkins, Derrick May, and Kevin Saunderson) developed a quicker, more futuristic style of music called "techno", influenced by Kraftwerk. Both house and techno attracted a following in the UK during the 1980s when unemployment was high. This, in turn, inspired the international **rave** (electronic music dance party) movement of the late 1980s and early 1990s, which was associated with the use of hallucinogenic drugs, including MDMA ("ecstasy"). Several large-scale rave parties drew thousands

Rave International electronic music dance party movement of the late 1980s and early 1990s; associated with the use of hallucinogenic drugs including MDMA (ecstasy).

Figure 5-21 Frankie Knuckles, 2012.

of youths to gather at impromptu and unauthorized concerts in fields or at abandoned warehouses.

In its earlier days EDM was not as commercially successful in the US as it was in Europe because it is not as music industry "friendly": the lengthy tracks don't easily fit in the typical US radio play spot or album track. Nevertheless, EDM developed a loyal underground fan base in the US. In recent years, EDM is moving toward mainstream success: the French electronic music duo Daft Punk won the 2013 Grammy awards for Record of the Year and Best *Pop* Duo/Group Performance of the Year (italics mine). Other recent EDM Grammy nominees or winners include Skrillex and The Chemical Brothers; in fact, the Grammy category "Dance/Electronica" since 2005 is a sign of the genre's rising mainstream profile.

DJ Juan Atkins, 2010: "Berry Gordy built the Motown sound on the same principles as the conveyor belt system at Ford's. Today their plants don't work that way—they use robots and computers to make the cars. I'm more interested in Ford's robots than Berry Gordy's music."[2]

Many subgenres of EDM exist and continue to proliferate. Two examples include "trance" and dubstep: trance is similar to techno but with more emphasis on the melodic line; dubstep, a Jamaican-influenced type from the UK, has a strong, pronounced bass line with a syncopated rhythm. EDM musicians frequently collaborate with pop and hip-hop and musicians; for instance, the French DJ David Guetta teamed up with hip-hop rappers Flo Rida and Nicki Minaj in "Where Them Girls At" (Guetta et al., 2010).

PLAYLIST OPTIONS
DISCO AND ELECTRONIC DANCE MUSIC

FIND

+ A video (or a short video excerpt if it's an extended performance) from one of the following disco or EDM performers:
  + Juan Atkins (aka "Model 500")
  + Avicii
  + The Chemical Brothers
  + Daft Punk
  + David Guetta
  + Frankie Knuckles
  + Kraftwerk
  + Giorgio Moroder
  + Skrillex
  + Donna Summer
  + The Village People
  + Zombie Nation

OBSERVE

+ Approximate date of the performance to determine whether this was during the disco era or a more recent time.
+ Electronic sound style.

ASK

+ Does your example merge electronic music with any other popular style?
+ What is the topic; does the song have a message? Or does it simply provide an opportunity to dance?

IV
DANGEROUS POETRY

Hip-Hop Culture and Rap

Rap music   A musical style from hip-hop culture that includes spoken rhyme over a rhythmic background and manipulation of preexisting recordings.

Hip-Hop   African American/Latino urban culture that originated in New York's South Bronx in the 1970s; rap music, scratching, and turntablism can be described as part of hip-hop culture.

Rap, a musical style that consists of spoken poetry over rhythmic accompaniment, emerged out of **hip-hop** culture in 1970s South Bronx, New York. Marginalized Blacks, Afro-Caribbeans, and Latinos created the hip-hop movement out of their own creativity and virtually nothing else, with very few resources. Graffiti art, poetry, break dancing, and sociopolitical commentary were as much a part of hip-hop as the music. This was a tight-knit community whose pioneers, such as **Afrika Bambaataa (b. 1957)**, sought to encourage artistic expression over gang violence and drugs.

Figure 5-23 Afrika Bambaataa, 2004.

The rap tradition itself has deeper roots in Black and Afro-Caribbean oral traditions of rhythmic speech over music, declamatory boasting, and "dozens" (trading insults). DJ Kool Herc and Grandmaster Flash were both born in the Caribbean and grew up in the Bronx to become early innovators as DJs in the US. The DJs brought their record collections to create music for dancers at local house parties or other public places. The funk rhythmic backgrounds created on drum machines and synthesizers shared links with disco, which developed at about the same time in uptown New York City. The DJs played "break" (percussion) sections of records for dancers who became known as "breakdancers."

Figure 5-24 Grandmaster Flash, 1999.

Reusing bits of preexisting recorded music in a process called "sampling" was a common practice among the hip-hop DJs, who also used "scratching" technique: manipulation of the vinyl recording under the needle to create pitched, percussive rhythmic sounds from the sampled music. Scratching was best accomplished with two turntables and a sound mixer. **Turntablism** became an important, sometimes virtuosic, mode of musical expression. "Beatboxing," percussive vocal or breath sounds that often imitate scratching, eventually became a popular rhythmic and expressive device as well. As the DJs' task became more complex, they brought in MCs (MC stands for "master of ceremony") or announcers, to interact with the dancers. The MCs rapped poetry with ever increasing complexity and depth of meaning. Taken altogether, the rhythmic sampled and scratched background with the

Turntablism The DJ's use of a two-turntable and mixer console as a musical instrument, especially in hip-hop, disco, and EDM music.

new poetic language and techniques of rap created a rich, polyrhythmic tapestry with formidable expressive power.

"Old school rap" (as we now call it) of the early 1970s through the mid-1980s emphasized the role of the DJs who "play" the turntables as music instruments. Turntablism never became commercially successful due, in large part, to the inherent legal problems of sampling preexisting published music, but the practice, nevertheless, developed an underground following. Equipment in software and audio engineering that caters to turntablists continues to be developed and sold while national and international turntablist competitions maintain a following into the twenty-first century. The old school rapping style was relatively simple and formulaic. Although sociopolitical messages have been integral to rap themes from the beginning, old school rap also emphasized dance and celebration. The Sugar Hill Gang's "Rapper's Delight" (1979) significantly raised rap's profile with the mainstream public. "Birthday Party" (Grandmaster Flash and the Furious Five, 1981) and "The Message" (Grandmaster Flash and the Furious Five, 1982) exemplify songs in both topics. Hip-hop's commercial development advanced dramatically during these years with popular representations of hip-hop art, fashion, and language. The film *Wild Style* (Ahearn, 1983) featured important figures from hip-hop culture, including Grandmaster Flash.

"New school rap" emerged in the mid-1980s with the success of **Run-D.M.C. (founded 1981)** and the subsequent founding of Def Jam Records in 1984. New school rap themes emphasized the message more than the party. The role of the MCs increased in importance with a more complex and aggressive rapping style, and the music became more pop and rock oriented than old school rap. Def Jam's producer Rick Rubin's idea for Run-D.M.C.'s collaboration with metal band Aerosmith led to a fascinating music video that dramatically bridged a large divide in fan bases. Separated by a metaphorical wall, the two bands loudly and competitively rehearse: the wall is torn down by Run-D.M.C. and together they perform a cover of Aerosmith's "Walk This Way" (Tyler and Perry, 1979; cover version, 1985) to the loud cheers of a hall full of fans. The collaboration, which generated crossover sales, was good business for both Run-D.M.C. and for Aerosmith. Def Jam, originally a modest, independent recording company before its 1985 contract with the major recording label Columbia, is credited with successfully marketing rap to a crossover mainstream audience while emphasizing controversial, realistic, and gritty urban-themed messages. Artists with Def Jam include LL Cool J, The Beastie Boys, Public Enemy, and, more recently, Kanye West and Rihanna.

Figure 5-25 Run-D.M.C., date unknown. From left, Jason Mizell, Darryl McDaniels, and Joseph Simmons.

"Gangsta rap" flourished in the mid-1980s on the West Coast with increasingly graphic portrayals of gangster life. "F--- tha Police" (Ice Cube, MC Ren, D.O.C.), released by N.W.A. ("Niggaz with Attitude") from their album *Straight Outta Compton* (1988) garnered world-wide attention and controversy for lyrics aimed so directly at law enforcement:

> F--- the police comin straight from the underground
> A young n--- got it bad cause I'm brown
> And not the other color so police think
> they have the authority to kill a minority ...

Some took this song as a real threat to law enforcement while others saw it as liberating free speech and a story that needed to be told. The need for authenticity, which had always been crucial to hip-hop culture, was especially valued among gangsta rap performers, many

Excerpts from Ice Cube, MC Ren, and The D.O.C., "Fuck tha Police," Straight Outta Compton. Copyright © 1988 by Priority Records.

Figure 5-26 Tupac Shakur, date unknown.

of whom maintained their personas as genuine gangsters. Taped gunshots, sirens, and other sounds provided intense realism to accompany controversial, violent, misogynistic lyrics. Controversy swirled outside the hip-hop community among concerned listeners in the general public and in law enforcement over the crude references to women, gays, drugs, and violence. Inside, a bitter feud developed between East Coast and West Coast rappers. The insults and threats that rappers expressed to each other in their songs and videos fueled sales and anger at the same time. Tragically, rappers **Tupac Shakur (1971–1996)** from California and Biggie Smalls/Notorious B.I.G. (1972–1997) from New York were both shot to death in the mid-1990s after publicly feuding with each other. Both murders remain unsolved at the time of this writing. (See Chapter 14, Music in the Middle East, "Palestinian Music: Voices of Resistance," for Shakur's influence on the Palestinian rapper group, DAM.) Gangsta rap dominated through the turn of the century with performers such as N.W.A., Ice-T, Snoop Dog, and 50 Cent.

In the meantime, other styles proliferated. Pop-oriented rappers such as dancer MC Hammer (b. 1962) and comedic actor **Will Smith "Fresh Prince" (b. 1968)** provided friendlier messages. After his success as a rapper, Will Smith starred in a television sitcom, *The Fresh Prince of Bel-Air* (1990–1996). But rap, by nature a text-driven form, proved itself versatile enough to diverge into less commercialized subgenres and to spread among many social groups throughout the country. Alternative rappers such as Arrested Development emphasize Black liberation. White rapper Eminem, who emerged in the late 1990s with particularly savage lyrics, has become one of the most controversial—and popular—rappers of any ethnicity. Female rappers express their own points of view; some of their albums contain messages that are especially challenging to rap's male-dominated status quo, such as **Queen Latifah's (Dana Elaine Owens, b. 1970)** "U.N.I.T.Y" from *Black Reign* (1993), which insists on respectful treatment of women.

Figure 5-27 Will Smith, 2016.

Figure 5-28 Queen Latifah performing "God Bless America" at Super Bowl 44, 2010.

As producers and performers take the 1985 Run-D.M.C. and Aerosmith collaboration lesson to heart, recent blends of rap with R & B, mainstream pop, rock, gospel, electronic music, and even country music continue to increase rap's mainstream popularity. The hybrid songs often feature combinations of rap and song with both electronic and traditional instrumental accompaniment that enrich the musical texture, and they convey lyrics that express a wide variety of messages. Justin Timberlake and Jay-Z recently collaborated on "Holy Grail" (Timberlake, Jay-Z, et al., 2013), which quotes grunge band icon Kurt Cobain's "Teen Spirit." The angst-ridden message of "Holy Grail" about the insidious price of success recalls the trapped feeling evoked in the 1977 Eagles song, "Hotel California":

[Verse 1: Justin Timberlake]
You take the clothes off my back
And I let you
You'd steal the food right out my mouth
And I'd watch you eat it
I still don't know why
Why I love you so much
Oh …

[Verse 3: Jay-Z]
Now I got tattoos on my body
Psycho bitches in my lobby
I got haters in the paper
Photo shoots with paparazzi
Can't even take my daughter for a walk …

PLAYLIST OPTIONS
HIP-HOP CULTURE AND RAP

FIND

- A rap song performance by one of the following performers:
  - 50 Cent
  - Afrika Bambaataa
  - The Beastie Boys
  - Missie Elliott

- Eminem
- Ice-T
- LL Cool J
- N.W.A.
- Public Enemy
- Queen Latifah
- Run-D.M.C.
- Will Smith "Fresh Prince"
- Snoop Dog
- The Sugar Hill Gang

OBSERVE

- Topic and tone of lyrics.
- DJ accompaniment style and the overall musical texture of the performance.
- Visual story or dance if your example is a video.

ASK

- What is the message of your example, and is it "authentic" or artificial?
- Is the poetry skillful and expressive?

CHAPTER 5 VOCABULARY & IMPORTANT FIGURES

Vocabulary

Alternative rock

Beat

Disco

EDM

Funk

Heavy metal

Hip-Hop

Mashup

New wave

Outlaw country

Polyrhythm

Punk

Race records (or race music)

Rap music

Rave

Remix

Turntablism

Important Figures

Aerosmith (founded 1970)

Afrika Bambaataa (b. 1957)

Beyoncé (b. 1981)

James Brown (1928–2006)

Mariah Carey (b. 1970)

Aretha Franklin (b. 1942)

Whitney Houston (1963–2012)

Michael Jackson (1958–2009)

Elton John (b. 1947)

Frankie Knuckles (1955–2014)

k. d. lang (b. 1961)

Paul Simon (b. 1941)

Lynyrd Skynyrd (founded 1964)

John Cougar Mellencamp (b. 1951)

Queen (founded 1970)

Queen Latifah (b. 1970)

Charlie Pride (b. 1934)

Prince (1958–2016)

Run-D.M.C. (founded 1981)

The Sex Pistols (founded 1975)

Tupac Shakur (1971–1996)

Patti Smith (b. 1946)

Will Smith "Fresh Prince" (b. 1968)

Bruce Springsteen (b. 1949)

Sting (b. 1951)

The Village People (founded 1977)

Amy Winehouse (1983–2011)

ENDNOTES

[1] (From NPR Interview, "k. d. lang's 'Watershed' Moment," 5/2/08, http://www.npr.org/templates/story/story.php?storyId=90132700

[2] (As quoted in David P. Szatmary, Rockin' In Time: A Social History of Rock-and-Roll, 8th ed., Pearson, 2014, pp. 314–15.)

Image Credits

- Figure 5-1: Copyright © 2007 by D.L., (CC BY-SA 2.0) at https://commons.wikimedia.org/wiki/File:DJ_Hypnotize_and_Baby_Cee.jpg.
- Figure 5-2: Cherie A. Thurlby / Copyright in the Public Domain.
- Figure 5-3: Copyright © 2007 by Robbiework, (CC BY-SA 3.0) at https://commons.wikimedia.org/wiki/File:Willie_UK2K7_2.JPG.
- Figure 5-4: Oscar Espinoza / Copyright in the Public Domain.
- Figure 5-5: Copyright © 2006 by Charlie Llewellin, (CC BY-SA 2.0) at https://commons.wikimedia.org/wiki/File:Kdlang22_(cropped1).jpg.
- Figure 5-6: Copyright © 2008 by John Krupsky, (CC BY-SA 2.0) at https://commons.wikimedia.org/wiki/File:Carolinachocolatedrops.jpg.

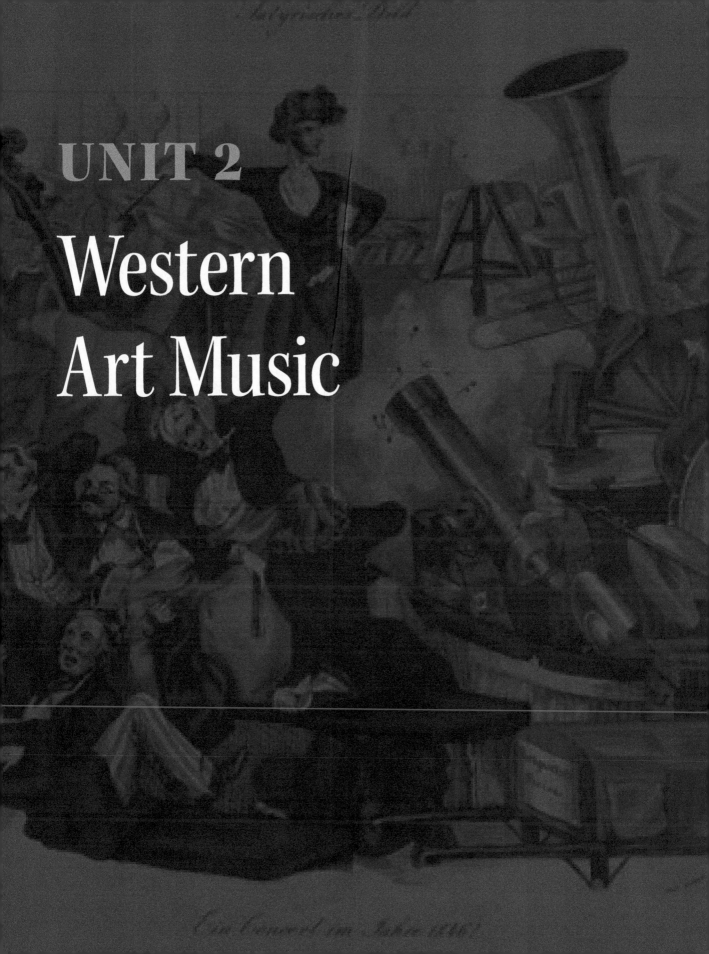

UNIT 2
Western Art Music

Introduction to Unit Two

This Unit's Story

Unit 2 traces the development of what most people call "classical" music from Greek antiquity to the present day. Readers will find descriptions of many of the most important musical styles from this great span of time in Europe within their historical and cultural contexts. Musical genres, or categories, are explained through their characteristic musical elements and functions. The personalities and techniques of important figures in music are explored in this unit as well.

Historians and teachers tend to carve history into segments—we usually call them "eras"—to make the large quantity of data easier to remember and understand. Some of these periods clump quite naturally into one general style or group of styles, such as the classic or romantic eras. Others are not so naturally categorized: Some of these "eras" have many styles that are very different from each other, such as the medieval and baroque eras. Nevertheless, this unit proceeds chronologically, and we will find stylistic trends with each of these eras. These era names will help in the study of Western music from the last two millennia, but just as with the Unit 1 (American Vernacular Music) musical styles, labels can be problematic: feel free to think beyond the categories.

Historical Eras in Music History

In the following definitions, "c." stands for the Latin *circa* ("approximately"); "BCE" stands for "Before the Common Era"; and "CE" stands for "Common Era." Composers' dates throughout this text will often have the *circa* abbreviation, as in "William Byrd (c. 1540–1623)"; fl. for floruit ("flourished"), when only career or life event dates are known, and birth or death dates are a mystery, as in "Comtessa de Dia (fl. late twelfth, early thirteenth century)"; and "b." for "born" for composers still living, as in "Philip Glass (b. 1937)."

Antiquity Used here to refer to classical Greek and Roman civilizations before the medieval era, c. eighth century BCE to fifth century CE.

Medieval Era The period of European history spanning approximately the fifth to the fifteenth centuries CE. This was a transitional period marked by the collapse of the Roman Empire, the Christianization of Europe, and the continuous development of national identities and boundaries.

Renaissance ("Rebirth") The period of European history from the end of the medieval era in the early fifteenth century to 1600, characterized by a renewed interest in classical cultures. This inspired what we now call the humanist movement, which sought to preserve and emulate ancient intellectual and artistic achievements.

Reformation Used here to refer to the Protestant Reformation, the sixteenth-century Christian religious movement that resulted in the establishment of Protestant churches and profound changes in Christian worship.

Counter-Reformation The Roman Catholic response to the Reformation, which included the Council of Trent (1545–1563) and various reforms.

Baroque Derived from "misshapen pearl" in Portuguese; Western European musical style c. 1600–1750; highly ornamented style.

Enlightenment (Age of Reason) Generally considered as lasting from the late seventeenth through the end of the eighteenth centuries, this rationalist movement sought to look beyond the Bible for answers to life's mysteries in philosophy, politics, science, scholarship, and the arts.

Classic Era European music between approximately 1750–1820. "Classical music" is generally used to refer broadly to all European art music, but music specifically of the classic era features aesthetic qualities inspired by classical Greek culture, such as reason, symmetry, and clarity.

Romanticism Used here to refer to the nineteenth-century European movement, characterized by a more subjective point of view than the rationalist classical era. Romantic music emphasizes intense emotional expression, literary programs, and the use of large musical forces.

Titles in Western Art Music

A song is entitled with the first line of its text, or lyrics. This means that for a genre with not just one but *two or three* different poems to be sung at the same time (such as the medieval motet), you'll see the title of each poem in succession, separated by a slash, as in Philippe de Vitry's (1291–1361) *In arboris/Tuba sacre fidei/Virgo sum.* Yes, a small group of singers sing different lyrics at the same time in the medieval motet: welcome to Western art music's obsession with **texture**. An instrumental work is generally labeled with its key and often its **tempo**: "Piano Sonata no. 14 in C Sharp Minor, op. 27, no. 2, *adagio sostenuto*" is the full title of the first and most famous movement of Beethoven's "Moonlight Sonata."

Musical Texture The melodic and harmonic relationship of musical lines, or voices; see Musical Elements Appendix.

Tempo The speed of a musical work; see Musical Elements Appendix.

Both instrumental and vocal works are usually given opus (Lat. "work") numbers and sometimes an additional catalogue number. This can make art music titles look cryptic to the uninitiated, but it's really just a desperate attempt to keep a complicated list of works organized. The catalogue number reflects the musicologist or organization responsible for the catalogue. For instance, Ludwig von Köchel (1800–1877) catalogued Mozart's works; therefore, each of his works uses a "K" number as one of its identifiers, such as in "Symphony no. 40 in G Minor, K550." Not all abbreviations come from the cataloguer's name: in the mid-twentieth century, German scholar Wolfgang Schmieder's (1901–1990) thematic catalogue of J. S. Bach's works uses "BWV" for *Bach-Werke-Verzeichnis* ("Bach works catalogue") as in "Lute Suite in G Minor, BWV 995."

Audience Etiquette with "Classical" Music

Don't miss opportunities for the ultimate musical experience: a live performance. Audience etiquette in art music performances—particularly with music from the seventeenth through the nineteenth centuries—is usually rather restrained compared to that of other types of music. Listeners are expected to be silent throughout the performance and even withhold applause at the ends of movements (sections) of extended works until the end of the very last movement. This means that sometimes when the music finishes with a resounding cadence and the most natural thing in the world seems to be to applaud, look around first: you might be the single (and very embarrassed) audience member clapping in the entire hall.

Put away any electronics. Even silenced electronics are distracting because of their glow. Can you imagine yourself onstage, trying to express the depths of an emotion with exquisitely fine-tuned physical movements calculated to produce the exact sound you've been perfecting for hundreds of rehearsal hours to audience members browsing Facebook and stealing your intellectual property (recording your performance without permission)? Performers and your fellow audience members need your courtesy and your attention.

All of this might seem like too much. Why put up with history lessons, foreign languages, cryptic titles, and, when we attend a live performance, all sorts of etiquette rules? Because when we explore this repertoire, we find music that can take us back—or forward—in time, music that can combine sheer athletic prowess with intellectual and emotional power, and music that offers immeasurable depth and excitement.

178

CHAPTER

6

Antiquity to 1600

I
ANCIENT ROOTS

Antiquity Classical
Greek and Roman civiliza-
tions before the medieval
era, c. eighth century BCE to
c. fifth century CD (Also see
Unit 2, Western Art Music,
Introduction).

Prehistoric and Babylonian Music

Traces of prehistoric music exist from as far back as 35,000 years ago in physical objects such as whistles and flutes found in European settlements and in visual images from the sixth millennium BCE in Turkish cave paintings of drummers and dancers. Actual instruments, parts of instruments, or carved images of instruments such as lyres, harps, lutes, pipes, drums, and bells survive from ancient Mesopotamia of the third and fourth millennia BCE. Artifacts of written texts leave clues

Opposite: Franco-Flemish tapestry, "Hearing" from the Lady and the Unicorn tapestry cycle. This sumptuous scene, which represents the sense of hearing, shows a courtly lady who plays a portative organ while her assistant works the bellows. The six tapestries in the series are housed in the Musée national du Moyen Âge in Paris.

about the significant role of music in ancient Babylonian cultures. Rituals such as weddings and funerals, the accompaniment of daily work, and entertainment included music, which is just as true for people today.

Ancient Greek Music (C. Eighth Century BCE to Fifth Century CE)

Later, during the first millennia BCE, music flourished in Hellenistic culture as an ever-present component of daily life. *Mousike* referred to the arts of any of the nine muses (Greek goddesses of learning and the arts), including history, drama, dance, and song; for the Greeks, poetry, rhythm, melody, and harmony were combined into one entity. Ancient literary drama and epic poetry may bring books and libraries to modern minds, but these works were likely sung. Terms that have lasted from the original Greek usage signal this probability: "lyric poetry," for instance, referred to poetry sung with lyre accompaniment, and "tragedy" incorporates the word, "ode"—the art of singing. "Hymn" is a Greek word that referred to a poem in praise of gods or heroes.

Greek musical pitches were organized into several different types of scales, called modes, each of which was associated with distinct melodies, rhythms, and topics. They were named after regions as in the "Dorian" or "Phrygian" modes. Vocal music was especially important, and Greek musical **texture** was sung **monophonically**, often with **heterophonic** or

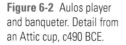

Figure 6-2 Aulos player and banqueter. Detail from an Attic cup, c490 BCE.

polyphonic instrumental accompaniment (see the Musical Elements Appendix on musical textures). Rhythm and meter closely follow the poetic rhythm in texted music. Musical instruments often symbolized particular aspects of life and were used to accompany the worship of specific deities. The **aulos**, a reed wind instrument with two pipes, was used in Greek tragic drama and was associated with Dionysis, the god of wine and ecstasy. The **lyre**, which usually had seven strings and was played with a plectrum, was used to accompany the worship of Apollo, god of light, learning, and the arts. The lyre was also used as an accompaniment to dance and poetry and was considered an important part of education. Famous musicians traveled throughout the Hellenistic world on concert tours and participated in competitions. Most performers were slaves or servants. Women were allowed to perform professionally on the lyre, but they were not permitted to compete.

Musical Texture The melodic and harmonic relationship between musical lines, or voices. **Monophony** consists of only a single musical line or voice, **heterophony** consists of a single musical line with simultaneous variation, **homophony** features one dominant melody with subordinate chordal accompaniment, and **polyphony** includes two or more independent musical lines; see Musical Elements Appendix.

Aulos An ancient reed instrument with two pipes, associated with Greek tragic drama and with the worship of Dionysis; see Musical Instruments Appendix.

Lyre An ancient stringed instrument, which was associated with the worship of Apollo; see Musical Instruments Appendix.

Figure 6-3 Muse playing the lyre. Detail from an Attic vessel, 440–430 BCE.

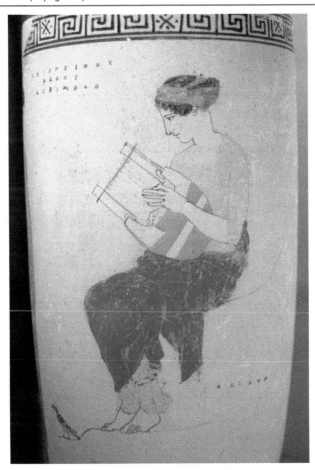

Mathematical Aspects of Music: Pythagoras

Pythagoras (c. 570–c. 490 BCE) recognized numerical ratios between musical intervals: according to legend, he noticed several blacksmiths pounding hammers of different sizes, which created variously pitched sounds. Were the pitches dependent on the strength of the blacksmiths or the size of the hammers? His request of the blacksmiths to trade hammers yielded his answer: hammer size determines the pitch, and if one hammer is exactly half the size of another, it will sound twice as high, creating the octave interval with a ratio of 2:1. All other musical intervals can be expressed in ratios as well, and this discovery became one of the foundations of modern **acoustics**, the science of sound. Pythagoras and his followers maintained that the mathematical law that governs musical intervals rules the cosmos as well, and they developed the concept of a relationship between planetary motions and musical intervals. The resulting mystical notion of "unheard music" created by the movement of heavenly bodies continues to fascinate people to this day; it is popularly known as **music of the spheres**.

Acoustics   The science of sound.

Music of the spheres   Mystical concept developed by Pythagoras and his followers of "unheard music" created by the movement of heavenly bodies.

Figure 6-4 Pythagoras shows his theory of intervallic ratios with blacksmiths, bells, glass harmonica, monochord, and pipes in this 1492 woodcut published by Francino Gaffurio.

Philosophical Aspects of Music: Plato and Aristotle

The Greek philosophers asserted that music affects the emotions and the characters of its listeners. For the education of children, **Plato (c. 429–347 BCE)** emphasized the importance of a balance between gymnastics, which develops strength, and music, which develops sensitivity and intellect, in forming good citizens. An education that only emphasizes gymnastics would lead to savagery, but a sole focus on music would lead to softness. In *The Republic* he quotes his teacher Socrates: "Then he who best blends gymnastics with music and applies them most suitably to the soul is the man whom we should most rightly pronounce to be the most perfect and harmonious musician ..."[1] Plato's student **Aristotle (384–322 BCE)** details the ways each musical instrument and each mode has specific effects on behavior and character in his *Politics*: "Rhythm and melody supply imitations of anger and gentleness, and also of courage and temperance, and of all the qualities contrary to these, and of the other qualities of character, which hardly fall short of the actual affections, as we know from our own experience, for in listening to such strains our souls undergo a change."[2]

PLAYLIST OPTIONS
ANCIENT MUSIC

FIND

- A historically informed performance by one of the following:
    - Atrium Musicae de Madrid
    - Richard Dumbrill
    - Ensemble Kérylos
    - Michael Levy
    - Musica Romana
    - Petros Tabouris

Or an example of ancient music:

- Vocal music, such as the Epitaph of Seikilos found on a tombstone
    - Lyrics, translated:
      As long as you live, be lighthearted.
      Let nothing trouble you.

> Life is only too short,
> And time takes its toll.[3]

- Lyre or other stringed music
- Aulos or other wind music

OBSERVE

- Musical texture: (monophonic, polyphonic, or heterophonic)
- Instrumental timbre (such as plucked stringed or wind instruments)
- Relationship between music and text in vocal music

ASK

- What is the likely original performance context: when, where, and for what reason was this music produced?
- If your example is vocal music, what does the text mean, and how does that influence the performance?

II
MEDIEVAL MUSIC (FIFTH CENTURY TO EARLY FIFTEENTH CENTURY)

Medieval Era The period of European history spanning approximately fifth to fifteenth centuries CE. also see (Unit 2, European Art Music, Introduction).

Historical context

Pagan Europe was Christianized during the earlier centuries of the Middle Ages. By the later Middle Ages, massive cathedrals had been built in the largest cities of a mostly Christian Europe, and smaller churches were prevalent throughout European societies. National monarchs and the church shared power over most of the continent. Arts such as painting, sculpture, stained glass, music, and literature flourished because the church patronized, or supported, their cultivation. Most of the surviving evidence of art, literature, and music we have from those centuries, in fact, comes from church sources because the church was the source of the wealth, education, materials, and storage that would make the legacy of these cultural achievements possible.

Sacred Music

The earliest Christians, most familiar with the **sacred** (religious) music of their Jewish tradition, gradually developed the foundations of Christian music with influences from Jewish liturgical practices of the time: they sang psalms from the Hebrew Book of Psalms and popular hymns, according to the calendar. Religious services in most synagogues and churches still feature hymns and psalm singing or psalm recitation to this day. Christians, however, developed the Mass liturgy, which commemorates Christ's last supper and serves the Holy Eucharist. The Mass worship service set to music is known as a **Mass setting**.

Plainchant, also known as **Gregorian chant**, was the musical expression of early medieval Christian worship in Mass and in other prayer services. Although some aspects of the earliest sacred musical style, such as rhythmic features, are unknown before the advent of notation, we know that it is **monophonic** and nonmetric because the chants are entirely text-driven. This leaves very few musical elements to express the meaning of the text. **Text-setting styles**, or ways of fitting words to melodies, however, are sometimes used as a mode of expression. **Melismatic** text-setting style, for instance, in which many notes per syllable of text are sung, is used for the emotionally charged word, "alleluia" ("praise God" in Hebrew). **Syllabic** settings with one note per syllable of text are used for chants that need to convey many words clearly, such as the Credo, or creed—the formal statement of beliefs.

Most plainchant composers are anonymous, but we remember **Hildegard of Bingen (1098–1179)** as one of the most notable figures of the Middle Ages in music and in many other fields as well. The abbess of a convent in Germany, she was distinguished for her scholarship, her artistic endeavors, her political insights, and her visions. Hildegard's plainchant style was unusually expressive for her time with a wider melodic range and a more flexible structure than the music of her contemporaries. She often set her own vivid and mystical poetry to her music. She wrote a morality play, a drama meant to teach virtues, which was sung to her music. *Ordo virtutum* (*The Virtues*) portrays various allegorical characters, such as the Virtues and the devil, engaged in a struggle over sin and repentance.

Sacred music Religious music.

Mass setting Mass worship service set to music.

Plainchant (Gregorian chant) Christian, monophonic sacred chant originating in medieval Christian worship traditions.

Monophony Musical texture that consists of a single musical line; see Musical Elements Appendix.

Text-setting styles Ways of fitting texts to melodies; **syllabic** text-setting matches one note to each syllable of text, and **melismatic** text-setting features many notes for each syllable of text.

Hildegard of Bingen: "God has implanted the living voice of the breath of life in reason, that is, the voice of rejoicing, which by good knowledge, sees and knows faith. That same voice is a well-sounding trumpet resonating with works of kindness, for it enjoys the embrace of divine love. This voice of divine love resounds in the symphony of all praises of salvation."[4]

Sacred music gradually began to develop rhythmic and **polyphonic** characteristics around the same time as the advent of notation, beginning from around the ninth century. Plainchant melodies, which had become associated with certain prayers over past generations, became foundations for additional, ornamental musical lines to be sung during passages that included significant sections of the text. In the earliest departures from purely monophonic chant, the additional lines adhere closely to the original melodies; for instance, they might proceed in parallel or similar motion within a fixed range of intervals. Over the next few centuries, the musical lines eventually become more independent of each other and then could finally be considered truly polyphonic.

Polyphony Musical texture that consists of two or more independent musical lines; see Musical Elements Appendix.

One genre in particular features an extreme form of polyphony: early medieval **motets** were polyphonic vocal works based on preexisting musical lines (often chants), with one or more additional texted musical lines. Those texts were different—in meaning and sometimes even language—and meant to be sung simultaneously with the original chant texts and musical lines. Although the original tune is often from plainchant with sacred Latin text, the additional line might be a secular French love poem, instead, which makes this genre a combination of sacred and secular music; eventually, even the original tune could be either sacred or secular. Interestingly, the two or three different texts in these polytextual motets usually have a point in common; for instance, the original sacred text might be about the Virgin Mary and the secular French text about a beautiful, chaste maiden. **Guillaume de Machaut (c. 1300–1377),** although more famous as a poet during his lifetime, was one of the most important composers of his day. His motets usually feature two additional texted lines of French poetry over an original foundational tune with sacred Latin text.

Motet A polyphonic vocal work. Early medieval motets often feature multiple texts sung simultaneously.

PLAYLIST OPTIONS
MEDIEVAL SACRED MUSIC

FIND

- A Medieval sacred work, such as:
  - A plainchant (also known as Gregorian chant) example

- Mass chant texts and translations are readily available online with "Mass translation" as the search term
- Hildegard's *Ordo Virtutum* religious drama
  - Text and translation readily available online.
- A medieval polytextual motet: texts and translations may be difficult to find online.
  - Machaut's *Aucune gent/Qui plus aimme/Fiat voluntas tua*
  - Philippe de Vitry's (1291–1361) *In arboris/Tuba sacre fidei/Virgo sum*

OBSERVE

- Meter or the lack of a meter
- Text-setting style (syllabic or melismatic)
- Melodic contour
- If your example is a motet: language/s and meanings of multiple texts
- Timbre: use of voices with or without musical instruments

ASK

- If your example is plainchant:
  - What is the role or prayer of that particular chant?
- If Hildegard's music is your example:
  - Did Hildegard compose the text as well? If so, what does it mean, and does her music express it in some way, such as through melodic contour and range?
- If your example is a motet:
  - If your example is vocal (some performances are instrumental), is there more than one text? If so, do the meanings of the texts correspond with each other in any way?
  - How do the musical lines interact with each other; do they seem to begin and end phrases together, or are they extremely independent?
  - Do the vowels and consonants between the different texts line up with each other sometimes, or do they present in a staggered effect?

Medieval Secular Music

Music-making in medieval European society, outside of the protective auspices of the church, crossed a wide range of social and economic strata. Traveling musician-entertainers often lived on the edge of poverty, marginalized by religious and civil society, while the more secure artisan class musicians formed professional societies known as guilds. Some poet-composers in France and Germany were aristocrats and even royalty.

Texts in **secular** music were generally in the vernacular languages and included epic poetry, such as *Beowulf* in England, or the Old Norse eddas. **Bards**, who sang, chanted, or recited poetry, were active throughout the Middle Ages. The harp and other stringed instruments were often used as instrumental accompaniment. "Bard" has come to mean "poet" today, but its original meaning in Celtic languages was closer to "praise-singer."

Minstrels were professional musician-entertainers throughout Europe. Some were itinerant, traveling from town to town to perform acrobatic feats, storytelling, comic sketches, and music. Others developed more security and status by organizing guilds. Their music included instrumental dances and **chansons**, which are secular polyphonic works. Although chansons were originally conceived as vocal works with song texts ("chanson" means "song" in French), medieval musicians performed chansons with either voices or instruments or a combination of both. **Pastoral** themes, which reference rustic topics, such as nature, countryside, and the rural life of peasantry and shepherds, are common in music as well as in drama, literature, and the visual arts throughout European history.

The "inventors of song"—**troubadours** from the Occitanian culture in what is now southern France and **trouvéres** from northern France—usually came from the upper classes, sometimes as high as royalty. Minnesingers ("singers of love") in Germany were aristocrats as well. Most of the songs of these poet-composers grew out of the literary ***fin' amors*** (ideal love, or courtly love) tradition, which expressed the pain of unrequited

Secular music
Nonreligious music.

Bard Originally "praise singer," an entertainer who sang, chanted, or recited poetry.

Minstrel Itinerant musician-entertainer in medieval Europe.

Chanson (Fr. "song") French secular vocal genre, often polyphonic and sometimes performed with instruments.

Pastoral Reference to rustic topics, such as nature, countryside, peasants, farmers, and shepherds.

Figure 6-6 In this detail from Cantigas de Santa Maria collection of images (c1280), we see instrumentalists with 2 bowed stringed instruments (vielles) and one plucked stringed instrument (citole). They could have been troubadours and/or minstrels.

Troubadours and trouvéres French aristocratic "inventors of song" or poet-musicians whose songs often expressed the *fin' amor* tradition.

Fin' amor (Occitan: "refined love") Popular theme in early modern European literature of idealized love, which expressed the pain of unrequited love, devotion to the beloved, and the refinement of the lover through a lifetime of suffering and service.

love, devotion to the beloved, and the refinement of the lover through a lifetime of suffering and service. The *fin' amor* theme was related to the medieval cult of chivalry and often indicated, particularly in the songs of the minnesingers, a veiled worship of the Virgin Mary. Other topics included politics, pastoral settings, bawdy songs, and the crusades. Troubadour and trouvére songs were collected in *chansonnières*, or songbooks; we don't know the melodies for most of the songs because only some notated examples survive. From the examples that do exist, we know that the melodic range is generally narrow, and the music displays a variety of forms and melodic contours to express the poetic meaning of the text. Rhythm is not indicated in these musical examples; meter, rhythm, and tempo most likely varied according to topic and textual meaning. Prominent troubadours include **Bernart de Ventadorn (c. 1130–c. 1200),** a humbly born troubadour who achieved renown for his *fin' amor* poetry and music, and **Comtessa de Dia (fl. late twelfth, early thirteenth century),** a *troubaritz*, or female troubadour, expresses the pain of unrequited love from a woman's viewpoint in her song, *A chantar.* **Richard the Lionheart (1157–1199)**, who reigned as King of England 1189–1199 during a time when English and French cultures were politically close, was also a trouvére.

PLAYLIST OPTIONS
MEDIEVAL SECULAR MUSIC

FIND

One of these:

- A performance of medieval epic poetry and drama, such as:
  - An Altramar medieval music album
  - Benjamin Bagby's *Beowulf* performance in the original language; an excerpt can be heard at bagbybeowulf.com
- A video of medieval dance and instrumental music; use search terms, such as
  - Medieval dance
  - *Estampie* or *istampita*
  - Medieval instrumental music

- A troubadour or trouvére song by one of these promi-
  nent poet-composers (texts and translations available
  online):
  - Bernart de Ventadorn's *Can vei la lauzeta mover*
  - Comtessa de Dia's *A chantar m'er de so qu'ieu non
    volria*
  - Richard the Lionheart's *Ja nun hons pris*

OBSERVE

- If your example is epic poetry:
  - Performance is recitation, chant, song, or a combi-
    nation of these
  - Use or absence of musical instruments
- If your example is instrumental dance music:
  - Prominent meter
  - Improvisatory passages, especially in repeated
    sections
- If your example is a troubadour or trouvére song:
  - Melodic contour
  - Use or absence of musical instruments

ASK

- If your example is an epic poetry performance:
  - How effective is the interpretation? Does it bring
    the drama to life?
- If your example is an instrumental dance music video:
  - If dancers are included in your example, what is the
    choreography like; are the dancers in pairs, or are
    they organized in larger groups?
  - How do the musical instruments compare with
    modern musical instruments?
- If your example is a troubadour or trouvére song:
  - Does this song feature *fin amour* poetry, which
    expresses unrequited but refining love?
  - In songs with instrumental accompaniment, what
    do the instruments do? Do they follow the voice
    in unison, do they elaborate when the voice is not
    active, do they create their own musical lines, or
    is the accompaniment some combination of these
    styles?

III
RENAISSANCE MUSIC: EARLY FIFTEENTH CENTURY TO 1600

Renaissance ("Rebirth") The period of European history from the end of the medieval era in the early fifteenth century to c. 1600, characterized by a renewed interest in classical cultures also see (Unit 2, European Art Music, Introduction).

The **Renaissance** ("rebirth") in Europe signaled a renewed interest in classical cultures, which inspired the humanist movement to preserve and emulate ancient intellectual and artistic achievements. Italian culture became the epicenter of the European Renaissance with classically inspired realism and the development of perspective in the visual arts. Throughout Europe, the transmission of ancient literature became even more important than it had been before, and the advent of printing in Europe led to much more widespread literacy. Printed music, in turn, led to wider dissemination of music and musical styles.

Traditional Sacred Music in the Renaissance

Polyphonic texture was the hallmark of traditional sacred music in northern Europe during the fifteenth and sixteenth centuries. Mass settings and motets continued their polyphonic development, although motets were no longer polytextual. In the Franco-Flemish region (which is now Belgium, Luxembourg, and parts of Holland and northern France), a number of composers rose to prominence. **Johannes Ockeghem (c. 1410–1497)** was particularly distinctive for his intellectual compositions that incorporated puzzles for the performers to unravel. He often wrote **canons**,

Canon (or round) Two or more musical lines, or voices, in strict imitation throughout a musical work or a section of a musical work.

for instance, which are polyphonic compositions in which two or more parts, or melodic lines, proceed in strict imitation throughout the entire work or section (more popularly known today as "rounds"). Although most canons are precisely notated to direct performers' successive entrances, Ockeghem sometimes leaves it up to the performers to figure out certain musical elements such as meter or pitch level in the different musical lines. His contributions include mass settings, motets, and secular works.

When wealthy Italian nobility supported the arts by offering employment, many talented musicians from northern Europe journeyed

Figure 6-7 Illuminated manuscript page of "Kyrie" ("Lord") from a mass setting by Johannes Ockeghem, Chigi Codex, late 15th century.

southward, setting in motion a blend of the northern polyphonic style with the more homophonic, informal characteristics of Italian music. The French composer **Josquin des Prez (c. 1450–1521)** was the most prominent of these imported talents, and his music reflects both styles, sometimes in alternation within the same work. Josquin also developed the **points of imitation** technique: in contrast to the canon technique of strict imitation throughout the musical work, imitative entries among the different musical lines last only briefly at the beginnings of phrases before the lines continue, each with its own distinct melodic contour. Josquin is particularly known for his many motets, and he also composed mass settings and secular music.

Points of imitation
Brief passages of imitation between musical lines; often at beginnings of text phrases in vocal music.

Reformation Music

Protestantism has been—and continues to be—profoundly influential ever since its beginnings in 1517 when **Martin Luther (1483–1546)** posted his complaints against corrupt Catholic practices on the door of a

Martin Luther: "After all, the gift of language combined with the gift of song was only given to man to let him know that he should praise God with both word and music, namely, by providing the word through music and by providing sweet melodies with words."[5]

Figure 6-9 Portrait of Jean Calvin by Titian (1490–1576).

church in Wittenberg, Germany. He set the entire **Reformation** movement in motion, which led to important theological changes, worship in vernacular languages, and more accessible church music for many Christians.

Luther was a theologian and a priest, and he was also a musician; he wrote sacred **chorales**, or German strophic hymns, and he encouraged his musician colleagues to write chorales, as well. Their melodies could be newly composed, based on plainchant tunes, or even reworked from popular songs with religious texts substituted to make them suitable for worship in church. For Protestants, music became more accessible than the old plainchant for two reasons: the text was in the vernacular (which was, of course, German for the first Lutheran chorales), and the music was organized in **strophic form** to enable everyone in church to learn the melody more easily. The entire congregation was expected to sing, and they were able to do this with very little education. A hallmark of Protestantism is a more direct, individual, relationship with God, and this powerful new tradition of hymnody was its musical reflection.

Early chorales were mostly monophonic, but eventually the melodies were supported by chordal accompaniment in a texture known as **homophony**. In this texture, we can hear one distinct melody, but chords are added which support the melody. Over these supportive chords, homophony has one dominant musical line or melody, unlike polyphony, which presents more than one independent musical line.

Other European reformers led movements in succeeding years, each with its own theological and stylistic characteristics. Swiss reformer **Jean Calvin (1509–1564)** and his followers held very strict views regarding music, which they distrusted for its powers to distract Christians from a virtuous life. Calvinist musicians set biblical psalms to monophonic melodies with rhythm and meter, but polyphonic music and, in many cases, musical instruments were discouraged or even forbidden in church services.

In England, Reformation era Christians were forced to switch religious affiliations back and forth as royalty switched their allegiance for and against the Roman Catholic hierarchy. Throughout the first half of the sixteenth century, the succession of English monarchs alternated one after the other

Reformation Used here to refer to the Protestant Reformation, the sixteenth-century Christian religious movement that resulted in the establishment of Protestant churches and profound changes in Christian worship (also see Unit 2, European Art Music, Introduction).

Chorale German strophic hymn.

Strophic form Song structure in which the same music is repeated for all stanzas of the text; see Musical Elements Appendix.

Homophony Musical text that features one dominant melody with subordinate chordal accompaniment; see Musical Elements Appendix.

Figure 6-10 Portrait of William Byrd.

Anthem Sacred polyphonic choral composition with English text, similar to the motet.

Counter-Reformation The Roman Catholic response to the Reformation, which included the Council of Trent (1545–1563) and various reforms.

beginning with Henry VIII, who broke with Rome in 1531, and ending with the reinstatement of the Church of England (Anglicanism) by Elizabeth I in 1559. In the meantime, composers needed to adapt to these changes by providing traditional Latin mass settings in Catholic services or **anthems**—sacred polyphonic choral compositions with English texts—for Anglican services. For most, obedience to royal religious mandates of the day, whatever they may be, was crucial not only to successful careers but also to personal freedom and safety. The celebrated English Catholic composer **William Byrd (c. 1540–1623),** however, was apparently allowed to continue to compose mass settings for recusant Catholics under Elizabeth I in spite of her Anglican rule. At the same time, he also accommodated the Church of England through his contributions to the development of Anglican service music and through his outstanding repertory of anthem compositions. Byrd is also renowned for his secular instrumental music (see "Secular Music," below).

Counter-Reformation Music

The Roman Catholic Church sought to address the issues raised by reformers through the Council of Trent, a conference of church hierarchy that convened throughout the years between 1545 and 1563. The council reaffirmed traditional Catholic doctrines but tried to purge abuses as well. They also saw the value of clarity in music: they recommended that liturgical music should feature less complex polyphony so that the text could be heard more clearly. **Giovanni Palestrina (c. 1525–1594),** a devout Catholic composer, addressed **counter-Reformation** concerns: he carefully constructed his polyphonic mass settings with compositional techniques that served to clarify the text, such as the creation of a distinct musical motive for each phrase, with great sensitivity toward text pronunciation and meaning. His music would later come to symbolize traditional polyphonic church music.

Figure 6-11 Frontpiece of the missal of Giovanni Palestrina (1554), which shows Palestrina presenting his musical work to Pop Julius III.

PLAYLIST OPTIONS
RENAISSANCE SACRED MUSIC

FIND

One of these:

* An example of pre-Reformation Latin sacred music, such as:

    * A movement from Ockeghem's *Missa Prolationum* (text and translation available online with "mass text and translation" as the search term)

    * Josquin's motet, *Ave Maria ... virgo serena* (text and translation available online with "Ave Maria ... virgo serena translation" as the search term)

- An example of Reformation music, such as:
  - A German Lutheran chorale (hymn): *Ein feste Burg ist unser Gott* ("A Mighty Fortress is Our God") by Martin Luther (text and translation available online.)
  - An English anthem: "Sing Joyfully Unto God" by William Byrd.
- An example of counter-Reformation music, such as:
  - A movement from Palestrina's *Missa Papae Marcelli* (text and translation available online with "mass text and translation" as the search term)

OBSERVE

- Text language: Latin or vernacular (German, English, French)
- Musical texture:

ASK

- If your example is pre-Reformation music:
  - Do you hear complete canons or points of imitation?
- If your example is Reformation music:
  - How does the Reformation composer reach out to "everyday" people who have not been educated in Latin or theology?
- If your example is Palestrina's counter-Reformation music:
  - How does Palestrina address the Council of Trent's recommendations for clarity in music?

Secular Music in the Renaissance

European society's most privileged families had already cultivated music for many generations by the sixteenth century, but the advent of commercial music printing in 1501, combined with a rising middle class, added a large new population of amateur music-makers. People of either gender in polite society were expected to read music, sing, perform an instrument, and dance. Notated music and instructive handbooks proliferated, and musical literacy flourished. In keeping with humanistic Renaissance ideals, music was meant to faithfully express the poetry in vocal music; thus, vocal genres became especially significant. Musical instruments were classified into two categories: *haut* ("high" or loud) for larger ensembles and *bas* ("low" or soft) for more intimate performances. Instrumental ensembles, or **consorts**, as they were known in England, could, of course, include both types of instruments.

The most important genre of sixteenth-century Italian secular music, the **madrigal,** is a secular polyphonic vocal work. The text is usually a single stanza of cultivated poetry; the great fourteenth-century Italian poet **Francesco Petrarch (1304–1374)**, for instance, was a favorite source. Topics concerning love are most common, and pastoral settings are common. Vivid **word-painting**, or musical expression of the text, is common in this vocal music: heaven, for instance, is often musically portrayed by a rising melodic contour, and pain can be expressed with harmonic **dissonance**. Madrigals were usually composed for four or five single voices, but instruments could be substituted for one or more of the parts. **Luca Marenzio (c. 1553–1599)** was one of the most prominent Italian madrigal composers.

Figure 6-12 Luca Marenzio, 1560.

Although the madrigal originated in Italy, the genre sparked a following in England after translations were published and sent to an eager English public. Composers in the British Isles, such as **Thomas Morley (c. 1557–1602)**, eventually developed their own, English, style of madrigal, which tended to be lighter and more humorous and often included passages full of the nonsense syllables, "fa-la."

Lute was a common accompaniment to vocal music in Europe. The French chanson, referred to above, continued to develop during the Renaissance as a polyphonic vocal work that could be performed by a vocal ensemble or by a solo voice with lute accompaniment. The same is true for the English lute song that emerged in the late sixteenth and early seventeenth centuries. Both cultures often use cultivated poetry, which is expressed with sensitive text declamation while the lute accompanies the voice with subtle nuance. **John Dowland (1562–1626)** was the most prominent lute song composer; he composed a rich repertory of solo lute music as well, and he was renowned for his music's characteristic depth, sophistication, and melancholy.

Consort A term used in England to refer to an instrumental ensemble.

Madrigal Secular polyphonic vocal genre in sixteenth-century Italy and England.

Word-painting Musical expression of the text.

Dissonance A combination of pitches that clash or sound unstable; the listener expects a resolution to follow a dissonant chord; see Musical Elements Appendix.

Lute A plucked stringed instrument with a rounded back that flourished in Europe from the late Middle Ages through the baroque era; see Musical Instruments Appendix.

Several types of instrumental music in the Renaissance were popular. Introductory instrumental works that preceded sacred or secular performances featured imitative or improvisatory passages or both styles in alternation. Common titles for these pieces include "fantasia," "toccata," and "prelude." Often, instrumental works had vocal models: many sacred and secular vocal works, such as motets and chansons, were arranged for musical instruments and often for a single solo lute. Variations on standard tunes were popular and would be for many centuries beyond the Renaissance. Dance types, many of which are composed in variation form, include the stately pavan in duple meter and the lighter, quicker galliard in triple meter.

Figure 6-13 *Musical Group on a Balcony* by Gerrit van Honthorst (1590–1656). In an unusual perspective, musicians play variously sized lutes to accompany a singer.

PLAYLIST OPTIONS
SECULAR MUSIC IN THE RENAISSANCE

FIND

One of these:

- A madrigal
  - An Italian madrigal, such as Luca Marenzio's *Solo e pensoso* with text by the great Italian poet, Petrarch (text and translation available online)
  - An English madrigal, such as "Fair Phyllis" by John Farmer.

- A French chanson or English lute song that was popular in its day:
  - Claudin de Sermisy's (c. 1490–1562) *Tant que vivray* (text and translation available online.)
  - A John Dowland lute song, such as *Flow, My Tears*

- An example of Renaissance instrumental and dance music
  - A video of Renaissance dance music; use search terms, such as
    - Renaissance dance
    - pavan
    - galliard
    - bransle
    - saltarello
  - An example of solo instrumental work, such as a lute work by Dowland or harpsichord music by Byrd.

OBSERVE

- Topic in vocal music
- Instrumentation
- Structure and meter, especially in dance music

ASK

- If your example is vocal music:
  - How does the music "paint" the text? What musical elements (such as melodic contour, texture, rhythm) are used?

- If your example includes musical instruments:
    - What musical instruments do you hear and, if more than one, what role do they each play in the texture? Harpsichord, lute, recorders, and viols (bowed stringed instruments) are common, accompanied by various percussion instruments to emphasize the rhythm and meter.
- If your example is a video of dance music:
    - What are the metric and rhythmic characteristics of the music?
    - Does the choreography organize dancers in pairs, or does it create circles or other patterns out of larger groups of people?

CHAPTER 6 VOCABULARY & IMPORTANT FIGURES

Vocabulary

Acoustics

Anthem

Antiquity

Aulos

Bard

Canon (or round)

Chanson (Fr. "song")

Chorale

Consort

Counter-Reformation

Fin' amor (Occitan: "refined love")

Homophony

Lute

Lyre

Madrigal

Mass setting

Minstrel

Monophony

Motet

Music of the spheres

Pastoral

Plainchant (Gregorian chant)

Points of imitation

Polyphony

Sacred music

Secular music

Text-setting styles

Texture

Troubadours and trouvéres

Word-painting

Important Figures

Aristotle (384–322 BCE)

Bernart de Ventadorn (c. 1130–c. 1200)

William Byrd (c. 1540–1623)

Jean Calvin (1509–1564)

Comtessa de Dia (fl. late twelfth, early thirteenth century)

John Dowland (1562–1626)

Hildegard of Bingen (1098–1179)

Josquin des Prez (c. 1450–1521)

Martin Luther (1483–1546)

Guillaume de Machaut (c. 1300–1377)

Luca Marenzio (c. 1553–1599)

Thomas Morley (c. 1557–1602)

Johannes Ockeghem (c. 1410–1497)

Giovanni Palestrina (c. 1525–1594)

Francesco Petrarch (1304–1374)

Plato (c. 429–347 BCE)

Pythagoras (c. 570–c. 490 BCE)

Richard the Lionheart (1157–1199)

ENDNOTES

[1] Plato's Republic Book 3, 412a, trans Paul Shorey, *Plato. Plato in Twelve Volumes* (Cambridge, MA: Harvard University Press, 1969).

[2] Aristotle's Politics, Book VIII, Part 5, trans. Benjamin Jowett, Internet Classics Archive, accessed April 29, 2012, http://classics.mit.edu/Aristotle/politics.8.eight.html.

[3] Epitaph of Seikilos, trans. Thomas J. Mathiesen, as quoted in David J. Rothenberg and Robert R. Holzer, *Oxford Anthology of Western Music* (New York, Oxford: Oxford University Press, 2013), Vol. 1, p. 1.

[4] Hildegard of Bingen, Letters, translated by Joseph L. Baird and Radd K. Ehrman, New York: Oxford University Press, 1994, vol. I, letter 70r, pp. 154–155. Image: Frontpiece of Scivias, Hildegard's book in which she describes her visions, showing Hildegard receiving a vision, dictating to her mentor Volmar, and sketching on a wax tablet.

[5] Martin Luther, Preface to Symphoniae Jucundae, from Luther's Works, Augsberg Fortress Publishers, 1965, pp. 321–324.

Image Credits

- Figure 6-3: Source: https://commons.wikimedia.org/wiki/File:Mousai_Helikon_Staatliche_Antikensammlungen_Schoen80_n1.jpg.

- Figure 6-4: Francino Gaffurio / Copyright in the Public Domain.

- Figure 6-5: Source: https://commons.wikimedia.org/wiki/File:Hildegard_von_Bingen.jpg.

- Figure 6-6: Cantigas de Santa Maria / Copyright in the Public Domain.

- Figure 6-7: Ockeghem / Copyright in the Public Domain.

- Figure 6-8: Lucas Cranach the Elder / Copyright in the Public Domain.

- Figure 6-9: Titian / Copyright in the Public Domain.

- Figure 6-10: Gerard van der Guch / Copyright in the Public Domain.

- Figure 6-11: Source: https://commons.wikimedia.org/wiki/File:Giovanni_Palestrina_and_Pope_Julius_III.jpg.

- Figure 6-12: Source: https://commons.wikimedia.org/wiki/File:Luca_conte_Marenzio,_Komponist_des_16._Jahrhunderts.jpg.

- Figure 6-13: Gerrit van Honthorst (1590-1656) / Copyright in the Public Domain.

CHAPTER

7

Baroque Music

Seventeenth- and eighteenth-century Europe was both a powerful and a turbulent time. Colonization of the New World enhanced the wealth of ruling and aristocratic classes, but the gulf between rich and poor was extremely wide. Religious friction between Protestants and Catholics ranged from uneasy peace to sustained war and savage bloodshed. Scientific discoveries and rational philosophical perspectives by Galileo, Descartes, and others challenged church doctrines and spurred the Enlightenment. Meanwhile, a richly creative artistic culture continued to bloom.

"**Baroque**" is a term that describes the highly ornamented seventeenth- and early- eighteenth-century styles, especially in the visual arts. Critics in later years, looking back on this era, first used this term but in a derogatory way. It probably originates from the Portuguese word for "misshapen pearl," and it came to connote an exaggerated manner: "over the top" or in bad taste. This extravagance is expressed in the richness of detail and in the drama of the baroque arts. Architecture is embellished with a dizzying array of trimmings and opulence, paintings often display extreme emotions with startling effects of light and color, and sculpture is imbued with motion and turmoil.

Baroque Derived from "misshapen pearl" in Portuguese; Western European musical style c. 1600–1750; highly ornamented style.

Opposite: An example of the ornate baroque style in a Roman church ceiling: Giovanni Battista Gaulli, Triumph of the Name of Jesus, 1676–1679. Ceiling fresco with stucco Figures, Church of Il Gesù, Rome.

Music was eventually included in the concept of a baroque era despite the wide range of musical styles throughout Europe. One common thread was the importance of the expression of **affects**—idealized emotional states—in music. Baroque Europeans placed great importance on the role of emotions. The expression of a single affect throughout a musical work or an entire movement in an extended work of music was a goal applied generally to musical genres—even instrumental music—throughout Western Europe.

Affect Emotional state; in baroque music, a common musical goal was the expression of a single affect throughout a work or movement.

I

ITALY

The Florentine Camerata and Accompanied Monody

The beginning of the baroque era in music finds its roots just before 1600 with another resurgence of humanism in Italian culture. A group of humanist musicians and theorists in Florence, known as the **Florentine camerata**, studied and cultivated Greek aesthetics and performance practices. They focused on the Greek tragedies; how were they performed? Inspired by their classical studies, they developed three practices, in particular, that would revolutionize Western art music: musical drama was sung continuously throughout the entire length of the work; music faithfully represented the text of the drama; and, in order to most vividly represent the text, musical texture was a single vocal line rather than the traditional polyphonic texture, with instrumental accompaniment. This development of **accompanied monody**, as it was called, became the basis for opera and for a more vertical, **homophonic**, concept of musical tonality.

We can think of homophonic music as "vertical" because it proceeds in chords, or stacks of notes rather than the more linear, or horizontal, polyphonic music. The homophonic style of accompanied monody was emphasized by the ***basso continuo***, which is continuous instrumental accompaniment, notated in a bass line (the lowest-sounding line in

Accompanied monody A single vocal line with instrumental accompaniment.

Homophony Musical texture that features one dominant melody with subordinate chordal accompaniment; see Musical Elements Appendix.

Basso continuo Continuous instrumental accompaniment notated in a bass line with single notes, numbers, and other symbols.

musical notation) with single notes, numbers, and other symbols. Musicians who read *basso continuo* know which chords are meant by these symbols and perform accordingly, with the same humanist goal as the vocalists to express the meaning of the text. Musically, the continuo functions much like the rhythm section in a modern rock or jazz band: it provides foundational rhythmic and harmonic accompaniment, typically with a combination of notated music and improvisation.

Singer and composer **Giulio Caccini (1551–1618)** was one of the camerata members who wrote vocal music in accompanied monody with basso continuo; his collection of songs, *Le nuove musiche* (1602), in fact, includes an illuminating introduction on performance practice for singers. He uses the term ***sprezzatura***, which he describes as a rhythmic, harmonic, and melodic freedom in order to more dramatically express the text:

> … it occurred to me to introduce a kind of music by which anyone could almost speak in music, using … a certain noble *sprezzatura* in the melody, passing sometimes over some discords while sustaining the pitch of the bass note … I have also come to call the style "noble" that, not subjecting itself to regular meter, often halves the duration of the notes, according to the meaning of the words. From this is born a line with *sprezzatura* ("disregard"), as it is called.[1]

Sprezzatura Rhythmic, harmonic, and melodic freedom in order to more dramatically express the meaning of the words in vocal music.

Opera

The Florentine camerata's idea to present staged drama, set to continuous music throughout, is now known as **opera**. A musical setting of a dramatic text, or **libretto**, an opera includes soloists, ensembles, chorus, and instrumental accompaniment. The drama begins with an **overture**, or instrumental introduction. The absence of spoken dialogue presents challenges to the librettist: if a typical song usually focuses on only one or two emotions of a single character, how can the audience learn all the plot points of an intricate story? **Recitative**, a speech-like style of vocal music, is the answer: ranging from quick, chatty dialogue to lyrical expressions of exciting events or heart-rending soliloquy, recitative communicates dramatic action as it happens. Since it is declamatory, recitative is chanted with great rhythmic freedom, unrestrained by any particular meter.

The **aria**, on the other hand, is closer to what most of us think of as a "song": during a pause in the action, the character expresses one or two emotions in a lyrical and melodious setting of a poem, usually according

Opera Staged drama based on a libretto, set to continuous music, which includes soloists, ensembles, chorus, and instrumental accompaniment.

Libretto (It. "little book") Lyrics, or text of an opera; a librettist is the author of the text.

Overture An instrumental introduction to an opera or other dramatic work.

Recitative Speech-like vocal music without strong meter that is often used to deliver plot points and dialogue in opera and other dramatic vocal works.

Aria (It. "air") Lyrical, melodious song, usually with a clear meter.

Figure 7-2 Jacopo Peri during his performance as Arion in 1589, by Bernardo Buontalenti (c1531–1608).

Figure 7-3 Portrait of Claudio Monteverdi (1630) by Bernardo Strozzi (1581–1644).

to a recognizable meter. Most Italian operas for the next several centuries alternate between recitative and aria sections—the plot points are conveyed as the action progresses in recitative, and the action stops when a main character (or occasionally two or more characters in ensemble) plumbs the depth of an emotion with a lyrical, metrical aria.

This marriage of music and drama, along with alternating recitative and aria passages, orchestral accompaniment, elaborate stage settings, and talented performers, creates one of the most powerful experiences in Western art music. Camerata member **Jacopo Peri (1561–1633)** composed the first opera that still survives (*Euridice*, 1600), and he is considered to be the innovator of recitative style in opera. **Claudio Monteverdi (1567–1643)** successfully used the camerata's innovations in his music and helped to bring about the *stile moderno* (modern style) in music that inspired immediate controversy but ultimately great changes in the foundations of musical theory and style. He enjoyed a long, distinguished career in Mantua and Venice and is especially known for his operas. In a later generation, the vocal music of singer and composer **Barbara Strozzi (1619–1677)** features recitatives and arias with breathtaking dramatic expression.

Castrato (castrati, pl.)
Male singer who is castrated before puberty to preserve his high vocal register.

Throughout the seventeenth and eighteenth centuries, many of the most celebrated opera singers were ***castrati***: males who were castrated before puberty to preserve their high vocal registers. The earliest documented cases of this amazing—and appalling—practice began before the

Figure 7-4 Orpheus and Eurydice, by Jacopo Vignali (1592–1664). This ancient Greek myth was a favorite topic for opera composers, including Peri and Monteverdi. Note the baroque rather than ancient Greek clothing style and the bowed stringed instrument (more representative of 17th century Italian opera) rather than the harp or lyre. Orpheus seems on the verge of looking back to his beloved Eurydice, which will break his promise and send her back to the realm of death forever.

Figure 7-5 *The Viola da Gamba Player*, thought to be composer Barbara Strozzi, by Bernardo Strozzi (1581–1644).

baroque era in the church, where women were not allowed to sing, but the choirs nevertheless needed to include high-voiced singers to perform music written for all vocal ranges. Opera listeners heard the best aspects of both genders in the *castrati*: high vocal register combined with strength and stamina. After years of rigorous training in technique and improvisation, the most successful castrati would be ready to take the stage, often as leading men in the most heroic operatic roles. Their heavily ornamented vocal style incorporated brilliant scales and breathtakingly sustained notes. Although most castrati were Italian, and critics from other European cultures expressed shock at the practice, audiences in many of these same European countries flocked to the astonishing performances of the best castrati, keeping the tradition widespread in Europe until the early nineteenth century. Most prominent baroque opera composers wrote *castrato* roles, which in modern performances usually need to be either sung by women or transposed to lower registers for men. The greatest celebrity *castrati*, such as **Carlo "Farinelli" Broschi (1705–1782)**, performed extensively, adored and well paid by their audiences.

Figure 7-6 Portrait of Carlo "Farinelli" Broschi (detail), c 1752, by Jacopo Amigoni (1682–1752)

Instrumental Music

The **concerto**, one of the most popular Italian baroque instrumental genres, is based on the contrast of instrumental groups with different timbres, such as strings versus winds, and also a variety of textures, such as polyphonic versus homophonic passages. The **concerto grosso** emphasizes all of these differences between a small group and a larger ensemble of instruments, and the **solo concerto** showcases a soloist against the entire ensemble, which was comprised of all or mostly stringed instruments, later known as the "orchestra" (to be described more fully in Chapter 8, Classic Era Music). Both types of concertos proceed with alternating passages of competition and conversation between the small group or soloist and larger group. Violinist **Arcangelo Corelli (1653–1713)** devoted his compositions—many of which are concertos—to the **bowed stringed** family of instruments, which gave him the rare distinction in his day of a composer whose fame rested on his instrumental music. **Antonio Vivaldi (1678–1741)** composed vocal as well as instrumental music, but he is best known for his solo concertos. He taught music in an orphanage, and his many students inspired him to write hundreds of concertos for a wide variety of soloists.

Concerto An instrumental work that contrasts orchestra with soloist or small ensemble, usually comprised of three movements.

Bowed stringed instruments Family of instruments which include the violin, viola, violoncello ("cello"), and double bass, which produces sounds primarily by means of a bow rubbed across strings that are stretched tightly over a resonator box; see Musical Instruments Appendix.

Figure 7-7 Thought to be a portrait of Antonio Vivaldi, 1723

PLAYLIST OPTIONS
ITALIAN BAROQUE MUSIC

FIND

- A vocal work, such as:
  - An opera
    - An excerpt of *L'Orfeo* by Monteverdi is recommended, based on the myth of Orpheus and Eurydice. (Synopsis and libretto with translation are available online.)
  - A solo aria by Caccini, Monteverdi, or Strozzi
    - Try Strozzi's *Che si può fare* from op. 8, no. 6 (text and translation available online)
- Or an instrumental work, such as:
  - A concerto grosso by Corelli
    - Videos that show live performances of Corelli concertos (which can be helpful to show the smaller, contrasting group of performers) are available online.
  - A solo concerto by Vivaldi
    - Vivaldi solo concertos, including "The Four Seasons" from op. 8, a set of concertos that imitate seasonal nature sounds, are widely available online.

OBSERVE

- Word-painting in vocal music.
- The differences between arias and recitatives in opera.
- Instrumental blend and contrast in concertos.

ASK

- If your example is vocal music:
  - How do the aria and recitative genres work together to dramatize a story?
  - In vocal music, can you discern the stylistic freedom of *sprezzatura*, which can cross boundaries in rhythm, harmony, and melody in order to express the words? Do you ever notice *sprezzatura* in today's popular music?

+ If your example is instrumental music:
  + What happens in your instrumental concerto example that shows conversation (blending) or competition (contrast) among the instruments?

II
SPAIN AND THE
NEW WORLD

If Italy dominated Europe in the early baroque era with its own brand of humanism, Spain dominated with wealth and power. Colonization of the New World as well as participation in the African slave trade made Spain richer and, at the same time, set up a conduit for influences to occur between many cultures. The music of what we now call Latin America after the sixteenth century carries traditions from Spain, Africa, and the Americas (see Chapter 11, Music in the Americas, for more on Latin America's "triethnic" heritage). Although historians have traditionally emphasized Spanish influence, the reality of cross-cultural influences should be remembered: *the influence traveled in all directions*. The development of art music in the New World is reflected by the wide variety of backgrounds and styles of its composers: Spanish or Portuguese composers who were trained in Europe or American musicians of indigenous or mixed descent each made music that combined features of European and New World traditions in various degrees of hybridization. The most distinct quality of baroque era Hispanic music on either side of the Atlantic is its diversity.

Vocal Music

Musical drama in the Hispanic baroque era is unlike that of Italy: dialogue that Italian opera would incorporate into recitative is generally spoken, and songs are typically strophic. The castrato tradition was shunned; women played most of the roles instead. Although a small number of operas were produced, the most popular secular vocal genre was the

Sor Juana Inéz de la Cruz: "I continued my studious effort to read and read some more, to study and study some more, with no teacher other than the books themselves...In this way I proceeded, always directing the steps of my study to the summit of sacred theology, as I have said; and to reach it, I thought it necessary to ascend by the steps of human sciences and arts, because how is one to understand the style of the queen of sciences without knowing that of the handmaidens? ... How to know whether Saul healing at the sound of David's harp came from the virtue and natural power of music or the supernatural ability God wishes to place in David? ... And without being very expert in music, how are we to understand the musical proportions and their beauty found in so many places...?"[2]

zarzuela, a light musical drama typically on a mythological topic. The zarzuela includes sung and spoken dialogue, and the accompaniment prominently features strummed and plucked harps and guitars.

The prevailing sacred vocal music genre was the **villancico**, which could also be secular but as church music it was—and still is—associated with special occasions, especially Christmas. Villancicos are performed by choirs and sometimes include soloists and continuo. Strummed and plucked harps and guitars are often prominent in the accompaniment just as with zarzuelas. The continuum of styles stretches from traditional European polyphonic imitative textures to homophonic, dancelike, and syncopated characteristics of the styles most influenced by American and African music. Spanish harpist **Juan Hidalgo (1614–1685)** composed theater, chamber, and sacred music, including many villancicos; as a prominent composer employed by royalty, he was particularly influential.

Some Spanish composers such as **Juan de Araujo (1646–1712)** relocated to South America and composed villancicos that were heavily influenced by indigenous American idioms; at the other end of the spectrum, composers of indigenous or mixed descent, such as the Mexican composer **Manuel de Zumaya (or Sumaya) (c. 1678–1755)**, wrote villancicos steeped in Renaissance and Baroque European techniques. Most baroque Hispanic musical styles fell somewhere in between these two extremes. **Sor (Sister) Juana Ines de la Cruz (c. 1648–1695)** should be remembered here even though she was not a composer. A highly educated and gifted poet, dramatist, and scholar, Sor Juana wrote many villancico texts, and she emphasized the importance of music in her writings.

Instrumental Music

Ostinato variations permeated instrumental music throughout Europe and the Hispanic world during the baroque era. From the Italian word for "obstinate," an ostinato is a repeating harmonic, melodic, or rhythmic pattern. A set of ostinato variations, also known as a **ground bass** or

Zarzuela Light musical drama typically on a mythological topic; this Hispanic genre includes sung and spoken dialogue with plucked string and continuo accompaniment.

Villancico A Hispanic sacred or secular vocal work for choir, which sometimes includes soloists and continuo; strummed and plucked harp and guitar are often prominent in the accompaniment.

Ostinato variations (ground bass) From the Italian word for "obstinate," an ostinato is a repeating harmonic, melodic, or rhythmic pattern. An ostinato variation set, also known as a "ground" or "ground bass," is a set of variations built on an ostinato pattern; the variations are often improvisational.

"ground," is a set of variations—often improvisational—built on an ostinato. Any musical element, most often the treble melody and rhythm, is varied over a compelling and familiar repeating bass line or chord sequence, giving the ostinato a similar role to today's twelve-bar blues.

A wide variety of ostinato types, known by different names, were popular across cultures. For instance, the chord sequence or bass melody pattern for the Italian "Romanesca" is related to the Spanish "*Guardame las Vacas*" and the English "Packington's Pound." The ostinato is discussed here while we explore Hispanic music, however, because of this form's special relationship to Hispanic music on both sides of the Atlantic: for instance, the *zarabanda* and *chacona* are said to have originated in the Americas before traveling to Spain, Italy, and, ultimately, France and Germany where they became popular dances known as the Sarabande and Chaconne, prominently featured in dance collections, or suites. Both dances originally featured lively, suggestive dance movements

Figure 7-9 A page of guitar tablature from Instrucciòn de Mùsica sobre la Guitarra Española by Gaspar Sanz, 1674. In this style of baroque guitar tablature, each line represents a string, and each number represents a fret ("0" denotes an open string). This is similar to modern guitar tablature.

that scandalized European visitors. Singers and dancers performed to improvisational instrumental accompaniment, particularly castinets and strummed guitars. Indeed, the dance genres' original mode of travel to Europe appears to have been via the guitar repertoire (see the Musical Instruments Appendix for more about early guitar).

The guitar was especially popular in Spain and other Hispanic cultures. Although it usually fulfilled its strummed accompaniment role for singers and dancers, another, more cultivated, plucked idiom reminiscent of lute music began to develop among guitarists during the seventeenth century, as well. **Gaspar Sanz (mid-seventeenth–early eighteenth centuries)** exemplifies this new hybrid guitar style in Spain. A priest, scholar, and musician who played organ as well as guitar, Sanz included many dances based on ostinatos in his published guitar works from 1674–75, which featured examples of the *zarabanda* and *chacona* in both strummed and plucked, or single note, styles. In a later generation, **Santiago de Murcia (c. 1682–c. 1740)**, a Spanish composer and theorist, is especially interesting for his culturally diverse repertoire and his links to Mexico. His 1732 Saldivar Codex No. 4 manuscript, which was found in Mexico in the late twentieth century, is comprised of many ostinato types, including the earliest known notated music of African American origin: *cumbés* and *zarambeques*. Murcia is believed to have traveled to Mexico sometime between 1718–1731. Ostinato variations were performed with musical instruments other than guitar, as well. For instance, the prominent Spanish composer and organist **Juan Bautista José Cabanilles (1644–1712)**, who wrote both choral and organ music, included ostinato variation sets in his organ music.

PLAYLIST OPTIONS
HISPANIC BAROQUE MUSIC

FIND

- An example of Latin American baroque music with search terms, such as:
  - "Mexican baroque"
  - "Latin American baroque"
  - "Hispanic baroque"
- Or a particular vocal work, such as
  - "*Los coflades*" by Spanish composer Juan de Araujo (text and translation available online)

- *"Celebran Publiquen"* by Mexican composer Manuel de Zumaya (text and translation available online)
- Or an instrumental work, such as
    - A Gaspar Sanz or Santiago de Murcia guitar work
    - Look for a video of a performer with a baroque (rather than modern) guitar under the search term, "baroque guitar."
    - A keyboard work by Juan Bautista José Cabanilles

OBSERVE

- Instrumentation: accompaniment to vocal music often includes plucked strings and, perhaps, percussion instruments.
- Meter and rhythm: simple or compound meters; often dance-like rhythms.
- Structure: listen for an ostinato or ground bass pattern in the bass melody or chord sequence. Common ground bass terms include "passacalles," "chaconne" or "chacona," and "folia."

ASK

- Where on the continuum is your example: does it sound European, or can you hear American and African influences?
- If your example is sacred music from the New World, do you think the topic is treated similarly or very differently than it would be treated in a Western European culture outside of Spain?
- If your example is baroque guitar music, do you hear vigorous strumming, plucked single notes, or a mixture of both styles?

III

FRANCE

Louis XIV (1638–1715) was the epitome of an absolute monarch; he increased French wealth and power during his reign through his centralized government at home and through his expansion of French colonialism in the Americas, Asia, and Africa. He also dominated French baroque culture and style. He was much more than a patron of the arts: heavily involved in theater and music, he took lessons on lute, guitar, and harpsichord, but, most of all, he danced.

Ballet is a formal, theatrical dance tradition that underwent an especially active period of development in France during the reign of Louis XIV. His passion for ballet inspired him—even after his ascension to the throne—to dance in dozens of theatrical productions. One of his stage roles was Apollo, the sun god: this gave rise to the "sun king" nickname that stayed with the monarch as a majestic epithet. Soon after his ascension, he founded a national academy of dance; this act, and the king's own daily dance rehearsals, ensured the prestige and the popularity of ballet in French music and culture; indeed, French has been the language of ballet ever since. Dancers are held to a rigorous tradition of technical mastery in graceful, fluid movements through choreography that demand athletic prowess and stamina.

All the arts flourished under the rule of Louis XIV; he imported the most exceptional talents of the region to his resplendent palace in Versailles where he produced extravagant, large-scale performances. Even before Louis XIV, music at the French court had been divided into 3 categories: *Music de la Grande Ècurie* (Music of the Great Stable), where large ensembles performed; *Musique de la Chapelle Royalle* (Music of the Royal Chapel), which offered performances of sacred music; and the smaller, more intimate performances of the *Musique de la Chambre* (Music of the Chamber). But this king's extraordinary cultivation of music, theater, dance, and many other artistic disciplines brought such glamour to his court that aristocracy both at home and abroad sought to emulate French style.

Figure 7-10 Louis XIV as Apollo the Sun King in 1653, art by Henri de Gissey (1621–1673).

Ballet Theatrical, formal dance tradition that originated in Europe.

Stage and Sacred Music

The monarch had formed a close friendship with a fellow dancer in one of his staged productions during his youth. **Jean Baptiste Lully (1632–1687)** came to France from humble circumstances in Italy as a young teenager who played violin and guitar. In France, he developed his talents in dance and composition. His lifelong friendship with the king provided the composer with power and influence. Lully's prestigious court position combined with his stature as a composer made his music emblematic of French culture—ironic for an Italian composer but, nevertheless, true.

Figure 7-11 Portrait of Jean-Baptiste Lully by Paul Mignard (1639–1691).

Lully dominated French stage music with his operas and ballets, which included sumptuous staging and costumes. Sizeable orchestras performed the overtures and dances that were included in all staged musical works, as well as the accompaniments in opera. Instrumental music, thus, became more important due to its significant role in all staged works, especially the ballet. Uneven or "dotted" rhythms (*long*, short, *long*, short ...) pervaded French instrumental music, which might have been encouraged at least, in part, by the necessities of French dance choreographies. Interestingly, this distinctive rhythm is often unnotated; musicians are expected to understand this as a stylistic trait, which is also often the case with the similarly uneven "swing" rhythm in twentieth-century jazz.

Lully's favor with the king ensured his sole publishing rights for stage music in France during the height of his career. With the support of the

Figure 7-12 Performance of Lully's opera Alceste at Versailles in 1674; drawing by Jean Le Pautre (1618–1682).

king, Lully developed this iconic French musical style—which included the uneven rhythms and the prominence of dance and instrumental music—that was to result in a lasting influence. Later, the organist, composer, and theorist **Jean Philippe Rameau (1683–1764)** was to perpetuate French musical influence not only with his own staged and instrumental compositions but also through his *Traitè de l'harmonie* (*"Treatise on Harmony,"* 1722), which codified much about the modern concept of tonality that is in use today.

Sacred music was also a strong presence in the French baroque era. Harpsichordist and singer **Elisabeth Jacquet de la Guerre (1665–1729)** composed in a variety of genres and was the first woman in France to write an opera. She is also known for her sacred **cantatas**, which are vocal works with instrumental accompaniment; performed by a solo vocalist or choir, this genre often includes more than one movement and has either a sacred or a secular topic. An especially gifted musician who performed for Louis XIV when she was only five years old, Jacquet de la Guerre grew up to be a prominent composer who dedicated most of her works to the king.

Figure 7-13 Portrait of Jean-Philippe Rameau, c1728, by Joseph Aved (1702–1766).

Cantata Vocal work with instrumental accompaniment. Performed by solo vocalist or choir, this genre often includes more than one movement and has either a sacred or a secular topic.

Figure 7-14 Portrait of Elisabeth Jacquet de la Guerre by François de Troy (1645–1730)

Solo and Small Ensemble Music

Dance Suite, or Suite Group of contrasting instrumental dances. Most dances have a simple two-part structure with each section repeated: AABB.

Great interest and importance was also placed on smaller, more intimate musical ensemble genres in the court of Louis XIV. Apart from the extravagantly staged dance productions, social dancing to the accompaniment of a soloist or small group of musical instruments was a favorite pastime at Versailles and, thus, with French aristocracy, in general. Chamber ensembles (small instrumental groups) accompanied the dancers with **dance suites**, which are groups of contrasting dances. The French dance choreographies were often highly cultivated, demanding a substantial amount of training and practice for the dancers. French dancing masters hired by aristocrats gave lessons regularly in households throughout

France and even beyond French borders. Dance suites incorporate popular dance types, each of which has a characteristic tempo and meter and sometimes an international theme, as well; for instance, the gigue, which recalls the English "jig," in **triple meter**, moves quickly. Sometimes additional names or whimsical words were also added to the titles. Most dances have a simple two-part structure with each section repeated: AABB. Preludes are sometimes unmeasured, without notated meter, encouraging performers to interpret the music relatively freely in an improvisatory manner. The French **sarabande**, descendent of the earlier lively triple meter *zarabanda* from Latin America, deserves special note here because by the middle seventeenth century in France, the dance had evolved into a dignified slow movement, still in triple meter but with a strong second beat due to its choreography. This later, stately, version of the dance was a typical component of the dance suite.

The baroque **lute**, which had increased in size, pitch range, and volume from the earlier Renaissance models, enjoyed immense popularity in early-seventeenth-century France. Cousins **Ennemond (1575–1651)** and **Denis Gaultier (1597 or 1603–1672)** were two leading composers who developed a distinctive French lute style—much of which was to become part of the fabric of French musical style for other instruments. Instrumental dance suites are staples of the baroque lute repertory, but another genre began with the Gaultiers. The ***tombeau***, a musical commemoration or lament on someone's death, used a slow tempo with musical depictions of mourning such as descending lines or sounds that recall tolling bells. These *tombeaux*, first composed by lutenists but soon taken up by keyboardists and others, to this day effectively recreate the pain of loss with exquisitely poignant dissonance and languishing melodies.

The lute's important role as an accompaniment for vocalists created a special circumstance that influenced lute—and ultimately French—musical style. In order to achieve a sonic balance with the louder human voice, lute players needed to develop a way to make their chords more audible. Once lute strings are plucked, the rate of sonic decay is very quick; this necessitated *re*plucking the individual notes of chords in order to keep the harmony present for as long as the voice needed accompaniment. For this reason, French baroque lutenists would **arpeggiate** their chords, playing each note successively, either ascending or descending, instead of all at once. In arpeggiation, the chords are "spread" or "broken" so that the lute can be heard against the voice. What began as a necessity in the quest for ensemble balance became an iconic idiomatic style—with or without a vocalist—that the French keyboardists were eager to emulate, and it eventually became an essential characteristic of French music.

Triple meter   A metric pattern of 3 beats, typically with the first beat accented as in *strong*, weak, weak; see Musical Elements Appendix.

Sarabande   Popular dance form, which originated as a lively triple meter dance in Latin America (*zarabanda*) and later came to be quite slow, with a strong second beat due to its choreography.

Lute   A plucked stringed, fretted chordophone with courses (double strings), a rounded back that flourished in Europe from the late Middle Ages through the baroque era; see Musical Instruments Appendix.

Tombeau (tombeaux, pl.)   A musical commemoration or lament on someone's death; typically characterized by a slow tempo with musical depictions of mourning such as descending lines or sounds that recall tolling bells.

Arpeggio (arpeggiate, v.; arpeggiation, n.)   Notes of a chord sounding successively, either ascending or descending, instead of all at once.

Figure 7-15 *The Love Song* by Antoine Watteau (1684–1721). The baroque guitarist strums an accompaniment to a love song during what is surely a flirtatious or romantic moment.

Harpsichord A keyboard stringed instrument popular in the Renaissance through baroque eras; see Musical Instruments Appendix.

The **harpsichord** was especially popular in baroque France. Keyboard composers produced the popular genres of the day: dance suites, ground bass variations, and *tombeaux*. They used the lutenists' broken chord style and continued to develop it as a keyboard idiom. Harpsichordist Jacquet de la Guerre, mentioned above, was an important presence in court as a keyboard composer. Her contemporary and another harpsichordist, **Françoise Couperin (1668–1733)**, was an influential composer and teacher. His published information on performance practices remains a major source to this day for French baroque ornamentation, or improvised embellishments. Although he is most known for his harpsichord music, he wrote a great deal of vocal music as well.

Figure 7-16 Portrait of François Couperin.

PLAYLIST OPTIONS
FRENCH BAROQUE MUSIC

FIND

- A video example of a staged work; synopses of operas are available online, and videos often include translated text:
  - Jean Baptiste Lully
    - Search "Lully dance" for a baroque dance video
    - Search "Lully opera" for an operatic excerpt
  - Jean Philippe Rameau
    - Search "Rameau opera" for an operatic excerpt

- ◆ An instrumental example, such as
  - ◆ Search "Elisabeth Jacquet de la Guerre harpsi-chord" or "Françoise Couperin harpsichord" for a keyboard example
  - ◆ Search "Gaultier Tombeau" for a lute tombeau by Ennemond or Denis Gaultier

OBSERVE

- ◆ If your example is a dance video: choreography and costumes
- ◆ If your example is a staged vocal work: aria and recita-tive alternation
- ◆ Structure: listen for an ostinato or ground bass pattern in the bass melody or chord sequence
- ◆ Arpeggiated, "broken" chord style in instrumental music
- ◆ Uneven rhythms, or "swing" style interpretation of conjunct melodies, in French instrumental music

ASK

- ◆ If your example is staged music:
  - ◆ How does French opera compare to Italian opera?
  - ◆ How prominent is the role of dance in French music? Is there a connection between French baroque dance and present day ballet tradition?
- ◆ If your example is instrumental music:
  - ◆ Did your example display the rhythmic "swing" or the broken chord style, which are characteristic of French performance practice in instrumental music?

IV
ENGLAND AND GERMANY

The English Civil War and the Thirty Years War during the seven-teenth century was particularly brutal for all involved in the British Isles and in central Europe, especially in Germany. The wars ravaged their economies, and significant portions of their populations perished either from violence or from war-related famine and disease. The legacy of these wars probably diminished the development of the kind of strong, individual national styles that we see in France and Italy. German baroque music for many years tended to lean heavily on sacred more so than secular music, perhaps, in part, owing to a need for comfort amid the devastating hardships of war.

National styles from earlier eras could still be heard, for instance, in the consonant harmonies of the English choral tradition and in the polyphonic musical textures of German and other northern European cultures. But Italian music was a powerful influence; in fact, travel to Italy was a rite of passage for many northern musicians, who often stayed long enough to study with Italian composers and absorb much of the culture. The new vocal styles inspired by the Florentine camerata—accompanied monody with basso continuo and the alternation of aria and recitative in dramatic music—established themselves as part of English and German musical styles as well. French music was also influential, particularly in regard to dance music that was either accompaniment to genuine dancers or "stylized" instrumental dance music (not necessarily actually danced). English and German composers worked to blend the various national styles that they knew into one cohesive mode of musical expression. It was even said by a prominent eighteenth-century musician that the "German style" was a combination of the best music of other nations.[3]

Vocal Music

"The British Orpheus" was the epithet given to **Henry Purcell (1659–1695)**, the leading English baroque composer. He is especially well known for his vocal music, which includes sacred music for Anglican services as well as secular dramatic music. His *Dido and Aeneas* is one of the few English operas written during this time. As is true of most of his contemporaries, his style was strongly influenced by Italian music. Purcell distinguished himself, however, in developing an expressive vocal and musical style with English texts.

The emphasis of German vocal music was sacred. Early in the German baroque era, **Heinrich Schütz (1585–1672)** studied in Venice as a young man. His music is a mixture of new homophonic Italianate styles with traditional Germanic polyphonic textures. He wrote one opera which is now lost, but his contributions mainly consist of sacred vocal music. A century later, composer and organist **George Frideric Handel (1685–1759)** also spent time learning his craft in Italy as a young man. After

Oratorio Large-scale sacred vocal drama similar to opera but not staged.

coming back to Germany, he relocated to England where he enthusiastically promoted Italian opera. English audiences, however, were not as interested. Therefore, the talented composer, who was also a practical businessman, developed a less expensive dramatic vocal genre that was to ensure his popularity with the English public for the rest of his long and distinguished career. The **oratorio** is a large-scale sacred vocal drama similar to opera but not staged (thus, quite a bit cheaper). An oratorio often includes a narrator and is usually based on a biblical story. Vocal and instrumental forces include chorus, vocal soloists, and orchestra. The Latin oratorio had already been a popular genre in Italy for many years, but Handel used English texts, which made him quite popular with English audiences. Handel was well known for his skillful and effective blend of German, Italian, French, and English styles in his music.

Figure 7-17 Portrait of Georg Friedrich Handel, attributed to Balthasar Denner (1685–1749).

Johann Sebastian Bach: "As Cantor of the St. Thomas School...I shall set the boys a shining example... serve the school industriously...bring the music in both the principal churches of this town into good estate...faithfully instruct the boys not only in vocal but also in instrumental music ... arrange the music so that it shall not last too long, and shall ... not make an operatic impression, but rather incite the listeners

Handel's contemporary, **Johann Sebastian Bach (1685–1750)**, was another composer and organist. Unlike the more cosmopolitan Handel, however, Bach stayed in Germany; he was a devout Lutheran who did not promote himself or his music beyond his efforts to earn a living for his large family. He held several different positions during his lifetime, but for much of his career, he worked as a music director for two churches in Leipzig at the same time. His regular tasks included his own organ performances and the training and direction of his choir and instrumentalists. This is already an impressive amount of responsibility for two churches at once, but remember that in addition to that, the music was *his*: he would have improvised at least part of his organ performances, and he composed prolific amounts of music for Sunday services. Although he composed several major extended sacred works such as The *Magnificat* and the *Mass in B minor*, his most significant contributions in sacred music are his many church cantatas, which in the Lutheran worship tradition are multimovement vocal works for soloists, chorus, and instrumental accompaniment. Each Sunday's scripture reading provides the topic. Many of Bach's church cantatas are based on **chorales** (see Chapter 6, Antiquity to 1600, "Reformation Music"). These **chorale cantatas** feature quotations of the hymn tune either woven into a polyphonic texture or clearly stated in a simple homophonic setting. Although he was well respected by his peers, his works were not published during his lifetime and were generally neglected after his death. A nineteenth-century concert of his works renewed interest in his music, and his popularity has grown ever since. He is now admired more than almost any other composer in Western art music for his prolific contributions, his mastery of polyphonic technique, his improvisational abilities, and his understanding of international styles.

Chorale German strophic hymn (Chapter 6, Antiquity to 1600).

Chorale cantata Cantata based on a chorale, which includes quotations of the featured hymn tune.

Fugue Polyphonic composition in which a **subject**, or theme, is imitated successively in several musical lines. The second statement of the subject immediately following in another musical line, or voice, is known as the **answer**, and the **countersubject** is the musical material of the original voice after the subject is finished, set against the answer in a new voice.

Instrumental Music

The most extraordinary achievement in German baroque instrumental music is the cultivation of polyphonic texture in fugues, especially in those by J. S. Bach. The **fugue** is a polyphonic composition in which a **subject**, or theme, is imitated successively in several musical lines or voices (see the related **fuging tunes** in Chapter 1, American Traditional Music, "Psalmody in Eighteenth-Century New England"). The second statement of the subject immediately following in another voice is known as the **answer**, and the **countersubject** is the musical material of the original voice after the subject is finished, set against the answer in a new voice. As the fugue progresses, the subject and other musical motives are manipulated in various ways in relation to each other but fit together, like pieces of a jigsaw puzzle. The original subject, for instance, could be presented backwards or inverted (upside down, with the opposite melodic contour). The result is a complex musical work that, in the hands of a brilliant composer such as J. S. Bach, can be both intellectually and emotionally powerful. Brief introductory works known as "preludes" or "toccatas" usually introduce the fugues.

Instrumental music in Germany—keyboard, lute, winds, and bowed strings—display a rich amalgamation of styles: French and Italian influence in the dances and German influence in polyphonic textures. By the eighteenth century, the lute was a larger and more resonant instrument as it neared its final years of prominence in Europe. Lutenist and composer **Sylvius Leopold Weiss (1686–1750)** wrote many multimovement sonatas and suites for the lute, and he was a renowned performer. Handel's instrumental music included keyboard music and the overtures from his many stage works, as well as sonatas and suites for variously sized ensembles. J. S. Bach wrote music for instrumental ensembles, as well, and, interestingly, several remarkable sets of sonatas and suites for solo instruments, including the cello and violin, without keyboard accompaniment.

PLAYLIST OPTIONS
ENGLISH AND GERMAN BAROQUE MUSIC

FIND

- A performance of a famous lament from Purcell's opera *Dido and Aeneas*: recitative "Thy hand, Belinda," and aria "When I am laid in earth" (libretto available online)
- Or a sacred vocal music excerpt from J. S. Bach, Handel, or Schütz (texts, translations available online)
  - Bach's chorale cantata *Nun komm, der Heiden Heiland*, BWV 62 (based on Luther's hymn of the same name)
  - Handel oratorio: *The Messiah*, which includes the famous "Hallelujah Chorus"
  - Schütz sacred concerto: *Saul, Saul, was verfolgst du mich* ("Saul, Saul, why do you persecute me?")
- Or a Bach keyboard fugue with search terms, such as:
  - "Bach prelude and fugue"
  - "Bach toccata and fugue"
  - "Well-Tempered Clavier"

- Or an instrumental concerto, dance suite, or sonata, such as
  - J. S. Bach Brandenburg Concertos
  - Handel *Water Music* or *Music for the Royal Fireworks*
  - Sylvius Leopold Weiss lute suites and sonatas

OBSERVE

- If your example is vocal music:
  - Italianate aria and recitative alternation
  - Combination of northern European style polyphony with the newer homophonic Italian style
  - In Purcell's lament, note the repeated descending bass in the instrumental accompaniment
- If your example is instrumental music:
  - In the fugue, the opening subject begins alone; listen closely to the subject as it is repeated throughout the work.
  - Find the contrasts between instrumental groups in Bach's concertos, and notice the French dance influence in Handel's majestic suites.
  - Listen for the sonorous, idiomatic arpeggios in Weiss lute works.

ASK

- If your example is vocal music:
  - Was the composer of your example able to vividly paint the text with music?
- If your example is instrumental music:
  - Instrumental concerto, dance music, or sonata: Do you discern an international influence?
  - A keyboard fugue: How does the composer use—and sometimes modify—the subject throughout the work, and how does the rest of the musical material fit with it? Does the subject ever appear in more than one voice at the same time?

CHAPTER 7 VOCABULARY & IMPORTANT FIGURES

Vocabulary

Accompanied monody

Affect

Aria (It. "air")

Arpeggio (arpeggiate, v.; arpeggiation, n.)

Ballet

Basso continuo

Bowed stringed instruments

Cantata

Castrato (castrati, pl.)

Chorale cantata

Concerto

Dance Suite, or Suite

Fugue

Harpsichord

Homophony

Libretto (It. "little book")

Opera

Oratorio

Ostinato variations (ground bass)

Overture

Recitative

Sarabande

Sprezzatura

Tombeau (tombeaux, pl.)

Villancico

Zarzuela

Important Figures

Juan de Araujo (1646–1712)

Johann Sebastian Bach (1685–1750)

Juan Bautista José Cabanilles (1644–1712)

Carlo "Farinelli" Broschi (1705–1782)

Giulio Caccini (1551–1618)

Arcangelo Corelli (1653–1713)

Françoise Couperin (1668–1733)

Florentine camerata (including Giulio Caccini and Jacopo Peri).

Denis Gaultier (1597 or 1603–1672)

Ennemond Gaultier (1575–1651)

George Frideric Handel (1685–1759)

Juan Hidalgo (1614–1685)

Sor (Sister) Juana Ines de la Cruz (c. 1648–1695)

Elisabeth Jacquet de la Guerre (1665–1729)

Jean Baptiste Lully (1632–1687)

Claudio Monteverdi (1567–1643)

Santiago de Murcia (c. 1682–c. 1740)

Jacopo Peri (1561–1633)

Henry Purcell (1659–1695)

Jean Philippe Rameau (1683–1764)

Gaspar Sanz (mid-seventeeth–early eighteenth centuries)

Heinrich Schütz (1585–1672)

Barbara Strozzi (1619–1677)

Antonio Vivaldi (1678–1741)

Sylvius Leopold Weiss (1686–1750)

Manuel de Zumaya (or Sumaya) (c. 1678–1755)

ENDNOTES

[1] Giulio Caccini, Preface to *Le nuove musiche* (The New Music), Florence: 1602, as quoted in *Source Readings in Music History*, Oliver Strunk, ed., Revised edition, Leo Trieitler, general editor, translation by Margaret Murata, New York and London: W. W. Norton, 1998, pp. 608, 616.

[2] In response to an unfavorable letter from the Bishop of Puebla (posing as a fictitious nun, Sor Filotea) regarding Sor Juana's literary scholarship and writings. From "Response of the Poet" in Sor Juana Inés de la Cruz: Selected Works, translated by Edith Grossman, W. W. Norton, 2014, pp. 165–166.

[3] Johann Joachim Quantz (1697–1773), *Versuch einer Anweisung die Flöte traversière zu spielen* (1752), as related in John Kmetz, et al. "Germany." *Grove Music Online. Oxford Music Online*, accessed May 25, 2012, http://www.oxfordmusiconline.com/subscriber/article/grove/music/40055.

[4] As quoted in Forney, Dell'Antonio, and Machlis, The Enjoyment of Music, 12th ed., W. W. Norton, p. 139.

Image Credits

- Figure 7-11: Paul Mignard / Copyright in the Public Domain.
- Figure 7-12: Jean Le Pautre / Copyright in the Public Domain.
- Figure 7-13: Joseph Aved / Copyright in the Public Domain.
- Figure 7-14: François de Troy / Copyright in the Public Domain.
- Figure 7-15: Antoine Watteau / Copyright in the Public Domain.
- Figure 7-16: Source: https://commons.wikimedia.org/wiki/File:Francois_Couperin_2.jpg.
- Figure 7-17: Attributed to Balthasar Denner / Copyright in the Public Domain.
- Figure 7-18: Elias Gottlob Haussmann / Copyright in the Public Domain.

CHAPTER 8

Classic Era Music

"Classical music" is the phrase most use to refer to any Western art music throughout history. But the term has specific connotations for the late eighteenth century: this aesthetic, inspired by classical (especially ancient Greek) culture, emphasizes intellect and reason rather than emotion; symmetry and clarity rather than drama and the unfamiliar; and simplicity rather than complexity. The entire classic era, in fact, is just a sliver of time when this aesthetic approach was at its height: sixty or seventy years between the end of the baroque era in 1750 and the early nineteenth century.

The classic era in music coincided with the later part of the **Enlightenment**, also known as the "Age of Reason." Science, philosophy, political ideology, and all of the arts were again inspired by humanism—this time with emphasis on reason and elegance. The eighteenth-century Western world was powerfully affected by the great revolutions in America and in France, which forced many to face the ideals of democracy. Philosophers, scientists, and scholars looked beyond the Bible for answers to life's mysteries, and a widespread movement to list, catalogue, and classify resulted in encyclopedias and taxonomic systems still used to this day. Artists emulated classical Greek realism, with a focus on structure and symmetry.

Classic Era   Western music between approximately 1750–1820 (also see Unit 2, European Art Music, Introduction).

Enlightenment (Age of Reason)   Generally considered to last from the late seventeenth through the end of the eighteenth centuries, this rationalist movement sought to look beyond the Bible for answers to life's mysteries in philosophy, politics, science, scholarship, and the arts (also see Unit 2, European Art Music, Introduction).

Opposite: Portrait of Elizabeth and Mary Linley, c1772, by Thomas Gainsborough (1727–1788).

Figure 8-2 Engraving by Benoît Louis Prévost from the 1772 edition of the Encyclopedie. Truth, top center, is surrounded by light and unveiled by the figures on the right, Philosophy and Reason.

Galant Classic era musical style characterized by sparse texture, short phrases, and simple, attractive melodies.

Empfindsam **(Ger. "sensitive" or "sentimental") style, or** ***Empfindsamkeit*** A classic era musical style which uses expressive effects that include "sigh" motives, chromaticism, and unusual rhythms to evoke emotions such as melancholy or nostalgia.

The aesthetic goals in late-eighteenth-century culture emphasized elegant, natural simplicity. **Galant** music exemplifies these qualities with its spare texture, short phrases, and simple, attractive melodies. ***Empfindsam***

(Ger. "sensitive" or "sentimental") style, or *Empfindsamkeit,* is another important—but very different, however—classic era musical style, which uses expressive effects that include "sigh" motives, **chromaticism**, and unusual rhythms to evoke emotions such as melancholy or nostalgia. *Sturm und Drang* (storm and stress) is an especially emotional style of music that was inspired by an eighteenth-century German literary movement. *Sturm und Drang* musical passages are characterized by sudden, extreme changes in volume and vigorous rhythms.

I
MUSICAL CHARACTERISTICS

A carefully balanced structure is the essential aspect of most classic era music, and the rest of the musical elements fall into place once this is recognized. Melodies tend to feature symmetrical phrasing; meters and rhythms are simple and rather predictable, and texture is mostly homophonic. Tonality is more **diatonic**—music that uses unaltered pitches from the scale—than it is in baroque or romantic music. Classic era musical style does not strive for emotional effect the way other styles do.

But this music is, indeed, capable of profound drama and emotion. Eighteenth-century opera reform helped renew the connection between music and text in staged productions; the superfluously ornamented aria style from the late baroque receded and a more idealistic style reminiscent of the sixteenth century's Florentine camerata emerged: operatic music again strived to express the words and the story rather than to simply impress.

Classical instrumental music achieves drama primarily through thematic development within many of the structures described in detail in the Musical Elements Appendix. Instrumental music has another strategy to hold our interest, however: passages often cycle through an array of topics that remind us of various settings and styles or even startle us. In a sharp contrast with baroque conventions, which aim to express only a single affect in an extended musical passage, classic era music often bounds from one extreme to the other, phrase by phrase. Horn motives signal a hunting party, melodies accompanied by bagpipe-imitating drones

Chromaticism ("chromatic," adj.) Music that uses altered pitches from the prevailing key. (See "diatonicism" for the antonym.)

Sturm und Drang (Ger. "storm and stress") An especially emotional style of music that was inspired by the eighteenth-century German literary movement. The music is characterized by sudden, extreme changes in volume and vigorous rhythms.

Diatonicism ("diatonic," adj.) Music that uses unaltered pitches from the prevailing key. (See "chromaticism" for the antonym.)

Pastoral Reference to rustic topics, such as nature, countryside, peasants, farmers, and shepherds (Chapter 6, Antiquity to 1600).

evoke **pastoral** settings, some consonant cadences make us think we are at church, and polyphony recalls the older medieval and Renaissance "learned" styles. Galant, *empfindsam*, and *Sturm und Drang* styles appear in—and sometimes dominate—these musical tours, as well.

PLAYLIST OPTIONS
BAROQUE AND CLASSICAL MUSIC COMPARISON

FIND AND COMPARE

* Solo keyboard works from different composers of the Bach family:
    * Baroque: Johann Sebastian Bach fugues or two-part inventions
    * Classical: Carl Philipp Emanuel Bach or Johann Christian Bach solo sonatas
* Or concerto slow movements (second movements) from a baroque and a classical composer:
    * Baroque: Vivaldi
        * Search "Vivaldi slow movement" and filter only concerto examples
    * Classical: Beethoven
        * Search "Beethoven concerto slow movement"

OBSERVE

* Instrumentation:
    * If your example is keyboard music, the instruments might differ—harpsichord or organ for the baroque music and piano for the classical music.
    * Symphonic music in the classic era features larger orchestras with a greater diversity of musical instruments than in earlier years. Most Vivaldi solo concertos feature violin as the solo instrument, and most Beethoven concertos focus on the piano; each highlights the favored instrument of his day.
* Texture:
    * The classical music of the Bach sons features only one clear melody at a time, unlike the imitative and often complex polyphonic puzzles of the elder Bach.
    * In the Beethoven concertos, we hear a much greater variety of affect and a more dominant single melody than we hear in the Vivaldi concertos.

ASK

- Do you hear a difference in the length and symmetry of musical phrases between your two examples?
- If your examples are concertos: how dominant is the solo instrument in the musical texture of each of your examples? Is there a difference in emphasis?

II
CLASSICAL COMPOSERS

Haydn

Joseph Haydn (1732–1809) was born into a working-class family in Austria. He sang in a boys' choir until he was seventeen, and afterward he worked diligently to learn composition with a combination of independent study and paid lessons. In 1761, he landed a position with the wealthy Esterházy family, where, for most of the rest of his life, he had an abundance of resources with which to direct performances and compose musical works in the lavish Esterházy country estate. Although his employment offered substantial reward and security, it should be remembered that he was a servant, obliged to please his employers. Haydn walked that delicate balance between his own creativity and his employers' interests with great skill, poise, and humor. Later in his career, Haydn was able to visit England twice; he performed his own compositions in London to much acclaim.

His music is elegantly rational but, at the same time, often unpredictable. Haydn combines his strong awareness of structure with an irresistible urge to surprise or "wink" at the listener. He does this by faking endings (the "Joke" quartet, for instance: *String Quartet* Op. 33 No. 2, 1781), placing suddenly loud chords where you'd least expect them (as in the second movement of the "Surprise" symphony, *Symphony No. 94*, 1791), or, in one instance, even including the stage direction to have orchestral members exit the stage before the music has

Joseph Haydn: "My prince was always satisfied with my works. I not only had the encouragement of constant approval but as a conductor of an orchestra I could make experiments, observe what produced an effect and what weakened it ... and take risks. I was isolated from the world; no one in my vicinity could make me lose confidence in myself or bother me, and so I had to become original."[1]

ended (in the "Farewell" symphony, *Symphony No. 45*, 1772). His wit is most often expressed in unexpected harmonies and sudden changes of emotion. Haydn also manipulates his **themes** in a process known as **thematic development**: a theme or motive gets altered and reshaped throughout a musical work using a variety of musical elements and styles. This technique enabled Haydn to give any melody—however simple—continuous interest and drama.

Haydn contributed to all the popular genres of the time, including oratorios and operas, but today, he is most well known for his instrumental music. He wrote many symphonies, string quartets, and sonatas and of such consistently high quality that his music maintains a strong presence on concert programs.

Theme   Melody or motive that recurs and has structural relevance throughout the work or movement; see Musical Elements Appendix.

Thematic development   The continuous alteration and expansion of a theme throughout a musical work or movement, utilizing a variety of musical elements and styles.

Mozart

The Austrian composer **Wolfgang Amadeus Mozart (1756–1791)** achieved fame as a child for his musical brilliance with the help of his father. Leopold was himself an accomplished musician as well as a true "stage parent" who took his young son Wolfgang, along with Wolfgang's sister Anna Maria ("Nannerl"), on tour. Europe was, thus, able to hear the talented Mozart children; Wolfgang's feats of musical memory and imagination astounded even the most skeptical listeners.

As a young man, his abilities continued to flourish through his contributions to the most popular genres of the day. He began employment as a court musician for the Archbishop of Salzburg when he was still a teenager, but, unlike Haydn, he did not adapt well to the expectations of his superior, and in 1781, he left for Vienna to pursue freelance work as a composer. For a while, his fame and great skill helped him make a living for himself and his family once he married. He taught music lessons, performed as a pianist, and composed for commissions. By the late 1780s, however, Mozart had fallen into debt, likely as a result of his extravagant lifestyle. His money troubles continued to worsen

Figure 8-4 Watercolor painting by Louis de Carmontelle (1717–1806) of 7-year old Mozart (at keyboard) with his father Leopold, and sister Maria-Anna ("Nannerl"). Leopold, a "stage dad," toured Europe with his children to perform as a family.

Wolfgang Amadeus Mozart: "People make a mistake who think that my art has come easily to me. Nobody has devoted so much time and thought to composition as I. There is not a famous master whose music I have not studied over and over."[2]

during the next few years despite his steadily growing number of outstanding musical works. Tragically, he didn't have time to recover from his financial setbacks; he died after a brief illness in 1791, shortly before his thirty-sixth birthday.

During his short life, Mozart established himself as a major composer of orchestral music, chamber music, opera, and sacred music. He is known for his "perfect" and elegant melodies and much more: special attention and repeated hearings reward listeners who notice a variety of textures, including polyphony, wide-ranging tours of topics, and, in the symphonic music, rich orchestration. In his collaborations with librettists such as **Lorenzo da Ponte (1749–1838)**, Mozart's operatic music heightens every detail of the personalities and situations of the stories.

In the twentieth century, Mozart's significance in classic era music, combined with his compelling and tragic biography, inspired *Amadeus*, a stage play by Peter Shaffer based on Mozart's life. The 1984 film version of *Amadeus* garnered many awards and familiarized a new generation with Mozart's music, leading to an even greater interest in the composer than was present before. Many details of Mozart's life are exaggerated—and some are downright fictionalized—to serve the riveting dramatic story, but the film captures the milieu of Mozart's world.

Figure 8-6 Engraving of librettist Lorenzo da Ponte by Michele Pekenino after Nathaniel Rogers (1788–1844).

Beethoven

The music of German composer **Ludwig van Beethoven (1770–1827)** signals a turning point in style: even though his music is based in eighteenth-century classical forms, Beethoven pioneered a more turbulent musical expression that developed into the romantic music of the nineteenth century. His career, usually delineated in three creative periods, was successful in spite of his complicated personal life and tragic hearing loss.

Ludwig van Beethoven: "But what mortification if someone stood beside me and heard a flute from afar and I heard nothing; or someone heard a shepherd singing, and I heard nothing. Such happenings brought me close to despair; I was not far from ending my own life—only art, only art held me back. Ah, it seemed impossible to me that I should leave the world before I had produced all that I felt I might, and so I spared this wretched life ..."[3]

Beethoven's childhood was difficult; his father's alcoholism burdened the family and eventually forced Ludwig to support his mother and brothers while he was still a teenager. But by the time he was seventeen, many—including Mozart—had already noticed his talent as a keyboardist and improviser. During his first period as a composer, up to about 1802, his music reflected the influence and ideals of earlier classical composers, such as Haydn and Mozart. Thematic development is pervasive in Beethoven's music throughout his career and betrays his debt to Haydn. By the end of his first creative period, however, Beethoven knew he was becoming deaf. This devastating condition, combined with a personality that was already temperamental, took its toll on Beethoven's personal life for the rest of his days.

The turbulent and innovative music of his second creative period demonstrated Beethoven's mission to express personal pain through his art. His music during this time was innovative, including many of the characteristics associated with later nineteenth-century romantic music: structural extensions, bold harmonies, and volatile dynamics accommodated more complex ideas and grand, heroic gestures. During this time, his prestige as an acclaimed composer attracted publishers and patrons in spite of his irascibility.

During his third creative period, which began in 1816, Beethoven's hearing loss continued to worsen and was probably severe or even profound by this time. Nevertheless, his music gained in depth and brilliance. Although his style maintained the tempestuous characteristics of his middle period, his latest music is especially known for its introspection and complexity. Plagued by ill health in his final years, Beethoven died at the age of fifty-six. (Signs of lead poisoning have recently been discovered in a lock of Beethoven's hair; this may have played a part in his death.) Over 10,000 people attended his funeral procession.

Beethoven's musical contributions include symphonies, concertos, piano sonatas, chamber music, sacred choral music, songs, and one opera: *Fidelio*. His music's great range of intense emotions, powerfully presented in cohesive classical structures, have enthralled listeners ever since. The heroic aspects of some of his music—especially his symphonic works—has made his music symbolic to many listeners ever since. The Allied forces in World War II, for instance, used Beethoven's famous opening motive for his Fifth Symphony, which has a rhythm that matches the Morse code for "V," as a symbol of victory. The "Ode to Joy" choral passage from Beethoven's Ninth Symphony, which celebrates the ideal of brotherhood, is particularly beloved around the world: it was adopted as the anthem of Europe in

1972, it was played by protestors at Tiananmen Square in 1989 before their ill-fated clash with the Chinese government, and every New Year season, the Japanese customarily attend performances of the Ninth Symphony.

The Classical Landscape

Listeners and scholars tend to focus on the three most prominent composers of the classic era, but a fascinating landscape of performers, librettists, critics, patrons, printers, and many other composers helped create and develop the classic style that made so much of the legacies of Haydn, Mozart, and Beethoven possible. The following comments describe a small sampling of significant classic era figures.

Carl Philipp Emanuel Bach (1714–1788) and **Johann Christian Bach (1735–1782)** (see playlist options, above) were both keyboardists and composers as was their father, the famous baroque German composer Johann Sebastian Bach—but they developed their own, more modern, styles. J. C. Bach was a friend of Mozart's and an important influence on Mozart as well, especially in regard to keyboard concertos. C. P. E. Bach influenced generations of musicians with his 1750 book, *Die Kunst das Clavier zu spielen* (*Essay on the True Art of Playing Keyboard Instruments*).

Although German culture was dominant in classic era music, many of the era's important talents came from other lands. Italian composer **Domenico Scarlatti (1685–1757)** worked for royalty in Portugal and Spain and wrote over 500 keyboard sonatas. His sonatas betray Spanish folk music influences and at least one sonata (K. 119) mimics popular Spanish instruments such as guitar and castanets. One of the earliest symphonists was **Giovanni Battista Sammartini (1700–1774)** of Italy, who helped establish symphonic forms and thematic development techniques. Czech composer **Johann Stamitz (1717–1757)** settled in Germany and developed the "Mannheim" style named after the German city in which he directed an orchestra. His symphonies were renowned for stylistic techniques that showcased his orchestra's brilliance, such as the crescendos (gradual increases in volume) and the rising motives (later called "rocket themes") that appear near the beginnings of his first movements. **Luigi Boccherini (1743–1805)** was an Italian composer and cellist especially noted for his chamber music and for his highly individual style.

Figure 8-8 Luigi Boccherini playing the cello, c1764, by Pompeo Batoni (1708–1787)

The opera world underwent significant changes during the classic era. In response to the criticism of showy baroque opera performances that forfeited dramatic coherence with excesses such as "suitcase arias" (popular singers' favorite arias which they carried around with them to sing in any other opera they desired), several reform movements emerged which sought to emphasize dramatic unity and, for the Italian librettist **Pietro Metastasio (1698–1782)**, a utopian portrayal of individuals and society. Metastasio's librettos led a powerful aesthetic trend toward the idea that dramatic performances should "elevate" the character of listeners rather than simply "entertain" them. German composer **Johann Adolf Hasse (1699–1783)** was particularly associated with Metastasio, having used his libretti for many of his operas. Hasse's wife, the Italian mezzo-soprano **Faustina Bordoni (1697–1781)**, was one of the most prominent singers of her day.

Figure 8-9 Portrait of Christoph Willibald Gluck by Joseph Duplessis (1725–1802)

Figure 8-10 Portrait of vocalist Faustina Bordoni by Bartolomeo Nazari (1699–1758).

Bohemian composer **Christoph Willibald Gluck (1714–1787)** was the reformer who engendered the most lasting influences on opera. His goal toward a "noble simplicity" shunned excessive virtuosity and ornamentation in favor of a return to the marriage of text and music reminiscent of Monteverdi and the early baroque Florentine camerata ideals. Mozart was influenced by Gluck's reforms, and he also used several Metastasio librettos. The librettist most associated with Mozart, however, was the Italian poet **Lorenzo da Ponte (1749–1838)**, who collaborated in several operas by Mozart and others.

The Swiss intellectual **Jean-Jacques Rousseau (1712–1778)** was most famous as a philosopher, but he was a composer as well. His aesthetic philosophy incorporated criticisms of French musical styles, which fed a controversy on the relative merits of French and Italian music. His *Dictionnaire de musique*, still an important reference work, was published in Paris in 1768.

Figure 8-11 Portrait of Jean-Jacques Rousseau (1712–1788) by Maruice Quentin de La Tour (1704–1788).

Johann Gottlob Immanuel Breitkopf (1719–1794) was a German printer and publisher who was also a technical and marketing innovator, leading his company to even greater success than his father, the founder of the business, had. He was a scholar and a philanthropist who hosted many of the day's luminaries in his home, including the German poet, Goethe. Under his direction, the publishing house commanded enough status to attract most of the major composers of the day. Later, the firm was bought by Hartel and became known as "Breitkopf and Hartel," which is still in business today; its current website greets visitors with "Welcome to the world's oldest music publishing company" on its homepage.

Figure 8-12 Portrait of Marianne von Martinez.

Marianne von Martínez (1744–1812) was a singer, keyboardist, composer, and teacher who lived and worked in close proximity to the greatest talents of the day. Metastasio, the librettist referenced above, lived in the same house and took charge of her education on the request of her family. He enlisted the help of the young, talented, struggling musician who lived in the attic—Joseph Haydn prior to his position with the Esterházys—to provide her with piano lessons. When she was older, she hosted *soirées* attended by Mozart and Haydn, among others. Even among these distinguished personalities, her talent shined; her compositions garnered praise from audiences and colleagues, and the prominent English music historian and critic **Charles Burney (1726–1814)** commended her expressive vocal performances.

Figure 8-13 Portrait of Charles Burney by Joshua Reynolds (1723–1792).

III
CLASSICAL GENRES

Orchestral Music

Orchestra A large ensemble of instruments, including strings, woodwinds, brass, and percussion instruments, with a conductor as the leader.

Percussion Family of instruments in which sound is produced variously by striking, shaking, and in other ways; see Musical Instruments Appendix.

Woodwinds A category of wind instruments in which the sound is produced when air vibrates through a tube; keys are stopped along the tube to change pitch; see Musical Instruments Appendix.

Symphony Multimovement work for orchestra; music written for this ensemble, usually in four movements.

Sonata form Dominant musical form in Western art music since the eighteenth century, typically used in the first movement of multimovement works; see Musical Elements Appendix.

Cadenza Solo virtuosic, improvisatory passage; especially common in concertos.

By the late eighteenth century, instrumental music in Western Europe enjoyed a higher status than ever before, especially in symphonic music, which refers to music performed by a symphony orchestra. The classical **orchestra** could have included as many as 30–40 members, depending on local resources and performance situations. Strings still dominated the orchestra, but **percussion** was added in the eighteenth century, and wind instruments—especially **woodwinds**—gained ground throughout the classic era. The two most common classic era symphonic genres are the symphony and the concerto.

The **symphony** is a multimovement work for orchestra, usually in four movements and—until Beethoven's Ninth Symphony—entirely instrumental. Formal characteristics of each movement typically correspond to the classical multimovement cycle; for instance, most first movements are in **sonata form** (see the Musical Elements Appendix for a detailed description of musical forms in the multimovement cycle). Symphonies are generally extended works, but the lengths of individual symphonies are widely variable. The earliest classical symphonies were generally brief; some lasted no longer than ten or fifteen minutes. Later classical symphonies lengthened as a result of more development and complexity, and with Beethoven, a symphony can last well over an hour.

Of all the popular baroque concerto types, classical musicians and audiences retained the solo concerto, which contrasts a soloist against the full orchestra and is generally in three movements, in fast-slow-fast order (see Chapter 7, Baroque Music, "Vocabulary," for "concerto" varieties). The soloist's virtuosic and improvisational musical passage toward the end of some concerto movements is known as the **cadenza**. This is the moment when orchestral accompaniment drops out (or is minimized) and all attention is given to the soloist, who delays the orchestral cadence with a suspenseful and often spellbinding display of the capacities of the solo instrument.

PLAYLIST OPTIONS
ORCHESTRAL MUSIC

FIND

- A symphonic or concerto movement by one of the following (search "[composer's name] symphony"):
    - Johann Stamitz in early classic era style
    - Haydn in mid-classic era style
    - Beethoven in late classic era style

OBSERVE

- Structure, such as sonata form in first movements, ABA, theme and variations, minuet and trio, rondo, or a combination of sonata and rondo form in other movements (see the Musical Elements Appendix for information on form).
- Thematic development:
    - Especially prominent in Haydn or Beethoven examples.
- If your example is a concerto:
    - Listen for a cadenza; if your movement has one, it will be toward the end of the movement.

ASK

- How are themes developed and transformed throughout the movement? Which musical elements are used to modify the themes?
- If your example is by Johann Stamitz: does it feature his signature rising motives and gradual crescendos, especially near the beginning? What kind of an effect would this have had on eighteenth-century audiences not used to such well-organized ensembles?
- If your example is by Beethoven: some of Beethoven's symphonic works have been labeled as "heroic." Does your example feature characteristics—such as dramatic key changes and thematic transformations, the prevalence of *Sturm und Drang*, or, in the Ninth Symphony, the sudden entrance of a chorus near the end—that support this idea?

Chamber Music

Chamber music Music for a small instrumental ensemble, usually one player to a part.

String quartet A chamber ensemble made up of two violins, viola, and cello; music written for this ensemble, usually in four movements.

Sonata Sectional or multimovement instrumental work for soloist or small ensemble.

Chamber music, which is music for small instrumental ensembles with one player to a part, flourished in the late eighteenth century. The ensemble could be a keyboard with one or more melody instruments, a wind ensemble, a bowed stringed ensemble, or other similar combinations. The two most popular ensemble types of chamber music are the string quartet and the sonata.

The **string quartet** is a multimovement work for two violins, viola, and cello, with the first violinist in the traditional role as leader of this ensemble. The **sonata** is a multimovement instrumental work for soloist or small ensemble. The soloist is often either a lone keyboardist or any other instrumentalist accompanied by a keyboardist; for instance, one can expect to see both a cellist and a pianist on stage if the recital program lists a cello sonata.

Chamber music reduces the texture to just a few musical instruments—and with some ensemble groupings of instruments within the same family, such as the string quartet, to only one characteristic musical timbre. For many listeners, this gives the musical message of the classic era, which was so focused on structure, a special clarity and power.

PLAYLIST OPTIONS
CHAMBER MUSIC

FIND

- A Haydn or Mozart string quartet movement
- Or Mozart's chamber ensemble, *Eine Kleine Nachtmusik* ("A Little Night Music"), K. 525
- Or the famous first movement of Beethoven's "Moonlight" sonata (Piano Sonata No. 14 in C sharp minor, op. 27 no. 2)

OBSERVE

- Structure, such as sonata form in first movements, ABA, theme and variations, minuet and trio, rondo, or a combination of sonata and rondo form in other movements (see the Musical Elements Appendix for information on form).

- Quick topic switches between graceful galant, polyphonic learned style, *Sturm und Drang*, and others.

ASK

- Many classic era chamber works were written for skillful amateurs; how might this have influenced classic era aesthetic preferences in musical melody, rhythm, and structure?
- If your example is a Haydn or Mozart movement: do you notice any unexpected—or all too expected—musical events that bring a smile?
- If your example is the first movement of Beethoven's "Moonlight" sonata: have you heard similar passages in music of other styles and times that emulate these sublime arpeggios?

Secular Vocal Music

Opera, a genre which emerged in the early-seventeenth-century Italian baroque era, continued to develop during the classic era. Comic opera became especially popular throughout Europe during the eighteenth century. These operas included spoken dialogue, light-hearted music interspersed with popular folk songs, and comic plots—sometimes with biting social and political satire. The language was typically in vernacular European languages throughout the regions in which comic opera was performed. A variety of terms were used to refer to national comic opera traditions including **opera buffa** in Italy, *singspiel* in Germany, and ballad opera in England.

Opera buffa Italian comic opera.

Originally inspired by the idealistic humanism of the early baroque era in the early seventeenth century, serious opera, or **opera seria**, developed throughout the seventeenth and early eighteenth centuries with a more revenue-generating emphasis on popularity and virtuosic display. In reaction to these baroque excesses, several eighteenth-century reform movements profoundly influenced the structures, musical styles, and topics of operas toward dramatic unity and the more classical aesthetic of simple elegance. *Opera seria* was more formal and lengthy than comic opera. Comic relief was relegated to humorous *intermezzo* performances of music during intermission between acts, which were unrelated to the main opera.

Opera seria Italian dramatic, serious opera.

Figure 8-14 Title page of Gluck's 1762 opera *Orfeo ed Euridice*

PLAYLIST OPTIONS
CLASSIC ERA OPERA

FIND

- A scene from Gluck's *Orfeo ed Euridice*
- Or a scene from Mozart's *Le Nozze di Figaro* ("The Marriage of Figaro")

- For videos, search "[title of work] [lyrics] or [subtitles]"
- Translated librettos are available online

OBSERVE

- Differences in musical style between arias and recitatives.
- Instrumental accompaniment styles that highlight personalities and events and support vocal melodies.

ASK

- How do musical word-painting techniques in your example help bring characters and events to life?
- If your example is Gluck's opera: what about this work recalls early baroque composer Monteverdi and his ideals besides the story?
- If your example is Mozart's opera and your scene includes an example of one of Mozart's famous ensemble numbers, does the music help you delineate personalities and situations between the characters?

Sacred Vocal Music

The late eighteenth century was a particularly secular era; it was, after all, considered the late years of the Enlightenment. Despite this fact, sacred music still flourished; musicians continued to compose and perform oratorios, mass settings, cantatas, and shorter sacred works such as psalm settings. The structures and topics of these genres were similar to what they had been in earlier centuries, but traditional styles such as polyphonic choral music were blended with newer musical characteristics in the late eighteenth century. Haydn's oratorios, for example, which owe so much to Handel, use the shorter and more regularized phrasing common in the classic era (see the Playlist Options comparison between baroque and classical music, above). Mozart and Beethoven also culminated their careers with major sacred works: Mozart worked on his *Requiem Mass in D Minor* (K. 626), which he wasn't able to finish, in his deathbed in 1791, and Beethoven regarded his *Missa Solemnis in D Major, Op. 123* (1819–1823) as his greatest work.

Figure 8-15 1808 performance of Haydn's *Creation*; Haydn is seated in lower center, wearing wig and hat. Watercolor by Balthasar Wigand.

PLAYLIST OPTIONS
SACRED MUSIC

FIND

- The opening of Haydn's oratorio *Die Shöpfung* ("The Creation")
- Or a movement from Mozart's *Requiem*, such as "Lacrimosa"
- Or a movement from Beethoven's *Missa Solemnis*
    - For videos, search "[title of work] [lyrics] or [subtitles]"
    - Translated librettos are available online

OBSERVE

- Texture: a blend of classical homophonic with more traditional baroque polyphonic textures.

- Word painting: more symbolic than in opera, which emphasizes character and plot.

ASK

- All of these examples are "crowning" works by their composers, who use the full palate of their creative skills to express religious mysteries. Do you recognize any personal compositional signatures and religious sensibilities of the composer in your example?
- Does your example betray any debt to the baroque oratorio composer, Handel, especially in regard to musical texture and word painting?

CHAPTER 8 VOCABULARY & IMPORTANT FIGURES

Vocabulary

Cadenza

Chamber music

Chromaticism ("chromatic," adj.)

Diatonicism ("diatonic," adj.)

Empfindsam (Ger. "sensitive" or "sentimental") style, or *Empfindsamkeit*

Galant

Opera buffa

Opera seria

Orchestra

Percussion

Sonata

Sonata form

String quartet

Sturm und Drang (Ger. "storm and stress")

Symphony

Thematic development

Theme

Woodwinds

Important Figures

Carl Philipp Emanuel Bach (1714–1788)

Johann Christian Bach (1735–1782)

Ludwig van Beethoven (1770–1827)

Luigi Boccherini (1743–1805)

Faustina Bordoni (1697–1781)

Johann Gottlob Immanuel Breitkopf (1719–1794)

Charles Burney (1726–1814)

Christoph Willibald Gluck (1714–1787)

Johann Adolf Hasse (1699–1783)

Joseph Haydn (1732–1809)

Marianne von Martínez (1744–1812)

Pietro Metastasio (1698–1782)

Wolfgang Amadeus Mozart (1756–1791)

Lorenzo da Ponte (1749–1838)

Jean-Jacques Rousseau (1712–1778)

Giovanni Battista Sammartini (1700–1774)

Domenico Scarlatti (1685–1757)

Johann Stamitz (1717–1757)

ENDNOTES

[1] Trans. Elaine Sisman in "Haydn, Shakespeare, and the Rules of Originality," in Elaine Sisman, ed., *Haydn and His World* (Princeton, NJ: Princeton University Press, 1997), p. 3, as quoted in Barbara Hanning, *Concise History of Western Music,* 4th ed. (New York: W. W. Norton, 2010), p. 345.

[2] W. A. Mozart, as quoted in Kristine Forney and Joseph Machlis, *The Enjoyment of Music* 10th ed., (New York: W. W. Norton and Company, 2007), p. 242.

[3] Ludwig van Beethoven, "Heiligenstadt Testament," from *Letter of Composers Through Six Centuries*, pp. 167–169. Krause Publications, 1967.

Image Credits

- Figure 8-1: Thomas Gainsborough / Copyright in the Public Domain.
- Figure 8-2: Benoît Louis Prévost / Copyright in the Public Domain.
- Figure 8-3: Thomas Hardy / Copyright in the Public Domain.
- Figure 8-4: Louis Carrogis Carmontelle / Copyright in the Public Domain.
- Figure 8-5: Barbara Krafft / Copyright in the Public Domain.
- Figure 8-6: Michele Pekenino / Copyright in the Public Domain.
- Figure 8-7: Julius Schmid / Copyright in the Public Domain.
- Figure 8-8: Pompeo Batoni / Copyright in the Public Domain.
- Figure 8-9: Joseph Duplessis / Copyright in the Public Domain.
- Figure 8-10: Bartolomeo Nazari / Copyright in the Public Domain.
- Figure 8-11: Maruice Quentin de La Tour / Copyright in the Public Domain.
- Figure 8-12: Source: https://commons.wikimedia.org/wiki/File:Marianna_Martines,_Pupil_of_P._Metastasio;_born_in_Vienna,_4th_day_of_May_1744,_Member_Academia_Filarmonica.jpg.
- Figure 8-13: Joshua Reynolds / Copyright in the Public Domain.
- Figure 8-14: Charles Monnet / Copyright in the Public Domain."

Liszt at the Piano by Josef Danhauser (1805–1845). In this powerfully symbolic scene of the romantic aesthetic, Franz Liszt sits at the piano facing a bust of Beethoven in front of a window that shows an approaching storm. At his feet is Countess Marie d'Agoult. Behind Liszt hangs a portrait of poet Lord Byron, in front of which stands Niccolò Paganini on the left with Gioacchino Rossini. Alexander Dumas and feminist Georges Sand are seated in front of a standing Victor Hugo or Hector Berlioz. To the left of them is a statue of Joan of Arc.

CHAPTER

9

Romantic Era Music

Enlightenment ideals left a powerful legacy for the nineteenth century. The American and French revolutions raised the value of democracy in the Western world after over two millennia of monarchy as the standard form of government in Europe. Enlightenment questions about the rights of marginalized populations, such as women and slaves, gained strength, and the individual—whether as a thinker and creator or as a tragic figure—was now more of a focus than ever before. Efforts to hammer out constitutions with more personal freedoms breathed new life into the development of national and cultural identities. Germany and Italy, for instance, each became unified nations in the nineteenth century. The European cosmopolitanism of the previous century changed drastically into a fascination for distinct ethnic traits of foreign cultures—an abiding interest, known as **exoticism**, that would drive romantic era literary, artistic, and musical themes for the rest of the century and beyond to the present day. Exoticism would bring mesmerizing power to the operatic stage in the nineteenth century.

Romanticism is a term that stems from European medieval epics in the vernacular, "romance" languages. By the nineteenth century, the term carried with it connotations of dramatic, wide-ranging emotions and themes rich with fantasy, horror, and exoticism. Nature—which could turn from peaceful to terrifying in a moment—was a compelling presence in romantic era aesthetics. Romanticism in literature was forged earlier than in music, partly by the late-eighteenth-century **Sturm und Drang** (Ger. "storm and stress") movement. One of the most important

Exoticism Evocation of foreign cultures in the arts.

Romanticism
Nineteenth-century European movement; romantic music emphasized intense emotional expression, literary programs, and the use of large musical forces (also see Unit 2 Western Art Music, Introduction).

Sturm und Drang ("storm and stress") style Musical style with sudden, extreme changes in volume, and with vigorous rhythms (Chapter 8, Classic Era Music).

Figure 9-2 *The Wanderer above the Sea Fog* by Caspar David Friedrich (1774–1840).

romantic literary figures was German writer **Johann Wolfgang Goethe (1749–1832)**, whose bestselling novella of tragic love, *Die Leiden des jungen Werthers* ("*The Sorrows of Young Werther,*" 1774) exemplified *Sturm und Drang*. Goethe's poetry provided perhaps the most beloved choices for nineteenth-century art song composers. The short stories and poems of American writer Edgar Allan Poe (1809–1849) embody darker, gothic romantic traditions with themes of horror, torment, and death—themes of interest to some nineteenth-century composers, including Berlioz and Schubert.

Visual artists expressed romanticism in haunting and evocative images. The landscapes of German painter Caspar David Friedrich (1774–1840) seem to symbolize the human condition and life itself. His haunting images of trees and rocks, often in the presence of human figures who stand by and watch, are both threatening and beautiful at the same time (see Figure 9-2). French painter **Eugéne Delacroix (1798–1863)** depicted the Spirit of the French Revolution with great drama in his 1830 *Liberty Leading the People,* which shows the heroism of a personified Liberty, holding the flag of the French Revolution aloft (see Figure 9-3). Delacroix's visits to North Africa resulted in a classic of exoticism: a colorful image of an Eastern harem in his 1834 *Women of Algiers in their Apartment*, which blends realism with European fantasy (see Figure 9-4).

Nineteenth-century music depicted all of these aspects of romanticism, especially in its emotional content. The forms and genres of the classic era remained a foundation: first movements were still often in **sonata form**, for instance, and solo **concertos** continued to flourish. The new preoccupation with emotional expression, however, changed proportions and pushed boundaries. The symmetrical phrasing, predictable rhythms, and diatonic harmonies of the previous century gave way to passionate lyricism, unpredictable rhythms, and colorful, chromatic harmonies.

Instrumental music, which rose in importance during the classic era, continued to gain status throughout the romantic era, and the size of

Sonata A multimovement instrumental work for soloist or small ensemble (Chapter 8, Classic Era Music).

Concerto An instrumental work that contrasts orchestra with soloist or small ensemble, usually comprised of three movements (Chapter 7, Baroque Music).

Figure 9-3 *Liberty Leading the People* by Eugene Delacroix (1798–1863).

Figure 9-4 *The Women of Algiers* by Eugene Delacroix (1798–1863). In this expression of exoticism, Delacroix highlights a sense of fantasy as well as fascination with foreign cultures.

the orchestra increased in numbers, variety of instruments, and volume. Newfound freedoms in musical structure and harmony served the burgeoning interest in nationalist ideals, exotic localities, and riveting story lines. The piano—larger, louder, and with a wider range in the nineteenth century—became music's emblem in the Western world. Its presence in the parlor was considered crucial to family and social life for the middle class and above. The broad array of nineteenth-century piano music for this instrument, ranging from beginning and intermediate level music for amateurs at home to bravura pieces for professional virtuosos on the concert stage, shows music's importance across many layers of nineteenth-century society.

I
SOLO AND SMALL ENSEMBLE VOCAL MUSIC

Art Song, Lied

Lied (Ger. "song," pl. *lieder*) or art song Nineteenth century German solo vocal settings of poetry with piano accompaniment.

Song cycle A set of songs, or *lieder*, unified in some way, usually by poet and theme.

The simple word, "song," became the name of one of the most important musical genres in the nineteenth century. **Lied** means "song" in German, but during the eighteenth and nineteenth centuries, it came to signify a specific genre: a musical setting of German poetry, performed by solo voice and piano accompaniment. **Art song** is a more international term that includes similarly expressive songs set to poetry in a variety of languages. Although the German version enjoyed dominance, this genre was popular throughout Europe. Groups of songs known as **song cycles**, unified by topic or musical style, were often performed together.

Composers made musical settings of poems by the best German romantic poets; Goethe was one of their most popular poets. Topics reflected perennial interests in love and nature, with additional—and sometimes wrenching—detours into fantasy and horror (see Schubert's *Erlkönig*, below). The role of the piano transcends itself in nineteenth-century lied:

more than a mere background accompaniment, the piano paints pictures with sound effects, expresses aspects of emotion beyond, or "underneath," those expressed by the vocalist, and even occasionally becomes a character in the story.

Musical expression of the poetry was reflected in every musical element, especially with the very structure of the song. **Strophic form**, which repeats the music with every stanza of text, gives listeners enough familiarity to sing along with ease. Strophic form is not very expressive, though. When the topic changes, as it often does in nineteenth-century romantic poetry, the music does not. **Through composed form**, however, features different music for every line of the poem; no repeated sections occur in this form. This is the ultimate in expression: every nuance of meaning for each line of poetry can be expressed. **Modified strophic form**, a combination of strophic and through composed forms, is a compromise. If a composer wants the listeners to have some feeling of familiarity but needs flexibility with the lines that reflect changes in emotions and meanings, this form allows for those changes. Art song composers used all these structures and more.

Franz Schubert (1797–1828) was the most prominent lied composer and the genre's pioneer. He came from a humble Austrian family and sang with the Vienna Boys Choir as a child. He was expected to follow in his father's footsteps and become a schoolteacher. After just a few years of teaching, however, he soon switched to music and devoted himself to composition for the rest of his short life. He wrote quickly, and his music became known for its unforgettable melodies and emotional depth. His genres included symphonies, sonatas, chamber works, choral works, and—for which he is most well known—over 600 lieder. Wealthy patrons hosted "Schubertiads," or concert parties, in their homes where Schubert's songs and other works were performed. He died at the young age of 31 after several years of illness.

Schubert's style includes both traditional and innovative elements. While his symphonic music follows the classical influences of Haydn,

Figure 9-5 Portrait of Franz Schubert by Wilhelm August Rieder (1796–1880); 1875 oil painting after his 1825 watercolor.

Strophic form   Song structure in which the music is repeated with each stanza of text (see Musical Elements Appendix).

Through composed   Music without repeating sections; each stanza is musically distinct.

Modified strophic form   Texted vocal music that combines features of strophic and through-composed forms.

Figure 9-6 Schubertiade by Julius Schmid (1854–1935).

Mozart, and early Beethoven, much of his piano and vocal music includes romantic expressive devices such as more harmonic dissonance and less predictable phrasing. Schubert is particularly known for his lieder's evocative piano accompaniments. Two song settings of Goethe poems provide vivid examples: In the supernatural horror story, Erlkönig ("The Erlking"), the piano takes on the role of a galloping horse, and in Gretchen am Spinnrade ("Gretchen at the Spinning Wheel"), the piano portrays the spinning wheel during a monologue about love. The piano parts to both of these songs successfully manipulate the listener's tension level at the same time that they paint vivid pictures of the action.

Parlor Song

Parlor song Song meant for amateur performance; usually strophic ballads with sentimental topics and simple musical settings.

As the piano became *de rigueur* for middle-class homes in many parts of the world, a less formal type of song became popular. Known as the **parlor song** in North America, it was named after the room in the

American home dedicated to entertaining guests. The songs were usually strophic ballads with fairly simple musical settings for amateurs to easily play for enjoyment. Performers were free to vary the melodies and accompaniments, as with folk music. Topics are often sentimental and steeped in social traditions, which we hear in one of the most popular songs of the century: *Home, Sweet Home* (1823) by Henry R. Bishop (1786–1855). It was written for the staged melodrama, *Clari, or the Maid of Milan*, to express a poignant moment in the plot when the heroine decides to go home despite the temptation to become a "fallen woman." There must not have been a dry eye in the house (see Chapter 2, Music for Stage and Screen, "Influence from Abroad: Operetta and Melodrama").

American "tunesmith" Stephen Foster (1826–1864), whom we met in Unit 1, American Vernacular Music, for his minstrelsy songs (see Chapter 2, American Music for the Stage and Screen, "Influence from Home: Minstrelsy"), is also well known for his parlor songs, such as *Jeanie with the Light Brown Hair* (1853). Foster, who wrote both words and music, may have been thinking about his wife Jennie, from whom he was briefly separated at the time. The text expresses heartsick nostalgia, with references to nature that seem to idealize his lost love. The music's AABA phrase pattern prefigures Tin Pan Alley structure (see Chapter 2, American Music for the Stage and Screen, "The Composers: Roots in Tin Pan Alley"). Foster's songs are currently enjoying a revival on today's recital programs.

PLAYLIST OPTIONS
NINETEENTH CENTURY ART AND PARLOR SONGS

FIND

A video or audio performance of:

* A prominent German lied composer or specific work, such as
  * Franz Schubert
    * *Erlkönig* ("Earl King"), D328
    * *Gretchen am Spinnrade* ("Gretchen at the Spinning Wheel"), D118
  * Clara Schumann
    * *Geheimes Flüstern* ("Secret Whispers")

- ◆ Robert Schumann
  - ◆ *Dichterliebe* ("A Poet's Love") song cycle, which include songs such as *Im wonder-shònen* ("In the Marvelous Month of May")
- ◆ An American parlor song, such as
  - ◆ *Home! Sweet Home!* by Henry R. Bishop
  - ◆ *Jeanie with the Light Brown Hair* by Stephen Foster

OBSERVE

- ◆ Piano accompaniment.
- ◆ Vocal style, which can range from operatic to popular or folk-song styles.

ASK

- ◆ Does the piano help paint a picture? Is it a character in the story?
- ◆ What is the song structure; strophic for sing-alongs, through composed for more freedom to express the text, or is it a modified strophic for aspects of both types?

II
CHAMBER MUSIC AND INSTRUMENTAL MINIATURES

Chamber music Music for a small instrumental ensemble, usually one player to a part (Chapter 8, Classic Era Music).

String quartet A multimovement chamber work for two violins, viola, and cello. (Chapter 8, Classic Era Music).

Sonata Sectional or multimovement instrumental work for soloist or small ensemble (Chapter 8, Classic Era Music).

If instrumental music finally came into its own during the eighteenth-century classic era, it flourished among the nineteenth-century romantics with even more prestige and emotionally expressive idioms. For many, instrumental music on a modest scale was the most meaningful. Intimate and refined, small ensembles or soloists could encapsulate the musical message most powerfully. Nineteenth-century musicians continued to cultivate **chamber music** genres popular in the previous century, such as the **string quartet** and the **sonata**. With the stronger nineteenth-century presence of the piano, interest in ensembles such as **piano trios** and **piano quintets** grew to make these some of the romantic era's most significant chamber works.

More innovative were **miniatures** and **character pieces**. Usually played by solo piano or another instrument such as violin or guitar, these were distinctively romantic era contributions. A miniature, often programmatic, is as short as a song or a poem and, in fact, is usually meant to be just that in the abstract medium of instrumental music. Character works, often also miniatures, are descriptive, can express subtle emotions such as nostalgia, and are entitled variously with names of tempos, dances, emotions, and characters. Although many nineteenth-century composers wrote chamber and miniature works, the following figures are most notable for their work in these genres.

The Mendelssohns

Born to a prominent Jewish family in Germany who had converted to the Lutheran Church, two siblings helped to create the early romantic era soundscape in different ways. **Fannie Mendelssohn Hensel (1805–1847)**

Piano trio   A chamber ensemble of or composition for piano and two other instruments, usually violin and cello; a work composed for this chamber ensemble.

Piano quintet   A chamber ensemble of or composition for piano and four other instruments, usually string quartet.

Miniature   In music, a short, often programmatic instrumental work especially popular in the romantic era meant to be the abstract musical equivalent of a poem.

Character piece   Descriptive, usually short instrumental work, especially popular in the romantic era.

Figure 9-7 Portrait of Fanny Hensel, 1842, by Moritz Daniel Oppenhiem (1800–1882).

Figure 9-8 Portrait of Felix Mendelssohn, 1829, by James Warren Childe (1780–1862).

composed mostly songs and piano pieces. She was a respected pianist, known for her precocious musical talent and her masterful interpretations of works by earlier composers such as J. S. Bach. Although a professional career for a woman of her social status would not have been considered suitable by her family, she was able to showcase her musical abilities by performing at her own salons, or gatherings of invited guests. The large music room in her home regularly hosted prominent citizens in business, politics, and the arts.

Her younger brother, **Felix Mendelssohn (1809–1847)**, also a pianist, became a prominent composer. He absorbed the musical styles of Mozart and Beethoven and enjoyed a close friendship with the romantic poet Goethe; these influences lent his music its classic era aesthetic foundations combined with a more romantic emotional power. He composed music in many of the most popular genres of the day, and he conducted and organized performances as well. Perhaps the most famous set of piano miniatures of the early nineteenth century was his *Lieder ohne Worte* ("Songs Without Words"), published in 1832. These 48 short pieces meant as musical poems exemplified the romantic aesthetic idea that instrumental music surpassed words in emotional expression.

Chopin and Lizst

Two virtuosos from Eastern Europe—acclaimed, touring pianists who also composed—reflected nineteenth-century romanticism in their lives as well as in their music. They each infused the classical repertory with Eastern European melodies and rhythms from their heritages in Poland and Hungary, and with their charismatic performances, they both helped to ensure the primacy of the piano in nineteenth-century solo instrumental concert music.

Fryderyck Chopin (1810–1849) composed almost exclusively piano music for players across the spectrum from amateurs to virtuosos. His short piano character pieces include études (Fr. "studies," a deceptive title for music that highlights specific technical issues but which, in Chopin's case, could also be virtuosic concert works) preludes, and others. He also wrote longer works for solo piano, such as his Ballades. His highly expressive music makes use of **rubato** (It. "robbed or stolen time"), or

Rubato (It. "robbed or stolen time") Rhythmic flexibility for the sake of expression (also see Musical Elements Appendix).

Franz Liszt (left) on Fredrick Chopin (right): "In his playing, the great artist performed in delightful ways. He played with a stirring heart overcome with shyness and breathless shuddering, as if his heart believed it was near a supernatural being whom he cherished indescribably and incomprehensibly. Like a boat moving upon a mighty wave, he let the melody surge up and down. At times the movement was almost indeterminate, as if an airy apparition had just appeared unexpectedly in this tangible and palpable world. In his compositions, he established the manner that gave his virtuosity such a special character, which he termed Tempo rubato: a "stolen," randomly disconnected tempo that is smooth, abrupt, and languishing at the same time, flickering like flames that waver when they touch the mist, like billowing grasses bending under softly blowing air, like the treetops that tilt arbitrarily here and there with the movement of the wind."[1]

rhythmic flexibility. Rubato is present, to some degree, in most musical performances, but it is especially compelling in Chopin's expressive melodies and mercurial rhythms.

Although he moved from his native Poland to establish his career in Paris after 1831, he was, nevertheless, loyal to Poland's ongoing struggle for independence. He expressed his nationalist sentiments artistically through his compositions based on Polish dances, in particular, the mazurka and the polonaise. He was an introvert who favored the intimate salon setting as a venue for his performances more than the large concert hall. Close friends with many of the leading composers, artists, poets, and writers of his time, he had a long-standing romantic relationship with feminist author George Sand (Aurora Dudevant, 1804–1876). Chopin died young of tuberculosis in 1849 after years of failing health.

Hungarian composer **Franz Liszt (1811–1886)** was a charismatic performer who inspired cult-like devotion among his fans. He wrote hundreds of piano works; his *Hungarian Rhapsodies* (1851–53), which evoke Romany and Hungarian folk music, are particularly well known. As both a composer and a virtuoso performer, he forged new, expressive piano techniques. This was during a time when the piano's volume and range was increasing; Liszt furthered these developments and exploited the expressive possibilities.

In contrast to more conservative composers such as Johannes Brahms (see below) and Mendelssohn, Liszt was an innovator in all aspects of his music, especially regarding harmony and formal structure. Modern performance conventions emerged with Liszt's career, including the term **recital** for a solo or small ensemble musical performance. The term also communicates art music's new protocol practiced by Liszt and his contemporaries: memorized performances of music by past composers. During the first part of his career, Liszt concertized extensively and maintained a flamboyant persona in his active social life. In 1865, however, he entered religious orders, in stark contrast to his former lifestyle. He continued to compose, perform, and teach for the rest of his life as "Abbé Liszt."

Recital Solo or small ensemble musical performance.

Robert Schumann: "A genuinely musical art form always has a focal point towards which all else gravitates, on which all imaginative impulses concentrate. Many composers place it in the middle (like Mozart), others reserve it for nearer the close (like Beethoven). Wherever it lies, the effect of any composition is dependent upon its dynamic influence. If one has been listening, tense and absorbed, there should come a point where, for the first time, one breathes freely; the summit has been reached, and the view is bright and peaceful--ahead and behind."[2]

Clara Wieck Schumann, 1853: "There is nothing that surpasses the joy of creative activity, even if only for those hours of self-forgetfulness in which one breathes solely in the realm of tones."[3]

The Schumanns and Brahms

Robert Schumann's (1810–1856) first goal as a young German musician was to be a concert pianist. An injured right hand, however, forced him in other directions toward composition and music criticism. His music was inspired by traditional forms and past composers, especially J. S. Bach. But Schumann also used the full romantic era's palette of emotional expression in his vocal and instrumental music, much of which was driven by his intense love of literature. Tragically, he suffered severe mental illness in his final years, and he died after an extended hospitalization.

Schumann's music was often especially imaginative. The setting of his *Carnaval* (1834–35, op 9) piano miniatures is a masked ball: each piece is entitled with the name of a dance, character (including his future wife, Clara), or social interaction. Schumann's music vividly portrays its varied topics. His published essays educated the public on music, advocated for other talented musicians such as Brahms (see below) and Schubert, and engaged the art music community in aesthetic dialogue.

The German pianist and composer **Clara Wieck Schumann (1819–1896)** met her husband Robert through her father, who was also Robert's piano teacher. She was a renowned pianist and a talented composer who complemented traditional forms with the more adventurous harmonies and sweeping melodies of the romantic era. As a composer, she is most well known for her piano and chamber works She limited her professional work, however, in deference to Robert's career and to her obligations as a parent: she mothered eight children with Robert, not all of whom survived her. After her husband's death, Clara concertized and taught piano in order to support her children. She was also a tireless supporter of her late husband's work; she almost completely stopped composing her own music after his death, but she continued to perform and curate his music.

A German composer from a family of humble means, **Johannes Brahms (1833–1897)** studied piano and music theory privately on scholarship and, in the meantime, earned money as a teenager performing music in restaurants, parties, and the theater. His culture's **vernacular music** was part of his musical language ever since. As a young man, he met the Schumanns in 1853, who recognized his talent and helped launch the younger composer's career. When Robert was hospitalized after a suicide attempt in 1854, Brahms helped take care of the Schumann children for a time while Clara went back to work

Vernacular music
The music that is most accessible, or familiar, to most people in a given culture (Unit 1 Introduction, American Vernacular Music).

Johannes Brahms, 1869: "...in a theme for variations, almost the only thing that actually has meaning for me is the bass. But that is sacred to me, it is the firm footing upon which I then build my tales. What I do with the melody is merely playing around, or ingenious-playing around...When I vary the melody, I can hardly do more than be clever or charming, or lend depth to a beautiful thought, albeit with

as a performer in order to earn money. He was a life-long friend to Clara after Robert's death, and he died less than a year after Clara's death.

Brahms became one of the most respected and influential composers of the nineteenth century. Profoundly influenced by Beethoven, his musical style is mostly traditional in structure but with deeply emotional romantic qualities. His music's rich textures and subtle rhythmic complexities are expressed in his symphonic, vocal, and solo piano music and, perhaps, most completely in his chamber music, the genre which many consider to be his greatest legacy.

A Voice from the Americas

The music of **Louis Moreau Gottschalk (1829–1869)** was filled with melodies and rhythms of the Americas. Born to a mother with Caribbean heritage, he grew up in New Orleans within the rich musical traditions of **Creole** culture. He studied music in Paris while still a child in 1841, and he toured Europe as a composer-pianist, 1845 to 1852. Chopin was impressed with Gottschalk's abilities after hearing him perform in 1845 before Gottschalk's sixteenth birthday. In 1853, Gottschalk debuted in New York City and spent the rest of his career as a performer and composer in the Americas. He was most well known for his piano music. His style draws from many kinds of American music, including Caribbean, folk, and popular songs. Notable piano solos include *Bamboula: Danse des Negres*, op 2 (1846–48) from early in his career while he was still in Europe and *Le Banjo,* op 15 1854–55, which imitates the banjo and quotes the Stephen Foster's popular song "Camptown Races." As the first internationally prominent art music composer from the Americas and a tireless concertizer, Gottschalk brought the vibrant sounds of America to stages on both sides of the Atlantic.

Figure 9-13 Photo of Louis Moreau Gottschalk.

Creole A cultural group, especially in Louisiana, that includes people of European and Afro-Caribbean descent; this term can also refer generically to a mixture of cultures and languages (Chapter 1, American Traditional Music).

PLAYLIST OPTIONS
CHAMBER MUSIC AND
INSTRUMENTAL MINIATURES

FIND

A video or audio performance of

- Chamber music by
  - Clara Wieck Schumann (Piano Trio G minor)
  - Johannes Brahms (Quintet for piano and strings F minor, Opus 34)
- Piano music by
  - Robert Schumann (*Carnaval,* 1834–35, op 9)
  - Fannie Mendelssohn Hensel (*Das Jahr,* "The Year," 1841)
  - Felix Mendelssohn (*Lieder ohne Worte*, "Songs Without Words")
  - Fryderyck Chopin (one of the études or nocturnes)
  - Franz Liszt *Hungarian Rhapsodies* (1851–53)
  - Louis Moreau Gottschalk (*Le Banjo,* op 15 1854–55)

OBSERVE

- The melody for instances of *rubato*
- Harmonic dissonances and their resolutions

ASK

- Is your example relatively traditional, sticking with classic era forms? Or is it especially innovative? Does it feature elements of tradition *and* innovation?
- What does the music say about the composer's cultural background and temperament?

III
CHORAL AND
ORCHESTRAL MUSIC

While romanticism inspired intimate songs, miniatures, and chamber music on one side of the continuum, music on a grand scale pushed the boundaries on the other side further than ever before. With the unprecedented choral entrance in Beethoven's *Symphony No. 9* (1824) as the watershed moment, large-scale drama distinguished nineteenth-century romantic music with larger ensembles, louder soundscapes with more **timbral** variety, and longer musical works.

Timbre Tone color, or quality (see Musical Elements Appendix).

Choral Music

Amateur choirs became popular among the general public. Their repertory of past composers favored Handel, J. S. Bach, and Haydn. Especially notable is the Handel and Haydn Society, which was founded in Boston in 1815. Choir director and music educator Lowell Mason (see Chapter 1, American Traditional Music, "Further Developments in American Sacred Music") was among its leaders, and the ensemble continues to perform to this day although it changed from amateur to professional status in the late twentieth century. **Part songs** became especially popular in the nineteenth century. Short choral works, divided into soprano, alto, tenor, and bass ranges ("SATB") of homophonic songs, typically featured sentimental or patriotic topics and were performed either without instruments *a cappella* or with keyboard accompaniment.

Part song Short choral work, divided into the following vocal parts in order of highest to lowest "SATB" pitch ranges: **soprano**, **alto**, **tenor**, and **bass** (pronounced "base"). (Also see Chapter 1, American Traditional Music.)

One of the most significant performances of the nineteenth century took place when Mendelssohn conducted J. S. Bach's *St. Matthew's Passion* in 1829. He launched a Bach revival and a new interest in music of the past: perhaps the first glimmer of the "early music" movement. *A German Requiem* (1868) by Brahms is one of the many notable large-scale choral works of the nineteenth century. Although it is a deeply spiritual work, Brahms broke with tradition when he set nonliturgical texts of his own choice instead of the traditional Catholic mass prayers.

Orchestral Music

One hundred years earlier, at the beginning of the eighteenth century, orchestral music was polite entertainment and a relative equal among other genres. By the beginning of the nineteenth century, however, it had become the main feature of the performance and far too dramatic to be considered polite. Thanks, in large part, to the legacy of Beethoven's symphonies, orchestral music entered its most prestigious time in the nineteenth century. Its status continued to increase throughout the century, which saw the establishment of many public symphony orchestras, most notably in London, New York City, and Vienna. The balance of repertory changed during the nineteenth century from mostly living composers to past idols, giving rise to a musical "canon," a near-sacred list of revered musical works ("strictly imitative music" is another, different meaning of the word).

The romantic symphony orchestra was also larger than before; it increased from around 40 to about 90 players throughout the century. New instruments joined the orchestra, especially brass instruments such as the tuba and trombone. Woodwinds and brass instruments became more equivalent to the string section than they had been in the eighteenth century. Nineteenth-century orchestral performances include an assortment of old and new genres. The solo **concerto's** importance continued unabated. Still a showcase for virtuosos, the concerto maintained its three-movement structure. Mendelssohn's *Violin Concerto in E minor* op 64 (1844) is one of the most popular from that period, perhaps performed more than any other violin concerto to this day.

Although the **symphony** after Beethoven was still based on classical forms, its proportions were changed to accommodate the music's emotional messages. Romantic composers were not as interested in symmetry as earlier composers were and much was expanded and lengthened. Nineteenth-century musicians and listeners believed in a variety of different, and sometimes conflicting, aesthetic goals for symphonic music. Conservative composers such as Brahms, for instance, maintained faith in the power of **absolute music**: music alone, without story, was enough to move the soul. Brahms used traditional forms recast with romantic expressive devices in his music. The fourth movement of his *Symphony No 4 in E minor*, op 98 (1884/85), which is based on a baroque ground bass structure, is a powerful example.

A more innovative view sought **programmatic music**, which references a story or setting outside of the music. The music of French composer-conductor **Hector Berlioz (1803–1869)** is a striking example

Concerto An instrumental work that contrasts orchestra with soloist or small ensemble, usually comprised of three movements (Chapter 7, Baroque Music).

Symphony Multimovement work for orchestra; music written for this ensemble, usually in four movements. (Chapter 8, Classic Era Music).

Absolute music Music without extra-musical references; see Musical Elements Appendix (Chapter 8, Classic Era Music.)

Program music Instrumental music with extra-musical references, such as a story or pictorial idea.

of that idea. His *Symphony Fantastique* (1830) shocked audiences with a program that included a man's obsession for and, in an opium dream, murder of a woman, his execution, and their meeting after death at a grotesque and horrifying witches' sabbath. The music was entirely instrumental and without words, but Berlioz wrote the detailed program in concert pamphlets to be handed out before the performance. He hired many musicians to perform the symphony; instrumentalists crowded the stage, with disproportionately loud sections of brass and percussion. This created a sonic power far beyond what audiences were accustomed to, and Berlioz was mocked for this in a contemporary cartoon (see Figure 9-14).

His use of ***idée fixe*** (Fr. "obsession") magnifies the story's passions. As a recurring theme with specific references—in this symphony, it

Idée fixe Term associated with Berlioz, often translated as "obsession"; similar to *leitmotif*, *idée fixe* is a musical motive representing a person or idea.

Figure 9-14 *A Concert in the Year 1846* By Andreas Geiger, after an earlier drawing by Grandville. Berlioz is caricatured here for his crowded, noisy orchestras and for his conducting style.

Quadruple meter A metric pattern of 4 beats, typically with the first beat accented and the third beat secondarily accented, as in *strongest,* **weak,** *strong,* **weak**; see Musical Elements Appendix.

Triple meter A metric pattern of 3 beats, typically with the first beat accented, as in *strong,* **weak, weak**; see Musical Elements Appendix; see Musical Elements Appendix.

symbolizes his beloved and object of his obsession—it returns in various forms as the story unfolds. For instance, it is introduced in **quadruple meter** during the first movement when the man sees the woman for the first time, but in the second movement entitled "A Ball," it is in a waltz-like **triple meter.** The complete *idée fixe* melody is presented every time with one exception: at the protagonist's execution, his final thoughts of his beloved are sharply cut off with the guillotine's blade.

Perhaps most shocking of all is that the story is semiautobiographical. Berlioz, who left medical school to devote himself to music, frequented the theater in Paris where he watched the English actress Harriet Smithson portray Shakespearian characters. He became obsessed with Smithson and idealized her as his "Ophelia" from Shakespeare's *Hamlet*. She spurned his advances for years before their short-lived marriage. Although his music was controversial, he achieved success in Europe. He wrote a treatise on the art of orchestration in 1844 and a variety of musical works, most of them programmatic.

Programmatic music can also evoke a national or ethnic identity, without any particular storyline. As we have already seen with Chopin and Liszt, Eastern European composers became an important presence in the nineteenth century, and **Antonín Dvořák (1841–1904)** was one of their strongest voices. He used folk-like melodies and rhythms from

Figure 9-15 Photo of Antonin Dvořák.

his native Czechoslovakia in works such as the *Slavonic Dances* for piano four hands or orchestra (1878 and 1886/87). A remarkable aspect of Dvořák's body of work is his American music. During his time in the United States in the 1890s, he carefully studied American musical idioms: he listened to Native American music, and he asked Black conservatory student H. T. Burleigh (who would later become a prominent American singer, composer, and arranger) to sing spirituals and plantation songs for him. Dvořák eloquently portrayed the musical styles of both of these marginalized groups, which the American musical establishment generally considered unimportant at the time, in his Symphony No. 9 *From the New World* (1893). Dvořák transcended the expressions of his ethnic background to teach Americans the value of their own folk music and to provide an example of its crafted portrayal in art music.

Symphonic poems (also **orchestral poems**, **tone poems)** are single movement programmatic orchestral works. Programmatic overtures, such as Mendelssohn's *Midsummer Night's Dream* (1826), prefigured this genre before Liszt invented the term for his own works in the mid-nineteenth century. The symphonic poems of the late-nineteenth-century composer Richard Strauss (1864–1949) achieve particular depth and sophistication. In his *Also sprach Zarathustra* (*Thus Spoke Zarathustra*) op 30 (1896), inspired by philosopher Friedrich Nietzsche's work, Strauss meant to convey in music "an idea of the evolution of the human race from its origin, through the various phases of development ..."[5] The opening brass fanfare of this work was used in Stanley Kubrick's *2001: A Space Odyssey* (1968), based on a short story by Arthur C. Clarke.

Symphonic poems (also orchestral poem, tone poem) Single movement programmatic orchestral work.

PLAYLIST OPTIONS
NINETEENTH-CENTURY CHORAL
AND ORCHESTRAL MUSIC

FIND

A video or audio performance of
- A particular choral work, such as
  - *A German Requiem* (1868) by Brahms
  - *Elijah, op 70* (1846–47) by Felix Mendelssohn
- Or a particular orchestral work, such as
  - *Symphony No 4 in E minor*, op 98 (1884/85) by Brahms
  - *Symphony Fantastique* (1830) by Berlioz
  - Symphony No. 9 *From the New World* (1893) by Dvořák
  - *Midsummer night's dream* (1826) by Mendelssohn
  - *Also sprach Zarathustra* (*Thus Spoke Zarathustra*) op 30 (1896) by Richard Strauss

OBSERVE
- Structure of the musical work
- Size of and makeup of the ensemble: which instruments and/or voices are performing, and what roles do they play relative to each other

ASK
- Is your example programmatic or absolute music? What are the relative merits of either type?

IV
OPERA AND DANCE

Although Italian, French, and German operatic traditions dominated in the nineteenth century, talents throughout Europe emerged to create a variety of national styles. The stories reveal much about the way Europeans saw themselves in the world: exoticism romanticized unfamiliar places and people. Borrowed melodic and rhythmic motives and colorful sets and costumes interacted to evoke far-off places and times. Both the music and the storylines were typically stereotyped and molded to the political and cultural bias of the storytellers.

Italian Opera

Bel canto
(It. "beautiful singing") "Beautiful singing" style of Italian opera, characterized by a prominent, expressive vocal melody with subservient orchestral accompaniment.

Coloratura
(It. "coloring") Elaborately ornamented style in vocal music, especially opera, which typically includes many notes rapidly executed. The term is also a reference to singers who specialize in this style, as in "coloratura soprano."

Verismo (It. "realism")* Realistic style in Italian operatic topics, which include vivid and often controversial portrayals of social hardship, cultural bias, and violence.

The **bel canto** (It. "beautiful singing") ideal can be considered Italian opera's most enduring legacy. The beauty of the vocal melody is emphasized while instrumental accompaniment is subordinate to the vocal music. *Bel canto* often uses **coloratura** passages: rapid, scale-like runs of ornamental notes performed by virtuosic singers, some of whom, such as "coloratura sopranos," specialize in this technique. Italian operas feature all-too-human characters across the socioeconomic spectrum with which their audiences can sympathize. Engaging stories include both comedy and tragedy in a kaleidoscope of settings and situations. The Italians maintained a strong contrast between recitative and aria. By the nineteenth century, they had developed scene "complexes" of recitatives, arias, vocal ensembles, and choruses with orchestral accompaniment to enhance the drama.

Giuseppe Verdi (1813–1901) was the most prominent Italian opera composer of his century. Although he experienced personal tragedy with the deaths of his wife and two children from illnesses early on, he eventually remarried and produced a total of 26 operas in his long and distinguished career. His settings range from the exoticism of *Aida* (1871), set in ancient Egypt, to the more realistic *La traviata* ("The Fallen Woman,"1853), which had much in common with the later **verismo** (realistic style), because of its unflinching focus on the moral hypocrisy of Verdi's own Italian society. Shakespeare was a favorite source for Verdi; *Macbeth* (1847) and *Otello* (1887) are among several works based on the English poet's dramas. Verdi also became a national hero during Italy's reunification as the new nation's most prominent composer.

German Opera

German opera provided a stark contrast to its Italian counterpart. Literature, history, and Germanic myth provided the plots, which emphasized the triumph of good over evil. Instrumental music held a much more important role than in Italian operas: themes could appear first and sometimes exclusively in the orchestra. Occasional passages of spoken dialogue combined with background music showed the influence of theatrical melodrama. (This would, in turn, influence the development of the twentieth-century eerie speech-like style, *Sprechstimme*, which will be described in Chapter 10, Modern Art Music, to follow.)

Figure 9-16 Portrait of Giuseppe Verdi by Giovanni Boldini (1842–1931).

Born the same year as Verdi, **Richard Wagner (1813–1883)** wrote music that was utterly different. Instead of the Italian recitative-aria dichotomy, vocal music in Wagner's operas occupied a middle ground between the two styles, creating an almost continuous vocal melody that was more declamatory than the Italian aria. The orchestral music was prominent to an often equal or greater degree than the vocal music. Wagner's harmonic style in his instrumental music was, in fact, profoundly influential in Western art music of the late nineteenth and early twentieth centuries. His delayed—and sometimes entirely absent—resolution to dissonance paved the way for the experimental compositions of later composers that would dismantle traditional tonality.

Leitmotifs (Ger. "leading motive") invest Wagner's dramas with powerfully effective aural associations. A musical motive that represents a character, item, emotion, setting, or idea in the drama, the *leitmotif* can be transformed, varied, and combined to suit each dramatic situation. It often first appears in the orchestra and only later, if at all, in the vocal melodies. It is a common tool for film score composers today, especially for film cycles, such as the *Star Wars* series by John Williams (see Chapter 2, American Music for Stage and Screen, "Film Music's Function").

Wagner wrote his own libretti, most of which were based on Germanic history and mythology. His four-opera cycle, *Der Ring des Nibelungen* (The Ring of the Nibelungs), written during the 1850s through the 1870s,

Leitmotif Term associated with Wagner and similar to *idée fixe*, *leitmotif* is a musical motive representing a person, place, object, or idea.

Richard Wagner: "True drama can be conceived only as resulting from the collective impulse of all the arts to communicate in the most immediate way with a collective public...Thus the art of tone... will realize in the collective artwork its richest potential ... For in its isolation music has formed itself

is based on Nordic mythology. The Ring operas opened at Bayreuth Festival Theater, which was built to Wagner's specifications. An annual festival dedicated to Wagner's music is still held annually in the town of Bayreuth to this day.

Figure 9-18 Scene from Wagner's *Götterdämmerung* ("Twilight of the Gods") by Josef Hoffman (1831–1904) for the original production.

Wagner was a controversial figure, however, to a degree that discredits his music for many. Born in Leipzig and raised with his earliest influences in theater and literature, his musical training did not begin until he was in his teens. A talented student, he quickly became a composer and conductor. He was also a political activist, and, in 1848, a participant in a failed uprising in Dresden. He fled to Switzerland, and while he was there, he wrote articles on politics and art that passionately espoused his nationalist perspectives. His anti-Semitic essay, "Judaism in Music" (1850), along with his later writings that claimed the superiority of the Aryan race, inspired Nazi Germany over 80 years later to use Wagner's music to symbolize its own nationalist sentiments. As a result, Israel banned performances of Wagner's music for many years, and his concerts continue to generate controversy there and elsewhere.

Figure 9-19 1875 Photo of Georges Bizet by Etienne Carjat (1828–1906).

Stage Music Beyond Italy and Germany

Spectacle was important in French opera, which included dance in its grand displays of choruses and orchestral music. **Georges Bizet (1838–1875)** wrote the music to *Carmen* (1875). Its colorful melodies and syncopated rhythms evoke the exotic setting of a Spanish Romani community. The title character's frank sexuality and violent death, however, make this an example of *verismo,* as well, and also created intense controversy at the time. Nevertheless, *Carmen* remains one of the most famous and beloved operas in the repertory.

Two prominent nineteenth-century composers of stage music came from Russia with very different styles. **Modest Mussorgsky (1839–1881)** was one of a group of composers known as "The Mighty Five" who spurned the Western European musical establishment in favor of a more independent and idiomatic Russian approach although they appreciated and were influenced by many innovative composers from Eastern and Western Europe, such as Chopin, Liszt, and Berlioz. His Russian-language opera, *Boris Godunov* (1874), is based on a historical plot about the sixteenth-century tsar for whom the opera is named. It is especially famous for its coronation scene, which includes elements of Russian folk melodies.

Although **Piotr Il'yich Tchaikovsky (1840–1893)** wrote music that was much closer to Western European influences, he, too, included Russian folk-like melodies in his music. Tchaikovsky wrote one opera, but he is most famous for his ballets, which include *Swan Lake* (1876), *Sleeping Beauty* (1889), and *The Nutcracker* (1892). His musical style's ideal partnership with dance, along with its fairytale charm, earned Tchaikovsky's place as the nineteenth century's most important ballet composer.

Light, comedic operetta, which is shorter than serious opera and includes spoken dialogue, was in demand throughout Europe. England produced the famous collaboration that is still popular today. Composer **Arthur Sullivan (1842–1900)** collaborated with librettist W. S. Gilbert (1836–1911) to create a series of hilarious operettas that quickly became international favorites, many of which mercilessly mocked pompous grand opera conventions. One of their most famous songs is the **patter song** "I am the very model of a modern major general" from *Pirates of Penzance* (1879), which is meant to be sung as quickly as is humanly possible for comic effect.

Patter song Vocal style in which many syllables of text are sung as quickly as possible for comic effect.

Figure 9-20 Mezzosoprano Celestine Galli-Mariá who played the role of *Carmen* in the first production, 1875. Portrait by Henri Lucien Doucet (1856–1895).

Figure 9-21 A scene from Act II of Tchaikovsky's *Swan Lake*, Tblisi, Georgia, 2007.

Figure 9-22 A scene from Opera Australia's production of *Pirates of Penzance*, 2007.

PLAYLIST OPTIONS
NINETEENTH-CENTURY OPERA

FIND

A video performance, with translation if needed, of a scene from an opera or operetta, such as

- Rossini's *Il barbiere di Siviglia* (The Barber of Seville, 1816)
- Verdi's *La traviata* ("The Fallen Woman," 1853) or *Aida* (1871)
- Giacomo Puccini's *Madama Butterfly* (1904)
- Wagner's *Tristan und Isolde* (1857–59) or his first opera from the Ring cycle, *Das Rheingold* ("The Rhine Gold," 1857)
- Bizet's *Carmen* (1875)
- Mussorgsky's *Boris Godunov* (1874)
- Gilbert and Sullivan's *Pirates of Penzance* (1879) or *The Mikado* (1885)

OBSERVE

- Melodic style; aria-recitative alternation, or something different.
- Role of instrumental music relative to the vocal music.

ASK

- What is the setting of the story, and how does the music evoke the place and time? If the setting is "exotic," what does it say about the European attitude toward and relationship with the foreign culture?
- If this is a comic scene: what is the ultimate target of the joke? (It could be a social class, a personality type, or even opera itself.)

CHAPTER 9 VOCABULARY & IMPORTANT FIGURES

Vocabulary

Bel canto (It. "beautiful singing")

Character piece

Coloratura (It. "coloring")

Exoticism

Idée fixe

Leitmotif

Lied (Ger. "song," pl. *lieder*) or art song

Miniature

Modified strophic form

Parlor song

Part song

Patter song

Piano quintet

Piano trio

Program music

Recital

Rubato (It. "robbed or stolen time")

Song cycle

Symphonic poems (also orchestral poem, tone poem)

Through composed

Verismo (It. "realism")

Important Figures

Hector Berlioz (1803–1869)

Georges Bizet (1838–1875)

Johannes Brahms (1833–1897)

Fryderyck Chopin (1810–1849)

Eugéne Delacroix (1798–1863)

Antonín Dvořák (1841–1904)

Johann Wolfgang Goethe (1749–1832)

Louis Moreau Gottschalk (1829–1869)

Franz Liszt (1811–1886)

Felix Mendelssohn (1809–1847)

Fannie Mendelssohn Hensel (1805–1847)

Modest Mussorgsky (1839–1881)

Franz Schubert (1797–1828)

Clara Wieck Schumann (1819–1896)

Robert Schumann (1810–1856)

Arthur Sullivan (1842–1900) (Composer of the "Gilbert and Sullivan" collaboration, with lyricist W. S. Gilbert (1836–1911)

Piotr Il'yich Tchaikovsky (1840–1893)

Giuseppe Verdi (1813–1901)

Richard Wagner (1813–1883)

ENDNOTES

[1] From "Chopin's Virtuosity," in The Collected Writings of Franz Liszt: F. Chopin, edited and translated by Janita R. Hall-Swadley, Scarecrow Press, 2011, p. 126.

[2] From "The Prize Symphony" (1836), as printed in Schumann on Music: A Selection from the Writings, edited and translated by Henry Pleasants, Dover Books on Music, 2011.

[3] As printed in Nancy B. Reich, *Clara Schumann: The Artist and the Woman,* Ithica and London: Cornell University Press, 2001, p. 215.

[4] From a letter to Adolf Schubring, as printed in Styra Avins, *Johannes Brahms: Life and Letters,* Oxford and New York, Oxford University Press, 1997, pp. 283–284.

[5] As quoted in Hugh Macdonald, "Symphonic poem," Grove Music Online. Oxford Music Online. Oxford University Press, accessed December 27, 2016, http://www.oxfordmusiconline.com/subscriber/article/grove/music/27250.

[6] As printed in Kristine Forney, Andrew Dell'Antonio, and Joseph Machlis, The Enjoyment of Music, 12th ed., W. W. Norton, 2015, p. 339.

Image Credits

- Figure 9-1: Josef Danhauser / Copyright in the Public Domain.
- Figure 9-2: Caspar David Friedrich / Copyright in the Public Domain.
- Figure 9-3: Eugene Delacroix / Copyright in the Public Domain.
- Figure 9-4: Eugene Delacroix / Copyright in the Public Domain.
- Figure 9-5: Wilhelm August Rieder / Copyright in the Public Domain.
- Figure 9-6: Julius Schmid / Copyright in the Public Domain.
- Figure 9-7: Moritz Daniel Oppenhiem / Copyright in the Public Domain.
- Figure 9-8: James Warren Childe / Copyright in the Public Domain.
- Figure 9-9a: Franz Hanfstaengl / Copyright in the Public Domain."
- Figure 9-9b: Louis-Auguste Bisson / Copyright in the Public Domain.
- Figure 9-10: Josef Kriehuber / Copyright in the Public Domain.
- Figure 9-11: Franz von Lenbach / Copyright in the Public Domain.
- Figure 9-12: C. Brasch / Copyright in the Public Domain.
- "Figure 9-13:
- Mathew Brady / Copyright in the Public Domain."
- Figure 9-14: Source: https://sgtr.files.wordpress.com/2011/06/berlioz.jpg.
- Figure 9-15: Source: https://commons.wikimedia.org/wiki/File:Dvorak.jpg.
- Figure 9-16: Giovanni Boldini / Copyright in the Public Domain.
- Figure 9-17: Pierre Petit / Copyright in the Public Domain.

Where do we come from? What are we? Where are we going? Primitivist painting by Paul Gauguin (1848–1903)

CHAPTER
10

Modern Art Music

Twentieth-century Europe began with the legacy of late romanticism. Passionate and agonizing themes in the works of composers who bridged the turn of the century, such as Gustav Mahler and Richard Strauss, provide signs that the cult of emotion was still one of the most powerful forces in art music. Poe's nineteenth-century horror stories inspired twentieth-century musical settings, such as Serge Rachmaninov's choral symphony, *The Bells* (1913).

Fin de siècle (Fr. "end of the century") literary and artistic movements, however, fueled by new ways of imagining the older concepts of exoticism, nature, and human emotion, rocked the boat and launched the **avant-garde**. Sigmund Freud's (1856–1939) explorations of the subconscious significantly influenced the Western world's trajectory into modernism. As colonized nations around the world sought the same freedoms lionized by the European Enlightenment, exoticism seemed to pivot into **nationalism** even among the European colonizers themselves. The devastating effects of two world wars inspired passionate—and often bitter—artistic expressions of trauma and profound disillusionment. Mass migrations, in large part to American shores, brought an abundance of European talents in music and many other fields to the US by the mid-twentieth century. This chapter describes the stories and selected works of a number of composers personally affected by war and its aftermath.

The twentieth century brought new technology that enabled people to hear—and later see—each other almost instantly. As a result, science

Avant-garde (Fr. "Vanguard")
Ultramodern, experimental art; in music associated with a wide variety of composers, especially Schoenberg and Cage.

Nationalism Used here in regard to musical style, the musical expression of national or ethnic identity.

and the humanities, including music, transcended local communities with new paradigms of "cultural or "national" identities. In this chapter, we will hear twentieth-century music give voice to the nostalgia, angst, broken-heartedness, resilient faith, and unbounded creativity of its musicians and listeners.

I
EARLY TWENTIETH-CENTURY ART MUSIC

Early-twentieth-century art music began with a foundation of romantic idioms from various nationalist perspectives. Wagner's influence was particularly powerful for the most prominent Germanic composers. Gustav Mahler (1860–1911) showed both Beethoven's and Wagner's influence in his expansive symphonic music, some of which include large choruses: his *Symphony No. 8 in E flat Major* (1906–7) is nicknamed "Symphony of a Thousand." Richard Strauss (1864–1949) devoted himself to opera after mastering the symphonic poem genre (see Chapter 9, Romantic Era Music, "Nineteenth-Century Choral and Orchestral Works"). His stage works carry Wagner's ideas forward with the use of leitmotif and harmonically complex music in his operas, such as *Salome* (1905), on the brutal and hedonistic story of John the Baptist's execution.

Visual and Literary Arts Inspire Music

Grounded in nineteenth-century styles, art music composers were also ready to move forward with new perspectives and musical techniques. Some of the most innovative musical styles had roots in visual and literary artistic movements, especially impressionism, primitivism, and expressionism.

Debussy and Impressionism

The impressionist painters of late-nineteenth-century France were downright revolutionary in their break with tradition. They rejected the formal styles of the past: instead of posed portraits of families sitting still with hands folded, they painted spontaneous scenes of people going about their daily lives. They rejected the photographic realism of the earlier nineteenth-century painters and, instead, emphasized the "first impression" of a subject with light and color. Although many critics of their time denounced them, this artistic movement inspired some of the most influential compositions of the early twentieth century.

French composer **Claude Debussy (1862–1918)** developed a musical style that paralleled the impressionists' fascination with light, color, spontaneity, and ambiguity.

Figure 10-2 *Girls at the Piano*, 1892, by Pierre-Auguste Renoir (1841–1919).

Figure 10-3 *Dance at the Moulin de la Galette*, 1876, by Renoir.

We see spontaneous interaction, as well as the importance of music and the piano at home in Renoir's *Young Girls at the Piano* (1892) (see Figure 10-2). While the glass in the bottom right foreground of Renoir's *Dance at the Moulin de la Galette* sparkles (see Figure 10-3), the overhead lamps create speckles of light over everyone, expressing movement and

Figure 10-4 *Impression, Sunrise*, 1872, by Claude Monet (1840–1926).

celebration in a brilliant array of color. The musical analogy to color and light in the visual arts can be **timbre** and pitch range in music. Timbre, also known as "tone color," became a profoundly important musical element in Debussy's orchestral music. The sonic qualities of individual musical instruments are highlighted as distinct personalities.

The blurred boundaries in Monet's *Impression, Sunrise* helped earn **impressionism** its name from a disapproving critic. Water, hazy sky, and smoke seem to melt together to obscure the places where one begins and the other leaves off. Debussy blurs boundaries in music with meter, a musical boundary in time. In what has been called **floating rhythm**, his music often avoids any clear definition of metric pattern: much of his music is **nonmetric**.

Harmony is also obscured in Debussy's music when dissonances are not resolved, and our sense of "home" as a point of return in the music is obscured. He avoided the familiar **chord progressions** that lead listeners through the predictable circle of "home," "away from home," and back to "home." He also broke with longstanding musical practices of his time when he used **scale** patterns from other places and other times. This created the unfamiliar sounding melodies and harmonies of his music. Debussy was innovative even as a student at the Paris Conservatory where he was known to look beyond Western art music for styles and movements in all of the arts and in the world beyond France. He became fascinated with Indonesian music when he heard a Javanese gamelan ensemble perform at the Paris Exhibition of 1889, and he later used similar melodies and rhythms in his music.

Debussy's compositions include orchestral, piano and chamber music, and French art songs. One work in particular generated intense controversy when it was choreographed and performed by the Russian ballet in Paris. *Prélude à "L'après-midi d'un faune"* ("Prelude to The Afternoon of a Faun," 1891–94; performed 1912), based on the symbolist poetry of Stéphane Mallarmé, is about a mythical creature, half man and half goat, who wakes up in the forest after an erotic dream, wondering whether he only dreamt about his encounter with nymphs … or was it real? The suggestive choreography and lead performance by Vaslav Nijinsky (1889/90–1950) shocked Parisian audiences. The music is a single movement programmatic instrumental work that mesmerizes listeners with its sensuous emphasis on tone color and its fluid, perpetually undefined rhythms and harmonies.

Timbre   Tone color, or quality; see Musical Elements Appendix.

Impressionism   Late-nineteenth-century French visual arts movement, featuring paintings that emphasize the "first impressions" of their subjects.

Floating rhythm Ambiguous rhythm and meter.

Nonmetric   Music with little or no discernible metric pattern; see Musical Elements Appendix.

Chord progression A series of chords; see Musical Elements Appendix.

Scale   An ascending or descending series of pitches, arranged in a specific pattern of intervals; see Musical Elements Appendix.

Figure 10-5 Vaslav Nijinsky as the Faun in Debussy's *Prelude to The Afternoon of a Faun*, 1912. Photo by Adolf de Meyer (1868–1946).

Primitivism and Stravinsky

In the year following Debussy's *Prélude* performance, Nijinsky choreographed and starred in a ballet by another composer who was deeply influenced by Debussy. The fury—and, according to some reports, even physical violence—between audience members on opening night of *Le Sacre du printemps* ("The Rite of Spring," 1913) brought the performance to a halt. The ballet, by Russian composer **Igor Stravinsky (1882-1971)**, is set in the distant, pagan past; a virgin sacrifices herself to appease the gods. It is not a traditional fairy tale, like Stravinsky's earlier ballets. In his own words, Stravinsky "wished to express the sublime uprising of Nature renewing herself—the whole pantheistic uprising of the universal harvest."[1]

Ostinato (It. "obstinate")
A repeating musical pattern (Chapter 7, Baroque Music).

His music shows Debussy's influence through his colorful, expressive orchestration. In *The Rite of Spring*, however, these traits are magnified through Stravinsky's own innovative style: pounding, dissonant **ostinato** passages, embedded in rich, complex textures are played by a large orchestra supplemented with heavy brass and percussion instruments. The quiet passages also express difficult emotions, such as anxiety and terror. The work is famously difficult to perform for both instrumentalists and dancers, but it has become an iconic favorite of early-twentieth-century orchestral literature. At the time, however, it was another assault on conservative Parisian audiences, reminiscent of Berlioz's *Symphonie Fantastique* almost a century before.

Primitivism Late-nineteenth-century visual arts movement inspired by the idea of an ancestral society close to nature, without the trappings of Western civilization.

Stravinsky's topic and musical style in *The Rite of Spring* has been described as **primitivist** after another visual arts movement inspired by the idea of a primal, ancestral society close to nature and without the trappings of modern civilization (see Figure 10-1). Primitivism can be seen as an outgrowth of nineteenth-century exoticism. Stravinsky was not tied to one style, however; he was also deeply influenced by impressionism and Debussy's music, and he explored experimental techniques described below; his strikingly original music is difficult to categorize. After leaving his native Russia in 1911, Stravinsky lived in Europe before moving to the United States during World War II. During his long career, he wrote orchestral works, vocal and dramatic works, and chamber music. His work is considered a major twentieth century-influence.

Expressionism Early-twentieth-century movement in visual arts, literature, and music, which emphasized the hidden emotions, such as anxiety and shame.

Expressionism and Schoenberg

Austrian composer **Arnold Schoenberg (1874–1951)** was also a painter; he was, in fact, an influential member of German **expressionism** in both

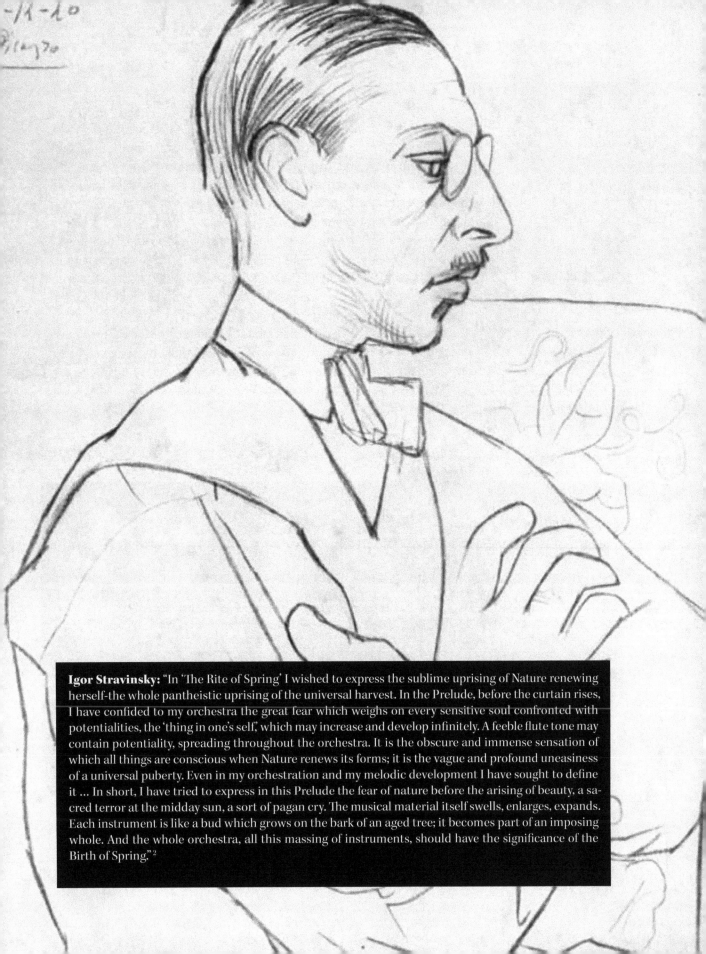

Igor Stravinsky: "In 'The Rite of Spring' I wished to express the sublime uprising of Nature renewing herself-the whole pantheistic uprising of the universal harvest. In the Prelude, before the curtain rises, I have confided to my orchestra the great fear which weighs on every sensitive soul confronted with potentialities, the 'thing in one's self', which may increase and develop infinitely. A feeble flute tone may contain potentiality, spreading throughout the orchestra. It is the obscure and immense sensation of which all things are conscious when Nature renews its forms; it is the vague and profound uneasiness of a universal puberty. Even in my orchestration and my melodic development I have sought to define it ... In short, I have tried to express in this Prelude the fear of nature before the arising of beauty, a sacred terror at the midday sun, a sort of pagan cry. The musical material itself swells, enlarges, expands. Each instrument is like a bud which grows on the bark of an aged tree; it becomes part of an imposing whole. And the whole orchestra, all this massing of instruments, should have the significance of the Birth of Spring."[2]

visual arts and in music. Expressionism was different from impressionism: the French focused on surface aspects of light and color, and on the "first impression" of the visual world. Expressionists, however, wanted to bring out what was hidden. Perhaps influenced by Sigmund Freud's (1856–1939) early-twentieth-century theories of the subconscious, expressionists depicted unwanted, distorted, and secret human emotions, such as anxiety and shame.

The *Pierre lunaire* song cycle, op. 21 (1912) exemplifies this style. Schoenberg set to music Albert Giraud's (1860–1929) poems about Pierrot, a comical theatrical character from European theater. The traditional Pierrot character was a sad clown; the expressionist lens adds neurosis, anxiety, and terror. In "*Der Mondfleck*" ("The Moonspot"), for instance, the clown mistakes a bright reflection of the moon on his black coat for a white spot that he must repeatedly try to wipe away. In "*Enthauptung*" ("Beheading"), Pierre imagines that he is beheaded by the moon, which is shaped like a scimitar.

Figures 10-7 & 10-8 Arnold Schoenberg self-portrait, 1910. And Arnold Schoenberg, 1927. Photo by Man Ray (1890–1976).

Figure 10-9 *Anxiety*, 1894; expressionist painting by Advard Munch (1863–1944).

Schoenberg's earliest compositions, such as *Verklärte Nacht* ("Transfigured Night," 1899), used the lush, tonal harmonies of the late romantic era. Absolutely no tonal center, however, exists for the *Pierre lunaire* songs. Schoenberg was experimenting with **atonality** at the time in which there is no hierarchy of pitches or chords and no "home" to return to. *All* the music is "away from home" and unfamiliar. Melodies, rhythms,

Atonality Music without tonality or total center and, thus, no distinction between dissonance and consonance.

and harmonic textures in atonal music often sound random in atonal music; performers and listeners are challenged to find points of reference that would make the music meaningful. Furthermore, Schoenberg uses the eerie **Sprechstimme** (Ger. "speaking voice") performance style for this work. Influenced by melodrama (see Chapter 9, Romantic Era Music, "German Opera"), *Sprechstimme* is a vocal style somewhere in between the spoken and sung voice. It can be rhythmically exact, but it is pitched more like either an exaggerated spoken voice or a whine rather than like a singing voice. No subject could be more suited to these experimental techniques than Pierrot, the clown who experiences nightmarish images.

By the early 1920s, Schoenberg began to develop a new, and completely different, tonal language. In the **twelve-tone** or **serialist method** (also called **serialism**), a **tone row**, or series of all twelve pitches used in Western music, are arranged in an order chosen by the composer. The musical work progresses strictly on the tone row: the notes must proceed in order. Chords can include groups of notes on the row because they are played at the same time, but the rule is to never jump ahead or behind on the row. The row can be used backwards, however, or upside down, in patterns known as **retrograde** and **inversion**, respectively, and even in **retrograde inversion**, the combination of the two (see Figure). Schoenberg's earliest twelve-tone composition is his *Piano Suite*, op 25 (1925), modeled on J. S. Bach's keyboard suites.

Figure 10-10 Schoenberg's tone row from Variations for Orchestra op. 31 (1928). "P" ("Prime") is the original tone row, "R" ("Retrograde") is the tone row backwards, "I" (Inversion) is the tone row inverted, or upside down with the opposite contour, and "IR" ("Retrograde Inversion") is the tone row both backwards and inverted.

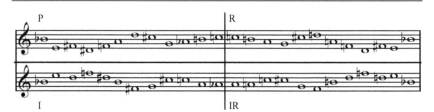

He was later to use twelve-tone music to powerful effect in his *A Survivor from Warsaw*, op. 46 (1947), for narrator, orchestra, and chorus. This work was based on the written account of a survivor of the horrific 1944 Warsaw Uprising during World War II. With expectations of Soviet support that never materialized, the Polish resistance fought German forces for over two months in desperate conditions before their loss to the German occupation.

Sprechstimme (Ger. "speaking voice") Speech-like vocal technique characterized by melodramatic or eerie effect; especially associated with Schoenberg.

Twelve-tone method, or serialism Twentieth-century method of composition devised by Schoenberg in which each of the 12 notes of the octave are placed in a particular order, or tone row, and are not repeated out of that order.

Tone row Particular arrangement of all 12 pitches of the octave in serialist compositions.

Retrograde Melody or tone row presented backwards.

Inversion Melody or tone row presented introverted (upside down).

Retrograde inversion Melody or tone row presented both backwards and inverted (upside down).

The twelve-tone method attracted many composers throughout the twentieth century. Many, including Stravinsky, experimented with it for a time, and some used it for their entire careers. Music based on the twelve-tone method can sound random to listeners, but this depends on the tone row and on the composer's style. Schoenberg, who was born in Vienna, left Germany in 1933 when the Nazis came to power. He settled in the US and became a professor at UCLA for the remainder of his career.

Nationalist Perspectives

Expressions of **nationalism** in Western art music outside of Germany include the work of Spanish composers Isaac Albeniz (1860–1909) and Manuel de Falla (1876–1946), who channeled Andalusian folk music and flamenco idioms in their vocal, keyboard, and orchestral music. Ralph Vaughan Williams (1872–1958) infused his music with English folk songs and influences from past English composers. In Finland, Jean Sibelius (1865–1957) expressed his deeply felt patriotism with romantic symphonic and vocal music known for its lyricism.

Nationalism Used here in regard to musical style, the musical expression of national or ethnic identity.

Hungarian composer and pianist **Béla Bartók (1881–1945)** was also an ethnomusicologist who studied Hungarian folk music. He collected songs "in the field" in Hungary much like John and Alan Lomax did in the US (see Chapter 1, American Traditional Music, "The Lomax Family and the American Folk Music Revival"). The encroaching German domination in Eastern Europe, however, prompted him to emigrate to the US in 1940, which cut short his research. He lived his remaining years in New York City's concrete jungle, sorely missing his homeland.

Polytonality Two or more tonalities occurring simultaneously.

Figure 10-11 Béla Bartók, 1927.

The Hungarian folk music Bartók studied strongly influenced his compositions. He sometimes quoted folk tunes, and many of his melodies and rhythms simply evoke Eastern European folk music style. But he was also a modernist and well educated in art music traditions of the past. His music is known for its clear and often symmetrical classical structures, **polytonal** harmonic language, and innovative, constantly changing meters. His *Concerto for*

Figure 10-12 Bartók collecting folk songs in Eastern European countryside with a gramophone, 1908.

Figure 10-13 Amy Beach.

Orchestra, BB 123 (1943) juxtaposes modern and folk elements throughout its five movements. The fourth movement is notable for its lyrical quotation of the popular Hungarian song, *Szep vagy, gyönyörű vagy Magyarország* ("You are lovely, you are beautiful, Hungary").

To be a "nationalist" composer in the United States would always mean many things. Americans who bridged the nineteenth and twentieth centuries were already referencing a multitude of musical styles from Europe and the Americas, including a range of Black musical genres and glimpses of Native American songs.

The works of **Amy Marcy Beach (1867–1944),** which were inspired by nineteenth-century German romantic traditions, do not seem to be nationalist at first glance. Her *Piano Quintet* (1907), for example, is based on a Brahms theme, embellished with her own more adventurous harmonies. Her *Symphony* op 32 (1897), however, was subtitled "Gaelic

Symphony" for its inclusion of melodies from the British Isles, and much later in her career, she included Inuit (Native American) melodies in her *String Quartet* (1929). Beach was married to a prominent physician who supported her work as a composer, a situation that provided ample time and opportunity for Beach to compose extended works. Large-scale projects are especially difficult for people who are marginalized or in some way isolated from equal education and opportunity as women generally have been in the field of composition. Beach, however, achieved international recognition during her lifetime.

Scott Joplin (c. 1867–1917) was Beach's contemporary and, in fact, may have been born the same year. He is well known for his **ragtime** piano compositions; however, he worked hard throughout his career on extended art music works such as opera and orchestral music, most of which has been lost. One opera exists (albeit without its orchestration) for which Joplin wrote both music and libretto in 1911: *Treemonisha*. Set on an Arkansas plantation run by former slaves in the 1880s, the heroine of the story opposes a group of men who practice phony magic in order to take advantage of her community. She champions education and becomes the leader of her community. The music includes a range of standard operatic styles, including recitatives, arias, ensembles, and choruses, but the opera also features American popular song and Black musical idioms, including a call and response spiritual scene, a barbershop quartet style **part song**, and a grand ragtime choral finale. Joplin was not able to produce *Treemonisha* during his lifetime; it would not be staged until 1972, 61 years after it was written. Its success resulted in a posthumous Pulitzer Prize for Joplin in 1974.

Band music became especially popular in the United States after the Civil War. Composed of wind and percussion instruments, **marching and concert bands** sprang up in local communities across the country, performing the thunderous, energetic music that became an iconic symbol of American patriotism in the early twentieth century. **John Philip Sousa (1854–1932)** conducted a US Marine Corps band until 1890 when he left to organize his own band. Sousa composed music for his band, including

Ragtime   Syncopated musical genre popular in the late nineteenth and early twentieth centuries (Chapter 3, Jazz).

Part song   Short choral work, divided into soprano, alto, tenor, and bass ranges ("SATB") (See Chapter 1, American Traditional Music, and Chapter 9, Romantic Era Music).

Marching band, concert band   Ensembles composed of wind and percussion instruments and which often specialize in marching music.

Figure 10-14   *Treemonisha* sheet music cover, 1911.

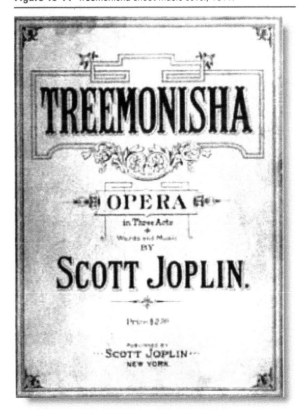

Figure 10-15 John Philip Sousa, 1900. Photo by Elmer Chickering (1857–1915).

the official national march of the United States, *The Stars and Stripes Forever!* (1892). Known as "the March King," Sousa toured with his band tirelessly; between 1892 and 1931, they logged thousands of performances throughout the US, several European tours (the first of which may have provided Europe's first introduction to ragtime), and one world tour. His band marches are sectional works; before the final section is the striking and contrasting duel-like exchange between instrument families called the **break strain** or **dogfight**. He often included counter-melodies in his band music, which added an extra level of artistry and interest. Sousa was a seasoned musician who also arranged music written by others for his band, composed his own operettas, and once conducted a Gilbert and Sullivan operetta performance.

American composer, organist, and businessman **Charles Ives (1874–1954)** worked outside of the mainstream in relative isolation but, nevertheless, became a significant figure in American art music. Born in Connecticut to a bandleader father, Ives grew up with the sounds of American marching band music, parlor songs, minstrel show tunes, and Protestant hymns. Ives is placed here under the "nationalist" heading because much of his music shows these influences through quotation and paraphrase, but his style was extremely multifaceted. He was also an experimental composer of great depth who used traditions and techniques from Western art music.

Ives, who was first trained by his father, was active musically from a very young age. He played organ in church professionally from the age of 14 and later studied music formally while he was a student at Yale. His career was unusual; he worked in the insurance business and composed in his spare time after work and on weekends. He was an inspired composer, however, who created a widely varied body of work that included both instrumental and vocal music.

An example of a light work inspired by the parlor song genre is *Memories* (1897), a short song in two parts: "Very Pleasant," in patter style with a whistled passage, and the nostalgic "Rather Sad." His symphonic poem, *The Unanswered Question* (1908), however, demonstrates his experimentalist and philosophical leanings. He ascribes symbolic meaning to the musical instruments in this excerpt from his forward to performers in the published score: "The trumpet intones 'The Perennial Question of Existence,' and states it in the same tone of voice each time. But the hunt for 'The Invisible Answer' undertaken by the flute and other human beings, becomes gradually more active, faster and louder…"[3] The texture of this mesmerizing work is multilayered: the trumpet's statement is punctuated by occasional active, agitated sounds from woodwinds, all against a backdrop of slow-moving chords played by bowed stringed instruments.

Two Black American composers came to prominence in the 1930s, both of whom grew up in Little Rock, Arkansas, not far from each other. Despite the turn of the century's encroaching Jim Crow laws throughout the South that mandated segregation, their community offered (albeit only temporarily) relative safety and opportunity during their childhoods—conditions that surely helped to nurture these two significant American talents.

Florence Beatrice Price (1887–1953) demonstrated her abilities early enough to enroll in the New England Conservatory in Boston by the age 14 to study keyboard and composition. After her studies, she spent most of her career in Chicago. She focused on her extended works, such as symphonies, concertos, and chamber music, but acknowledgment from publishers was difficult. To support herself and her two children, she taught, performed on theater organ for silent films, wrote popular music and teaching pieces, and orchestrated arrangements for WGN, Chicago's premier radio station.

Figure 10-17 Marian Anderson, photo by Carl Van Vechten.

In 1932, she won a competition for her *Symphony in E minor*, and at its 1933 premier by the Chicago Symphony Orchestra, she became the first Black American woman to have an orchestral work performed by a major American orchestra. Perhaps the climax of her career, however, was in 1939, when vocalist **Marian Anderson (1897–1993)** included works by Price in her Lincoln Memorial performance in front of 75,000 people. This was an even more triumphant moment for Anderson, who had been denied access to the stage in Constitution Hall, the originally planned venue for her concert, because she was a Black singer. In the controversy that ensued, Eleanor Roosevelt and others arranged the Lincoln Memorial concert, which included Price's setting of the spiritual, *My soul's been anchored in de Lord*. Price wrote over 300 pieces, including her powerful setting of the Langston Hughes poem, *Song to the Dark Virgin*. Most of her works remain unpublished.

Florence B. Price: "My dear Dr. Koussevitzky: Unfortunately the work of a woman composer is preconceived by many to be light, froth, lacking in depth, logic and virility. Add to that the incident of race—I have Colored blood in my veins—and you will understand some of the difficulties that confront one in such a position...The few times I have been able to overcome this handicap in the past and to manage to get a score examined I have met with most gratifying results, as you will note in the comments of critics quoted in my folder. Now that duties connected with caring for parents and children have been lifted from my shoulders, I do so want to make tangible progress and to get examined and performed some of my accumulated scores. In keeping with one last promise to myself that I shall no longer <u>hang back</u> [underline Price's], I am now being so bold as to address you. I ask no concessions because of race or sex, and am willing to abide by a decision based solely on worth of my work. Will you be kind enough to examine a score of mine? Very truly yours, Mrs. Florence B. Price."[4]

On the surface, her style is generally romantic, but her infusion of Black musical idioms and topics adds deeper, and sometimes sharper, levels of meaning and depths of expression.

William Grant Still (1895–1978) studied composition formally at university and also worked with W. C. Handy arranging music for Handy's dance band (see Chapter 3, Jazz, "Blues"). Still broke racial barriers and gained prominence as a composer when his *Afro American Symphony* premiered in 1931 by the Rochester Philharmonic Symphony just two years before Price's premier in Chicago. Notably, his symphony included not only Black folk idioms but also jazz and blues: "I knew that I wanted to write a symphony; I knew that it had to be an American work; and I wanted to demonstrate how the blues, so often considered a lowly expression, could be elevated to the highest musical level."[5] Still's 150 compositions include stage, orchestral, and vocal works. He achieved international recognition and became known as the "Dean of Afro-American Composers."

PLAYLIST OPTIONS: EARLY TWENTIETH CENTURY ART MUSIC

FIND

+ An excerpt of a video performance of one of the stage works described in this section, such as

  + Strauss: *Salome* (1905)

  + Debussy: *Prélude à "L'après-midi d'un faune"* ("Prelude to The Afternoon of a Faun," 1891–94)

  + Stravinsky: *Le Sacre du printemps* ("The Rite of Spring," 1913)

  + Schoenberg: *A Survivor from Warsaw*, op. 46 (1947)

  + Joplin: *Treemonisha* (1911)

- An excerpt of a video or audio performance of an instrumental work described in this section, such as
  - Mahler: *Symphony No. 8 in E flat Major* ("Symphony of a Thousand," 1906–7)
  - Bartók: *Concerto for Orchestra*, BB 123 (1943)
  - Beach: *String Quartet* (1929)
  - Sousa: *Stars & Stripes forever!* (1892)
  - Ives: *The Unanswered Question* (1908)
  - Price: *Symphony in E Major* (1932)
  - Still: Afro-American Symphony (1931)

OBSERVE

- Topic
- Tonality (or the absence of it)

ASK

- What does the topic reveal about the composer's world view?
- Do you notice tension between tradition and modernism in your example?

II

MID-TWENTIETH-CENTURY ART MUSIC

Experimental composers continued to explore new and unusual ideas as the mid-twentieth century's *avant-garde*. Other composers used the idioms of the past as a foundation in ways that blend tradition, modernity, culture, and personal struggle. Nationalists continued to champion their countries and ethnicities with musical styles and topics.

Experimental Composers

What is music? Compositions by **John Cage (1912–1992)** seem to ask this question. Cage, who studied with Schoenberg among others, used the twelve-tone method early in his career before going on to explore other musical languages. He used nontraditional instruments such as tin cans, an electric buzzer, and electronically amplified noises in his own percussion ensemble. He composed for **prepared piano** in which a variety of objects are inserted between some of the strings, causing distinctive percussive sounds and at least partially muted pitches. The published score to his *Sonatas and Interludes* (1946–48) for prepared piano provides instructions to the pianist regarding which objects to place between the strings, and where to put them. This musical work shows a special focus on timbre. The theme, even though it has no words as a strictly instrumental solo piano work, is the portrayal of the eight permanent emotions of Indian aesthetics: the erotic, the heroic, the odious, anger, mercy, fear, sorrow, and wondrous.

Cage was strongly influenced by Asian aesthetics and musical practices throughout his career. He sometimes used the South Asian rhythmic system of **tala** (see Chapter 15, Music in India and Japan, "India's Music") in which music is organized into units of time rather than in the metric patterns of traditional Western art music. Later, inspired by Japanese Zen Buddhism, Cage developed his most radical aesthetic approach, which urged listeners to focus on the present moment rather than on the music of the past. The role of silence became significant in his music at this stage.

These ideas led to his pioneering concept of "chance" in music. Cage uses divination methods from the ancient Chinese text, the *I-Ching* ("*Book of Changes*"), in his *Music of Changes* for piano (1951) in which a coin toss determines the performance order of composed segments of music and an equal number of segments of silence. The order of performance in this work, therefore, is left completely up to chance.

One of Cage's most controversial works is *4'33"* (1952), which he originally planned to entitle *Silent Prayer*. The performance is indeed silent throughout the four-and-a-half-minute time frame of the work. Nevertheless, the score divides the work into three movements, each of which simply states the performance instruction familiar to orchestral musicians, *tacet* (Lat. "be silent"). The premiere performance in upstate New York included outdoor seating, which would have included ambient sounds of nature amplified by the utter silence on stage. What is the point? Perhaps Cage, an iconoclast, wanted to divert his audience from the traditional, reverential act of listening to respected composers

Prepared piano Piano music in which the piano has been "prepared" with items such as bolts, clips, and rubber bands placed in the strings, affecting the timbre; especially associated with John Cage.

Tala Metric and rhythmic structure in South Asian music; one specific rhythmic cycle (Chapter 15, Music in India and Japan).

John Cage: "What happens, for instance, to silence? That is, how does the mind's perception of it change? Formerly, silence was the time lapse between sounds, useful towards a variety of ends, among them that of tasteful arrangement...or that of expressivity, where silences in a musical discourse might provide pause or punctuation...Where none of these or other goals is present, silence becomes something else—not silence at all, but sounds, the ambient sounds. The nature of these is unpredictable and changing. These sounds (which are called silence only because they do not form part of a musical intention) may be depended upon to exist. The world teems with them, and is, in fact, at no point free of them...There are, demonstrably, sounds to be heard and forever, given ears to hear. Where these ears are in connection with a mind that has nothing to do, that mind is free to enter into the act of listening, hearing each sound just as it is..."[6]

and performers and to surrender to the sounds that happen around us, instead. Other composers, many of whom were influenced by Schoenberg and Cage, made experimentation a hallmark of their work.

Since American composer **Ruth Crawford Seeger's (1901–1953)** efforts to try new ways to use twelve-tone technique in the early 1930s, composers have been experimenting with **total serialism** in which twelve-tone techniques are applied to musical elements other than pitch. **Milton Babbitt (1916–2011)**, for instance, applied serial technique to rhythmic duration. An example of this is the live vocal performance combined with prerecorded electronic sounds in his *Philomel* (1964). The plot is based on a tale from Ovid's *Metamorphoses* in which, like so many of the stories, the characters transform into birds. It is a disturbing tale, not for the squeamish, but rich material for modern music. **Pierre Boulez (1925–2016)**, who was also a prominent conductor, applied dynamics and articulation in his work with serial techniques.

Other experimental composers did not use twelve-tone technique and went in other directions, instead. **György Ligeti (1923–2006)** pioneered **micropolyphony** in his vocal and instrumental music, which features densely textured **polyphonic** lines. His complex music is famously hard to perform. Director Stanley Kubrick used excerpts from several of Ligeti's works, including *Lux aeterna* (1966), in the 1968 film, *2001: A Space Odyssey*. **George Crumb (b. 1929)** uses unorthodox performance practices and innovative notation in his powerfully expressive works. One of his most famous works, *Black Angels: Thirteen Images from the Dark Land* for electric string quartet (1970), was, at least in part, a protest against the Vietnam War.

One of the most significant and original composers of the twentieth century, French composer and organist **Olivier Messiaen (1908–1992)** was a devout Catholic who sought to express religious faith and a sense of the eternal through his music. Heavily influenced by the impressionistic aspects of music by Debussy and Stravinsky, Messiaen used colorful harmonies and timbres and nonmetric rhythms. Like Debussy, Messiaen was interested in musical scales and rhythms from medieval Europe and from other parts of the world. But Messiaen went beyond the ambiguous tonality of Impressionism into **post-tonal** territory with complex rhythmic patterns that sometimes seem to

Total serialism
Compositional method popular among some composers in the mid-twentieth century in which twelve-tone technique is applied to musical elements other than pitch.

Micropolyphony A term associated with Ligeti; densely textured polyphonic lines.

Polyphony Musical texture which features two or more independent lines, or voices; see Musical Elements Appendix.

Figure 10-20 Olivier Messiaen, 1930.

Post-tonal music
Music of the twentieth century and later that is not tonal, such as atonal or serialist music.

simulate timelessness and an entirely unique treatment of melody. He was fascinated by birds, creatures with spiritual symbolic meaning for Messiaen, and over many years, he created rhythmic and melodic patterns to imitate a great variety of specific birdsongs in his music.

His chamber work, *Quartet for the End of Time* (1941) for violin, clarinet, cello, and piano, is a dramatic example of both his compositional virtuosity and his faith during a brutally difficult episode in his life. While serving in the French army during World War II, he was captured by the Germans and interned at a German prisoner of war camp. There, he met three other musicians, for whom, along with himself on keyboard, he wrote this quartet. The title refers to the apocalypse in the Bible's *Revelation*. The work is in eight movements, each one with a title and a description. For instance, the first movement is entitled *Liturgy of Crystal* ("The awakening of the birds"), and the last movement, *Praise to the Immortality of Jesus* ("The ascent toward God"). On a cold night in January 1941, and with one of the cello strings missing, Messiaen and his ensemble performed the work for 5,000 other camp inmates. Messiaen continued to compose in the years following the war. He described his compositional style in *La technique de mon langage musical* (*The Technique of My Musical Language*, 1944).

Nationalist Composers

Serge Prokofiev (1891–1953) and **Dmitry Shostakovich (1906–1975)** were both Russian composers in the Soviet Union although Prokofiev lived outside Russia for a time. They both used traditional styles of the past, blended with modern techniques. Prokofiev wrote film scores and operas as well as symphonies; Shostakovich focused on his symphonic works although he wrote in other genres as well. They both had to cope with heavy restrictions on artistic freedom as did many in all of the arts in the USSR during the twentieth century. This has complicated their legacies with ongoing debates on whether their artistic decisions were authentic or in some way coerced by the government. The craftsmanship and beauty of their music, however, as well as the poignancy of their situations, has ensured the lasting popularity and influence of their music.

Figure 10-21 From left: Sergei Prokofiev, Dmitri Shostakovich, and Armenian composer Aram Khachaturian.

One of the most prominent American composers of the twentieth century was **Aaron Copland (1900–1990)**. He experimented with the 12-tone method early in his career, but his language later developed into a tonal, accessible language that has become emblematic of American music. He absorbed many American idioms, including western folk music, sacred music, and jazz. His variations on the Shaker hymn, "'Tis the gift to be simple," from the ballet suite, *Appalachian Spring* (1943–44), is especially famous. Copland wrote chamber, symphonic, and stage works, as well as film scores. He is especially known for his ballets.

Figure 10-22 Aaron Copland, 1970.

The career of English composer **Benjamin Britten (1913–1976)** was marked by his humanitarian concerns as a pacifist during World War II and as a gay composer who wished for tolerance. Complete openness about his homosexuality in early to mid-twentieth-century England would have ended his career and sent him to jail, or worse. He likely expressed himself, however, under cover of an allegory about what it must be like to be surrounded by a hostile society in his opera, *Peter Grimes* (1944–45). A fisherman is accused of a crime and, chased by a mob from his own village, driven to suicide. Britten, his life partner tenor Peter Pears (1910–1986) who would perform the part of Peter Grimes, and librettist

Benjamin Britten, 1964: "When I am asked to compose a work for an occasion, great or small, I want to know in some detail the conditions of the place where it will be performed, the size and acoustics, what instruments or singers will be available and suitable, the kind of people who will hear it, and what language they will understand—and even sometimes the age of the listeners and performers. For it is futile to offer children music by which they are bored, or which makes them feel inadequate or frustrated, which may set them against music forever; and it is insulting to address anyone in a language which they do not understand…But we shouldn't worry too much about the so-called 'permanent' value of our occasional music. A lot of it cannot make much sense after its first performance, and it is quote a good thing to please people, even if only for today. That is what we should aim at—pleasing people today as seriously as we can, and letting the future look after itself." [7]

Montagu Slater (1902–1956) all helped shape the overall story. Disturbing contradictions in the title character's personality adds depth and power to the drama.

Britten rejected extreme, avant-garde musical techniques because he placed great value on the accessibility of his music to everyone, including amateurs and children, chiefly through his choral music. Yet his music is unmistakably modern: he uses a tonal musical language but in nontraditional ways. For instance, he might repeat a dissonant interval in such a way that it becomes part of the structure and the "center" or "home" of the musical work, as he often does in the *War Requiem* (1961–62), to express the central message of tragedy.

Britten was open about his pacifism in his *War Requiem*. He combined the traditional Latin Requiem mass with poetry by Wilfred Owen (1893–1918), an English soldier who was killed in France during World War I. The use of Owen's poetry with its bitter commentaries to interrupt the Latin text was a statement in itself. Owen's 1918 draft preface of a collection of poems is a devastating indictment of war:

> "This book is not about heroes. English poetry is not
> yet fit to speak of them.
> Nor is it about deeds, or lands, nor anything about
> glory, honour, might, majesty, dominion, or power,
> except War.
> Above all I am not concerned with Poetry.
> My subject is War, and the pity of War.
> The Poetry is in the pity."[8]

Owen had hoped to publish his book of war poems the following year, but he perished in battle at the age of 25 before he could fulfill his ambitions. Britten used an excerpt of the words above as a preface to the score of his *War Requiem*. The first performance, which had been commissioned for the opening of the new cathedral at Coventry (the old cathedral had been destroyed in 1940 during a World War II bombing raid), included a multinational cast of soloists as a symbol of reconciliation: English tenor Peter Pears, German baritone Dietrich Fischer-Dieskau, and Russian soprano Galina Vishnevskaya were meant to sing at the opening. (The Soviets forbade Vishnevskaya's travel to the opening concert, however, so English vocalist Heather Harper replaced her at the last moment. Vishnevskaya was allowed to travel the following year to record the work with Pears and Fischer-Dieskau.) The 1962 performance at the new cathedral's opening was a historic moment, therefore, not only for Britten but for England.

PLAYLIST OPTIONS
MID-TWENTIETH-CENTURY ART MUSIC

FIND

- An excerpt of a video or audio performance of one of the experimental works described in this section, such as
  - Cage: *4'33"* (1952)
  - Babbitt: *Philomel* (1964)
  - Ligeti: *Lux aeterna* (1966)
  - Crumb: *Black Angels: Thirteen Images from the Dark Land,* for electric string Quartet (1970)
  - Messiaen: *Quartet for the End of Time* (1941)
- An excerpt of a video or audio performance of one of the nationalist works described in this section, such as
  - Shostakovich: *Symphony No. 5* (1937)
  - Copland: *Appalachian Spring* (1943–44)
  - Britten: *War Requiem* (1961–62)

OBSERVE

- Tonality, or the lack of it
- Performance practices, such as instrumentation
- Programmatic references in instrumental music

ASK

- Does your example have a clear message?
- What does the composer say about community or nation if this is a nationalist work?

III
LATE TWENTIETH AND EARLY-TWENTY-FIRST CENTURY ART MUSIC

The visual arts continue to be a significant influence on music while the latest generations of composers exhibit a plethora of styles and techniques. Musicians forge new topics, notably in acoustics and the environment, and the boundaries between "art" and **"vernacular"** music begin to fade as old paradigms shift.

A style that repeats the barest essentials, **minimalism** is another movement that originated in the visual arts. The monochrome paintings by Yves Klein (1928–1962) and the repeating, interlocking shapes of Frank Stella (b. 1936) are two early examples (see Figure 10-24). Minimalist music, which features repeating or slowly changing basic musical elements, has strong connections with vernacular and world musical styles. It is, in many ways, a reaction against serialism and other extremely rational and relatively inaccessible styles that alienated audiences earlier in the twentieth century.

One of the early pioneers of this style, **Philip Glass (b. 1937)** frequently uses **ostinato** technique with repetitive and very slowly changing patterns over time. His music emphasizes melody and consonant harmonies. Glass absorbed influences from South Asian musical processes through Indian sitarist Ravi Shankar (1920–2012), especially in terms of rhythmic organization (see Chapter 15, Music in India and Japan, "Music of India"). Glass's opera, *Einstein on the Beach* (1976, in collaboration with Robert Wilson, libretto by Knowles, Childs, and Johnson), does not feature a traditional story line and eliminates many other operatic conventions.

Vernacular music
The music that is most accessible, or familiar, to most people in a given culture.

Minimalism Musical style characterized by repetitive or slowly changing basic musical elements.

Figure 10-24 IKB 191 (International Klein Blue), monochrome painting by French painter Yves Klein (1928–1962).

Figure 10-25 Philip Glass, 2007.

This was a radical departure from the modern conception of opera.

Glass is also a film composer; his music for the Qatsi Trilogy films with director Godfrey Reggio are outstanding examples of the marriage between minimalist music and visual media. These films, also without conventional storylines, feature images of people around the world going about their daily lives. The second in the trilogy, *Powaqqatsi: Life in Transformation* (1988), shows people from the Southern Hemisphere at work, in transit, and in celebration. Opposite from the usual film score process, much of the music was composed before the film was shot, and, in some cases, the camera crew listened to Glass's music as they filmed. His mesmerizing score includes melodic and rhythmic idioms from South Asia and other parts of the world. The entire concept of the film trilogy, including the music, rejects the traditional Western idea of structure as does the visual aspect of film itself. Since the late twentieth century, Glass has exerted a significant influence on opera and film music. Two other important minimalist composers include John Adams (b. 1947) and Steve Reich (b. 1936).

Finnish composer **Kaija Saariaho (b. 1952)** uses techniques from **spectral music** in which the acoustic properties of sound (sound spectra) are used as the conceptual basis of musical compositions instead of the traditional concepts of musical elements such as rhythm and melody. These ideas developed from the experiments of early and mid-twentieth-century electronic music composers in Europe. Her opera, *L'amour de loin* (2000), has for its topic a twelfth-century troubadour and his experience of *fin' amor* (see Chapter 6, Antiquity to 1600, "Medieval Secular Music"), artfully blending avant-garde music with medieval references.

John Luther Adams (b. 1953) is an American percussionist and composer, based for many years in Alaska. His passionate focus on nature and the environment led him to pioneer a style known as **sonic geography** in which geographical space and environmental sounds of nature are integral aspects of the music. One can hear waves slowly crashing in his orchestral work, *Become Ocean* (2013). At the University

Spectral music Music in which the acoustic properties of sound (sound spectra) are used as the conceptual basis of musical compositions instead of traditional concepts of musical elements such as rhythm and melody.

Sonic geography Music in which geographical space and environmental sounds of nature are integral aspects of the music. Sonic geography is especially associated with John Luther Adams.

of Alaska's Museum of the North, Adams created a sound and light environment exhibit entitled *Place Where You Go Listen* in which colors and sounds change with the sun, moon, seismic vibrations, and the aurora borealis.

American composer **Jennifer Higdon (b. 1962)** wrote her poignant orchestral tone poem *blue cathedral* (2000) as a memorial to her younger brother, Andrew Blue Higdon. Her music is neoromantic but also modernist, with a focus on timbre. She says of this work, "I wanted to create the sensation of contemplation and quiet peace at the beginning, moving toward the feeling of celebration and ecstatic expansion of the soul, all the while singing along with that heavenly music."[9]

Figure 10-26 Jennifer Higdon with her cat, Beau.

American violinist **Caroline Shaw (b. 1982)** was the youngest ever recipient of the Pulitzer Prize in 2013 for her *Partita for Eight Voices*. Her music is an eclectic blend of vernacular and improvisatory idioms, with traditional art music influences as well: each of the partita's four movements is named after baroque dance genres, such as "sarabande" (see Chapter 7, Baroque Music, on the sarabande, "Instrumental Music").

Sarabande Popular dance form, which originated as a lively triple meter dance in Latin America, and later came to be quite slow in baroque Europe (Chapter 7, Baroque Music).

**PLAYLIST OPTIONS
LATE TWENTIETH AND EARLY
TWENTY-FIRST CENTURY ART MUSIC**

FIND

- A video or audio performance of one of the works described in this section, such as
  - Glass: Powaqqatsi: *Life in Transformation* (1988)
  - Saariaho: *L'amour de loin* (2000)
  - Adams: *Become Ocean* (2013)
  - Higdon: *blue cathedral* (2000)
  - Shaw: *Partita for Eight Voices* (2013)

OBSERVE

- Tonality, or the lack of it … or whether tonality is even an issue here
- The performance context and genre

ASK

- What counts as musical elements in your example… only the traditional concepts, or something new?
- What does your example say about the possibilities for art music of the future?

CHAPTER 10 VOCABULARY & IMPORTANT FIGURES

Vocabulary

Atonality

Avant-garde (Fr. "Vanguard")

Break strain (or "dogfights")

"Dogfights"

Expressionism

Floating rhythm

Impressionism

Inversion

Marching band, concert band

Micropolyphony

Minimalism

Nationalism

Part song

Polytonality

Post-tonal music

Prepared piano

Primitivism

Retrograde

Retrograde inversion

Sonic geography

Spectral music

Sprechstimme (Ger. "speaking voice")

Tone row

Total serialism

Twelve-tone method, or serialism

Important Figures

John Luther Adams (b. 1953)

Milton Babbitt (1916–2011),

Béla Bartók (1881–1945)

Pierre Boulez (1925–2016)

Amy Marcy Beach (1867–1944),

Benjamin Britten (1913–1976)

John Cage (1912–1992)

George Crumb (b. 1929)

Aaron Copland (1900–1990)

Claude Debussy (1862–1918)

Philip Glass (b. 1937)

Jennifer Higdon (b. 1962)

Charles Ives (1874–1954)

Scott Joplin (c. 1867–1917)

György Ligeti (1923–2006)

Olivier Messiaen (1908–1992)

Florence Beatrice Price (1887–1953)

Serge Prokofiev (1891–1953)

Kaija Saariaho (b. 1952)

Arnold Schoenberg (1874–1951)

Caroline Shaw (b. 1982)

Dmitry Shostakovich (1906–1975)

Ruth Crawford Seeger (1901–1953)

John Philip Sousa (1854–1932)

William Grant Still (1895–1978)

Igor Stravinsky (1882–1971)

ENDNOTES

[1] Igor Stravinsky, "What I Wished to Express in "The Rite of Spring," copyright in the public domain.

[2] Igor Stravinsky, "What I Wished to Express in 'The Rite of Spring." From the English translation by Edward B. Hill in the Boston Evening Transcript, February 12 1916, of a Stravinsky interview with Ricciotto Canudo the morning after the premiere, for Montjoie, May 29, 1913; reprinted in V. Stravinsky and Craft, Stravinsky in Pictures and Documents, pp. 524–526.

[3] As quoted in Mark Evan Bonds, *Listen to This*, Upper Saddle River, NJ: Prentice Hall, 2009, Chapter 41, pp. 368–373.

[4] Price's Nov. 6, 1943, letter to Boston Symphony Orchestra conductor Serge Koussevitzky. Her letter was not answered.

[5] As quoted in Eileen Southern, *The Music of Black Americans: A History*, 3rd ed, New York: W. W. Norton, p. 434.

[6] John Cage, "Changes," in Silence: Lectures and Writings, Middletown, CT: Wesleyan University Press, 1961, pp. 22–23 and 31–32, as printed in

Burkholder, Grout, and Palisca, A History of Western Music, 9th ed., p. 941.

[7] From "On Receiving the First Aspen Award," Britten's acceptance speech in Aspen, Colorado, July 31, 1964, as posted on the Aspen Music Festival website: https://www.aspenmusicfestival.com/benjamin-britten/, accessed 6/17/17.

[8] As published by the Wilfred Owen Association, accessed on January 7, 2017, http://www.wilfredowen.org.uk/Biography/preface.

[9] Forney, Dell'Antonio, and Machlis, *The Enjoyment of Music,* 12th ed., New York: W. W. Norton, 2015, pp. 552–553.

Image Credits

- Figure 10-1: Paul Gauguin / Copyright in the Public Domain.
- Figure 10-2: Pierre-Auguste Renoir / Copyright in the Public Domain.
- Figure 10-3: Pierre-Auguste Renoir / Copyright in the Public Domain.
- Figure 10-4: Claude Monet / Copyright in the Public Domain.
- Figure 10-5: Adolf de Meyer / Copyright in the Public Domain.
- Figure 10-6: Pablo Picasso / Copyright in the Public Domain.
- Figure 10-7: Arnold Schoenberg / Copyright in the Public Domain.
- Figure 10-8: Copyright © 1927 by Man Ray, (CC BY-SA 2.0) at https://commons.wikimedia.org/wiki/File:Arnold_schönberg_man_ray.jpg.
- Figure 10-9: Edvard Munch / Copyright in the Public Domain.
- Figure 10-10: Hyacinth / Copyright in the Public Domain.
- Figure 10-11: Source: https://commons.wikimedia.org/wiki/File:Bartók_Béla_1927.jpg.
- Figure 10-12: Source: https://commons.wikimedia.org/wiki/File:Bartok_recording_folk_music.jpg.
- Figure 10-13: George Grantham Bain Collection, Library of Congress / Copyright in the Public Domain.
- Figure 10-14: Scott Joplin / Copyright in the Public Domain.
- Figure 10-15: Elmer Chickering / Copyright in the Public Domain.

UNIT 3
World Music

Introduction to
Unit Three

This Unit's Story

What is "world" music? This term, born in a Eurocentric mind-set, can have many meanings, but it generally refers to "non-Western music": music of cultures other than Western Europe and modern North America. As a term that lumps all "other" music into one category for Westerners, it is extraordinarily practical and dangerous at the same time.

The goal of this unit is to introduce students to selected musical techniques and genres, as well as major figures in music from a variety of cultures around the world. Student listening skills that have been enhanced from the beginning of this text continue to deepen with what will be for many listeners their least familiar styles of music. But while we take advantage of the practicality of our topic, how do we address its dangers? We must examine our own attitudes about cultures other than our own, and the ways cultures interact while we explore these musical traditions. This examination begins with the definition of several terms important to Unit 3, World Music, including a more inclusive musical instrument classification system than the orchestral-based description of instruments from Unit 2, Western Art Music.

Important Terms in World Music Study

Cultures have used many varieties of musical instrument classifications: medieval and Renaissance Europe divided instruments into loud and soft dynamic levels, and later Europeans grouped instruments roughly according to their orchestral sections. Around the world, instruments have been classified according to the material out of which they are made, their function, and even their origination myths.

Early-twentieth-century musicologists Erich von Hornbostel (1877–1935) and Curt Sachs (1881–1959) developed a system in which musical instruments are classified according to sound production. The **Hornbostel-Sachs Instrument Classification System** is particularly valuable for the study of musical instruments across a wide variety of cultures and historical eras.

Aerophones, such as flutes, panpipes, and trumpets, produce sound by vibrating air. Guitars, harps, and bowed stringed instruments are **chordophones**, which generate sound by means of one or more tightly stretched strings. **Idiophones** generate sound from the substance of the instruments themselves; examples include castanets, rattles, and the triangle. **Membranophones**, or drums, produce sound with a stretched membrane over a hollow resonator. **Electronophones**, such as synthesizers, generate sound electronically.

Ethnomusicology: The study of social and cultural contexts in music-making, as well as of the music itself. The ethnomusicologist goes beyond the question, "*What* are we listening to?" to ask contextual questions, such as "*Why*, and *when*, is this music performed?" and "*What does this music mean to the culture*?" This is often true of the "musicologist," as well, but most musicologists focus on the Western art music traditions introduced in Unit 2, European Art Music; whereas, ethnomusicologists study and teach about music throughout the world in a wide variety of cultures.

Ethnocentrism: Perception or judgment that is limited by one's own cultural point of view, often with a presumption of superiority. An ethnocentric attitude is natural, but it can be harmful without self-examination and familiarity with people from cultures different from one's own. Genocide, ethnic cleansing, and war are the most dramatic examples of the results of ethnocentrism, but its pervasive presence in everyday life affects each of us in important ways, such as in academic success, employment, and social status. Our own ethnocentrism can block our interest and understanding of unfamiliar musical styles. When we listen attentively to music of other cultures, we take an important step toward understanding traditions different from our own.

Diaspora   (Greek, "scattering of seeds"): The migration or dispersion of a group of people beyond their original homeland. Historically associated with the migration of Jews outside Palestine, this term can apply to any culture or group that is dispersed. The dispersion may be the result of a wide variety of causes, such as forced expulsion, economic necessity, or simply attraction to another location. Music can show the effects of diaspora in a given culture; music can also be a telling measure of a society's cohesiveness, despite diaspora.

Each chapter in this unit explores just a small portion of what each region has to offer. Through brief musical examples, we can catch glimpses of the ways other people live, think, and express themselves. The musical languages are not the same; that old saying that music is a "universal" language is *not* true. But no matter where we come from, we turn toward music with our families and friends for meaningful or whimsical events: we hold weddings to music, funerals to music, heal or hurt each other with music, work or play to music, and we fall in love to music. We'll be surprised by our many differences, but perhaps the biggest surprise will be what we share: our powerful bond with music.

Aztec dancer, Howard County Maryland Pow-wow, 2007.

CHAPTER 11

Music in the Americas

I

INDIGENOUS MUSIC IN NORTH AMERICA

N ative American music in North America is considered to be an
expression of nothing less than the natural world. This is why
Native American performers receive music from nature (or
dreams and visions) rather than compose it themselves. Ceremonies
are considered simultaneously ancient and modern because they origi-
nate from nature or the Creator.

"Native American" is used here to mean the great variety of indigenous peoples in the Western Hemisphere, which include hundreds of
cultural groups and languages, and diverse lifestyles adapted to regional
conditions. The paradigm of musical production noted above seems to
hold true generally across North America, but specific musical elements
and performance practices differ widely.

The author owes special thanks to Mario Rey, PhD, who guided the
preparation of Chapter 11 in great detail.

Figure 11-2 Indigenous culture areas within continental US.

Music: Concept and Meaning

Evidence of North American musical life before European colonization includes musical instruments and pictographs of musicians and musical instruments from as far in the past as the seventh century CE. The most valuable scope of research in Native American music, however, is music-making after European contact. Very little documentation exists from before the arrival of Europeans because oral rather than literary tradition was pervasive throughout North America, and instruments were made out of natural substances such as wood and animal hide, which deteriorated quickly.

Ethnomusicologist **Francis Densmore (1867–1957)**, one of the pioneers in the study of Native American music, collected songs, discussed their cultural context, and analyzed various aspects of their musical elements in the early twentieth century. Although many scholars are currently engaged in the study of indigenous North American music, Densmore was an important figure because of her distinguished career of original fieldwork and thoughtful analyses. A great deal of these songs would have been lost forever had she not collected them in her lifetime because of the sweepingly destructive threats to Native Americans and their traditions since colonization by Europeans began.

Music is profoundly connected with everyday life and sacred ritual in Native American traditions. As in other cultures, love is one of the most popular topics. Additional subjects include nature, history, belief systems, and often all three combined; indeed, it would be difficult to separate these. Nature and man-made items are revealed in realistic detail or as symbol, and historical events are not necessarily separated from the spirit world and belief systems. Patriotism and courage are also emphasized in music: powwow music often features flag songs and national anthems (see more about the powwow, below).

As was noted above, musical composition essentially consists of "capturing" music from nature or the Creator in dreams and visions rather than the traditional Western European paradigm as the exclusive product of human imagination. Music is considered to have supernatural power; the Nehalem Tillamook in the Pacific Northwest have a word that means either "one's power" or "one's song," and the Navajo's Changing Woman *sings* the world into being. Some songs are secret or tied to specific seasons or times of day or only "owned" by one performer or tribe who may or may not grant permission to others to perform them.

Transmission is passed on from master to student in what is known as **oral tradition** rather than written tradition. Examples of musical notation

Oral tradition
Transmission of skills and information in spoken rather than written form (Chapter 1, American Traditional Music).

Frances Densmore at the Smithsonian Institution in 1916 during a recording session with Blackfoot leader Mountain Chief for the Bureau of American Ethnology: "It is a custom that songs connected with ceremonial acts shall be sung only by those who have received them in dreams, or who have inherited or purchased the right to sing them."[1]

are rare; most traditional musical performance is a mixture of memorization with some improvisation and some intentional arrangement or composition. The criteria for musical quality concerns success in its role within the fabric of the ceremony or social activity rather than virtuosic physical prowess or intellectual complexity. Spiritual power and its fruits, such as healing and fertility, are central to the definition of musical value. "Musicians," whose entire vocations center on the musical arts, do not necessarily exist as such in this context. Shamans, or ritual specialists and healers, are the people most likely to lead performances, but music is not exclusive to a few; it is a participatory action among those present.

Musical Characteristics

Regional similarities of musical style exist within cultures from areas that roughly correspond to natural geographic boundaries, such as the eastern woodlands east of the Mississippi River or the coastal plains cultures. Dance is fundamental in much of the music and celebrations among the indigenous peoples of North America. Patterns are often circular, and the ceremonies typically feature choreography, elaborate regalia, accessories such as feathers and masks, body paint, and idiophones such as rattles or bells that are either held or sewn onto the dancers' clothing. Every visual and sonic aspect of the ceremony is likely to carry symbolic meaning. Readers should note that the word, "costume," to describe the clothing of indigenous peoples is inappropriate because it implies that the wearer is pretending as in "Halloween costume." Instead, "clothing," "dress," or "regalia" more respectfully signify authenticity.

The most important instruments in Native American music generally are the human voice first and foremost, followed by various types of flutes, rattles, and drums. Although vocal styles vary among regions, high-pitched and falsetto ranges are especially popular throughout North America. Descending melodic contour throughout the course of a song is extremely common in Native American music; listeners can hear a gradual, or **terraced descent**, in which each successive phrase takes place in a progressively lower pitch range. Undulating contours are also common.

Terraced descent
Gradually descending melodic contour in which each successive phrase takes place in a progressively lower pitch range.

Figure 11-4 Dancers at Zuni Pueblo, c1871–1907; Oliver La Farge: "If you stay on [at the dance], and if you keep quiet, the rhythms of drum, song, and dance, the endlessly changing formations of the lines of dancers, the very heat and dust, unite and take hold. You will realize slowly that what looked simple is complex, disciplined, sophisticated. You will forget yourself. The chances are then that you will go away with that same odd, empty, satisfied feeling which comes after absorbing any great work of art." Oliver La Farge, "New Mexico," 1952, reprinted in Tony Hillerman, ed., The Spell of New Mexico, Albuquerque: University of New Mexico Press, 1976 (reprint ed. 1984).

Vocable In music, vocal sound without literal meaning.

Vocables are common in music throughout North America: they are typically constructed of sounds starting with the consonants H, W, Y, N, and S, followed by a vowel. Vocables may only appear briefly, they may be interspersed throughout a song among meaningful words, or the song may consist exclusively of vocables. Shouts and imitations of natural and animal sounds are common; these sounds may be ornamental or they may emphasize structural points.

Melodies are thought to stem from scales that divide the octave into two, three, four, five, or six notes. The **pentatonic** (five-note) **scale** in particular has been observed in cultures throughout the world, especially in North America and Asia. This concept of the "pentatonic" scale, therefore, carries the danger of being considered as the only fundamental scale in some cultures and one with a fixed set of intervals. A closer look, however, at the variety of Native American and Asian styles yields a multitude of intervals and nuances within pentatonic scales.

Pentatonic Scale
Five-note scale.

Scale An ascending or descending series of pitches, arranged in a specific pattern of intervals; see Musical Elements Appendix.

Rhythmic style and complexity vary among regions. Rhythmic duration in dance music naturally reflects choreographic requirements. Songs often begin with a slow and stately drum pattern before gradually increasing in speed and volume. Musical form is typically sectional and strophic, with a repetition of short phrases. The structure of dance music is determined by its ceremonial function and choreography. Poetic structure in texted music also helps determine the musical form just as in other parts of the world.

Recent Music

Before European settlement in North America, Native American cultures treated territorial boundaries flexibly in order to interact in trade, hunting, and other purposes. One of the most significant and devastating effects of colonization was the European paradigm of "borders" and the forced resettlements of Native Americans into reservations or cities. Powwows became an important gathering for displaced Native Americans in the twentieth century as a way to connect with each other and to preserve their cultures. The **powwow** has become a celebratory and often com- memorative event, rich in cultural display, many of them open to all people. Powwows typically feature dance processionals, drum circles, flute

Powwow (pow-wow)
Native American social gathering for cultural activities, including music, dance, food, and crafts.

Figure 11-5 Grand Entry at the 1983 Omaha powwow.

R. Carlos Nakai, 1988: "I was born in Flagstaff in north-central Arizona, right next to the volcano, and spent a lot of time there, on the Navajo reservation, on and near the Hopi reservation, and places where all my relatives lived. The later part of my years I spent down along the Colorado River with the Mohaves, and the Chemhuevis, the Yumans, Cocopas, and the Quechans. I think most of my time I was spending in things that dealt with music. In the culture that I belong to there were singers, or people that were storytellers, individuals who deal with one perspective or another of culture. So I was more or less immersed in it without my conscious awareness. The exposure has gone anywhere from Country and Western to early Rock and Roll, the early American music, Mohave music, and Navajo music, and Hopi music, and you know, just whatever, whoever was around at the moment. All the way to gospel songs. I think that's a pretty broad exposure to different involvements."[2]

music, and an MC who provides explanations of ceremony details and traditions.

Despite the work of Densmore and others, Native American musical traditions did not have a significant influence on European American music until the twentieth century and before. Native American dispersion, isolation, and oppression are the most likely causes for this cultural silence. The late twentieth century, however, witnessed a resurgence of interest in Native American cultures from both inside and outside the community of indigenous peoples.

Present-day musicians working in the full range of genres compose music with widely varying levels of traditional expression. Music with unmistakably Native American inspiration by Brent Michael Davids (b. 1959), for instance, is expressed functionally as art music for chamber ensembles, orchestras, and films. Some popular musicians, including Robbie Robertson (b. 1943) and Rita Coolidge (b. 1945), "crossed over" into Native American inspired music after achieving success in more mainstream popular styles. Others, such as **Carlos Nakai (b. 1946)** and the vocal ensemble Ulali (founded 1987), have from the very beginning completely identified themselves and their music as Native American.

**PLAYLIST OPTIONS
COMPARISON BETWEEN TRADITIONAL AND
CROSSOVER NATIVE AMERICAN MUSIC**

FIND
- A video example of traditional Native American music and dancing with search terms, such as:
  - "Powwows.com"
  - "[tribal name] dance"
  - "[tribal name] powwow"
  - "[tribal name] drum circle"

  Tribal names can include Cherokee, Inuit, Navajo, Sioux, Wampanoag, and many others

- Compare with an example influenced by other styles. Prominent recent musicians and ensembles include
  - Rita Coolidge or Walela
  - Brent Michael Davids
  - Carlos Nakai

- Robbie Robertson
  - Search "Robbie Robertson Native American"
- Ulali

OBSERVE

- Vocal style
- Melodic range and contour
- Form
- Ceremonial clothing if your example is a dance or powwow video
  - Use the terms "clothing," "dress," or "regalia" to signify authenticity, which is more respectful than "costume."
- Drum accompaniment to dance
- Modern influences in a crossover performance, especially in regard to
  - Instruments
  - Vocal style
  - Topics

ASK

- What signifiers, such as the intermittent shaking of a rattle or a topic that references indigenous beliefs, do you hear that connects your crossover example with Native American traditions? What is the performance context: a powwow? A ticketed concert? A recording?
- Do stylistic changes or adaptations of traditional indigenous musical styles diminish or nourish Native American culture?

II
LATIN AMERICAN MUSIC

L atin America consists of Central America, South America, and those regions in North America and the Caribbean where Latin cultures predominate. The term is deceptive: Latin America is not

Figure 11-7 Latin America political map.

just "Latin." Post-Columbian colonization, the slave trade from Africa, and mass immigration infused strong indigenous American civilizations with European and African cultures. This "triethnic" heritage continues to develop in unique proportions in each region throughout Latin America so that some indigenous cultures remain relatively unaffected to this day whereas other regions are profoundly influenced by African—more so than by European—cultures.

Indigenous Cultures

Panpipes Set of end-blown flute aerophones of varying lengths bundled together; see Musical Instruments Appendix.

Charango Small guitar-like fretted chordophone, popular in the Andes; see Musical Instruments Appendix.

Advanced political and agricultural development characterized many cultures of the regions we now call "Latin America" before European contact. Indigenous civilizations created magnificent architecture and art, practiced highly developed belief systems, and used written forms of communication.

Panpipe aerophones show a strong historical—and prehistoric—presence in South America. They are usually performed in ensembles, often with membranophones, idiophones, and vocalists. No evidence of pre-Columbian chordophones, however, is known to exist; Europeans introduced the small guitar-like **charango**, now popular as a folk instrument in some

Figure 11-8 Andean Panpipe player; Pasto Mother Earth parade song.

regions of the Andes. Rhythmic and melodic textures interact with each other, helping to create structure and interest. Dance is a pervasive cultural presence throughout indigenous cultures in Latin America. The music generally features syncopated, percussive rhythms with less improvisation than is used in other regions of the world and a fairly limited melodic range.

Sacred music in pre-Columbian cultures included musicians specifically trained and paid to perform at ceremonies and festivals, especially in Mayan and Incan cultures. The rites of shamans included music or, at least, sounds that could be considered either prayer or music (as is true of sacred music elsewhere). The sounds are often repetitive and can mimic the sounds of animals. Secular music was also prominent; for instance, flutes and drums would often accompany Peruvian work songs. Throughout Central and South America, celebrations of seasons and life events include music to this day.

Post-Columbian indigenous peoples in Latin America were profoundly influenced by Christianity and by European music. Christian tradition mingled with native cultures as can be seen in festivals with elements of both indigenous and Christian features. Evidence of the synthesis of more than one culture or belief system is prevalent throughout Latin America, and the proportion of European influence in present-day indigenous music is impossible to define with certainty.

PLAYLIST OPTIONS
SOUTH AMERICAN INDIGENOUS MUSIC

FIND
- A video or audio performance of panpipe or charango music with search terms, such as
  - South American panpipe music
  - Sikuri (Aymaran language term for "panpipe") music
  - Charango

OBSERVE
- Distinctive timbre of your example's instrument
- Melodic range and phrase length
- Rhythm
- Role of each instrument and voice if your example is an ensemble
- Level of influence from other cultures

ASK

- What is the performance context of your example?
  - An educational or cultural event?
  - A live performance for profit?
  - A recorded performance?
- Do you hear nontraditional influences, such as modern popular music, in your example?

Guitarrón Large bass guitar popular in Mexico, especially in mariachi ensembles; see Musical Instruments Appendix.

Accordion A free-reed aerophone with keyboard and folded bellows that are controlled by the player's arms; see Musical Instruments Appendix.

***Tejano* (Tex-Mex) music** Mexican popular musical style along the border with Texas.

Conjunto A small Latin American ensemble that often includes accordion and guitar.

Mexico

Both European and indigenous influences characterize most Mexican and Central American music. European dance types are performed with musical instruments of European origin, such as the accordion, violin, and trumpet, but also with musical instruments that have undergone distinctively Latin American development, such as the **guitarrón** and other types of guitars.

Border Music

German and Eastern European immigrants significantly influenced music in the border regions of Mexico and the United States. This can be heard in the use of **accordion** and in European dances such as the polka and the waltz. That influence can be heard today in ***Tejano* (Tex-Mex)** music, which is performed by a ***conjunto***, a small ensemble that often includes accordion and bass guitar. Polka and other European dance rhythms are usually prominent as is the accordion itself. Melody is the primary and sometimes sole concern for accordionists because the bass guitar takes the supportive chordal and rhythmic roles. Prominent *Tejano* performers include **Ramón Ayala (b. 1945)** and the band *Los Tigres del Norte*.

Love is a typical subject of *Tejano* songs. The tension and difficulty inherent in the Mexican-American sociopolitical experience, however, is an unavoidable topic because this music has been in the hearts of the working class since its beginnings. For

Figure 11-9 Tejano performer Ramón Ayala with his accordion, 2012.

instance, the lyrics for Los Tigres del Norte's "La Jaula de Oro" ("The Golden Cage," 1983) express the despair of an immigrant who misses his homeland. *Tejano* music has become emblematic of the Mexican-American condition.

Mariachi Music

Although **mariachi** music originated in western Mexico, its wide popularity has made this genre emblematic of Mexican culture in general. Ensemble instrumentation typically fulfills the three basic functions of the musical texture: melody (trumpet or violin), harmonic accompaniment (guitar and harp), and the bass line (*guitarrón*). The rich, mellow vocal delivery of strophic songs is punctuated by high-spirited hoots and shouts. Mariachi ensembles commonly perform at life-event celebrations such as weddings and the *quinceañeras* (female fifteenth-birthday celebrations) that are customary in some Latin American cultures.

Mariachi Traditional Mexican folk music that includes vocalist with trumpet or violin on melody, guitar or harp as harmonic accompaniment, and *guitarrón* on the bass line.

Figure 11-10 Mariachis playing at the Tenampa in Mexico City, 2010.

PLAYLIST OPTIONS
MEXICAN MUSIC

FIND

A video or audio performance of

- An example of *Tejano* (Tex-Mex) music with search terms, such as
    - Ramón Ayala
    - *Los Tigres del Norte*
    - *Tejano* accordion polka
- Or an example of mariachi music with search terms, such as
    - Mariachi Los Camperos
    - *Mariachi Divas*
    - *Mariachi Vargas*

Those not fluent in Spanish can add "translation" or "subtitles" to search term

OBSERVE

- Instrumentation and the role of each instrument (melody, harmony, or rhythm)
- Polka style dance rhythms, especially in border music
- Vocal hoots and whistles, especially in mariachi music

ASK

- Do you notice any electrified instruments in your example, which would indicate a later, less traditional, style?
- What is the topic? Romance, life events, work, and Mexican-American sociopolitical experience (especially in border music) are prevalent subjects.

Call and response
The alternation between leading and responding groups or individuals in music or speech; common in many cultures and often improvisatory (Chapter 1, American Traditional Music).

Interlocking rhythms
Multiple layers of rhythmic lines that seem to intersect and interact with each other; (Chapter 13, Music in Sub-Saharan Africa).

Improvisation The creation of music during performance; common in many cultures and genres, it is a hallmark of American jazz (Chapter 3, Jazz).

The Caribbean

African influence on Latin American music is unmistakable and especially prominent in Atlantic coastal regions. We can hear it in **call and response** singing, **interlocking rhythms**, and **improvisational** performance practices (see Chapter 13, Music in Sub-Saharan Africa). West African religious traditions in particular, with music as part of the package, spread to Latin American regions, especially Cuba, Haiti, and Brazil.

Calypso

Calypso likely originated from the work songs of enslaved Africans in Trinidad and Tobago. This Afro-Caribbean musical genre came to be heavily associated with carnival celebrations as well, functioning as dance music accompanied by **steel bands**. Song texts are a distinctive feature in calypso's history: sociopolitical commentary and even news stories were transmitted through calypso songs. Hard work, struggles with colonialism, and poverty are typical subject matter of the songs, along with the perennial topic of love. Prominent calypso performers include Aldwin "Lord Kitchener" Roberts (1922–2000), Slinger "Mighty Sparrow" Fransciso (b. 1935), and **Harry Belafonte (b. 1927).**

Calypso Afro-Caribbean dance music genre accompanied by steel bands; song texts often express sociopolitical commentary.

Steel bands
Caribbean ensemble of tuned steel drum (or pan) idiophones, especially popular in calypso music; see Musical Instruments Appendix.

Figure 11-11 Army Sgt. 1st Class Rafael Roman, of the Puerto Rican National Guard uses a hammer to tune a steel drum, Guantanamo Bay, 2009.

Harry Belafonte: "Just as Belafonte hit record stores, so did the debut album by some kid from Memphis named Elvis Presley. His first single, "Heartbreak Hotel," had already topped the charts. On that same May 5 Billboard album chart, his was number one to my number two. Different as our sounds were, I could see that in one way, at least, we were on parallel tracks. Elvis was interpreting one kind of black music—rhythm and blues—while I found my inspiration in black folk songs, spirituals, and calypso, and also in African music, which would one day be put under the heading of world music."[3]

Ska and Reggae

A new upbeat, highly syncopated Caribbean dance music genre developed from calypso and jazz idioms, with a brass section included in the band. "Ska" originated in 1964 with the Skatalites, a Jamaican band. Inspired by the Rastafari movement, this genre developed a spiritual dimension as well, and topics often centered on social justice.

The upbeat tempo of ska bands later slowed to create its offspring genre **reggae**, which dropped the brass section by the late 1960s. The Wailers, which included **Bob Marley (1945–1981)** and Peter Tosh (1944–1987), was one of the first reggae bands. The social commentary inherited from ska became a hallmark of this newer genre. Ever since its beginnings, reggae music has powerfully influenced commercial popular music in the United States: its characteristic syncopated rhythmic pattern can be heard in many of North America's best-selling songs at any given moment. Songs that espouse social justice topics in the style of early ska and reggae music, however, have since dwindled.

Figure 11-13 Bob Marley in concert, Dalymount Park, 1980.

Reggae Jamaican musical genre characterized by syncopation and social justice topics.

Salsa

An amalgamation of Latino-Caribbean and North American jazz idioms developed in the Caribbean and in New York City Latino communities during the mid-twentieth century, which came to be known as **salsa** after the spicy sauce used in Latin American cuisine. Salsa music, which is functional as both dance and song, is usually in duple meter with a fairly simple chord sequence. The highly syncopated, polyrhythmic accompaniment style often results in brilliant and exciting performances. Instrumentation typically includes Cuban percussion such as **bongos**, piano, bass, brass instruments, and saxophone. Topics include descriptions of Latino life in the United States. Prominent salsa performers include **Celia Cruz (1925–2003)**, Tito Puente (1923–2000), and Rubén Blades (b. 1948).

Salsa An amalgamation of Afro-Caribbean and North American jazz dance music with syncopated, polyrhythmic instrumental accompaniment.

Bongos (bongo drums) A pair of small Afro-Cuban membranophones joined together; see Musical Instruments Appendix.

Celia Cruz: "I'm a fan of all types of Cuban music: Lucumí songs (which we also call "Afro"), son, rumba, cha-cha, bolero, mambo, danzón, and so forth. As a matter of fact, Cuban music, from the Baroque to the atonal, is so varied that it has something for every taste. I truly believe that music is Cuba's greatest gift to the world, and I learned to appreciate it at home, since music was very important in our family. Music and dance are integral factors of the Cuban national character; my family was only an extension of this core Cuban relationship with music."[4]

PLAYLIST OPTIONS
MUSIC OF THE CARIBBEAN

FIND

A video or audio performance of one of the following:

- Calypso
  - Harry Belafonte
  - Lord Kitchener
  - Mighty Sparrow
- Ska or Reggae
  - Bob Marley
  - Peter Tosh
  - Skatalites
  - Wailers
- Salsa
  - Ruben Blades
  - Celia Cruz
  - Fania All Stars
  - Tito Puente

Those not fluent in Spanish can add "translation" or "subtitles" to search term

OBSERVE

- Syncopation and polyrhythms
- Instrumental and vocal texture
  - Large or small ensemble
  - Electrified or acoustic

ASK

- Is the topic of your example simply about love or day-to-day work, or does it carry a serious sociopolitical message?
- Do you notice any improvisation in your performance example?

South America

Tango

Its strong association with Argentina belies the many threads of origin for this genre, which include African, Iberian, Caribbean, and even Eastern European roots. Enslaved Africans in Argentina are known to have used the term "tango" during colonial times to refer to percussion instruments and a specific dance. In the nineteenth century, it came to be associated with the most impoverished districts of Buenos Aires and also with influences from the cowboy-like rural Argentine *gaucho* culture. By the early twentieth century, the **tango** had already achieved international recognition, which continues to grow today.

Figure 11-15 Tango performance in Buenos Aires, 2005.

Perhaps the most distinctive musical element of the tango is its sharply dotted rhythm (contrasting long and short durations), which is typically presented in duple meter. The tango's structure is influenced by the European polka. Twentieth-century ensembles usually highlight the **bandoneón**, often with bowed strings, and rhythm sections that include guitars, percussion, and piano. The striking, male-dominated choreography has been likened to the motions of a knife duel, but the lyrical melodies and vocal texts are intensely romantic. Among the many popular tango performers, two of the most celebrated in the history of the genre include early-twentieth-century vocalist Carlos Gardel (1890–1935) and mid-to-late twentieth-century composer, bandoneón player and bandleader **Astor Piazzola (1921–1992)**.

Figure 11-16 Astor Piazzolla with his bandoneon, date unknown.

Bossa Nova

Brazilian popular music became internationally successful with the rise of **bossa nova**, an innovative genre based on Afro-Brazilian samba rhythms but with a new and more complex pattern of syncopation. "Bossa" connotes "flair" or "ability;" this style expresses an offhand sophistication that impressed North American jazz musicians. Most popular from the late 1950s through the mid-1960s, the genre has inspired many jazz and popular musicians ever since.

The earliest bossa nova performances featured an almost whispering vocal part with only guitar accompaniment. This was an innovative vocal style strikingly different from the more robust delivery of earlier popular Brazilian music. The subdued, often complex melody fostered a distinctive blend with the guitar's elegant harmonies and intricately syncopated rhythms. Bossa nova lyrics can be sophisticated as well, and even the sonic qualities of the text are often especially well integrated with melody and rhythm. The earliest and most influential bossa nova musicians include Gilberto Gil and **Antonio Carlos Jobim (1927–1994)**. Charlie Byrd (1925–1999) was one of the earliest jazz artists from the United States to perform in bossa nova style.

Bossa nova
A musical genre based on Afro-Brazilian samba rhythms but with a more complex pattern of syncopation.

Tropicalia

The late 1960s Brazilian band, Tropicalia, provided the musical expression for what came to be known as the **tropicalia movement**, which included

Tropicalia movement
A controversial artistic movement launched by the 1960s Brazilian band Tropicalia, which favored international influences rather than a return to native authenticity.

literary and visual arts, as well. The movement's compelling and politically charged ideals favoring international influences in art, rather than a return to native authenticity, sparked controversy and even government repression including the incarceration of band members Gilberto Gil (b. 1942) and Caetano Veloso (b. 1942).

By definition, tropicalia is an amalgam of styles popular in the late 1960s, ranging from Brazilian and Caribbean popular genres to psychedelic rock and jazz. Rhythms are generally based on Afro-Brazilian influences but can be unpredictable and driven by declamatory melodies, with expressive and compelling lyrics. Tropicalia continues to be widely discussed in cultural studies and is still influential among some American musicians; for instance, the track entitled "Tropicalia" on popular musician Beck's 1998 album, "Mutations," clearly references the then thirty-year-old movement.

PLAYLIST OPTIONS
SOUTH AMERICAN MUSIC

FIND

A video or audio performance of one of the following:
- Tango
  - Carlos Gardel
  - Astor Piazzola
  - Tango dance
- Bossa Nova
  - "Desafinado"
  - "The Girl From Ipanema"
  - Antonio Carlos Jobim
- Tropicalia
  - Gilberto Gil
  - Tropicalia

Those not fluent in Spanish can add "translation" or "subtitles" to search term

OBSERVE
- Instrumentation:
  - Bandoneón in tango music
  - Guitar chords blending with voice in bossa nova
  - International influences in tropicalia

- Rhythmic patterns
  - Dotted rhythms in tango
  - Rhythmic pattern in bossa nova accompaniment
  - North American rock and jazz influences in tropicalia

ASK

- Should musicians stick to time-honored traditions, or should they welcome influences from other cultures? The choice between "authentic" tradition and international influence is most dramatically made in the Tropicalia movement, but all three of these genres answer that question in their own ways. What is your personal answer?

Art Music in Latin America

Art music influenced by European musical traditions as described in Unit 2, Western Art Music, took root in post-Columbian Latin America due to the aggressive colonization and missionary work of the European powers. Influences, however, traveled in all directions: Indigenous, European, and African musical idioms have shown themselves in art music of the Americas throughout the centuries since European contact. Seventeenth- and eighteenth-century composers were trained in Spain or in the New World, and some were of indigenous or *mestizo* (both indigenous and European heritage) descent. The particular blend of influences from the triethnic heritage described earlier in this chapter was unique to each composer.

Spanish born and trained Tomás de Torrejón y Velasco (1644–1728), for instance, who composed the earliest surviving New World opera, *La purpura de la rosa,* held close to Spanish traditions. The music of Spaniard Juan de Araujo (1646–1712), on the other hand, displays striking New World and even African idioms, such as in his **villancico,** *Los coflades.* Manuel de Zumaya (c. 1678–1755) is an example of a *mestizo* composer who mastered European polychoral techniques as can be heard in his villancicos, including *Celebran Publiquen.*

Modern composers in Latin America negotiate between at least three contexts. Nationalism is expressed through American idioms, such as the use of samba rhythms or harmonies built on pitches of the open strings of a guitar in symphonic music. Second, historical art music provides models of traditional Western art music forms and genres.

Villancico A Hispanic sacred or secular vocal work for choir, which sometimes includes soloists and continuo; strummed and plucked harp and guitar are often prominent in the accompaniment (Chapter 7, Baroque Music).

Atonality   Music without tonality or total center and, thus, no distinction between dissonance and consonance (Chapter 10, Modern Art Music.)

Serialism (See "Twelve-tone method")   Twentieth-century method of composition devised by Schoenberg in which each of the twelve notes of the octave are placed in a particular order, or tone row, and are not repeated out of that order; (Chapter 10, Modern Art Music).

Avant-garde aesthetics and compositional techniques of modernist art music, such as **atonality** and **serialism**, provide the third context. All of these aspects in one proportion or another can be found in most Latin American art music.

PLAYLIST OPTIONS: LATIN AMERICAN ART MUSIC

FIND

A video or audio performance of music by one of the following composers:

- Tomás de Torrejón y Velasco
  - Excerpt from the opera, *La purpura de la rosa*
- Juan de Araujo
  - Excerpt from the villancico, *Los coflades*
- Manuel de Zumaya
  - Excerpt from the villancico, *Celebran Publiquen*
- Leo Brouwer (Cuba)
  - *El Decameron Negro*
- Carlos Chavez (Mexico)
  - *Xochipilli: An Imagined Aztec Music*
- Alberto Ginastera (Argentina)
  - *Estancia*
  - Or try Ginastera's Piano Concerto No. 1, 4th movement and compare with Emerson, Lake, and Palmer's interpretation of it in "Toccata"
- Heitor Villa-Lobos (Brazil)
  - *Bachianas Brasilieras*

OBSERVE

- Wide variety of instrumental forces
  - Full orchestra
  - Chamber
  - Vocal
  - Guitar
- The role of rhythm, syncopation, and polyrhythm

ASK

◆ Does your example most evoke indigenous cultures, post-Columbian nationalist expressions, traditional European art music, or modernist techniques?

The celebrated Brazilian composer Heitor Villa-Lobos (1887–1959) was inspired by Brazilian popular street music—especially *chôros*, or street bands—as well as by historical Western art music. Among his many works for vocal, orchestral, and chamber ensembles, he paid homage to J. S. Bach, whose work he regarded as the fount of universal folklore, in his *Bachianas Brasilieras;* a series of compositions for a variety of instrumentations, melding traditional European tonality and polyphonic techniques with Brazilian influences.

The music of Mexican nationalist composer, conductor, and music commentator **Carlos Chavez (1899–1978)** is infused with romanticism, modernist techniques, and New World expressions. In his search for a new identity in Mexican musical culture, pre-Columbian elements represented a significant source of inspiration. "Xochipilli: An Imagined Aztec Music" is noteworthy in that it evokes music before European contact with indigenous instruments.

Argentinian composer Alberto Ginastera (1916–1983) is one of the most renowned twentieth-century composers of the Americas. His music is rich with New World references, especially of folk music from *gaucho* (rural Argentine cowboy-like culture) traditions as can be heard in the orchestral music from the ballet, "Estancia." At the same time, Ginastera explored modernist techniques, such as serialism, atonality, and, in his later years, neo-expressionism.

Leo Brouwer (b. 1939) is one of Cuba's preeminent musicians as a composer, concertizing guitarist, and conductor of the Cuban National Symphony Orchestra. Brouwer has written orchestral, vocal, chamber, and film music, as well. His compositional style has fluctuated between intensely avant-garde techniques and a more traditional harmonic language. Many of his guitar solos such as *Elogio de la danza* and *El Decameron Negro* maintain an important place in classical guitar repertoire.

Leo Brouwer: "To be useful is something incredible, because you're at the service of the world. Humans, when they communicate, when they teach, when they show, when they give...they're doing one of the most beautiful things in life...Perhaps my roots in solitude, of being an orphan—it forces me to these reflections."[5]

CHAPTER 11 VOCABULARY & IMPORTANT FIGURES

Vocabulary

Accordion

Bandoneón (button accordion, concertina)

Bongos (bongo drums)

Bossa nova

Calypso

Charango

Conjunto

Guitarrón

Mariachi

Panpipes

Pentatonic Scale

Powwow (pow-wow)

Reggae

Salsa

Steel bands

Tango

Tejano (Tex-Mex) music

Terraced descent

Tropicalia movement

Vocable

Important Figures

Ramón Ayala (b. 1945)

Harry Belafonte (b. 1927)

Leo Brouwer (b. 1939)

Carlos Chavez (1899–1978)

Celia Cruz (1925–2003)

Francis Densmore (1867–1957)

Antonio Carlos Jobim (1927–1994)

Bob Marley (1945–1981)

Carlos Nakai (b. 1946)

Astor Piazzola (1921–1992)

ENDNOTES

[1] Francis Densmore, Teton Sioux Music, Smithsonian Institution Bureau of American Ethnology, Washington: Government Printing Office, 1918, pp. 159–160.

[2] Christian F. Feest, "It's Not Just Music: An Interview with R. Carlos Nakai," Native American Studies 2:2, January 1988.

[3] My Song: A Memoir of Art, Race and Defiance, by Harry Belafonte with Michael Shnayerson, Vintage Reprint ed., 2012, p. 151.

[4] From Celia: My Life, by Celia Cruz with Ana Cristina Reymundo, Harper Entertainment, 2005, p. 26.

[5] "'To Be Useful Is Something Incredible': Leo Brouwer Reflects on his Legacy" from NPR's Deceptive Cadence, 4/11/17, by Betto Arcos.

Image Credits

- Copyright © 1980 by Eddie Mallin, (CC BY 2.0) at https://commons.wikimedia.org/wiki/File:Bob-Marley.jpg.
- Figure 11-1: Copyright © 2007 by Jeff Kubina, (CC BY-SA 2.0) at https://commons.wikimedia.org/wiki/File:Pow-Wow_Maryland.jpg.
- Figure 11-2: USGS / Copyright in the Public Domain.
- Figure 11-3: Harris and Ewing / Copyright in the Public Domain.
- Figure 11-4: John K. Hillers / Copyright in the Public Domain.

Hula kahiko performance in Hawaii Volcanoes National Park, 2004.

12 Music in Oceania

Oceania consists of Australia and three west Pacific island groups: Melanesia, Micronesia, and Polynesia. In this region, fully modern Western societies are juxtaposed with indigenous communities that practice some of the oldest cultural traditions on the planet. People began to migrate from Southeast Asia to Melanesia and Australia about 50,000 years ago when lower sea levels provided more land bridges and shorter distances between islands. Several waves of settlers spread throughout Oceania. The relationship between people and nature is central to traditional Oceanic belief systems, and music holds a prominent place in the myths and ceremonies that express these beliefs.

Drastic changes swept Oceanic cultures with the arrival of colonialism and Christian missionary activity from the late eighteenth through the twentieth centuries. Indigenous Oceanians had no defense against the deadliest import of the newcomers: a variety of pathogens that quickly diminished populations, often by more than half upon arrival. The newcomers' politics, religions, and cultures dominated indigenous traditions, in some places driving them underground or eradicating them altogether. Today some regions of Oceania—such as Hawaii and parts of Australia—are fully accessible and linked with the rest of the world, but other regions are isolated with indigenous groups that survive as hunter-gatherers or subsistence farmers. Many indigenous people experience unique combinations of traditional and modern lifestyles. English and French are the most common official languages throughout Oceania; hundreds of indigenous languages and dialects exist, however, in this distinctively island sector of the world.

Figure 12-2 Regions of Oceania

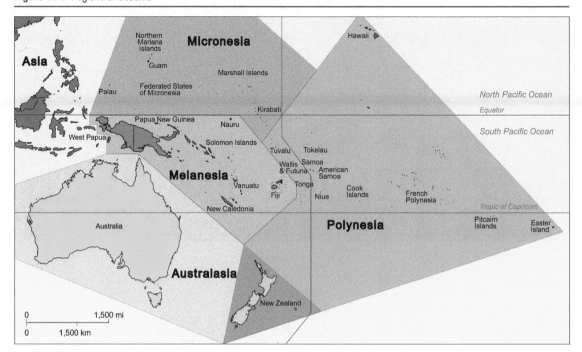

I
AUSTRALIA

Aboriginal Regarding indigenous peoples, or earliest inhabitants of a land; used often to describe indigenous Australians.

Australia is both a continent and a nation, with much of its population concentrated along its eastern and southeastern coasts. **Aboriginal** peoples who have inhabited the continent for at least 40,000 years developed a society rich with traditional belief systems, visual and musical arts, survival practices adapted to the varied Australian environments, and family-centered social networks. British colonization and rule over the continent in the eighteenth century was followed by nineteenth-century gold rushes that attracted immigrants from around the world. Australia is now a world power, prominent in business, sciences, and the arts, but it has a troubled history with its own indigenous peoples. In recent years, the government has attempted to address the devastating effects of colonization on aboriginal populations and traditions.

Traditional Culture

Aboriginal Australians may represent the oldest continuous culture on earth. They are traditionally hunter-gatherers who have developed rich and varied belief systems expressed in art, music, and dance. **Dreamtime (The Dreaming)** is an Australian aboriginal reference to the sacred time of the creation of the world. It is a continuous, living spiritual force that represents many facets of aboriginal belief systems and myths. Dreamtime's power can be tapped through ritual music, dance, and journeys. **Songlines** are groups of "small" songs often linked together in a series but with a wide range of functions and symbolic meanings. Songlines often transcend individual cultures to include a variety of languages and geographical areas within aboriginal Australia; in this way, they are "song maps" of ancient chants that can direct journeys and evoke Dreamtime myths and ancestors. Performances occur in the context of dance or during activities such as travel, healing, and everyday tasks. Music plays an important role in Aboriginal ceremonial events, or **corroborees**, which can also include storytellers and dancers decorated with body paint.

The most celebrated traditional Australian musical instrument is the **didjeridu** (often shortened to "didj"). This large aerophone, three to seven feet long and about one to three inches in diameter, is made out of

Dreamtime Australian aboriginal spiritual belief system and concept of creation.

Songlines (history song, song series) In aboriginal Australian traditions, groups of "small" songs often linked together in a series but with a wide range of functions and symbolic meanings.

Corroboree Aboriginal ceremonial events, which can also include storytellers and dancers decorated with body paint.

Didjeridu (didgeridoo, didjeridoo, didj) Large aerophone made out of eucalyptus wood; performers use circular breathing technique for continuous sound. The didjeridu has come to represent all Australian aboriginal cultures as a pan-Aboriginal cultural symbol; see Musical Instruments Appendix.

Figure 12-3 Indigenous Australian playing the didjeridu.

Circular Breathing
Didjeridu technique in which the player inhales through the nose and blows air out into the instrument at the same time, so the sound is continuous; see "Didjeridoo, Musical Instruments Appendix.

Clapsticks   A pair or set of wooden sticks used as idiophones to strike each other, especially as a rhythmic accompaniment to didjeridoo performance; see Musical Instruments Appendix.

eucalyptus wood hollowed out by termites. Performers use a technique called **circular breathing** in which the player inhales through the nose and blows air out into the instrument at the same time, so the sound is continuous. Traditional performers often imitate nature and animal sounds through airflow punctuated with vocalizations such as hums or growls. This instrument is traditionally taboo for females, but recently women have begun to perform it outside of traditional ceremonies. Although the didjeridu likely originated in some cultures specific to northern Australia, it has come to represent all Australian aboriginal cultures as a pan-Aboriginal cultural symbol. Still an iconic traditional instrument, it has also become a strong presence in popular and modern art styles. The didjeridu is traditionally performed along with singers; **clapsticks** provide a steady pulse and a metric framework for the celebrants.

British Colonization

Both science and power motivated Britain's Captain James Cook when he led expeditions to the South Pacific between 1768 and 1779. He brought along prominent scientists and artists to record the flora and fauna of the Australian coast and other Oceanic regions, but he also meant to find and claim the "Southern Continent" for Britain. In 1788, the British established a penal colony in eastern Australia. Convicts transported from the British Isles were mostly nonviolent and political prisoners, some of whom sang antiauthoritarian "outlaw" ballads such as "Moreton Bay or a Convict's Lament." The lyrics to "Moreton Bay" may have been written by convict **Francis "Frank the Poet," MacNamara (c. 1810–1861)**:

> ... For three long years I was beastly treated,
> And heavy irons on my legs I wore,
> My back from flogging it was lacerated,
> And oft-times painted with crimson gore ...[1]

Gold rushes in the nineteenth century attracted people from around the world in an immigration boom that increased throughout the rest of the nineteenth century. They brought their customs along with them, which included music from Europe and Asia. American-style minstrelsy and vaudeville shows became popular staged entertainment. British culture, however, was by far the dominant influence throughout Australia. British settlers who worked in rural settings such as sheep ranching sang ballads known as **bush songs**. Often sung unaccompanied to calm the sheep, the songs were sometimes supported by instruments such as the harmonica (also known as mouth organ in Australia), tin whistle, button accordion, or fiddle. These songs were similar in style and structure to traditional music of the British Isles. Collector **A. B. "Banjo" Paterson (1864–1941)** published *Old Bush Songs* in 1905. Paterson was also a songwriter; he wrote the lyrics to the most well-known Australian song, "Waltzing Matilda." The actual story of the song—not quite as well known outside of Australia as its cheerful melody—is about an itinerant worker who drowns himself rather than submit to authority after he's accused of a theft ("you'll not take me alive!") and then haunts the area. The story might be based on late-nineteenth-century clashes between shearers and the government; whether it is or not, it has the undeniably Australian spirit of struggle for freedom and survival in a harsh environment. Today "Waltzing Matilda" is an unofficial national anthem and a song that represents Australia around the world.

For aboriginal people, European contact caused mass deaths from disease followed by many years of hardship under British colonial rule. Discriminatory laws and policies regulated most aspects of life for aboriginal people, including where they could live, what they could do for a living, and whom they could marry. The Australian government's infamous "half-caste" policies throughout much of the twentieth century forced the removal of children of mixed descent from their own families in an effort to assimilate them into white society. Those children became known as the "stolen generations." One among them was singer-songwriter **Archie Roach (b. 1956)**, whose song "Took the Children Away" expresses the anguish this caused in such lines as

Bush songs Ballads sung by nineteenth-century Australian settlers, similar in style and structure to traditional music of the British Isles.

Figure 12-4 Cover of The Old Bush Songs, edited by A. B. Paterson.

Archie Roach: "Music I think is important...I can't imagine a world without music...It's important for everybody, not just indigenous people...I think the message I'm trying to get out now is that some of us have been carrying a big burden all our lives, and it's been weighing us down and making us sick, you know?...We need to work toward healing and being as strong and as healthy as we can be."[2]

Sent us off to foster homes
As we grew up we felt alone
Cause we were acting white; yet feeling black … "[3]

Today aboriginal lifestyles range from thoroughly traditional to modern, and most experience a combination somewhere along a continuum between the two. Although recent reforms and a highly celebrated government apology to indigenous peoples in 2008 signal a better direction, many in Australia still cope with the loss and marginalization that comes with such a difficult modern history.

Western Influences

Well-marketed recordings from the US of the Carter Family, Jimmie Rodgers, and other US country music artists in the 1930s resonated with Australians, inspiring their own country music industry that still flourishes today, complete with steel guitar accompaniment, yodeling, and lyrics about simple rural life. Prominent early Australian country mu-

sic figures Tex Morton (Robert William Lane, 1916–1983) and Slim Dusty (David Gordon Kirkpatrick, 1927–2003) fostered cowboy and trucker images, respectively. Mid-to-late twentieth-century country singer-songwriters include pop-country crossover star Olivia Newton-John (b. 1948), "Australia's Queen of Country Music" Jean Stafford (b. 1950), and country-folk singer John Williamson (b. 1945), whose popular "True Blue" expresses Australian values with its title as well as with its lyrics. Kasey Chambers, Lee Kernaghan, and Melinda Schneider are a few of the many country musicians who represent the latest generation of Australian country music.

The Beatles, who triggered the British Invasion in the US, inspired rock and roll in Australia as well. The pub-rock movement in Australia developed by the late 1970s, beginning with bands such as Billy Thorpe & the Aztecs and, later, with Men at Work, INXS,

Figure 12-6 John Williamson, 2012.

Midnight Oil, and others in the 1980s. Reggae's musical characteristics and themes of social justice are a strong influence in Australian pop music and especially in the music of aboriginal bands such as Coloured Stone. The integration of rock music with indigenous music is exemplified by the music of Yothu Yindi, a band that is composed of both aboriginal and nonaboriginal musicians. Traditional songs with guitar accompaniment, exemplified by The Bushwackers, created a pub-based folk music scene.

Art Music

The nineteenth-century gold rushes fostered concert music, especially among wealthy settlers. Amateur choral, instrumental ensemble, and opera music became popular. Celebrated Australian opera singers of the nineteenth and twentieth centuries include Nellie Melba (Helen Porter Mitchell, 1861–1931) from Melbourne and coloratura soprano Joan Sutherland (1926–2010). Both of them achieved wide international fame. Early-twentieth-century composers include Percy Grainger (1882–1961) and Peggy Glanville-Hicks (1912–1990), both known for their originality.

Figure 12-7 Joan Sutherland, 1975.

Composers who found inspiration in Australian history and aboriginal themes include Margaret Sutherland (1897–1984), whose opera *The Young Kabbarli* includes an aboriginal singer; John Antill (1904–1986), known for his 1946 orchestral ballet *Corroboree*, which aspired to authentic aboriginal choreography; and Peter Sculthorpe (1929–2014), whose orchestral composition *Kakadu* evokes the northern Australian landscape and Aboriginal chant.

For the latest generation of musicians, traditional world musical styles and art music intersect. Instrumentalists perform didjeridu in a variety of styles and contexts, and composers integrate aboriginal or other world musical traditions with experimental art music. Performance artist David Young (b. 1969) and aboriginal didjeridu virtuoso and composer William Barton (b. 1981) are especially notable. Today Australia maintains six state symphony orchestras and is home to the iconic Sydney Opera House. Designed by Utzon and finished in 1973, it is really a center that houses facilities for opera, ballet, theater, and symphony orchestra concerts.

Figure 12-8 Sydney Opera House.

PLAYLIST OPTIONS
MUSIC OF AUSTRALIA

FIND

A video or audio performance of

- Indigenous traditional music and dance, especially didjeridu performances:
  - iDidjaustralia: https://www.youtube.com/user/ididjaustralia/about
  - Jeremy Donovan, traditional player
  - Adèle and Zalem, nontraditional duo
- Iconic traditional Australian songs of European settlers:
  - "Moreton Bay or a Convict's Lament," words attributed to Francis MacNamara ("Frank the Poet," c. 1810–1861)
  - "Waltzing Matilda," lyrics by A. B. Paterson ("Banjo Paterson," 1864–1941)
- Australian musicians
  - Country and Traditional:

- Tex Morton, Slim Dusty, Olivia Newton-John, Jean Stafford, John Williamson, Kasey Chambers, Lee Kernaghan, or Melinda Schneider
- Pub-rock:
  - Billy Thorpe & the Aztecs, Men at Work, INXS, Coloured Stone, or The Bushwackers
- Art:
  - Vocalists Nellie Melba (Helen Porter Mitchell, 1861–1931) or Joan Sutherland
  - Composers Percy Grainger, Peggy Glanville-Hicks, Margaret Sutherland, or John Antill
- Eclectic:
  - Performance artist David Young, singer-songwriter Archie Roach, or didjeridu virtuoso and composer William Barton

OBSERVE
- Genre and instrumentation
- Topics
- Rhythmic and melodic aspects

ASK
- Influences can include cultures from other parts of the world, sociopolitical messages, and even nature. What are the influences that affect this performance?

II
MELANESIA

Named by Europeans in the early nineteenth century, Melanesia ("Black Island") has a great diversity of cultures across its mountainous terrain and coral atolls. In fact, this region has the highest density of quantity and concentration of languages on earth: they are estimated to number over 1,300. Ancestors from Southeast Asia arrived in separate settlements over a 5,000–50,000-year span. Melanesia is a region of islands within Oceania, comprised of separate nations and dependencies. But many of Melanesia's cultures, which often do not correlate with modern political boundaries, remain almost completely isolated in mountain villages.

Traditional Music

With such an abundance of languages and societies, musical traditions vary widely as well. Some musical instrument families, however, have been noted throughout the region. **Slit drums** are variously sized log idiophones that are struck rhythmically by the players. They are hollowed-out logs with narrow slits cut long-ways in the middle, up to about 20 feet long, often with carved semblances of animals or deities at the ends. Melanesians also play the **susap,** a bamboo idiophone mouth harp. Aerophones, including panpipes, and hour-glass shaped membranophones are also common in Melanesia. These instruments are used to accompany dance in special performances, or **singsings**, that can last for many hours and include elaborately decorated clothing and masks. Singsings can mark community or individuals' life events, and they can also celebrate meetings between cultures. The rhythms expressed particularly by the log idiophones and the membranophones can be quite complex and multilayered (see **interlocking rhythms** in Chapter 13, Music in Sub-Saharan Africa). Traditional Melanesian music and dance is represented at the Festival of Pacific Arts, which is held every four years and features Oceanic performances.

Slit Drums Log idiophones struck rhythmically; see Musical Instruments Appendix.

Susap A bamboo mouth-harp idiophone.

Singsing Special performances that can last for many hours and include elaborately decorated clothing and masks.

Interlocking rhythms Multiple layers of rhythmic lines that seem to intersect and interact with each other (Chapter 13, Music in Sub-Saharan Africa).

Western Influences

Missionaries and other settlers brought chordophones—especially the guitar—and Western musical styles. In the 1920s, **bamboo bands** became popular. Sets of variously sized bamboo tubes tied together are end blown or struck, often in ensemble with panpipes, guitar, and voice, with rhythms that are influenced by popular music. These bamboo bands are still popular today, especially in the Solomon Islands. In the late twentieth century, Melanesian music absorbed rock and reggae musical styles to accompany indigenous language songs.

Bamboo Bands Ensembles featuring bamboo tube aerophones and other instruments that became popular in the 1920s in Melanesia, influenced by popular music; see Musical Instruments Appendix.

III
MICRONESIA

Micronesia ("Small Islands") consists of more than 2,000 small islands in four main island groups from both volcanic and coral origins and a tropical marine climate. The first settlers came from Indonesia over 3,000 years ago, followed by Melanesians about 1,000 years later. Magellan's 1521 arrival was the first known European contact. Micronesians have a variety of lifestyles, depending on geographic conditions as well as a variety of cultures. Over ten indigenous languages and many dialects are spoken, along with English and Japanese. Christianity's strong influence over Micronesian cultures is one result of the European colonization since the seventeenth century. As with Melanesia, Micronesian political and cultural boundaries are often not the same.

Conch shell trumpet
Traditional Oceanic aerophone, often used for signaling. Air is blown through a hole in the side or tip; see Musical Instruments Appendix.

Traditional musical instruments, mostly aerophones and idiophones, include **conch shell trumpets** used for signaling, several types of indigenous flutes, and bamboo or wooden sticks used in "stick dances" that often depict combat. Vocal music and dance is especially important in Micronesia. In fact, some communities hold song and dance competitions in lieu of combat. Dance in Micronesia is often a visual enhancement of sung poetry: movements enhance the texts. Dancers are rehearsed, often organized in ranks, and synchronized in both movement and choral song. These song and dance performances are often associated with birds, seafaring, fertility, and tattooing. Props can include paddles, head ornaments, and the bamboo or wooden sticks for stick dances.

Missionaries and settlers from outside Oceania introduced foreign instruments to Micronesia in the nineteenth and twentieth centuries, especially guitars, ukuleles (see below, under "Hawaii"), mandolins, harmonicas, accordions, and organs. Although Protestant missionaries forbade dancing, indigenous dance movements are routinely performed in many churches. Cassette tape recordings, which disseminated popular music from the West, were popular in late-twentieth-century post-colonial Micronesia. Today rock, country, reggae, and other styles played in bands comprised of Western instruments such as guitar, drums, and electronic keyboards are a strong presence. A renewed interest in indigenous tradition, however, is finding its voice in the Oceania's Festival of Pacific Arts and other regular events.

Figure 12-9 Micronesian school students perform a traditional Micronesian dance.

PLAYLIST OPTIONS
MUSIC OF MELANESIA AND MICRONESIA

FIND
- A video or audio performance of
  - Melanesian slit drums
  - Melanesian bamboo band music
    - Especially from the Solomon Islands
  - Micronesian dance
  - Micronesian stick dance
  - "Melanesian music"
  - "Micronesian music"

OBSERVE
- Genre and instrumentation
- Dance regalia and choreography
- Rhythmic and melodic aspects
- The presence or absence of Western influences

IV
POLYNESIA

Polynesia ("many islands") covers a wide geographical area of eighteen island groups in the Pacific, including Aotearoa (New Zealand), Rapa Nui (Easter Island), and the US state of Hawaii. The earliest settlers migrated from Asia and Southeast Asia to Melanesia and eventually spread into the Polynesian islands. Today the islands are home to both original and more recent settlers from around the world. Indigenous languages are supplemented throughout Polynesia, most commonly with English, French, and Spanish.

Polynesian cultures vary, but music and dance are important throughout the islands. Life events such as weddings, funerals, and historic occasions inspire ceremonial performances. Small groups of synchronized dancers narrate poetry not only through song but also with choreographed motions in either standing or seated dances. These performances commonly express their social hierarchies and belief systems. In order to keep the poetic messages clear, performers do not dramatize or "act out" the stories in their choreography; instead, the hand, wrist, and arm movements sign specific words and phrases. Melody and harmony are not as important in Polynesia as they are in European musical traditions, so foreign audiences and scholars can misunderstand the music as "simple" or "primitive" while they miss the nuanced and multifaceted poetic meanings. This section will focus on the music and dance of Hawaii and Aotearoa (New Zealand).

Hawaii

Original settlers thought to be Polynesians came from islands to the south of Hawaii in several waves starting about 650 CE. Captain James Cook's arrival in 1778 marked the first known European contact. American and

Figure 12-10 Hula kahiko performance in Hawaii Volcanoes National Park, 2005.

European traders colonized Hawaii soon afterward, capitalizing on trading opportunities in whaling and other industries. By the twentieth century, the US had overthrown the Hawaiian indigenous monarchy and annexed the islands, which eventually became the fiftieth state in 1959.

Traditional Music

Mele, the foundation for much of Hawaiian music and dance, are poetic song texts that can be sacred or secular, with a vast array of topics, including genealogical songs that trace lineage, name songs that honor people, love songs, and welcome songs. Mele accompanied by dance are typically in duple meter, and mele without dance are generally **nonmetric** chants. Vocal styles vary according to topic; some styles feature prominent vibrato. Hawaiian dance, called **hula**, is often used with or instead of song to express mele. The dancer sings, and, in seated dances, also plays rhythmic idiophones or membranophones. Hand, wrist, and arm movements convey the words, phrases, and, at times, rich,

Mele Traditional Hawaiian poetic song texts, with a vast array of topics.

Nonmetric Music with little or no discernible metric pattern; see Musical Elements Appendix.

Hula Traditional Hawaiian dance, often used with or instead of song to express mele (poetic song text). Hand, wrist, and arm movements convey the words, phrases, and rich, multilayered meanings of the mele in graceful gestures.

multilayered meanings of the mele in graceful gestures. Hula clothing can include decorative accessories such as leis (flower necklaces). The most common traditional musical instruments include the conch for signaling, membranophones, and rattle idiophones. Hula dancers often accompany themselves with both instruments.

Western Influences

Nineteenth-century Christian missionaries suppressed indigenous culture, including language, music, and traditional beliefs. The missionaries condemned hula, in particular, as vulgar. Under their influence, many Christianized Hawaiians embraced Western culture. They learned Christian hymns and other Western songs, which strongly influenced Hawaiian popular music idioms in the next century. This caused traditional music and hula to go underground until a late-nineteenth-century revival emerged with new, Western-influenced styles that featured strophic poetry and songs, ukulele (see below) and guitar accompaniment, and Victorian gowns worn by hula dancers.

An especially important indigenous musician during the revival was also Hawaii's last monarch: **Lili'uokalani, Queen of Hawaii (1838–1917)**. Author, composer, vocalist, and instrumentalist, as well as a political figure and ruler from 1891 until the US takeover in 1893, Lili'uokalani was a creative force as well as an advocate for both indigenous and Asian Hawaiians. She resisted the US colonialism already underway and sought to preserve traditional culture, especially through her music. Although her notated, strophic songs built upon European harmonies reflected her Western-style musical training, she also composed many traditional chants that blended Hawaiian and European musical idioms. Her most well-known song, "Aloha Oe" ("Farewell to Thee"), written while she was under house arrest during the US takeover, is still popular today.

The two chordophones most associated with Hawaii today—the ukulele and the steel guitar—are not indigenous to Polynesia. Portuguese settlers introduced a small, four-stringed folk guitar to Hawaii in the 1870s that soon became known as the **ukulele (Hawaiian "jumping flea")** on the islands, also known as the "uke." When Hawaiian ukulele players toured the US mainland in the late nineteenth and early twentieth centuries, it became a beloved symbol of a quickly disappearing idyllic tropical lifestyle. Vaudevillians strummed this portable instrument throughout their concert tours, ensuring the ukulele craze of the early twentieth century, as well as its recent revival.

Ukulele, uke (Hawaiian "jumping flea") A small, four-stringed folk guitar chordophone introduced to Hawaii by Portuguese settlers in the 1870s; see Musical Instruments Appendix.

Lili'uokalani, Queen of Hawai'i: "No especial change was perceptible in my treatment or mode of life by reasons of my trial and sentence. Though I was still not allowed to have newspapers or general literature to read, writing-paper and lead-pencils were not denied; and I was thereby able to write music, after drawing for myself the lines of the staff. At first I had no instrument, and had to transcribe the notes by voice alone; but I found, notwithstanding disadvantages, great consolation in composing, and transcribed a number of songs. Three found their way from my prison to the city of Chicago, where they were printed, among them the "Aloha Oe" or "Farewell to Thee," which became a very popular song."[4]

Steel guitar (Hawaiian guitar) Chordophone on which glissando sounds are produced by a sliding steel bar. Originally developed in Hawaii, the instrument is also a virtually indispensable component of country music in the US and around the world; see Musical Instruments Appendix.

The **steel guitar** (**Hawaiian guitar**), a chordophone on which glissando sounds are produced by a sliding steel bar, became as inseparable with the Hawaiian sound as the ukulele. It was popularized in the late nineteenth century by Joseph Kekuku, who experimented with sliding his comb or his penknife on the strings of a guitar. Its roots, however, may go back much further: ethnomusicologist Mantle Hood traces its possible origin to an Indian immigrant who recreated an ancient South Asian chordophone. Hood compares the traditional Hawaiian vocal style featuring vibrato and falsetto with steel guitar characteristics, implying a natural affinity. He makes an interesting distinction between the fact that the mele (poetic text) is most important to traditional Hawaiians and that the distinctive sound of the slide guitar is most important to listeners outside of traditional Hawaiian society. Thus, the steel guitar creates a bridge for non-Hawaiians to Hawaiian meaning.[5] Disseminated throughout the US by touring musicians, the steel guitar took hold in country music on the mainland. The instrument gradually developed into a horizontal table with several necks, pedals, and knee levers to facilitate its signature slide between pitches. The steel guitar, still strongly associated with Hawaii, is now, at the same time, a virtually indispensable component of country music in the US and around the world.

Hawaiian-themed entertainment on the mainland boomed throughout the twentieth century and beyond, marketed with entrancing images of a tropical Hawaiian paradise on ukulele and steel guitar instruction book covers, travel brochures, and film posters. Hawaiian music has developed its own identity through a variety of styles and popular entertainers. Iconic figures in Hawaiian music include "Don Ho" (Donald Tai Loy Ho 1930–2007), a nightclub singer whose commercial style had roots in big band music, and Eddie Kamae with the Sons of Hawaii, a band active in the 1960s through the 1990s, featuring ukulele and steel guitar.

The legacy of singer and ukulele player **Israel "Iz" Kamakawiwo'ole (1959–1997)** is treasured by Hawaiians. He expressed indigenous awareness in an accessible and sincere "Jawaiian" (Hawaiian reggae, or "island music") musical style, which has roots in reggae and became popular in the 1990s among indie labels in Hawaii. Although his song topics include ancient Hawaiian legends, his covers of "Somewhere Over the Rainbow" and "What a Wonderful World" have become internationally popular. More recently, the Japanese-American ukulele virtuoso **Jake Shimabukuro**

(b. 1976) has risen to prominence as a Hawaiian musician. In 2006, a video of his instrumental arrangement of "While My Guitar Gently Weeps" by George Harrison became viral and catapulted him to worldwide fame. Since then, he has shown his prowess in his own compositions as well as his instrumental covers of rock, jazz, and classical music. These two renowned musicians use the ukulele in

Figure 12-12 Jake Shimabukuro, 2010.

vastly different ways.

Aotearoa (New Zealand)

The last stop in the Polynesian migration was Aotearoa (New Zealand), settled by around 1300 CE. This nation, comprised of two large and several smaller islands, is renowned for the beauty and variety of its landscapes, which include high mountains, plateaus, narrow inlets or "fiords," and beaches. Tribes of **Maori**, separated by these natural geographic features, practice distinctive local styles of woodcarving, music, dance, and body art.

Maori   Indigenous people of Aotearoa (New Zealand).

Traditional Music

Moteatea—Maori traditional chant, song, or sung poetry—is a core musical practice among Maori that is meant to connect performers and

Moteatea   Maori traditional chant, song, or sung poetry. Traditional songs are performed in unison, with melodies in a narrow range.

listeners with their spiritual selves and remind them of the meaning of past events and their present condition. Moteatea performance, which also functions as speech, can help resolve disputes between individuals or tribes. Traditional songs are performed in unison, with conjunct melodies in a narrow range.

The Maori use traditional musical instruments, including idiophones made of materials such as animal bones and teeth, jade, and wood. Flute music was associated with life events and healing. The last surviving player who learned in the traditional way died in the 1960s, but a revival has been underway by Maori musicians since the late twentieth century instigated, in large part, by traditional flute-maker Brian Flintoff and scholar-performers Hirini Melbourne (1949–2003) and Richard Nunns (b. 1945).

Haka A war dance and chant, which has become an iconic Maori display of spirit and courage.

Dance is especially important to Maori as it is with Polynesians in general. The **haka**, a war dance with chant, has become an iconic Maori display of spirit and courage. From wide, battle-ready stances, performers stamp their feet rhythmically and aggressively. They begin the dance with

Figure 12-13 Maori warriors perform a Haka for US Secretary of Defense Leon Panetta during his visit to Auckland, New Zealand, 2012.

quivering motions that are thought to connect the dancer's body and mind, bringing the dance to life. Arm and hand gestures throughout the dance convey information. Facial expressions are fearsome, with wide-open eyes and protruding tongues. The text is chanted and shouted rather than sung. The haka includes many subtypes and individual compositions. Although it is clearly warlike, it can also be performed for celebration, commemoration, or political comment. Since 1888, the All Blacks New Zealand rugby team has performed hakas before their games in order to confront and intimidate their opponents.

Western Influences

During the eighteenth and nineteenth centuries, Europeans and Americans introduced European harmonies to the Maori when they began trading and missionary activities in the region. The sailors' hornpipes and whistles attracted the Maori, who had their own strong tradition of flute music. While they were Christianized, they learned hymns and practiced choral singing. Touring choirs and instrumental ensembles, such as the Fisk Jubilee Singers and John Philip Sousa's band from the US, became especially popular, helping to spark the formation of choral societies and brass bands among the Maori. Choral competitions featuring hymns, anthems, and oratorios began in the late nineteenth century and continue to this day.

Modern Aotearoa (New Zealand) boasts a vibrant musical life across the continuum of vernacular through art musical genres. Prominent art music composers include **Dame Gillian Whitehead (b. 1941)**, whose modernist atonal works are influenced by elements of her Maori heritage, and Jack Body (1944–2015), an arts advocate who intensively mined East and Southeast Asian musical idioms for his compositions. Lyric soprano **Dame Kiri Te Kanawa (b. 1944)** earned international fame in the 1970s with her mellifluous vocal quality in a wide range of operatic roles. The Atamira Dance Company (created in 2000) is a contemporary dance troupe that references indigenous Maori themes and musical instruments. **Moana Maniapoto (b. 1961)** of Moana & the Tribe is a singer-songwriter, and the first non-American to win the US-based International Songwriting Competition: she won in 2003 with "Moko." Her songs, which explore Maori traditions and concerns, show influence from reggae, R&B, and other popular idioms. Maori cultural competitions and festivals are regularly presented throughout Aotearoa (New Zealand) to foster the revival and preservation of indigenous performance arts.

Dame Gillian Whitehead: "Sometimes I hear a finished idea but at other times I only know the kind of soundscape or the sound world I want, and I have to find the way to get to it. One way I've worked is by setting up a pattern of pitches that stretches my imagination as I need to build something that can involve them all in a musical way. Sometimes even within a single piece there are some bits that I know very clearly and other parts that I have to explore, that may take a lot of time to get right. In a couple of pieces I've written recently, it's been difficult to determine where the piece starts. I started working on the piece and thought no, it starts further back, so I go further back and then I write something that encompasses that bit and the next bit—but no, it starts even further back. And that's been quite a new experience for me. Because in the past I could always start at the beginning and go on from there. But now the question seems to be, just how far back do I have to start?"[6]

PLAYLIST OPTIONS
MUSIC OF POLYNESIA

FIND

A video or audio performance of
*   Hula dance
    *   Especially Merrie Monarch Festival videos
    *   Visit the Merrie Monarch Festival's website for information & videos: http://merriemonarch.com
*   "Aloha Oe" ("Farewell to Thee") by Lili'uokalani
*   Hawaiian performers
    *   Don Ho
    *   Eddie Kamae and the Sons of Hawaii
    *   Israel "Iz" Kamakawiwo'ole
    *   Jake Shimabukuro
        *   Especially his landmark video, "Ukelele Weeps" (cover of Harrisons's "While My Guitar Gently Weeps")
*   Maori haka
    *   Traditional context
    *   All Blacks (New Zealand rugby team) pregame haka
*   New Zealand musicians
    *   Dame Gillian Whitehead, composer
    *   Jack Body, composer
    *   Dame Kiri Te Kanawa, vocalist
    *   Atamira Dance Company
    *   Moana Maniapoto of Moana & the Tribe, singer-songwriter

OBSERVE

- Topics
- Dance regalia and choreography
- Rhythmic and melodic aspects
- Interplay of Western, Asian, and Polynesian influences

ASK

- How has Polynesian music influenced Western culture?

CHAPTER 12 VOCABULARY & IMPORTANT FIGURES

Vocabulary

Aboriginal

Bamboo Bands

Bush songs

Circular Breathing

Clapsticks

Conch shell trumpet

Corroboree

Didjeridu (didgeridoo, didjeridoo, didj)

Dreamtime

Haka

Hula

Maori

Mele

Moteatea

Singsing

Slit Drums

Songlines (history song, song series)

Steel guitar (Hawaiian guitar)

Susap

Ukulele, uke (Hawaiian "jumping flea")

Important Figures

Israel "Iz" Kamakawiwo'ole (1959-1997)

Dame Kiri Te Kanawa (b. 1944)

Francis MacNamara ("Frank the Poet," c. 1810–1861)

Lili'uokalani, Queen of Hawaii (1838–1917)

Moana Maniapoto (b. 1961)

A. B. Paterson ("Banjo Paterson," 1864–1941)

Archie Roach (b. 1956)

Jake Shimabukuro (b. 1976)

Dame Gillian Whitehead (b. 1941)

ENDNOTES

[1] Simon McDonald: Traditional singers and musicians in Victoria: Wattle LP, 1962.

[2] Interview available on at archieroach.com at http://www.archieroach.com.au/archie_roach_videos.html accessed 6/22/17.

[3] Archie Roach website, accessed March 12, 2016, http://www.archieroach.com.au/song/took-the-children-away-2/.

[4] From Hawaii's Story By Hawaii's Queen by Liliuokalani, Boston: Lee and Shepard, 1898, Ch XLVI, "Sentenced—My Prison Life."

[5] Mantle Hood, "Musical Ornamentation as History: The Hawaiian Steel Guitar." *Yearbook for Traditional Music,* Vol. 15, *East Asian Musics* (1983), pp. 141–148.

[6] From "Ways of Looking and Listening," Gillian Karawe Whitehead talks to film director Gaylene Preston, 2001.

Image Credits

- Figure 12-1: Copyright © 2004 by Ron Ardis, (CC BY-SA 2.0) at https://commons.wikimedia.org/wiki/File:Hula_Kahiko_Hawaii_Volcanoes_National_Park_01.jpg.

- Figure 12-2: Copyright © 2014 by Cruickshanks, (CC BY-SA 3.0) at https://commons.wikimedia.org/wiki/File:Oceania_UN_Geoscheme_Regions.svg.

- Figure 12-3: Copyright © 2011 by Steve Evans, (CC BY 2.0) at https://commons.wikimedia.org/wiki/File:Australia_Aboriginal_Culture_009.jpg.

- Figure 12-4: A. B. Paterson / Copyright in the Public Domain.

- Figure 12-5: Copyright © 2011 by Bruce, (CC BY 2.0) at https://www.flickr.com/photos/theholygrail/5440296950.

- Figure 12-6: Copyright © 2012 by Eva Rinaldi, (CC BY-SA 2.0) at https://commons.wikimedia.org/wiki/File:John_Williamson_Guitarist.jpg.

- Figure 12-7: Copyright © 1975 by Allan Warren, (CC BY-SA 3.0) at https://commons.wikimedia.org/wiki/File:Dame_Joan_Sutherland,_by_Allan_Warren.jpg.

- Figure 12-8: Copyright © 2008 by David Iliff, (CC BY-SA 3.0) at https://commons.wikimedia.org/wiki/File:Sydney_Opera_House_-_Dec_2008.jpg.

- Figure 12-9: U.S. Department of State / Copyright in the Public Domain.

- Figure 12-10: Copyright © 2005 by Ron Ardis, (CC BY-SA 2.0) at https://commons.wikimedia.org/wiki/File:Hula_Kahiko_Hawaii_Volcanoes_National_Park_02.jpg.

- Figure 12-11: Menzies Dickson / Copyright in the Public Domain.

- Figure 12-12: Copyright © 2010 by Joe Bielawa, (CC BY 2.0) at https://commons.wikimedia.org/wiki/File:Jake_Shimabukuro_(5151354125).jpg.

- Figure 12-13: Copyright © 2012 by Erin A. Kirk-Cuomo, (CC BY 2.0) at https://commons.wikimedia.org/wiki/File:Haka_performed_during_US_Defense_Secretary%27s_visit_to_New_Zealand_(1).jpg.

- Figure 12-14: Copyright © by Gareth Watkins.

Drummers in Ghana, 2012.

CHAPTER

13 Music in Sub-Saharan Africa

A frica, the world's second largest continent, features vast and widely varied regions that include grasslands, deserts, rainforests, and islands along its coast. Diamonds, gold, and oil are some of Africa's most important mineral resources. Africans live in a great variety of environments, such as in cities, in outlying homesteads, and in migrant worker or nomadic camps. Almost 3,000 distinct ethnic groups live in Africa. Hundreds of indigenous languages are classified into four language families throughout the continent. Swahili is one of the indigenous languages, and it is also a "trade language" or *lingua franca* in parts of Africa among a variety of cultures that would not otherwise be able to communicate. It became useful in this way by incorporating influences from a variety of languages.

Powerful kingdoms began to emerge as early as c. 3500 BCE on the Nile River in Egypt and then, later, beginning in c. 500 CE, throughout the rest of the continent. Outside of these kingdoms, smaller, "stateless" societies have existed, some of them with governing hierarchies. European colonialism, which began in the seventeenth century, led to the establishment of many national boundaries that crossed cultural groups and created the prominence of English, French, Portuguese, and other European languages. Millions of Africans were victimized and displaced by slave-trading over many centuries. This resulted in a major portion of the African diaspora throughout the world. Although slavery is now widely considered illegal and immoral, the sale and forced labor of an

405

Figure 13-2 Political map of Africa.

estimated 21 million people continues to this day on many continents, including Africa.[1]

Indigenous belief systems throughout the continent are wide-ranging but some aspects in common include the idea of one supreme creator god, with intermediate deities or spirits that might live in nature such as water, rocks, and trees. Colonialism and immigration disseminated Christianity and Islam throughout Africa ever since the origin of those religions. Islam, for instance, took an early foothold in Northern Africa but has a presence throughout much of the rest of Africa as well. Christianity, also widespread throughout the continent, shows its presence especially in the Ethiopian Coptic Church and in South Africa where the South African National Anthem is partly based on a Christian hymn.

The concept of "music" in Africa has many differences from its meaning and practice in Western culture. Music is part of an interwoven texture of arts that include song, instrumental performance, dance, and drama. All of these arts, with music included, are practiced in daily work, social, and political life. Everyone is invited and often expected to participate with at least some basic knowledge and proficiency rather than to sit quietly as an audience. In music, as in other pursuits, oral—rather than written or notated—tradition is valued and cultivated. A common Western impression that cultures without written communication are "primitive" has caused Westerners to underestimate much about Africans, including the rich, complex features of African music.

Musical elements in Africa tend to emphasize interaction and spontaneity. For instance, **improvisation** is a hallmark of African music. Social interaction in music is exemplified by **call and response**, the alternation between leading and responding groups or individuals in music or speech, which often includes improvisation. Rhythmic textures are among the most cultivated and complex in the world: multiple layers of rhythmic lines seem to intersect and interact with each other in what can be called **interlocking rhythms**. Distinctive varieties of timbre, pitch, tempo, and volume among the drums and idiophones can make a rich rhythmic texture uncannily transparent despite its complexity. Still, this demands a radically different way to listen for most Westerners: instead of delineating melody, harmony, and individual rhythms, traditional polyrhythmic ensemble music needs to be heard in its totality. The resulting sound picture creates a different and more complete impression than the sum of its parts.

This chapter explores music-making in two major sub-Saharan areas of the African continent: the region of West Africa and the nation of South Africa. Northern African music, which tends to be more aligned with Middle Eastern Arabic music, will be examined in a section on Egyptian music-making in Chapter 14, Music in the Middle East.

Improvisation The creation of music during performance, common in many cultures and genres; (Chapter 3, Jazz).

Call and response The alternation between leading and responding groups or individuals in music or speech.

Interlocking rhythms Multiple layers of rhythmic lines that seem to intersect and interact with each other.

I

ENCOUNTERS, COMMUNICATION, AND SYNTHESIS: MUSICAL INSTRUMENTS IN WEST AFRICA

West Africa features desert and savannah (grassland) to the north and forested regions in the south. Some of the earliest African societies emerged in this region, such as the Akan culture and the Mali Empire. West Africa was also the epicenter of the Atlantic slave trade. Although much of the continent suffered the effects of slave trading, most of the kidnapped Africans bound for the Americas are believed to have left Africa in ports along the West African coastline. Today memorials stand in tribute to this history, most notably the *Maison des Esclaves* ("House of Slaves") with its Door of No Return, a UNESCO World Heritage site in Dakar, Senegal. France and England dominated in this region during the colonial era, but Spain and Portugal also had claimed territories. Throughout the second half of the twentieth century, African nations achieved independence. Today Islam is the most widespread religion; however, Christianity and African traditional religions are also practiced in the region.

West African music features rich polyrhythmic textures, influences from beyond West Africa, and strong family traditions. A hereditary class of oral historians known as **griots** carry on the musical and literary traditions of the culture. The emphasis varies among regions and individuals, but their role goes beyond musical performance. Depending on the community, the griot is any combination of musician, storyteller, poet, historian, and praise singer. The term, "griot," is French, and is used by Westerners as an umbrella term for several different subtypes throughout West Africa.

***Griot* tradition**
A hereditary class of oral historians who carry on the musical and literary traditions of the culture in Western Africa.

Encounter I: Ancestor of the American Banjo?

The banjo, one of the principal instruments in American bluegrass and old-time country music, has roots in Africa. Out of several West African lutes that could reasonably be considered ancestors to the banjo, evidence for the **akonting** is especially compelling, thanks to the collaboration between Swedish banjo historian Ulf Jagfors and Gambian akonting scholar-performer Daniel Laemouahuma Jatta. It is a gourd pierced with a long pole that is made out of a bamboo-like woody grass called *bangoe* in Manding, a West African language. A short drone string (meant to be played without changing its pitch) and two or more long strings are stretched along the pole that is used as a neck. This very type of stringing, in which the thumb is meant to play the drone string and the fingers to play the long strings in down-stroke style, was used in the early American banjo and is strikingly similar to a traditional plucking technique known as "clawhammer."

Akonting A long-necked plucked chordophone from Africa, likely an ancestor to the American banjo; see Musical Instruments Appendix.

Figure 13-3 *The Old Plantation*, 18th century watercolor in the Rockefeller Folk Art Center in Williamsburg, VA, atributed to John Rose.

Laemouahuma "Daniel" Jatta (Pictured standing next to a print of William Sidney Mount's The Banjo Player, 1856.): "My goal is to set a center in The Gambia, which can be the gateway for everyone who wants to understand these folk cultures that are the foundation of our music, culture, and history. To understand it and be able to use it as it was used before, to develop our societies in all forms. Because the instruments and the cultures that were able to create all the thinking we have today is a kind of a creative knowledge that is in them that we must look into again, to be able to come back with the creativity that was there before. Unless we do that with an institution that is prepared to involve these people who still have the knowledge, we cannot be able to go beyond what we have."[2]

The akonting is considered a "folk" rather than a griot instrument; one does not have to be from a griot family in order to play it. In the eighteenth-century watercolor *The Old Plantation* (see Figure 13-3), we see an instrument similar to both the akonting and the banjo. The accompanying drum, the stick dance, and the turbans in the painting indicate Mandinkan or Jola cultures from the same region of West Africa as the akonting. American banjo virtuoso Béla Fleck traveled to Africa for his documentary, *Throw Down Your Heart*. He jammed with African musicians, including members of the Jatta family in The Gambia, who play the akonting and other traditional instruments.

Encounter II: A Griot Instrument Goes Global

Kora   A Western African plucked-string harp chordophone; see Musical Instruments Appendix.

The **kora** is a harp made from a large gourd covered with cowhide and pierced with a wooden pole that serves as a neck. Nineteen or twenty-one strings extend from the neck to the gourd. Unlike the akonting, the kora is not a folk instrument; instead, it is traditionally considered to be the domain of male griots, who can use it to accompany both male and female praise singers. It also stands on its own as a soloistic instrument, which can dazzle listeners with melodic and rhythmic intricacies in the hands of a virtuosic player. The Diabaté family of Mali, who can trace seventy-one generations of their griot heritage, are renowned players. **Toumani Diabaté (b. 1965),** in particular, has achieved international fame not only with his virtuosity but also through his collaborations with musicians of other cultures and styles. Influenced as a child by Western musicians such as Jimi Hendrix and Led Zeppelin, Diabaté formed his Symmetric Orchestra. The name is a reference to his idea of a perfect balance between tradition and modernity, according to his website. His band includes both traditional and modern instruments. His concert career is

Figure 13-5 Toumani Diabaté with kora, 2009.

rich with cross-genre collaborations, including the flamenco group Ketama, the blues and jazz musician Taj Mahal, and singer-songwriter Björk.

Communication: Talking Instruments in the Asanti Tradition

Musical instruments are often used as spoken language in West Africa. Speech sounds such as inflection, rhythm, and accent are recreated on drums, trumpets, flutes, whistles, and stringed instruments. The sounds can be uncannily recognizable as words, but they are not exact; much depends on both spoken and musical dialect, the style of the musician, and the instrumental idiom. For instance, talking drums reflect accent and the number of syllables in the phrase with more precision than melodic instruments, which more clearly recreate the inflected pitches. Musicians also can elaborate on the words and phrases melodically, rhythmically, or in other ways. The "talking drums" of the Akan are well known, but perhaps **talking instruments** ("surrogate speech" is used by some scholars) would be a better term because of the use of so many instruments this way in addition to drums.

Similar practices exist throughout Africa and in other parts of the world, but talking instruments are especially popular among the Akan people in Ghana and Côte d'Ivoire (Ivory Coast). Twi, the **tonal language** of the Akan, is especially well suited as a foundation for the performance of talking instruments: in a tonal language, inflection and accent help determine the meaning of a word, so musical elements such as pitch and accent are already important aspects of speech. Many African and East Asian languages are tonal but English and most other European languages are not.

What do these talking instruments say? In Akan performances, they usually convey proverbs imbued with layers of subtle meanings. The Akan culture, which likely has connections with the kingdoms of Ghana and Mali from the Middle Ages, holds traditional beliefs that place importance on a High God, good and evil spirits, and the influence of ancestors. Sounds emanating from musical instruments, which the Akan believe are imbued with good spirits, can protect people from evil spirits. One needs to understand not only the language but also the culture to be able to decode the proverbs. We have an example in a passage "spoken" by

Talking Instruments
Western African musical instruments that are used to create speech-like sounds such as inflection, rhythm, and accent.

Tonal language
Language in which inflection and accent help determine the meaning of a word.

Figure 13-6 Fontomfrom drums, which are used as "talking drums," Ghana, 2017.

pitched **membranophones**, below. Note the several layers of meaning, which include a literal description of the human intersection with nature, the high value placed on ancestry, and a testament to one creator:

> The river crosses the path,
> The path crosses the river,
> Who is elder?

Membranophones
Musical instruments which produce sound by vibrating stretched skins, or membranes over a hollow resonator; most of these are drums; see Musical Instruments Appendix.

The path was cut to meet the river,
The river is of old,
The river comes from
"Odomankoma" the Creator.[3]

Synthesis: Diverse Threads in the Tapestry of West African Popular Music

Highlife: The Roots of Modern Popular Music in West Africa

Highlife West African early to mid-twentieth-century music that blended African idioms with European and American—especially Caribbean—influences.

European colonial presence in West Africa brought with it the musical influences of Christian missionaries, military bands, sea shanties, and other styles based in Western European music. By the early nineteenth century, West Africans had begun to acquire instruments such as pianos, guitars, Americanized banjos, and band instruments. They used them to play music that blended African idioms with European and American—especially Caribbean—influences.

Throughout the early twentieth century, dance music, which was associated with "high society" parties, developed and became known as **highlife**. The music was typically in simple duple meter with a steady tempo for the dancers. Melodies were catchy and often joyful, in syncopated rhythm. The song texts—written in a West African language or in English—were most often about love but some included sociopolitical references. Castanets, maracas, and drums dominated the rhythm section, with wind instruments and guitars on the melody.

During World War II, swing music inspired highlife bandleaders such as **E. T. Mensah (1919–1996)**, who toured West Africa with his band "The Tempos." Mensah's 1957 performance in Ghana with the renowned American jazz trumpet player Louis Armstrong signified a poignant connection between American jazz and African highlife. By the late twentieth century, however, West African popular music in Africa had developed into other styles, dominated by a new generation of performers.

Music in West Africa Today

The various strands of musical sources in West Africa—folk and griot traditions, colonial music, the blend of Africa and the West in highlife, and the influences of both Islamic sacred music and of Caribbean music—come together in a lavish tapestry of styles. Prominent West African musicians of the late twentieth century learned much from their diverse musical soundscape, but they also became innovators who have developed throughout their own careers and are currently influencing many others. The following represents only a sample of today's notable West African musicians.

"King" Sunny Adé "KSA" (b. 1946) is a Nigerian singer-songwriter and guitarist associated with the Yoruban popular dance musical genre, **jùjú.** A blend of traditional Yoruban talking drum and praise-singing styles with American and South Asian popular music, jùjú uses both traditional and modern electronic instruments, with a vocal chorus of praise singers.

Jùjú Yoruban popular dance musical genre of Nigeria, which uses both traditional and modern electronic instruments, with a vocal chorus of praise singers.

"The golden voice of Africa," singer-songwriter **Salif Keita (b. 1949)** is from Mali and a noble descendent of a thirteenth-century Mandinkan Empire founder. His decision to become a musician, however, as well as his albinism, drastically set him apart. Albinism is a congenital absence of pigment in the skin, hair, and eyes, which results in a different, much lighter color than in those without albinism. Many Africans born with albinism suffer discrimination and sometimes violence due to widespread superstitions about the condition. Keita's most important influences include traditional African music, Caribbean and other Western popular styles, and Islamic sacred music. His 2009 album *La Différence*, which includes a plea for acceptance and respect of albinos and all people, won "Best World Music" album in 2010.

Senegalese singer-songwriter and percussionist **Youssou N'Dour (b. 1959)** is a hereditary griot. He became known early in life as a talented praise singer and quickly developed an international following. He is especially known for developing and popularizing **mbalax**, a fusion of Western popular music with traditional Senegalese rhythms. The documentary, *I Bring What I Love*, describes the controversy surrounding his 2004 album of Islamic sacred music, *Egypt*.

Mbalax A fusion of Western popular music with traditional Senegalese rhythms.

Salif Keita on performing in France: "I had not only left a country for another, I had left a whole continent for another. Therefore, I was somewhat expecting challenges...I came up against a wall, which was Show Business. I had no hammer to break that wall and besides, it was not by using force that it would be brought down. What was needed was experience and knowledge of the milieu. Composing in Africa was the easiest thing. You have a melody, in your lyrics, you speak about someone. You repeat words that have been said for ages, for hundreds and thousands of years. You repeat the same things. Whereas here, you must say what is essential in the least amount of time...I like that. You are losing some habits but you are learning something that can be useful to you for the rest of your life."[4]

Figure 13-8 Youssou N'Dour performing in Warsaw, Poland, 2009.

Angélique Kidjo (b. 1960), of Benin, is a singer-songwriter nicknamed "Queen of African crossover pop." Her influences include American jazz and popular music, Latin American styles, and African styles.

Figure 13-9 Angélique Kidjo, 2006.

PLAYLIST OPTIONS
MUSIC OF WESTERN AFRICA

FIND

A video or audio performance of
- Akonting music (African banjo-like instrument)
  - Daniel Jatta
- Kora music (see Diabaté, below)
- Talking instruments, especially
  - Fontomfrom talking drums
  - "talking drums imitate speech"
- Notable West African musicians
  - "King" Sunny Adé "KSA"
- Singer-songwriter, guitarist
- "jùjú music" genre
- Toumani Diabaté
  - Kora player
  - Symmetric Orchestra
- Salif Keita ("The golden voice of Africa")
  - Singer-songwriter
    - Angelique Kidjo ("Queen of African crossover pop")
  - Singer-songwriter
  - E. T. Mensah
  - Bandleader
  - Highlife genre
    - Youssou N'Dour
  - Singer-songwriter, percussionist, griot
  - Mbalax genre

OBSERVE

- Instrumentation; instrumental features and performer technique
- Improvisational performance
- Interlocking rhythms, or layers of meters and rhythms

ASK

- Did the performance include audience participation in any way?

> ◆ Did the performance reveal Western influences? If so, which musical elements show these influences, and in what way? What stays traditional?

II
THE TRANSFORMATIVE POWER OF SONG: VOCAL MUSIC IN THE NATION OF SOUTH AFRICA

The region of Southern Africa features a series of plateaus surrounded by the Great Escarpment, which in some parts take the form of mountain ranges. Centrally located within the Southern African plateaus are the sandy expanses of the Kalahari Desert. The region's two largest rivers, the Zambezi and the Limpopo, drain eastward into the Indian Ocean.

Musical aspects in common with groups elsewhere in Africa include the prevalence of polyrhythms, similar musical instruments such as types of xylophones, and improvisatory performance practices. In Southern Africa, music is defined by the presence of metered rhythm, so drumming or rhythmic chanting is considered music, but nonmetric vocal singing is not.

The nation of South Africa (not to be confused with the region of Southern Africa) encompasses the southernmost tip of the continent. No less than eleven languages are classified as "official" here, including Afrikaans, English, Xhosa, and Zulu. The most popular out of all the official languages is Zulu; the Xhosa and Zulu cultures are the most prevalent groups in the country.

Afrikaners, descendants of seventeenth-century Dutch settlers who speak Afrikaans (a derivation of Dutch), ruled South Africa together with British colonists throughout the colonial period. For most of the second half of the twentieth century, the nation of South Africa was officially a racially divided nation under the policy of **apartheid** ("apartness" in Afrikaans). Although colonial forces had already subjugated indigenous

Apartheid A system of racial segregation and discrimination enforced by the South African government from 1948–1991 in which the rights of non-Whites were severely curtailed.

South Africans long before, apartheid went beyond that in a historically racist political framework: racial discrimination was, in fact, written into law.

Between 1948 and 1991, the South African government enforced this system of segregation between the White minority and the non-White majority throughout the nation. Residential and business sections in cities were demarcated for either Whites or non-Whites. Public facilities such as buses and restrooms were carefully labeled for either Whites or non-Whites. Even social contact between Whites and non-Whites was regulated when allowed at all. Apartheid did not just separate people, however; it discriminated against non-Whites with much lower standards of citizenship and services across all aspects of life, including education, healthcare, employment, and political representation.

These policies triggered protests and uprisings, and the government responded with bloody crackdowns and political imprisonments. Many

Figure 13-10 Apartheid-era sign on beach in Durban, South Africa, 1989, in English, Afrikaans, and Zulu.

nations around the world censured South Africa and some, including the US, imposed sanctions on the government until apartheid fell in the early 1990s. Music, in its role as a medium of protest, demonstrated its power to inspire strength in apartheid's victims at the same time that it conveyed an awareness of apartheid's brutality to the world outside.

Song as Expression and Dignity

Weekend choral singing in South Africa began among male migrant workers in the late nineteenth century. After a long, hard week in factories or in mines, the workers, far from home and living in all-male hostels, became singers. They formed **a cappella** choirs and competed against each other through the night. The competitions increased throughout the twentieth century and continue to this day. Their performances eventually included detailed **choreography** and fashion shows with handsome suits, shoes, hats, and white gloves. Successful choirs enjoy an improved social status.

The leader ("controller") directs the choir ("the chord") in a call and response style. Most sing in the bass range with one or two higher voices, and the leader is often a tenor. Musical textures include polyphony and hymn-like homophonic four-part harmonies. Intricate polyrhythms, vocal sound effects, and visually arresting choreography add interest and power to the performance. Most of these workers come from the Zulu ethnic group that is prevalent in Southern Africa. Zulu vocal polyphony and distinctive leg stomps and kicks provide a foundation of stylistic characteristics to these performances. Other influences overlay that foundation, including European harmonies from the Christian hymns and other songs that missionaries taught Africans in colonial times.

This choir music genre was named **mbube** (Zulu, "lion") after the name of one of the genre's earliest recorded songs. **Solomon Linda (1909–1962)** and his group, the Evening Birds, recorded *Mbube* in 1939. The song's winding trail through the music industry in the US began when song collector and media theorist Tony Schwartz received the song from a South African correspondent and passed it along to Pete Seeger (see Chapter 1, American Traditional Music) and the Weavers, who used it as their basis for "Wimoweh" in 1951. The Tokens 1961 version, renamed "The Lion Sleeps Tonight," became a hit, reaping large profits. By its 1994 inclusion in Disney's *Lion King* animated feature film, the song had been covered by over a dozen artists and was well known. Yet Solomon Linda died in poverty soon after the song's initial success. The 2002 PBS

A Cappella (lt. "in the chapel style") Vocal music unaccompanied by musical instruments. (Unit 2, Western Art Music, Introduction).

Choreography
The sequence of dance movements or the notated version of dance movements (Chapter 2, American Music for Stage and Screen).

Mbube **(Zulu, "lion") and** *isicathamia* **(Zulu, "to walk stealthily like a cat")** A South African choir music genre in which the leader directs the choir in a call and response style. Popular competitions brought the genre to prominence with the Solomon Linda's Evening Birds and Joseph Shabalala's Ladysmith Black Mambazo.

documentary *A Lion's Trail* raised important questions on artistic ownership and international copyright law.

Mbube's choreography and music softened under the influence of
Ladysmith Black Mambazo leader **Joseph Shabalala (b. 1941)**. He
emphasized rhythmic accuracy with hushed but precise vocal harmonies.
The group's crouching, tip-toeing motions—in sharp contrast to mbube's
more common forceful stomps—earned its new genre name, **isicathamia** (Zulu, "to walk stealthily like a cat"). Shabalala, who grew up near
the town of Ladysmith, moved to Durban as a young man and worked as
a mechanic. But he was inspired to sing, and he was fiercely competitive.
He named his group after his hometown, adding the words "black" (after a
Zulu symbol of strength, the black ox) and "mambazo" ("axe," with which
to cut down the competition). Long, disciplined rehearsals perfected their
technical prowess, and they indeed vanquished their competitors. By
the time the celebrated American singer-songwriter Paul Simon invited
Shabalala to collaborate in 1985, Ladysmith Black Mambazo was already
a successful ensemble.

Figure 13-11 Ladysmith Black Mambazo performing in Innsbruck, Austria, 2008.

Joseph Shabalala, just weeks after the deaths of his wife and daughter: "Singing is just like kneeling down and praying. I remember the first day when I listened to harmony. It calmed my heart. And from that day, up to today, music is just like my pillar. I just lean against that harmony."[5]

Simon's *Graceland* (1986) project, however, propelled them to international attention. The music of the album and tour was eclectic, featuring a spectrum of African and American musical genres and artists. Besides Ladysmith Black Mambazo, the album's collaborating musicians included Senegalese griot Youssou N'Dour and American pop singer Linda Ronstadt. The subsequent tour included Miriam Makeba (more about Makeba, below). Simon's visit to South Africa was controversial: most other artists stayed away to protest apartheid with a cultural boycott. Furthermore, some critics worried that Simon's collaboration would result in an exploitation of African music to generate money for the American music industry.

The album, however, was a critical success, earning two Grammys and international praise. Ladysmith Black Mambazo continued its own international career; the ensemble is still active at the time of this writing. Its repertoire is continually enriched with new collaborations but also still informed by its Zulu roots. Their topics, expressed in Zulu or English lyrics, remain centered on themes of peace, unity, and love.

Song as Protest and Liberation

Origins of the New National Anthem

In 1897, a Methodist choirmaster of Xhosa descent wrote the Christian hymn, *Nkosi Sikelel' iAfrika* ("Lord, Bless Africa") for his young students. Enoch Mankayi Sontonga (1873–1905) taught at a mission school near Johannesburg and may have heard an American touring choir led by a Fisk Jubilee Singers alumnus. Even if he did not catch the performance, he was likely influenced by the Christian hymn "Jubilee" tradition of four-part choral arrangements, popularized by international choir performances (see Chapter 1, American Traditional Music, "Spirituals"). He wrote both the music and one stanza of lyrics in the Xhosa language. Seven more stanzas would later be written by Samuel Mqhayi, and in 1942, Moses Mphahlele added a Sesotho language version.

The comforting hymn took root, and by 1912, it was sung even at political meetings that advocated for the rights of black Africans. When apartheid was established later in the century, the hymn became a symbol of resistance. The South African government saw the hymn as subversive and banned it, which only gave it more power as a protest song. After apartheid's fall, a shortened version of *Nkosi* was paired with the Afrikaner hymn *Die Stem van Sud Afrika* ("The Call of South Africa"): together they became the new national anthem in a powerful symbol of reconciliation. *Nkosi* is sung in the indigenous African languages of Xhosa, Zulu, and Sesotho; *Di Stem* is sung in Afrikaans and English.

Miriam Makeba: Mama Afrika

South Africa produced many musical talents throughout the twentieth century, and vocalist **Miriam "Mama Afrika" Makeba (1932–2008)** became one of the entire continent's brightest stars. She sang for seven years in her school chorus as a child, and as a young woman, she was invited to sing with local jazz bands. Popular music in Southern Africa, as elsewhere on the continent, developed its own fusion between local African roots and Western styles such as jazz, rock 'n' roll, and reggae. The resulting hybrid style in South Africa is called ***mbaqanga***. A typical band consists of a lead vocalist (such as Makeba) or a melody instrumentalist backed by electric guitars, drums, and sometimes accordion or violin.

Mbaqanga South African hybrid popular music style of the mid-twentieth century that was a fusion between local African roots and Western styles such as jazz, rock 'n' roll, and reggae.

The lyrics of *mbaqanga* songs were mostly in English and Bantu languages, purposely avoiding Afrikaner, the official language of South Africa during apartheid years. Even though most songs were not overtly political, that very absence of Afrikaner carried an implicit message of resistance. Makeba, who included traditional songs in her repertoire, was able to signify her cultural identity for herself and her listeners without directly confronting the government during the early days of her career. That was to happen later.

Her 1959 performances in the film *Come Back Africa* and in the jazz opera *King Kong* brought her sudden international fame. As her career flourished in the years following with European and American tours, she revealed a versatile range of styles and collaborations with instrumentalists and other vocalists, including Americans Harry Belafonte, Paul Simon, Nina Simone, and another prominent South African musician, trumpet player Hugh Masekela (with whom she was briefly married). Makeba was an outspoken critic of apartheid, and in 1964 she was invited to speak about it at the UN General Assembly. In response, the South African government banned her concerts and forced her to make the choice whether to return home and relinquish her right to travel or to stay away and never come home again. She remained an exiled performer throughout the rest of the apartheid years, continuing to raise international awareness about apartheid in her concerts.

One of the most popular songs in her repertoire, a traditional wedding song known in the West as "The Click Song," introduced Westerners to the clicking sounds of the Xhosa language. Its true title is *Qongqothwane*, and it tells the story of a beetle who makes clicking sounds and can revolve the top part of its body in any direction. The song is meant to bring good luck to the wedding couple, but another layer of meaning is that the beetle can point the way to a better future in troubled times.

Later career accomplishments include the 1986 Dag Hammerskjöld Peace Prize, her 1988 autobiography, *Makeba: My Story*, and her 1992 appearance in the film version of the 1987 musical about the Soweto uprising and its deadly aftermath, *Sarafina!* The musical is notable for its candid representations of the South African government's violent reaction to a student protest. Amazingly, the stage version of *Sarafina!* opened in South Africa and toured in the US while apartheid was still in effect. After apartheid's fall, Makeba returned back home to South Africa. She appeared in the 2002 Hirsch documentary *Amandla!* about the role of music in the struggle to end apartheid.

Voëlvry: Young White South Africans Against Apartheid

Anti-apartheid sentiments surged among a new generation of white South Africans in the 1980s. The Afrikaner protest movement, known as **Voëlvry** (Afrikaans, "free as a bird" or "outlawed") was promoted by the South African record label Shifty Records and their signed artists, especially the Gereformeerde ("Reformed") Blues Band, led by **Ralph Rabie (1960–2002)**, whose stage name was Johannes "Kerkorrel," after the name of a Dutch organ trademark. Both the name of the band and the stage name of its leader were meant to mock the Dutch Reformed Church, a dominant presence in the lives of Afrikaner families. The band members were mostly well educated and from middle class homes with strict religious upbringing. Their music conveyed hard-hitting lyrics in rock and punk styles. One of their songs, "Sit Dit Af" ("Shut it Down"), made a mocking reference to a television network's favorable coverage of President Botha.

Voëlvry recalled American antiwar and civil rights activism from twenty years earlier. Young Afrikaners had more than apartheid on their agenda: the government was drafting Whites into military service to be deployed in Black townships and in border wars. The protesters rejected their elders' plans, but they struggled to answer how they would replace those plans: what should their true role be in the nation's future?

Voëlvry (Afrikaans "free as a bird" or "outlawed") Afrikaner youth protest movement of the 1980s, promoted by the South African record label Shifty Records and their signed artists, including bandleader Ralph Rabie and singer-songwriter Roger Lucey.

Miriam Makeba: "It is strange, but the song that boosts my career higher than it has ever been, and the tune that makes me known to people and countries that have never heard of me before, is also one of my most insignificant songs. I wrote "Pata Pata" in 1956, back in South Africa. It is a fun little song, with a nice rhythm. I just made it up one day, and I was thinking of a dance that we do at home. Pata means "touch" in Zulu and Xhosa...It is my first truly big seller. All of a sudden, people who never knew I have been in America since 1959 are asking me to be on their television shows and play at their concert halls in 1967...I go to Argentina for a concert, and everywhere I travel in South America they are singing my song. Versions are recorded all over the world in several languages. I will say one thing about success: It feels good."[6]

The story of South African singer-songwriter **Roger Lucey (b. 1954)**, whose career was thwarted by a government agent, exemplifies one possible "road" (a prominent metaphor in his work) forward for South Africans.

In the late 1970s, Lucey, another Shifty Records label artist, began performing original music in an eclectic style. His music showed the influence of Bob Dylan with elements of folk, country, and rock musical styles. He wrote blunt lyrics that confronted his society's hypocrisies. As a White man, Lucey did not suffer consequences at first, but his performance of "Lungile Tabalaza," provoked a government response. The song was about an event that had triggered worldwide condemnation of South Africa at the time: a young Black man had fallen five stories to his death during a police interrogation in 1978. The South African Security Police assigned a young officer named Paul Erasmus to silence Lucey, and so Erasmus began a relentless campaign of "dirty tricks" to ruin Lucey's musical career.

Erasmus confiscated most of Lucey's published albums, and he made anonymous threats to venue owners so that they would turn away Lucey and his band even after they had been contracted to perform. These and other tactics ended Lucey's career, and his personal life suffered greatly. Although he continued to write songs, he did not perform them publicly for many years. In the meantime, Erasmus, who was obligated to file detailed reports, spent hours listening to Lucey's music and, as a result, he secretly became a fan. In the early 1990s, he resigned his position, and in 1995, he began to publish a detailed account of his actions against Lucey.

The two men met for the first time in the 2002 documentary on their encounter, *Stopping the Music: A Story of Censorship in Apartheid South Africa*.[7] After some conversation, Lucey performed "The Road Is Much Longer" (1979) for Erasmus, which includes these lines:

> *"And a truck driver stops for a rap for a ride*
> *So you get in and you talk about work 'til the miles*
> *And the roar of the horses gets in between*
> *But the scars on his knuckles they show you where he's been."*

They have since formed a friendship and have collaborated to represent Freemuse, an international organization that advocates and defends freedom of expression for musicians and composers.

Nelson Mandela

South African leader **Nelson Mandela (1918–2013)** has much to say on the importance of song in his own life and among fellow South Africans in his autobiography, *Long Walk to Freedom* (1994). Rarely does he describe staged musical performances with quiet audiences as is customary with Western music. Instead, he relates many instances of group singing or of call and response singing in which he acts as either leader or member of the responding group.

His childhood memories of traditional Xhosa ceremonies, which include group singing and dancing, are vividly portrayed. Later, as an attorney who had established Johannesburg's first Black law practice in 1952, his work with families drew him into the anti-apartheid cause. At first, he advocated peaceful protest, but under a brutally repressive regime, Mandela and many other South Africans found themselves repeatedly faced with the ultimate question between pacifism and violent resistance for the sake of survival and freedom. Mandela marked his own turning point with a song:

> *I stepped across the line: I said that the time for passive resistance had ended ... at that point I began to sing a freedom song, the lyrics of which say, "there are the*

Figure 13-14 Nelson Mandela, 2000.

enemies, let us take our weapons and attack them." I sang the song and the crowd joined in … in the heat of the moment I did not think of the consequences.[8]

In 1964, Mandela was sentenced to life in prison where he spent the next 27 years. He describes much singing during his incarceration; sometimes as work songs during hard labor, and often at bedtime, when the prisoners would sing freedom songs. He remembers that Vuyisile Mini (1920–1964), the musician, union organizer, and anti-apartheid activist who would later be executed, led fellow prisoners in freedom songs daily.

As the key figure of the anti-apartheid movement, Mandela was eventually able to negotiate his own release and, with his political party and supporters, build a new government after apartheid's fall. He was never considered a professional musician or a musicologist. Like many Africans, however, he regarded music a shared, participatory art:

The curious beauty of African music is that it uplifts even as it tells a sad tale. You may be poor, you may have only a ramshackle house, you may have lost your job, but that song gives you hope. African music is often about the aspirations of the African people, and it can ignite the political resolve of those who might otherwise be indifferent to politics. One merely has to witness the infectious singing at African rallies. Politics can be strengthened by music, but music has a potency that defies politics.[9]

PLAYLIST OPTIONS
MUSIC IN THE NATION OF SOUTH AFRICA

FIND

A video or audio performance of
- Mbube (Zulu, "lion") or isicathamia (Zulu, "to walk stealthily like a cat")
  - Solomon Linda and The Evening Birds (mbube)
  - Joseph Shabalala and Ladysmith Black Mambazo (isicathamia)
  - Paul Simon with Joseph Shabalala and Ladysmith Black Mambazo
    - *Graceland* (1986)

- Versions of "The Lion Sleeps Tonight" ("Mbube," or "Wimoweh"), including
  - Solomon Linda and the Evening Birds original version ("Mbube," 1939)
  - Pete Seeger and the Weavers ("Wimoweh," 1951)
  - The Tokens ("The Lion Sleeps Tonight," 1961)
  - Disney version from *The Lion King* ("The Lion Sleeps Tonight," 1994)
  - PBS documentary, *A Lion's Trail*, 2002, on the song's trail through the American music industry
- *Nkosi Sikelel' iAfrika* ("Lord, Bless Africa")
  - Before apartheid: Christian hymn
  - During apartheid: resistance song
  - Post-apartheid: New South African national anthem
- Notable South African musicians
  - Miriam Makeba ("Mama Afrika")
    - Vocalist and activist
    - *Mbaqanga* genre
    - "*Qongqothwane*" ("Click Song")
  - Ralph Rabie ("Johannes Kerkorrel")
    - Gereformeerde Blues Band
    - *Voëlvry* movement
  - Roger Lucey
    - Singer-songwriter
    - *Voëlvry* movement
    - *Stopping the Music: A Story of Censorship in Apartheid South Africa* Documentary (Doug Mitchell, 2002)

OBSERVE

- Vocal style
- Ensemble interaction
- Topics

ASK

- Does the performance resist apartheid in a direct or indirect way?
- If the American music industry has an impact on the African performance or the performer/s, do you believe it is mostly to the Africans' advantage or disadvantage? Is it a balance?

CHAPTER 13 VOCABULARY & IMPORTANT FIGURES

VOCABULARY

Akonting

Apartheid

Call and response

Griot tradition (jali, jalolu, jeliya, or jelilu)

Highlife

Interlocking rhythms

Jùjú

Kora

Mbalax

Mbaqanga

Mbube (Zulu, "lion") and *isicathamia* (Zulu, "to walk stealthily like a cat")

Talking Instruments

Tonal language

Voëlvry (Afrikaans "free as a bird" or "outlawed")

Important Figures

"King" Sunny Adé "KSA" (b. 1946)

Toumani Diabaté (b. 1965)

Salif Keita (b. 1949)

Angelique Kidjo (b. 1960)

Solomon Linda (1909–1962) and The Evening Birds

Miriam "Mama Afrika" Makeba (1932–2008)

Nelson Mandela (1918–2013)

E. T. Mensah (1919–1996)

Youssou N'Dour (b. 1959)

Joseph Shabalala (b. 1941) and Ladysmith Black Mambazo

ENDNOTES

[1] See the International Labour Organization Report, 103rd Session, 2014; The Global Slavery Index estimates the number to be as high as 45.8 million people: http://www.globalslaveryindex.org/findings/.

[2] "An Interview with Laemouahuma (Daniel) Jatta," by Chuck Levy, 2012.

[3] See Michael B. Bakan, *World Music: Traditions and Transformations*. McGraw-Hill, 2007, pp. 187–188; translation from Daniel Agyei Dwarko in Roger Vetter, *Rhythms of Life, Songs of Wisdom*, CD Booklet, Smithsonian Folkways SF CD 40463, 1996.

[4] Outcast to Ambassador: The Musical Odyssey of Salif Keita, by Cheick M. Cherif Keita, CreateSpace Independent Publishing Platform, 2011, p. 88.

[5] "A Wise Man Keeps on Singing," Interview with David Thomas, The Telegraph, 27 June 2002.

[6] Makeba: My Story, by Miram Makeba with James hall, New American Library, 1987.

[7] See Doug Mitchell, *Stopping the Music: A Story of Censorship in Apartheid South Africa.* A Cutting Grooves Production, 2002.

[8] Nelson Mandela, *Long Walk to Freedom*. South Africa: Macdonald Purnell, 1994; Little, Brown and Company ebook edition 2008, p. 157 (Chapter 17).

[9] Op. cit., p. 178 (Chapter 21).

Image Credits

Instrumental ensemble, 1908. Instruments from left: percussion instruments including a riqq (tambourine) on the player's lap, qanun, violin, ney, 'ud, and cello.

CHAPTER

14

Music in the Middle East

T he very term "Middle East" is problematic. It is not a continent; instead, it is a region that includes parts of Asia and North Africa. It is also not a name that Middle Easterners gave themselves; the British defined the region with this term as they did with "Near East" (regions closer to Europe) and "Far East" (regions closer to the Pacific) by its orientation from England. Arabic terms include the *mashriq* ("the place where the sun rises") for the Arab world east of and including Egypt and the *maghrib* ("the place where the sun sets") for North Africa west of Egypt. Whatever the name, three of the world's most prominent religions found their origins here. It is a crossroads between three continents that has hosted great diversity and intense confrontations throughout history. In this chapter, we focus on music in ancient Anatolian, Egyptian, and Mesopotamian cultures and among modern Egyptians, Israelis, and Palestinians.

Figure 14-2 Map of "traditional Middle East" and "Greater Middle East".

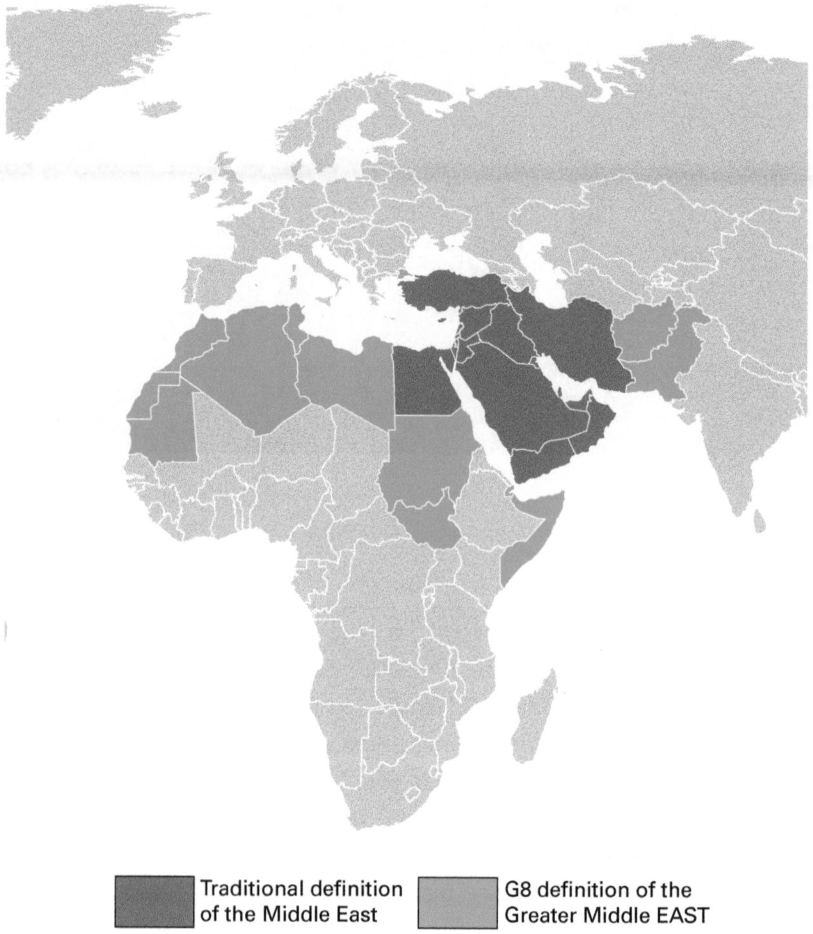

| Traditional definition of the Middle East | G8 definition of the Greater Middle EAST |

I

THE DISTANT PAST

A rich variety of cultures spread along timelines as well as geographical regions in what the world now calls the Middle East. Societies in Mesopotamia, Anatolia, and Egypt were the first regions on earth where hunters and gatherers gradually began to domesticate plants and animals, where settlements flourished to become cities, and where traders began to use written language. The webs of influence between these cultures created the foundation for much of the modern world's language, science, and art.

Figure 14-3 Early societies formed in Mesopotamia, Anatolia, and Egypt.

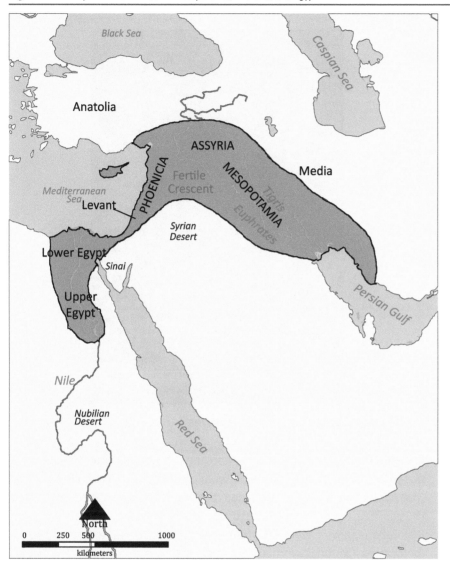

Our earliest images of music-making in the region come from Anatolia, the western and central portion of modern-day Turkey (Anatolia on the map, Figure 14-3). Archeologists have discovered clusters of mud-brick dwellings from as early as c. 8000 BCE. A common theme in engravings and murals appears to be group dancing during cult worship, and drummers are included with dancers or hunters in some images. Later, the Hittite culture (c. 1650–c. 1500 BCE) produced Inandik pottery, which shows musicians with lutes, harps, and cymbals; cymbal players appear to be females, and the other musicians are apparently males.

Figure 14-4 Early Hittite vase with depictions of man with stringed instrument and woman with cymbals, dated from the first quarter of the second millennium BCE.

The Mesopotamian region between the Tigris and Euphrates Rivers, parts of modern-day Iraq and Syria, hosted a succession of ancient cultures, including the Akkadians, Sumerians, Babylonians, and Assyrians. In the range of time between c. 3300 BCE to c. 65 BCE, these Mesopotamian cultures produced the earliest known writings about music. Their topics included descriptions of musical instruments, tuning instructions, music theory, performance practice, song texts, and poetry. Pictograms (pictorial symbols) for harps and musicians go back as far as the fourth millennium BCE.

The world's earliest named poet and composer, Sumerian high priestess **Enheduanna (fl. c. 2300 BCE),** composed hymns. The texts to some of her hymns still exist but without her melodies. She was the daughter of King Sargon and a high priestess dedicated to the Moon god in the temple complex of Ur. After her father's fall from power, her hymns express pain and anger at her own forced exile. Her texts indicate that she sang and played a musical instrument, the "harp of lamentation," which was probably a lyre.

Over two hundred years later in c. 2070 BCE, Sumerian ruler Shulgi composed a hymn in which he claims with great detail the ability to play

Enheduanna (ancient bas-relief depicts Enheduanna): "O lady, the harp of mourning is on a hostile shore, Dragged over the rocks. When the people of the city hear my sacred song, They are ready to die." As quoted in Janet Roberts, "Enheduanna, Daughter of King Sargon: Princess, Poet, Priestess (2300 B.C.)."[1]

and tune the lute, harp, and lyre, portions of which are delivered here with a flourish of royal confidence:

> "... the firstborn son is a fashioner of words, a composer of songs, a composer of words ... they will recite my songs as heavenly writings ... Nothing is too complicated for me ... Even if they bring to me, as one might to a skilled musician a musical instrument that I have not heard before, when I strike it up I make its true sound known; I am able to handle it just like something that has been in my hands before."[2]

In Anatolia, Hittite cuneiform tablets mention music as part of their sacred and royal occasions. Egyptian literature includes many references to music, including songs about love and daily life. Lyrics and instrumental characteristics are detailed in Egyptian writings, but no evidence of musical notation has been found. Distinguished Greeks, including Pythagoras (c. 570–c. 490 BCE) and Plato (c. 429–347 BCE), studied in Egypt and praised their musical traditions.

Musical Instruments

Sistrum (plural: sistra)
A type of rattle popular in ancient Egypt; see Musical Instruments Appendix.

Our sources include musical artifacts, or objects made by humans: the remains of musical instruments have been discovered in Mesopotamia from the fifth millennium BCE. Prehistoric and ancient cultures throughout Eurasia and parts of North Africa used wind instruments made of metal, reed, wood, bone, and animal horns. Drums were made of both wood and metal. Idiophones included bells, clappers, clay rattles, cymbals. The **sistrum** (plural: sistra) is a type of rattle that was popular in ancient Egypt, especially in the worship of the Goddess Isis, to ward off evil spirits. It is a U-shaped object with a handle; loose-fitting, often metallic bars intersecting the "U" slide back and forth to produce sound when the hand shakes it (see Figure 14-6). Sistra are still used in the Ethiopian church, and similar instruments are used in sub-Saharan Africa. Stringed instruments included harps, lutes, and lyres (see Figure 14-7). Carved animal heads or deities—in some cases made out of precious metals—often decorated lyres, harps, and other musical instruments (see Figure 14-8). The Musical Instruments Appendix provides more information on all of these instrument types.

Figure 14-6 Woman holding a sistrum: fragment of Egyptian wall painting, c1250–1200 BCE.

Figure 14-7 Three Egyptian musicians, Tomb of Nakht, Thebes, c1422–1411 BCE. From left: aulos (pipes), lute, and harp.

Who Performed?

Men and women, slaves and celebrities, soloists and ensembles performed music. The Babylonians left records of hundreds of musicians who lived and worked throughout the fabric of society. Music sounded in the temples, workplaces, nurseries, taverns, and military. Some musicians

Figure 14-8 Mesopotamian lyres, dated c2550–2450 BCE, on display at the British Museum.

owned land and traveled as trusted diplomats; others were captives from war, trained to sing for their owners' entertainment. Shepherds played reed pipes while lutenists played in taverns with other instrumentalists and dancers. Idiophones attached to priests' clothing and horse trappings show that music accompanied ceremonies and processions.

Monophony Musical texture that consists of only a single musical line or voice.; see Musical Elements Appendix.

Homophony Musical texture that features one dominant melody with subordinate chordal accompaniment; see Musical Elements Appendix.

Aulos An ancient reed instrument with two pipes, used in Greek tragic drama and associated with the worship of Dionysis; see Musical Instruments Appendix (Chapter 6, Antiquity to 1600).

Music Theory

Scholars in the Babylonian Tablet House during the 1800s BCE taught their students music along with math, language, and other subjects. Their writings delineate musical texture with terms such as "like one" for **monophonic** singing and "teamwork" for **homophonic** part-singing. Astonishingly, seven-note scales similar to most of the later Greek modes—which form the basis of modern Western scales—date from at least as far back as the Akkadians in the twenty-second century BCE. Later, central Anatolia was settled by Hellenists such as the Phrygians and Lydians. Phrygian **aulos** players became famous far beyond their own borders, disseminating elements of music theory and probably performance practices throughout Greek culture.

PLAYLIST OPTIONS
MUSIC FROM THE DISTANT PAST

FIND

A video or audio performance of
- Michael Levy on ancient lyre
- Richard Dumbrill, scholar on ancient music
- Peter Pringle, vocalist and instrumentalist
- "Hurrian Hymn No. 6" (c. 1400 BCE), ancient Mesopotamian musical fragment, considered world's oldest known melody

OBSERVE
- The timbre and visual features of ancient instruments
- The meaning of the words if the performance is texted
- Melodic contour
- Rhythmic and metric features of the music

ASK

+ What aspects of the performance is "reconstructed" by scholarship and musical preference, and what is reasonably certain from the source?

+ Does this music offer meaning or interest to listeners today?

II
EGYPT

A land of contradictions, Egypt is a modern country with one of the longest histories of advanced civilization in the world. Although the map shows its location as a North African country, it is more culturally aligned with the eastern part of the Middle East, known as the *mashriq*, rather the rest of North Africa, the *maghrib* (see map, above).

Egypt's awe-inspiring pyramids are the most conspicuous evidence of a society from several millennia BCE that cultivated organized religion, agriculture, government, writing, and the arts. Alexandria's position on the Mediterranean helped make it a crossroads of trade and culture during Egypt's Greco-Roman period. The Library of Alexandria, which housed hundreds of thousands of papyrus rolls, offered Egyptian, Greek, Hebrew, and Buddhist literature. It was the most famous and, perhaps, the most important library of the ancient world before its destruction sometime during the late fourth century CE.

Egyptians gradually assimilated the Arabic language and Islamic faith during the Islamic era, which was ushered in with a seventh-century Arab invasion. Many centuries later, Egypt was transformed again when the French invaded in 1798. Napoleon arrived armed not only with military troops but also with scientists and scholars; this inaugurated a period of European fascination with Egyptian history as well as colonization. British colonial presence followed in 1882 and lasted until the mid-twentieth century when Egypt became independent in 1952. As a result of its many intrinsic strengths and outside influences, Egyptian culture ever since has blended traditional Arab and modern Western practices, styles, and aspirations.

Arabic Music Theory

Melodies in Middle Eastern music are based on the **maqam (pl. maqamat)**. Literally "place" or "position," *maqamat* are modes or types of scales, each with characteristic intervals, melodies, rhythms, topics, and symbolic associations. The *maqam* divides the octave into more notes than the Western scale; in fact, many *maqamat* have 24 pitches per octave: twice as many as the Western scale's 12 pitches. That means that for each key on the piano, these Arabic melodies would have two pitches. Some pitches are fixed in the *maqam* system, but others are variable. Musicians often display their virtuosity by improvising within the *maqam* structure in ways that express the meaning of the text or function of the music.

Various regions in the Middle East, such as Arabic, Persian, Turkish, and Sephardic (Southern European and Middle Eastern) Jewish cultures, have developed different *maqam* styles. Music outside the Middle East has been influenced by the *maqam* system: South Asian music, Spanish flamenco music, Jewish sacred music, and Eastern European Yiddish klezmer traditions (see below, under "Klezmer from the European Diaspora") all use modes similar to *maqamat*. Modern Western popular and art music also show influence of the *maqam* system.

Maqam (pl. maqamat)
An Arabic mode or a type of scale, with characteristic intervals, melodies, rhythms, topics, and symbolic associations.

Sacred Expressions

Sacred music in the Arabic world is one of the most important expressions of the *maqam*. The **adhan**, or Islamic call to prayer, is traditionally sung from a minaret to initiate each of five daily prayers. Styles of the *adhan* vary widely; some are extremely **melismatic** with wide ranges. Given that the *maqam* has so many more notes per octave than the Western scale, this allows a considerable range for the singer to develop his expression of the *adhan*. The singer, called the **muezzin**, is specially trained and enjoys an honored status as the prayer-caller. Value is placed on a precise and clear delivery of the text and its pronunciation, but the *muezzin* is also expected to have a virtuosic ability to ornament the melody of the *adhan*. For the faithful, the *adhan* is considered prayer more than as "music" just as is true of the sacred expressions (however melodious or rhythmic) of many other religions, such as Buddhism, Christianity, and Judaism.

Adhan   Islamic call to prayer.

Melismatic text-setting style   A text setting style in which many notes per syllable are sung (Chapter 6, Antiquity to 1600).

Muezzin   A Muslim prayer caller, who is a trained singer.

Secular Music

Poetry is the driving force for much of Egyptian secular music. In vocal music meant for entertainment, the poem marks the beginning of the compositional process when a poet is commissioned. After the poem's creation, a composer fashions a melody that expresses its meaning, and performers interpret the poem and music. A traditional Egyptian concert from some time in the past century might be described as follows:

We begin with a rhythmically free, improvisatory instrumental solo, or **taqsim**, on the **'ud**, the plucked stringed predecessor of the European lute. The instrumentalist (traditionally a male) has a chance to display his virtuosity in musical style as well as instrumental technique in this intro-duction to the song's *maqam*. Then we hear the vocalist's **mawwal**, or improvisatory and melismatic interpretation of the poem, to heighten drama of the poetry. Although the vocalist can be either male or female, the feminine pronoun will be used here to remember **Umm Kulthum (1904–1975)**, the most acclaimed vocalist of the Arab world in the twentieth century (see below, under "Umm Kulthum"). She is accom-panied by an instrumental ensemble including **ney** (flute), **qanun** (large zither) **riqq** (frame drum), 'ud, and Western violin (see Figure 14-1).

With these forces behind her, the vocalist interprets the text with ornamental elaborations and repetitions in a performance that can last an hour or more. Listeners show their excitement and urge reiterations of their favorite passages, and she responds. During the most emotional moments of the concert, audience and musicians become swept up in **tarab**, an ecstatic musical experience.

Taqsim An introductory, improvisatory instrumental solo in Arabic music.

'Ud Plucked stringed Middle Eastern chordo-phone; the predecessor of the European lute; see Musical Instruments Appendix.

Mawwal A vocalist's improvisatory, melismatic interpretation of Arabic poetry.

Ney An Arabic flute aerophone; see Musical Instruments Appendix.

Qanun A large Arabic zither; see Musical Instruments Appendix.

Riqq An Arabic frame drum; see Musical Instruments Appendix.

Tarab An ecstatic musical experience in Arabic music.

Umm Kulthum

Kulthum learned to sing while listening to her father teach songs to her brother. In order to supplement his income for his duties at the local mosque, her father sang religious music for weddings and other events throughout the countryside. They were a poor family in a rural village, and he was grooming his son to join him in his performances. When he heard the strength of his daughter's voice, she became part of the family ensemble. But in order to avoid disapproval in his community for putting his daughter on stage, he dressed her as a boy for their performances. The audiences noticed her talent, and some encouraged her father to move the family to Cairo where music education and industry in Egypt flourished.

She was indeed successful in Cairo when the family moved there in 1923. She branched out from her repertory of religious songs with secular music and Arabic poems. Instead of singing with her father and brother, she began to solo with the kind of instrumental accompaniment described above. And, to complete her transformation, she dressed as a woman, in the Western styles popular among the wealthy ladies of the day in Cairo. Concerts were plentiful, and her recording career began in 1924, one year after her move to Cairo. With the advent of Egyptian radio broadcasting in the 1930s, she became an especially prominent performer over the airwaves and would be for the rest of her life.

In the late 1930s, Kulthum began to broadcast regular monthly concerts from a large garden in Cairo. Listeners appreciated her powerful voice and wide range. More than that, they were transfixed by her improvisatory and deeply emotional interpretations of the best Arabic poetry. Her skillful manipulation of structure, tempo, volume, rhythm, melody, and every other musical element evoked *tarab*, the powerful musical experience for Arabic listeners. Every first Thursday night of the month throughout the concert season, millions of Egyptians and others throughout the Arab world listened to her live radio broadcasts in their homes and in coffee shops. This became a favorite tradition for many decades through the rest of her career until the early 1970s.

Kulthum collaborated with the most respected composers and poets in Egypt. She herself was not considered a composer, but the quality of her improvisatory elaborations on others' compositions earned her renown as a creator as well as a performer. She also appeared in several Egyptian musical films. During her career, she became an outspoken advocate for Egyptians, known especially for her charity work on behalf of the Egyptian military. She befriended Egypt's president, Gamal Abdel Nasser (in office 1956–1970), who also had humble beginnings. By the time of her death, she was considered a major influence in the Arab world as a singer and a cultural figure. Many years later, she still inspires listeners through her recordings.

Umm Kulthum: "My father was uneasy. The idea that his daughter should sing in front of men he didn't know was difficult for him to accept, but my singing helped to support the family. So he dressed me in boys' clothes, and I sang this way for several years. I realize now he wanted to convince himself, and the audience too, that the singer was a young boy and not a young woman."[3]

PLAYLIST OPTIONS
MODERN EGYPTIAN MUSIC

FIND

A video or audio performance of
- The adhan, or Islamic call to prayer
- Umm Kulthum, vocalist
- *A Voice Like Egypt*, Virginia Daniel's documentary on Umm Kulthum
- Instrumental music: use "taqsim" or any of the musical instrument names, such as "'ud," "ney," or "qanun" as a search term

OBSERVE

- Meaning of the words in texted vocal music
- Vocal style
- Improvisatory flourishes in vocal or instrumental music
- The timbre of each instrument
- Audience response if that is included in the performance

ASK

- In vocal music, the process begins with the poem. What relevance do the words in this performance have outside of the Middle East, if any?
- If the performance included an instrumental ensemble, which instruments were dominant, or did they have relatively equivalent roles?

III
ISRAEL

Israel, a strip of land along the eastern Mediterranean coast, is at once old and new. It includes Jerusalem, where the second Temple of Jerusalem was demolished in 70 CE after a failed uprising against the Roman Empire. The city has been a symbol of home for Jews ever since. For many centuries, the Jewish **diaspora** was spread throughout the Mediterranean and beyond, including North Africa, the Middle East, and Europe. More recently, and especially during the twentieth century, many Jews came to live in the Americas.

Sacred Expressions

Such a wide-ranging diaspora has given rise to many different styles of worship. Theological and cultural differences among Jews gave rise to different religious sects and liturgical styles. Still, some common practices can be noted. Devout Jews regularly recite religious literature, especially the Torah, Jewish sacred scripture familiar to Christians as the first five books of the Old Testament from the Bible. These recitations are performed as chant in a form of heightened, melodious speech called **cantillation**. The *hazzan*, or cantor, leads the congregation in cantillation. Second only to the rabbi in the moral and religious leadership of the congregation, the *hazzan* is expected to have a fine voice, capable of melodious, free elaboration on traditional forms. Cantillation melodies generally come from oral tradition; some have been notated, but most are freely chanted. It should be remembered that cantillation is not considered "music," nor are the melodious sounds of the *hazzan* "singing." It is a sacred expression, more akin to prayer.

The use of musical instruments is avoided in the most orthodox synagogues, except for the **shofar**, a trumpet made from a ram's horn that is performed during the High Holy Days, or Jewish New Year: Rosh Hashanah and Yom Kippur. Other Jewish denominations, such as Reform and Conservative, use modern Western instruments during worship throughout the year, such as guitar, drums, flute, violin, and piano.

This author owes special thanks to Yale Strom, who provided corrections and information in great detail for this section.

Diaspora (Greek, "scattering of seeds"): The migration or dispersion of a group of people beyond their original homeland. Music can show the effects of diaspora in a given culture and can also be a telling measure of a society's cohesiveness despite diaspora (Unit 3, World Music, Introduction).

Cantillation Chanted recitation of religious literature in Jewish sacred music.

Hazzan Jewish cantor, who leads the congregation in cantillation.

Shofar A trumpet made from an animal's horn, traditionally used in Jewish High Holy Days liturgy; see Musical Instruments Appendix.

Europe and Israel

Ashkenazim   Northern
and Central European Jews.

Sephardim   Descendants
of Jews who left the Iberian
Peninsula after the 1492
expulsion.

The centuries of diaspora were marked by persecution and sometimes forced expulsions, especially in Europe. Those who lived in Northern Europe and their descendants are considered **Ashkenazim**; those who settled in the Iberian Peninsula and their descendants are known as **Sephardim.** Diasporas for both ethnic groups are spread widely throughout the world today. In the eighteenth century, the Russian monarchy restricted Ashkenazi Jews within the Eastern European region called the "Pale of Settlement" (see Figure 14-10).

In the late nineteenth century, European Jewish intellectuals founded the Zionist movement and began to settle the area then known as Palestine. "Zion" signified the city of Jerusalem, their long-lost home, to Jews. The genocidal Holocaust of World War II during the twentieth century inspired redoubled efforts to create a new homeland for Jews, and, in 1948, the United Nations declared the state of Israel. Throughout these years, waves of Jewish immigrants arrived from all over the world—especially Europe, North Africa, and the Middle East. The young

Figure 14-10 Pale of Settlement map, 1772–1917.

Figure 14-11 Itzhak Perlman, 1984.

nation faced a daunting project: to unite Jews who had lived thousands of miles apart in many different cultures for two millennia.

Ashkenazi Jews tended to dominate the melting pot of Israeli society; this ensured the importance of Western art music in Israel. Opera companies, orchestras, choirs, and music schools modeled after their European counterparts began to emerge in the late nineteenth and early twentieth centuries even before statehood. Today, Israel is the birthplace or home to many prominent educators, performers, and composers. A noteworthy example is the Israeli violinist **Itzhak Perlman (b. 1945),** one of the world's most respected and beloved musicians.

Klezmer from the European Diaspora

Others brought with them the folk traditions from their diasporic cultures. The improvisatory and highly ornamental dance music known as **klezmer** is a musical tradition of Ashkenazi Jews from Eastern Europe. The word "klezmer" is built from two Hebrew words: "kley" ("tool" or "instrument")

Klezmer Improvisatory and highly ornamental dance music of Ashkenazi Jews.

Figure 14-12 Klezmer musicians at a wedding in the Ukraine, c1925.

and "zmer" ("to make music"). Therefore, "klezmer" literally means "in-strument (or vessel) of music (or song)," and it came to refer to musical instruments and instrumentalists. By the seventeenth century, performers played violin, bass, *tsimble* (hammered dulcimer, also known as a cimbalom), and possibly a bass drum. Today's klezmer band usually features woodwinds, bowed strings, accordions, and other Western European instruments. Clarinets and violins, in particular, are used to imitate the human voice with uncanny realism in depictions, for instance, of laughter and sobs. This is no coincidence in a genre known for its spirited expressions of both joy and pain.

Klezmer musicians traveled between towns in Eastern Europe, performing for weddings and other life-cycle events, for entertainment, or for a range of other musical services. As is true of the Yiddish dialect—a Germanic language which includes Hebrew and Slavic elements—klezmer music developed among Ashkenazi Jews with many Eastern European influences. In fact, a cross-influence relationship developed with another marginalized ethnic group, the Roma (also known as "Gypsies," a term which is considered pejorative), whose music has notable similarities to klezmer and whose musicians include Jewish folk music in their repertories. The "doina" (or "doyne" in Yiddish), an improvisatory, melismatic vocal lament, is sung in parts of Eastern Europe, especially Romania, and is featured in klezmer repertory. Interestingly, the doina is related to the Arabic *taqsim*. Perhaps klezmer's most important influences, however, are melodies from the synagogue, rooted in modes that are similar to Arabic *maqamat* and strongly contrasting with common Western European scales. These are remarkable links to the Middle East after two millennia of diaspora.

With the mass migrations of the twentieth century, klezmer was disseminated around the world. Its influence was especially strong in the United States, in the melodies of American musicians such as Irving Berlin, George Gershwin, and Artie Shaw. Moreover, cross influences developed between jazz and klezmer musicians. But many immigrants in the middle twentieth century were anxious to assimilate into the societies of their new locations; they avoided secular aspects of their ethnic roots. Klezmer, along with the Yiddish language, generally began to diminish by the 1940s. The decline continued after World War II and the

Figure 14-13 Klezmer clarinettist Giora Feidman with ensemble, 2016.

devastating effects of the Holocaust: the influx of Jewish immigrants all but disappeared. Israel became a nation in 1948, and American Jewish culture became more focused on Hebrew—the national language of the new country—than on the Yiddish of their Ashkenazi roots. A new surge in popularity began in the 1970s, however, with the first wave of revivalists, among them clarinetist **Giora Feidman (b. 1936),** who came from an Eastern European family of klezmer musicians, and The Klezmorim, a high-spirited band from Berkeley, California. Today, ethnographer, filmmaker, and founder of the klezmer band Hot Pstromi **Yale Strom** contributes to the revival as both a performer and as a scholar of klezmer culture.

Pioneers

Many Zionist settlers aspired toward a culture as free of the diaspora "baggage" as possible. They promoted a national identity in various ways, perhaps most importantly in the adoption of Hebrew as their official spoken language. In a pioneering spirit, they developed new music for a new nation. **Erets-Israel ("land of Israel") songs** are folk songs in monophonic texture set to Hebrew texts. Many are in minor keys, which can suggest nostalgic or melancholy emotions. They originated either as Hebrew translations of songs from the diaspora or as newly composed melodies set to Zionist poetry. The Israeli national anthem, "*Hatikvah*" ("The Hope"), is one example of an Erets-Israel song. The text is by Hebrew poet Naphtali Herz Imber (1856–1909). In 1888, Samuel Cohen arranged the well-known European tune that originated from a sixteenth-century Italian song by Giuseppe Cenci. The words recall many years of diaspora with the goal in sight:

> "...With eyes turned toward the East, looking toward Zion, Then our hope—the two-thousand-year-old hope—will not be lost ..."

Erets-Israel ("Land of Israel") songs Israeli folk songs in monophonic texture, set to Hebrew texts.

Music of the Mizrahi

Israeli music today includes all of the genres recalled above, plus the full plate of popular styles prevalent in Western music since the twentieth century, including folk, jazz, rock, and rap music. Music of the *Mizrahi* (Hebrew: "Eastern") Jews, (Jews who are of Middle Eastern origin), however, and especially that of Jewish Yemenites, is of particular interest here. Many Jewish Yemenites emigrated to Israel soon after statehood in the mid-twentieth century. Their numbers were large enough to create a sizeable community in Israel. Music by Jewish Yemenites currently inspires wide attention and dissemination not only among Jewish Israelis but also among Muslims and others in the wider Middle East and beyond in Europe and the US. The musical styles are rooted in traditional Arabic instrumentation, performance practices, and tonalities but with a wide variety of modern Western and global influences.

Israeli singer-songwriter **Achinoam ("Noa") Nini (b. 1969)**, of Jewish Yemenite heritage, grew up in the US and emigrated to Israel as a young woman. She works with guitarist, arranger, and co-composer Gil Dor, who co-founded the Rimon School of Jazz and Contemporary Music. Together, their high-profile collaborations include albums with American jazz musician Pat Methany, English singer-songwriter Sting, and Arabic Israeli singer-songwriter Mira Awad. Noa, who wrote the theme song to the film, *Babel* (2006), cites her strongest influences from the American folk music revivalists of the 1960s, such as Paul Simon and Joni Mitchell. Her music also shows inspiration from Israeli and Jewish music, Arabic music, and Western art music. She is extremely versatile, able to sing in Arabic, English, French, Hebrew, and Yemenite, among other languages. Her topics include passionate calls for peace from a woman's point of view, including "There Must Be Another Way" (with Mira Awad, 2009), and "Mark of Cain" (1996) about a woman pregnant with her rapist's child.

International attention is turning to three sisters who recently founded **A-WA (Arabic, "yes," or "yeah;" active since 2015)**. Tair, Liron, and Tagel Haim combine traditional rural Yemeni women's songs with idioms from modern EDM, reggae, and Motown music. Their grandparents had immigrated to Israel from Yemen in 1949; the sisters grew up in a small village at the south end of Israel made up of Yemeni immigrants. Women in traditional rural Yemen did not read or write; therefore, the way they taught and preserved their culture was through their songs. A-WA wanted to sing these traditional songs and combine them with modern dance music. The group describes its name as a "cheer-up call" to enjoy life, with a mixture of old and new: in fact, their performance garb at the time of this writing combines traditional style robes with Converse shoes. To modernize traditional songs, they keep traditional themes, cut down on lengthy verses, and add catchy chorus sections. Tair has described their first song, "Habib Galbi" ("Love of My Heart," 2016), as an ancient song "passed down by women to their daughters. Each generation of women added new verses."[5]

Achinoam "Noa" Nini (pictured here with Gil Dor): "And that's when I started learning to juggle. A three ball juggle...music, matrimony, and ten years later, motherhood, once, twice three times...three children, three thousand concerts...three, is a magic number... :) By the way, that's another reason I never wanted to sing any song I didn't love, or do anything I didn't feel strongly about...how could I justify leaving my loved ones for fluff? For bogus? What for?? But for lighting my little flashlight into another hidden corner of the human sould, for creating something, for making the world a better place, for beholding a dance of hearts as music connects people on a higher level...ah! For that, I was willing to sacrifice...And I did..."[4]

Figure 14-15 A-WA sisters from "Habib Galbi" official video, 2015.

PLAYLIST OPTIONS
MUSIC OF ISRAEL AND THE JEWISH DIASPORA

FIND

A video or audio performance of

- Jewish sacred music; use one of the following search terms:
    - Cantillation
    - Hazzan or Jewish cantor
    - Jewish shofar
- European art music performance by Israeli performers, such as Itzhak Perlman, violinist
- Klezmer music, especially the following artists:
    - Giora Feidman, klezmer clarinetist
    - The Klezmorim band
    - "Itzhak Perlman Plays Klezmer" video
    - Yale Strom, klezmer violinist and scholar
        - with Elizabeth Schwartz
        - with the Hot Pstromi band
- Erets-Israel music, especially the Israeli national anthem, "*Hatikvah*" ("The Hope")
- *Mizrahi* music of Israeli Jewish Yemenites, such as
    - "Mark of Cain" by Noa and Gils Dor
    - "There Must Be Another Way" by Noa and and Mira Awad

- Ted Talk by Noa, January 2016.
- "Habib Galbi" ("Love of My Heart," 2016) traditional song arranged by A-WA

OBSERVE

- Cantillation: melodic contour
- European art music: place and circumstances of performance
- Klezmer or Erets-Israel music: Metric and rhythmic features
- Klezmer music: Instrumental timbres, melodic contours, and imitations of the human voice

ASK

- How much of the performance has roots in the Middle East? Europe?

The settlement and establishment of Israel, however, prompted a new diaspora, with its own musical expressions of resistance. It came from an ethnic group not mentioned in Israel's national anthem, *Hatikvah*.

IV

PALESTINIAN MUSIC: VOICES OF RESISTANCE

Conflict between Arab Palestinians and the incoming Zionist settlers erupted over many issues, including residency and political status. History, language, faith, and competing objectives separate them; these differences have led to violence, oppression, and far-reaching losses for everyone involved that continue to this day. The United Nation's recognition of Israel in 1948 included the partition of the West Bank and the Gaza Strip for Palestinians, which resulted in mass relocations for hundreds of thousands of people. Refugee camps sprang up inside Israel and in neighboring countries for Palestinians who had lost their homes.

The author owes special thanks to Miranda Fedock, who provided information on several sources on this topic.

Figure 14-16 Map of Israel and the Occupied Territories.

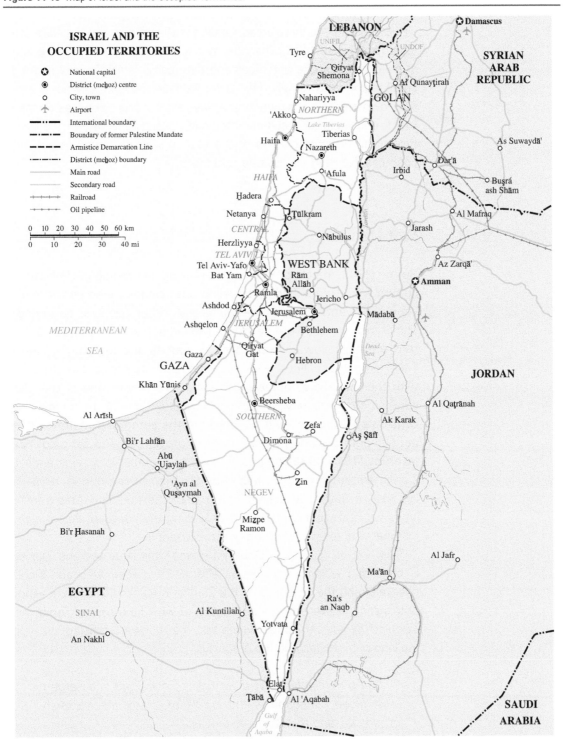

The fragmentation of their society has been profound. Palestinians are virtually locked into three areas: Israel, the West Bank, and the Gaza Strip (see map, Figure 14-16). The latter two are walled in, with Israeli control of checkpoints at the entrances and throughout Israel. Travel within this small region is extremely difficult for Palestinians, so many never leave their own areas. This situation severely restricts basic services, employment, education, and cultural interaction. Conditions vary in the wider Palestinian diaspora outside of the region, which includes neighboring countries, North Africa, Europe, and the US.

Past Traditions

Before 1948, much of the music-making in traditional Palestinian culture was exemplified by traveling poet-singers, who performed at life-cycle events such as weddings and other types of gatherings. Their lyrics, which were based on proverbs, historical stories, or current events, followed fixed rhyme schemes and rhythmic patterns. They sang these lines with music based on poetic structure but with the melodic elaboration (see *mawwal*, above and in the glossary) so common in Middle Eastern music. Many of the songs were considered "folklore" without credit to the authors. But some of the poet-singers became famous or even folk heroes. The songs of **Nuh Ibrahim (1913–1938)** helped to inspire a grassroots resistance to Zionist settlement and British control of the region during 1936–39. His use of colloquial dialect rather than the standard Arabic in his lyrics was particularly effective in reaching the hearts of Palestinians; his goal was to speak for the common people.

The text of his song, "Debate Between the Arab and the Zionist," is bitter and violent. The stanzas alternate between Arab and Zionist speakers, and the Arab shoots the Zionist in the end. A notable aspect of this song, however, is his delineation of what he meant by "Arab" and "Zionist." When the Zionist claims that the Arabs are chasing him from the land of his ancestors, the Arab says:

> *"Stop manipulating with words, as if you are submerged in sleep. Palestine is the cradle of Islam, the Messiah [Jesus], and the Prophets [Judaica]."*

Excerpt from Nuh Ibrahim, "Al-'Arabi wa al-Sahyuni ("Debate Between the Arab and the Zionist")," My Voice Is My Weapon: Music, Nationalism, and the Poetics of Palestinian Resistance, trans. David McDonald. Copyright © 2013 by Duke University Press.

For the Palestinians, "Arabs" referred to the native Muslim, Christian, and Jewish inhabitants; the "Zionists" were the new settlers from Europe. Ashkenazim Zionist settlers, in particular, were their true adversaries rather than all Jewish people.[6] Nuh Ibrahim was killed in combat with the British at the age of 25 in 1938 after only four years of singing. Some of his songs are still sung today, and his work inspired more songs of resistance after his death.

DAM

In the late 1990s, while two young Israeli Palestinian brothers found inspiration in American rappers' videos, one song in particular stood out. Tupac Shakur's "Holler If Ya Hear Me" (1993) shows a disturbing scene of police brutality set against the backdrop of a run-down neighborhood. "It looked like he filmed it in our home town, Lyd. Even though we didn't know English and we didn't get the lyrics, we made the connection."[7]

Tamer Nafar, with his brother Suhell Nafar and friend Mahmoud Jreri, who had already been experimenting with rap music, moved to sociopolitical topics in their own music. They began to practice and memorize the English words to American rap music covers and original songs. Although their understanding of English was limited, this was a solid platform on which to build their vocal, rhythmic, and stylistic skills. Soon, they began to create their own lyrics in Arabic. They named their group DAM; the initials stand for "Da Arabic MCs" but with two more levels of meaning: "dam" is Hebrew for "eternal" and Arabic for "blood." DAM became the first prominent Palestinian hip-hop group.

When they perform for diverse audiences, they are able to use a mix of English, Hebrew, and Arabic lyrics. Flexible as they are, however, they aim straight for the hearts of Palestinian youth with their use of the most current dialect, just as the poet-singer Nuh Ibrahim did in the 1930s, and their lyrics express Palestinian life and tragedy under an occupying force. Their 2001 Arabic song, "Min Erhabe" ("Who's the Terrorist?") asks the question with biting indictments:

> "Who is a terrorist? I am a terrorist?
> How can I be a terrorist if I live in my homeland? ...

Source: http://docplayer.net/54003401-Min-irhabi-who-is-the-terrorist-dam.html.

When I accused you, you jumped up and say:
'You too let children throw stones
Don't they have parents to keep them at home?'
What, did you forget you buried the parents
Under the stones of their own homes?
And now you call me a terrorist?"[8]

The "Min Erhabe" video shows disturbing scenes of brutality against Palestinians. It echoes Tupac's video in spirit, but real footage of Israeli armored vehicles and bulldozers take the place of the American squad cars in Tupac's dramatized video, and the backdrop is daytime in the Middle East rather than nighttime in an American city. "Min Erhabi" resonated with DAM's listeners: it was downloaded over a million times soon after its release in 2001, and DAM became famous throughout the Middle East.

DAM's success inspired others to the genre. In 2009, the first Palestinian hip-hop competition took place in Gaza with a satellite uplink transmitted to the West Bank. The electronic connection was crucial because travel between Palestinian districts is difficult and, sometimes, impossible. Even where permission is granted, travelers often need to take long detours on buses or cabs or go through more checkpoints. Indeed, the competition's jurors were not allowed to cross the checkpoint into Gaza, so they watched online from the West Bank. The fact that performers from both locations bonded throughout the competition was, in itself, a social milestone for the Palestinians separated from each other, who have long experienced tensions, if not bitter divides, between those who live in Israel, Gaza, and the West Bank.

DAM has increased bonds between far-flung Palestinians by collaborating with rappers in Gaza, the West Bank, and in other countries, such as in Europe and the US. Unless all the performers are able to be on tour outside of Israel and Palestine, the collaborations need to be online because of the Israeli travel restrictions. DAM has also collaborated with Israeli and other non-Palestinian groups. While DAM's topics continue to center on protest, they have recently published songs with strong messages about women's rights and violence against women, such as "Who You R," and "If I Could Go Back in TIme" in collaboration with the female Palestinian Israeli singer, Amal Murkus. The documentary *Slingshot Hip-Hop* documents their supportive collaborations with female rappers and their community work with Palestinian children, as well.

Tamer Nafar of DAM: "For me, stepping into politics, like my father used to say, it's like into a burning building. Hip-hop made me understand that I want to be a fireman."[9]

Figure 14-18 Amal Murkus, 2015.

PLAYLIST OPTIONS
PALESTINIAN HIP-HOP MUSIC

FIND

A video performance of
- DAM ("Da Arabic MCs"), using "DAM Rap" as a search term; significant videos include:
    - "Min Erhabi" ("Who's the Terrorist?"), the song that made the group famous in 2001.
    - "#Who_You_ R," featuring Maysa Daw
    - "If I Could Go Back In Time," featuring Amal Murkus
    - "God of Revolution"
- Documentary on Palestinian hip-hop music, such as
    - *Channels of Rage* (2003), directed by Anat Halachmi
    - *Slingshot Hip-Hop* (2005), directed by Jackie Reem Salloum
- Other Palestinian musicians, such as
    - Excentrik (Tarik Kazaleh), Palestinian-American
    - Shadia Mansour, British Palestinian

OBSERVE

- The meaning of the words
- Arabic musical elements, such as *mawwal*, improvisatory vocal flourishes

- ◆ If the performance is a video, note the environment and watch for symbolic props

ASK

- ◆ What are the topics of the performance?
- ◆ Some have suggested that Palestinian hip-hop is becoming more progressive than hip-hop in the US, especially in regard to women's issues. Do you agree?

CHAPTER 14: VOCABULARY & IMPORTANT FIGURES

Vocabulary

Adhan

Ashkenazim

Cantillation

Erets-Israel ("Land of Israel") songs

Hazzan

Klezmer

Maqam (pl. maqamat)

Mawwal

Muezzin

Ney

Qanun

Riqq

Sephardim

Shofar

Sistrum (plural: sistra)

Taqsim

Tarab

'Ud

Important Figures

DAM (Tamar Nafer, Suhell Nafer, and Mahmoud Jreri)

Enheduanna (fl c. 2300 BCE)

Giora Feidman (b. 1936)

Nuh Ibrahim (1913–1938)

Umm Kulthum (1904–1975)

Itzhak Perlman (b. 1945)

Yale Strom (b. 1957)

ENDNOTES

[1] Journale de Estudios Orientales, Transoxiana 8 –Junio 2004: http://www.transoxiana.org/0108/index08.html . Roberts cites the translations from editors Aliki Barnstone and Willis Barnstone, A Book of Women Poets from Antiquity to Now, Schocken Books, New York, 1992; the Barnstones adapted the translation by William W. Hallo and J. J. A. van Dijk from the original Sumerian script.

[2] The ETCSL project, Faculty of Oriental Studies, University of Oxford: http://etcsl.orinst.ox.ac.uk/cgi-bin/etcsl.cgi?text=t.2.4.2.02#, accessed 8/11/16; specific lines and hymns A Praise Poem, t.2.4.2.02 358–373; 154–174.

[3] A Voice Like Egypt, documentary film by Virginia Danielson, directed by Michael Goldman, Arab Film Distribution, 1996.

[4] from her Ted Talk transcript 1/24/16, available on noa-the-singer.blogspot.com at https://noa-the-singer.blogspot.com, accessed on 6/22/17.

[5] Ruth Eglash, "How Modern Jewish Singers are Keeping Ancient Yemeni Tradition Alive," *The Washington Post*, 1/8/2016.

[6] See David A. McDonald's translation and analysis of the song, in *My Voice is My Weapon: Music, Nationalism, and the Poetics of Palestinian Resistance*. Durham and London: Duke University Press, 2013, pp 46–51. He comments that this was typical of the poet-singers' lyrics of the time.

[7] Suhell Nafar describes the scene in Jackie Reem Salloum's documentary *Slingshot Hip-Hop, 2005*. Also see the documentary *Channels of Rage*,

directed by Anat Halachmi (2003), which shows DAMs relationship with Israeli rapper Ya'akov "Kobi" Shimoni, AKA Subliminal.

[8] English translation on DAM website: http://www.damrap.com/album/whos-terrorist-ارهابي-مين/116 accessed 8/9/16.

[9] From "Palestinian rapper Tamer Nafar on what hip-hop can and can't do for cultures in conflict," Interview by Tom Barnes, Mic Network Inc, published 3/13/17, available at https://mic.com/articles/170676/palestinian-rapper-tamer-nafar-on-what-hip-hop-can-and-can-t-do-for-cultures-in-conflict#.STElwg199, accessed 6/22/17.

Image Credits

▲ Sitar workshop, with tabla player in back, in Islamabad, Pakistan

◄ Japanese taiko drum

CHAPTER

15

Music in India and Japan

The vast continent of Asia is the world's largest, with the greatest diversity in geographical features, plant and animal life, and human culture. In this chapter, we focus on music in the South Asian nation of India, and in East Asia's Japan.

I

INDIA

South Asia consists of a number of nations, most prominently, India. The Brahmaputra, Ganges, and Indus rivers dominate the northern part of the Indian peninsula, which is bordered by the highest mountain range in the world: the Himalayans. Islam is the most prevalent faith in some countries, such as Afghanistan, Pakistan, and Bangladesh; Hinduism and Buddhism in others, such as India and Sri Lanka, respectively. Christianity, Sikhism, and other faiths are practiced as well in smaller numbers. Our focus is on music-making in India, in itself a widely diverse country with an ancient history almost as old as the Middle East's Mesopotamia. Indeed, evidence exists of trade—a powerful stimulant for cross-cultural influence—between India and Mesopotamia from as far back as the twenty-third century BCE.

473

Figure 15-2 Map of South Asia.

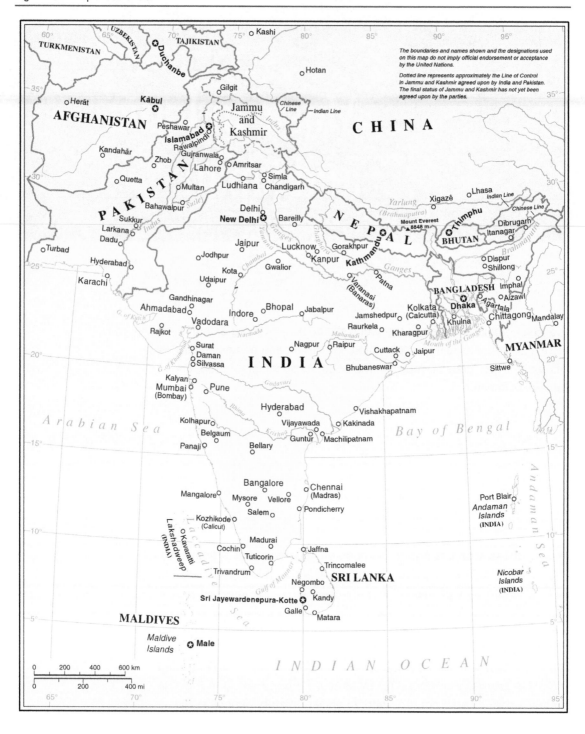

Today India is a widely diverse country whose people speak hundreds of different languages and dialects. The most common languages are Hindustani and English; the latter is one of the many cultural vestiges of British colonial rule, which ended in the mid-twentieth century. The caste system, a rigid, hereditary social hierarchy that includes the "untouchables" at its lowest level, was officially banned in the mid-twentieth century. With roots that go back roughly three thousand years, however, discrimination still persists. Furthermore, India's over-population poses great challenges despite the nation's growing economy with impressive contributions in technology and the arts. With over one billion people, its population is a close second to China's in about one third of the space.

Indian culture diverges into northern and southern regions. The **Hindustani,** or northern Indians, speak Hindi languages and represent a blend of Central and South Asian influences. Hinduism, Islam, and other faiths coexist in the North, leading to a more secular society. Hindustani music is known for its rich tradition of improvisatory instrumental performances, based on complex theoretical foundations. **Carnatic** Indians in the South mostly speak languages of the Dravidian family, such as Tamil. Predominantly Hindu, theirs is a more devout society. Religious and vocal music is especially important in the South, with less emphasis on instruments and improvisation.

Hindustani Northern Indian region and culture.

Carnatic Southern Indian region and culture.

India's Music

Indian art music, called "Indian classical music" in English, has been documented in theoretical treatises since the fourth century CE. Since musicians cultivated their art through oral tradition rather than through written notation, however, the melodies and rhythms are not recorded. Indian scales divide the octave into a total of about 22 pitches rather than 12 as in the West, which would mean that, similarly to the Arabic **maqam**, the South Asians would have almost twice as many recognized pitches per octave as the Western piano keyboard.

A **raga** (from Sanskrit with meanings that include "color" and "passion") is an Indian musical system of scale patterns and melodic figures. This brief definition, however, belies the depth of meaning and spiritual significance ragas have for South Asian musicians, who may devote themselves to many years of training in order to develop their understanding of raga structures and topics. Ragas have many extra-musical associations, such as time of day, emotions, colors, and deities.

Maqam (pl. maqamat) An Arabic mode or a type of scale, with characteristic intervals, melodies, rhythms, topics, and symbolic associations (Chapter 14, Music in the Middle East).

Raga South Asian musical system of scale patterns and melodic figures.

Meter The pattern of accents in a series of beats; see Musical Elements Appendix.

Rhythm In general: Those aspects of music that have to do with time, including beat, meter, accent, and duration. Specifically: The duration of individual notes and pauses; see Musical Elements Appendix.

Tala Metric and rhythmic structure in South Asian music; one specific rhythmic cycle.

The length of a single raga performance, which in northern India is improvised throughout, can vary widely from a few minutes to more than an hour, taking the listener through a wide range of emotions and references. A concert of several ragas can last as long as four hours or more. Ragas have captured the imaginations of poets and painters for hundreds of years. *Ragamala* ("garland of musical notes or colors") paintings from the fifteenth through the seventeenth centuries presented ragas as human figures with colorful backgrounds, often captioned by verses that told their stories (see Figure 15-3).

Meter and **rhythm** in South Asia, known as **tala**, can also refer to specific rhythmic patterns. Tala patterns are much more variable and complex than Western rhythms. They do not necessarily have regular accent patterns as Western meters do on most downbeats (the first beat, or "1" of every measure in Western music, is usually emphasized

Figure 15-3 Raag Deepak, in Ragamala by Sahibdin, 1605.

whether in duple, triple, or quadruple meters). Instead, the melodic shapes in each musical work help determine tala accent patterns. A single tala can be many beats long—sometimes over two dozen beats (in comparison to the most typical Western meters that are only 2, 3, or 4 beats long). Furthermore, these patterns are not notated; instead, they are memorized and counted in performance with hand-clapping and gestures. Audiences often clap along with the tala in performances.

Shiva, a Hindu deity, reveals the importance of music and rhythm for South Asians. In his role as Nataraja (Lord of Dance), he is traditionally shown holding a small drum, which represents the sound of the universe, the passage of time, and creative energy. His powerful dance is able to destroy and then renew the universe (see Figure 15-4).

Figure 15-4 Nataraja ("Lord of Dance") is a depiction of the Hindu God Shiva.

Performance

Raga ensembles typically consist of soloist melodic instrument or vocalist, **drone** accompaniment, and percussion. The **tambura** supplies the drone, which acts as a reference pitch from which the soloist develops the raga. The tambura can also provide rhythmic nuance with its plucking patterns.

In Carnatic raga performances, the soloist tends to be a vocalist, with a wind instrument or Western violin as the melodic accompaniment. Hindustani raga performances, however, often feature the **sitar** as both the soloist and the melodic accompaniment. Perhaps the most famous Indian instrument, the sitar is equipped with a main set of six or seven strings that the player plucks and an additional set of thirteen strings that vibrate sympathetically on their own, creating a rich, sonorous texture.

Drums provide accompaniment and occasional solos in raga performances, ranging from basic metrical cues to complex rhythmic conversation with other members of the ensemble. Drummers often chant their drum strokes as they perform in various genres, according to their tala pattern. In the north, Hindustani **tabla** players accompany sitar soloists in an interactive ensemble style developed and made famous by the Indian sitarist and composer, **Ravi Shankar (1920–2012).**

Drone   Sustained pitch or pitches

Tambura   A long-necked, unfretted drone lute; see Musical Instruments Appendix.

Sitar   A long-necked, fretted lute with extra strings that vibrate sympathetically, creating rich sonorities; see Musical Instruments Appendix.

Tabla   A pair of hand-played drums with contrasting shapes and pitches; see Musical Instruments Appendix.

Ravi Shankar

He became India's most renowned musician of the twentieth century. As a 10-year-old child, Shankar moved from his home in Northern India to Paris to join his older brother Uday Shankar's dance company. Their tours during the 1930s familiarized Ravi with the Western musical world. When the celebrated Indian musician Allauddin Khan (c. 1881–1972) joined the tour as a soloist, Shankar began a period of rigorous traditional training under Khan that lasted over seven years. He studied several instruments, especially the sitar, and became a sitar soloist by the age of nineteen.

Although Shankar was Hindustani, his cosmopolitan background encouraged him to synthesize a variety of styles. He used Carnatic rhythmic ideas, expanded the interaction between tabla players and soloists, and included tabla solo segments in his performances. As a virtuoso, he modified the sitar to increase its pitch range. During the 1950s, he performed on Indian radio as a composer and conductor, and he began to compose film scores.

By the 1960s, Shankar's stature aligned with a new era of fascination in the West for Indian culture. With high values placed on natural healing and on finding one's own inner path, the growing "counterculture" movement in the US embraced South Asian traditions such as yoga and meditation. The civil rights and antiwar movements signaled a new era of tolerance and peace to its optimistic members. Hallucinogenic drug use took on an almost spiritual importance to a generation striving to break free from what they saw as narrow mid-twentieth century moral, religious, and intellectual conventions. For many, Indian music provided the soundtrack.

Without understanding the complex structures and melodies of the ragas, Westerners perceived trance-like repetition, a lack of structure, and a breathtaking, seemingly limitless variety of pitches. Indian musicians and their traditional audiences, however, would have comprehended this music differently. The Western response was an expression of "exoticism," or "orientalism," in which Westerners are fascinated with Eastern cultures but only see them through an **ethnocentric** lens that stereotypes and limits understanding.

This fascination—inseparable from its ethnocentric limitations—was at play during Shankar's rise to fame in the West during the 1960s. Rock music was especially susceptible to Shankar's music. The stepped-up role of the tabla in his ensemble, along with Shankar's brilliant, improvisational virtuosity, inspired what came to be called "raga rock." **Arpeggiated** flourishes from Indian stringed instruments emerged in this subgenre of rock, sometimes accompanied by the sounds of the tabla or other percussion

Ethnocentrism
Perception or judgment that is limited by one's own cultural point of view, often with a presumption of superiority. Our own ethnocentrism can block our interest and understanding of unfamiliar musical styles. (Unit 3, World Music, Introduction).

Arpeggio (arpeggiate, v.; arpeggiation, n.)
Notes of a chord sounding successively, either ascending or descending, instead of all at once (Chapter 7, Baroque Music).

instruments. Shankar's most notable connection with American pop music came from his association with one of the Beatles band members. George Harrison's lessons under Shankar during the 1960s inspired Harrison to use Indian musical instruments and idioms in a way that transcended much of the common stereotyping. His "Love You To" from the album *Revolver* (1966), for instance, featured an unprecedented level of authenticity in its rendering of a song accompanied by an Indian ensemble.

Shankar's performances at the Monterey Pop Festival and Woodstock (1967 and 1969, respectively) ensured his superstar status in the US. Shankar made a lasting impression on musicians of other genres as well, among them jazz saxophonist and composer John Coltrane and minimalist composers Phillip Glass and Terry Riley. Shankar collaborated with American classical violinist Yehudi Menuhin (1916–1999) in their 1967 album, *West Meets East*, which was successful enough to warrant second and third volumes in 1968 and 1976. After George Harrison's death in 2001, Shankar organized and composed music for a tribute concert entitled *Concert for George*, which included both Eastern and Western musicians who were close to Harrison.

Two of Shankar's surviving children enjoy successful careers as performing and recording artists. Singer-songwriter Nora Jones (b. 1979), who grew up in Texas after her parents separated, performs a wide variety of American popular musical styles including jazz and country. Anoushka Shankar (b. 1981) is a sitar performer and composer who is interested in fusions of styles, including Indian, Western classical, and Western popular music.

Figure 15-5 Anoushka Shankar, 2014.

Ravi Shankar: "We are lucky in a way because the very nature of Hindustani classical music, which is based on oral tradition and improvisation, requires that our music is contantly transforming itself. Whenever I perform onstage, something spontaneously comes out that is new. I have made my recordings in the same way. In the West, these recordings would be considered original compositions, but they are all based on and resemble the old style. That's the beauty of our music."[1]

PLAYLIST OPTIONS
INDIAN MUSIC AND INFLUENCES

FIND

A video or audio performance of
- A traditional raga ensemble, such as a group led by
  - Ravi Shankar
  - Anoushka Shankar
- A sitar and tabla ensemble
- Western music influenced by Shankar and others, such as
  - "Love You To" (George Harrison, 1966) or "Within You Without You" (George Harrison, 1967)
  - Ravi Shankar with Yehudi Menuhin from *East Meets West* (1967)
  - Ravi Shankar with Phillip Glass from *Passages* (1990)
  - Shankar's *Concert For George* (2002), a culturally eclectic concert

OBSERVE

- Instrumental texture and timbre; vocal style
  - Drone instruments
  - Solo instruments or voices
  - Percussion instruments
- Metric and rhythmic features
- Melodic contour

ASK

- *For Indian traditional music performances:* Can listeners hear and interpret this music differently, depending on their level of familiarity with the music?
- *For culturally blended performances:* Aside from the question of whether you enjoyed the performance, can you see any possible disadvantage to anyone as a result of blending Indian and Western musical styles?

II
JAPAN

East Asia is home to more than one fifth of the world's population and a number of nations that include China, North Korea, South Korea, Mongolia, and our topic here, Japan.

Japan's four main islands and numerous smaller islands lie along Asia's eastern coast. Mountain ranges dominate much of Japan's geography and include many active volcanoes. Most of the population's ethnicity is Japanese; exceptions include the indigenous Ryukyuan and Ainu people and those with heritages from cultures outside of Japan. The vast majority of people speak Japanese in many

Figure 15-7 Map of Japan.

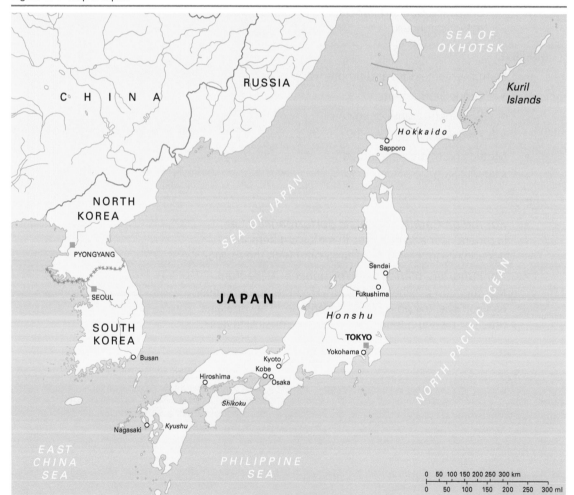

local dialects. Tokyo, the Japanese capital, is one of the world's most populous cities.

Religions include Japan's indigenous Shinto, along with Buddhism, Christianity, and others; many families practice a combination of belief systems. Japan's rich and distinctive cultural traditions have roots in mainland China and Korea, especially in regard to language and the arts, which includes much of Japan's traditional music and musical instruments. The high value placed on education in Japan has helped to preserve ancient traditions at the same time that it has buoyed modern technological advancement and economic prominence on the world stage.

Figure 15-8 Three women in Japanese tea house with wall hanging and plant display, c1910.

Japanese Aesthetics

Japanese aesthetics is marked by refined understatement and focus. The haiku poem, for example, which limits its seventeen syllables to three lines of five, seven, and five syllables, respectively, demonstrates an extraordinary economy. Both image and the empty space between images are important in Japanese visual arts, such as painting, flower arrangement, and calligraphy; the latter two are considered arts, far beyond their practical value. The natural world is another important element in Japanese aesthetics; we see its inspiration in expressions of transience and asymmetry in the art of bonsai, the cultivation of dwarf trees.

One tradition, in particular, brings together many aspects of Japanese aesthetics. First practiced by Zen monks and based on Zen Buddhist traditions, the tea ceremony is a highly formalized reception for guests in a peaceful setting that features paintings, flower arrangements, beautiful tea utensils, and, of course, tea. Harmony, respect, cleanliness, and tranquility are the qualities that have been emphasized in the tea ceremony for hundreds of years.

Figure 15-9 View from inside Okochi Denjiro Garden tea house, Kyoto.

Gagaku

Gagaku ("elegant music") A traditional Japanese musical genre that emphasizes preservation over change in every aspect of style, technique, and performance practice.

"**Gagaku**" is written in two Chinese characters that literally mean "elegant music." Although the claim that gagaku has not changed since its eighth century introduction into Japan is exaggerated, its repertory is rich with ancient and international roots that include Chinese and Persian melodies. Gagaku is a profoundly conservative genre that emphasizes preservation over change in every aspect of style, technique, and performance practice. Traditional Japanese music has generally been taught through oral tradition, with instruction and direct imitation until the modern use of notated music. Intensive preparation is emphasized, and improvisation is rare.

Gagaku Performance

Timbre The characteristic tone quality or tone color of sound; for instance, a trumpet and a violin may produce the same pitch, but the two sound sources have distinctly different timbres; see Musical Elements Appendix.

Timbre is an especially important musical element in gagaku: as instruments enter, one by one, their sonic characteristics are showcased and savored. A gagaku performance might begin, for example, with the

Figure 15-10 Traditional gagaku ensemble at the Kyoto Palace, Japan, 2013.

Ryuteki A transverse bamboo flute; see Musical Instruments Appendix.

Taiko A large, double-sided flat drum, sometimes hung on a frame; see Musical Instruments Appendix.

Hichiriki A small double reed bamboo pipe; see Musical Instruments Appendix.

Tone cluster A group of adjacent notes that sound simultaneously; the result is extreme dissonance (Chapter 10, Modern Art Music).

Sho A mouth organ made of 17 bamboo pipes with internal reeds; see Musical Instruments Appendix.

Biwa A fretted 4–5 stringed lute of Japan, played with a large plectrum; see Musical Instruments Appendix.

Koto A 13-stringed zither plucked by picks attached to thumb and fingers; see Musical Instruments Appendix.

Monophony Musical texture that consists of only a single musical line or voice; see Musical Elements Appendix.

Polyphony Musical texture that consists of two or more independent musical lines; see Musical Elements Appendix.

high-pitched, brilliant **ryuteki**, punctuated with intermittent strikes on the **taiko.** The pungent, oboe-like **hichiriki** takes up the ryuteki's melody, accompanied by a richly dissonant **tone cluster** from the **sho**. Now the **biwa** and **koto** players, with stately posture and choreographed arm movements, support the melodic line with arpeggiated chords. The tempo throughout is slow with no discernable meter, suggesting timelessness.

Musical textures in gagaku are decidedly linear and often **monophonic**. When more than one musical line sounds simultaneously, it is **polyphonic** but in a different way than in Western music: the lines are not necessarily harmonized or linked with each other in the way that Western composers historically lined up the separate voices as if fitting pieces of a puzzle together. Polyphony in gagaku resists the complete "fit" or resolution so common in Western polyphony. Instead, the relationship between musical lines is subtler and less measurable. This relative freedom from strict definition in Japanese musical texture is also true of rhythmic, metric, and structural musical elements, as well.

Zen Buddhist values of self-control and intense focus exert a powerful influence on performance practice in traditional music. Musicians typically kneel or sit cross-legged with straight backs and little or no facial expressions; they do not move to the music or show their emotions. Separate performers in musical ensembles often face in the same direction outward toward the audience rather than inward, toward each other.

PLAYLIST OPTIONS
GAGAKU MUSIC

FIND

A video or audio performance of
- Instruments separately or in pairs, such as
  - Hichiriki and sho
  - Biwa and koto
- A gagaku ensemble
  - Especially the official state ensemble: Gakubu, or Music Department of the Imperial Household
- A popular gagaku composition, such as
  - "Etenraku" ("Music of Divinity" "Music of Heaven" or "Music of Divinity")
- Gagaku with bugaku (dance)

OBSERVE

- The timbre of each instrument
- Percussive rhythmic gestures without a clear metric pattern
- Intense dissonance
- The fixed posture and slow, deliberate gestures of musicians

ASK

- How does gagaku exemplify Japanese aesthetics?

Shin'ichi Suzuki

Japanese musical culture today is spread across three realms: Japanese traditional music, Western music (including vernacular and art genres), and world musical traditions. Of these three, Japanese people have generally been most familiar with Western music for the past century or so, in large part due to the impact of Christian missionaries from the West. The influential twentieth-century educator, **Shin'ichi Suzuki (1898–1998)**, who grew up with Western art music, taught children around the world how to play violin with a seemingly simple philosophy centered on the idea of innate talent in all children.

Shinichi Suzuki: "Maybe music will save the world. That is, if we work for that purpose... there are people who think that Art exists for its own sake, but I do not think so. Art exists for the human species. I think that all of the people who love art, those who teach art, and all of you, should burn with the obligation to save the world. It is necessary to be concerned about the importance of educating a really beautiful human spirit."[2]

The son of a prominent Japanese violin maker, Suzuki studied violin as a youth and moved to Berlin to study under violinist Karl Klingler in 1921. While in Germany, he socialized with a number of celebrated artists and intellectuals, including Albert Einstein. This experience undoubtedly led him to reflect on the nature of talent: Is it intrinsic in everyone or just a special few? In Germany, he also met and married Waltraud Prange (1905–2000), who would later translate his most popular book into English (see below).[1] After his return to Japan in 1928, Suzuki first founded chamber and orchestral performing ensembles, and soon afterward, he began to teach music.

He was struck by the realization that most children of any nationality speak in their own language by the age of five. Children might fall behind in school subjects, such as mathematics, yet the vast majority can speak fluently. The fact that children acquire language very early and before school meant to Suzuki that, with the right environment, they are innately ready to learn. Something is wrong with the educational system, he believed, not the children.

Suzuki Method A musical education method created by Shin'ichi Suzuki (1898–1998) in which students are taught a variety of musical instruments with emphases on listening, repetition, group lessons and performances, and parental involvement.

He developed an educational philosophy based on the "mother-tongue method," later named "Talent Education," and known to Americans as the **Suzuki Method.** With the environment of early language acquisition in mind, he built his method of teaching children violin first by ear and repetition and later with notated music. Just as parents are constantly present with infants as they learn language, the method promotes parental involvement throughout lessons and practice. Group lessons and performances are also emphasized. Perhaps the most innovative aspect of Suzuki's philosophy, however, was his goal. Contrary to almost every Western musical approach, which aims for a professional level of musicianship, Suzuki instead strove to build character, intellectual awakening, and joy in his students.

Throughout the mid- and late twentieth century, Suzuki's method gained popularity and status as it demonstrated impressive results. His graded series of method books, stocked with Western traditional and art music tunes, were instantly accessible to an international audience in the West. Waltraud Suzuki's 1983 translation of her husband's *Nurtured By Love* introduced his philosophy to a wide English-speaking readership. Today, the Suzuki method is used throughout the world to teach a variety of musical instruments.

**PLAYLIST OPTIONS
SUZUKI METHOD**

FIND

A video of
- Shinichi Suzuki
- Suzuki violin group lesson
- Suzuki orchestra

OBSERVE
- The simplicity of the tunes
- Imitation and repetition

ASK
- Do you think this educational strategy would work with subjects other than music?

CHAPTER 15 VOCABULARY & IMPORTANT FIGURES

Vocabulary

Biwa

Carnatic

Gagaku ("elegant music")

Hichiriki

Hindustani

Koto

Raga

Ryuteki

Sho

Sitar

Suzuki Method

Tabla

Taiko

Tala

Tambura

Important Figures

Ravi Shankar, (1920–2012)

Shin'ichi Suzuki (1898–1998)

ENDNOTES

[1] From *My Music My Life* by Ravi Shankar, Mandala publishing, 1968, 2007, p. 168

[2] Shinichi Suzuki, Waltraud Suzuki trans, *Nurtured By Love: A New Approach to Education*, New York: Exposition Press, 1969.

[3] From "Ability development from age 0": As quoted in Hendricks 2011.

Image Credits

- Figure 15-1a: Uchohan / Copyright in the Public Domain.
- Figure 15-1b: Copyright © 2004 by Elijah van der Giessen, (CC BY 2.0) at https://commons.wikimedia.org/wiki/File:Taiko_drum.jpg.
- Figure 15-2: UN.org / Copyright in the Public Domain.
- Figure 15-3: Source: https://commons.wikimedia.org/wiki/File:Sahibdin_001.jpg.
- Figure 15-4: Copyright © 2015 by Mullookkaaran, (CC BY-SA 4.0) at https://commons.wikimedia.org/wiki/File:Nataraja_The_Lord_of_Dance_from_Thanjavur_Palace.jpg.
- Figure 15-5: Copyright © 2014 by Didier Chérel, (CC BY-SA 4.0) at https://commons.wikimedia.org/wiki/File:Concert_de_Anoushka_Shankar_du_6_août_2014_-_02.jpg.

- Figure 15-6: Copyright © 2014 by Markgoff2972, (CC BY-SA 4.0) at https://commons.wikimedia.org/wiki/File:Ravi_Shankar.jpg.

- Figure 15-7: Source: https://www.dreamstime.com/stock-photos-japan-north-korea-south-korea-political-map-capitals-tokyo-pyong-yang-seoul-national-borders-some-image39076613.

- Figure 15-8: University of Victoria Libraries / Copyright in the Public Domain.

- Figure 15-9: Copyright © 2012 by Noel Reynolds, (CC BY 2.0) at https://commons.wikimedia.org/wiki/File:Okochi_Denjiro_garden_tea_house_(7123923261).jpg.

- Figure 15-10: Copyright © 2013 by Miya.m, (CC BY-SA 3.0) at https://commons.wikimedia.org/wiki/File:Gagaku_orchestra01.JPG.

- Figure 15-11: Arthur Montzka, "Suzuki," https://suzukiassociation.org/media/dr-shinichi-suzuki-leads-student-violin-group/. Copyright © 2012 by Suzuki Association of the Americas. Reprinted with permission.

Appendix:
Musical Elements

Sound and Melody

Sound occurs when a force causes wave-like vibrations that are heard by an auditory receptor. **Pitch** is a word we use for the "highness" or "lowness" of a sound. Sound waves depicted on a sonogram show that high pitches have a higher frequency, and low pitches have a lower frequency. That is, high pitches create more waves in any given time period than lower pitches. The characteristic tone quality or tone color of sound is known as tone color or **timbre**; for instance, a trumpet and a violin may produce the same pitch, but the two sources have distinctly different timbres.

The distance between two pitches is known as an **interval**. Musicians use intervals as building blocks for chords, scales, and melodies. Music students are expected to name and recognize intervals by ear early in their course of study. A **scale** is an ascending or descending series of tones, arranged in a specific pattern of intervals. For instance, a major scale in Western culture is a series of seven different notes, each one whole step apart except for two specific intervals, which are half-steps. Scales help musicians recognize intervals, and they also help musicians learn to play their instruments.

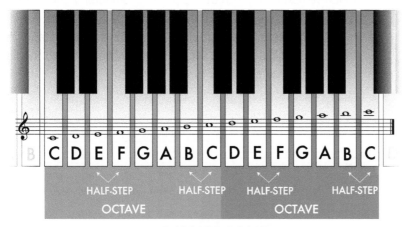

C MAJOR SCALE

A **melody** is a succession of musical pitches that has identifiable shape and meaning. Melodies can vary greatly in length and complexity, but some of the simplest melodies are capable of tremendous power over our emotions and memories. Each melody has its own set of characteristics. **Melodic range** is the distance between the lowest and highest notes of any given melody. Each musical instrument or human voice has its own range of pitches. Bass (pronounced "base") singers, for instance, have a much lower range than sopranos. **Melodic contour** is the shape of a melody, such as ascending, descending, or wavelike.

MELODIC CONTOUR

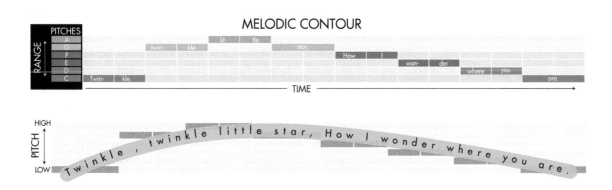

Melodic ideas that are sung are similar in some ways to thoughts that are spoken and written. In melodies, a unit of meaning within a larger structure is known as a **phrase**. The music between phrases that comes to a tentative rest (often a breathing place for singers) or the complete rest at the very end of the musical work is known as a **cadence**. The cadence between two phrases usually sounds inconclusive, but the cadence at the very end of a musical work or section sounds conclusive to the listener's ear as if one has "come home."

Rhythm and Meter

Music is an art that flows through time. We divide this time into **beats**, or subdivisions of beats, which are the basic units of musical time. Beats are often abstract concepts; they are elements in a blueprint for a structure in time around which individual notes occur. Have you ever tapped your foot to music—but at the very instant your foot touches the floor, there happens to be no music? You must have been tapping the beat—even when it was more of an idea than an audible note. Within and among the conceptual beats, the lengths of the individual notes and rests (silent pauses) vary. The duration of individual notes and rests is referred to here as the **rhythm**. Many combinations of rhythms occur in music, such as dotted rhythms (long-short patterns), or triplets (notes that occur in groupings of three). Different rhythmic patterns performed simultaneously are known as **polyrhythms**.

These rhythms operate within a larger framework, however, of regular beats. A series of beats typically has a pattern of accents, or **meter**. In Western musical notation, these are divided into **measures**, also known as bars, with bar lines throughout the music so that the musician can read the music more easily. Measures can be defined as a unit of a fixed number of beats in notation. Each of these measures, in other words, contains the same number of beats. This could theoretically be any number, but usually it is two, three, or four beats. Whatever the rhythm, we count to the same number in every measure, such as "two" in **duple meter**, "three" in **triple meter**, and "four" in **quadruple meter**.

But these measures aren't just about number: accent pattern is the essence of meter. Typically, the first beat in a measure has the strongest accent, and sometimes other beats in the measure have secondary accents. Conductors typically gesture with arm and hand, sometimes holding a baton, to indicate the patterns of strong and weak beats; see the conducting patterns corresponding to duple, triple, and quadruple meter in the illustrations below.

Duple meter is a metric pattern with two beats per measure, which typ-

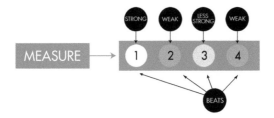

ically expresses the following accent pattern: ***strong***, weak.

DUPLE

Triple meter is a metric pattern with three beats per measure, which typically expresses the following accent pattern: ***strong***, weak, weak. The "waltz" is a dance in triple meter; check out the "Blue Danube" by Johann Strauss II (op. 314) or Bill Monroe's "Kentucky Waltz."

TRIPLE

Quadruple meter is a metric pattern with four beats per measure, which typically expresses the following accent pattern: ***strongest***, weak, *strong*, weak. Marches are often—but not always—in duple or quadruple meter; see *Sousa's Stars and Stripes Forever*.

QUADRUPLE

Nonmetric music has little or no discernable metric pattern. Chants, which are generally based rhythmically on their texts, are often nonmetric.

Meter doesn't always behave "typically," however. **Syncopation** shifts the accent from the expected first beat of the measure to somewhere else. For instance, a syncopated musical passage in quadruple meter might express the following accent pattern: weak, ***strong***, weak, ***strong***. Or it might even further subdivide the four beats into smaller rhythmic units so that the first beat alone can be: weak-***strong.***

Harmony

Harmony refers to the relationships and progressions of pitches that sound simultaneously in musical texture. A **chord** is a group of two or more different pitches sounded together. The notes in some chords sound more compatible with each other than in others. **Consonance** is a combination of pitches that seem to match, or sound stable, and **dissonance** is a combination of pitches that clash, or sound unstable; the listener expects a resolution to follow a dissonant chord.

The organization of pitches and harmonies in hierarchies is known as **tonality**. That term is also often used to indicate **major** and **minor keys** in Western music since the early eighteenth century, which are sets of pitches and harmonies built on seven-note scales with specific patterns of whole steps and half steps. Music in minor keys is often associated with unhappy or nostalgic feelings while the brighter sounding music in major keys is sometimes linked with more positive emotions.

A **chord progression** is a series of chords. Chord progressions usually use specific combinations of pitches to set up our expectations in certain ways. One of these chords feels like "home" to us because it generally begins and ends the progression, and it is usually consonant, or stable. The rest of the chords denote varying degrees of "away from home" because they are dissonant, or unstable; they have an unfinished feeling, which makes listeners wait for the resolution, or "home" chord.

The **twelve-bar blues** is a type of chord progression over the course of twelve bars, or measures, specific to American blues style; in its most basic form, it uses the following recurring series of chords: I I I I IV IV I I V V I I^1 over which a melody is varied. The twelve-bar blues chord sequence is a particularly powerful type of sequence for those of us who grew up in a culture in which the blues is prevalent. The types of chords and the number of chords in a blues progression, however, can differ widely; the progression portrayed here was only a starting point in the early years of the blues genre.

Chords used in the basic twelve-bar blues progression.

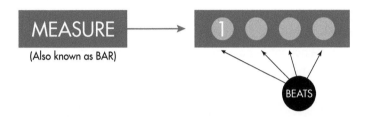

Twelve-bar blues structure and chord progression

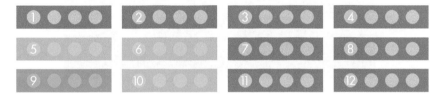

Example of a twelve-bar blues song passage

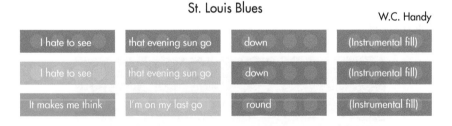

St. Louis Blues

W.C. Handy

Texture

When we hear one or more musical lines (also known as "voices" even when they are instrumental) and how multiple lines are related to each other, we hear **musical texture**.

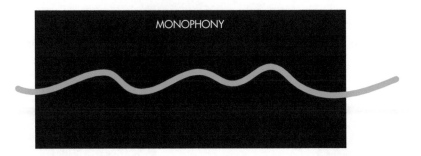

If we hear only a single singer or melody instrument, we know this is **monophony**, which features only a single musical line, or voice. But we can also hear monophony when many singers or musical instruments perform the same single musical line, with no accompanying chords and no competing melodies. Octaves can be considered monophonic texture. Medieval plainchant, also known as Gregorian chant, is an example of monophonic music.

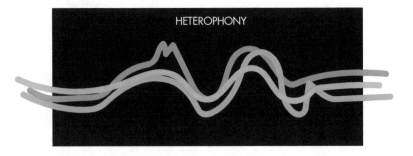

A single musical line with simultaneous variation or ornamentation is known as **heterophony**. When two or more singers sing the same melody, the texture is heterophonic when at least one of them embellishes the melody.

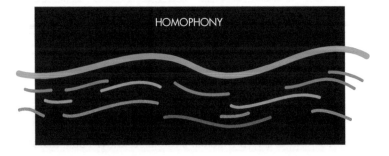

The most common musical texture in Western music today is **homophony**, which features one dominant melody with subordinate chordal accompaniment. A familiar homophonic setting is a singer who accompanies herself on a guitar: the vocal part of this performance is the melody, and the guitar often provides only the chordal accompaniment.

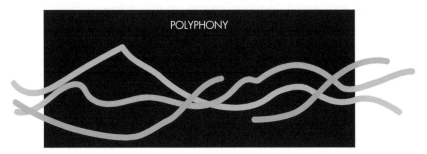

Sometimes, however, we hear a **countermelody** simultaneous to an original melody, which adds complexity and interest. This is a type of **polyphony** in which two or more independent musical lines, or voices, occur

Example of a familiar polyphonic round

"Row, Row, Row Your Boat," 1881.

simultaneously. Medieval and Renaissance sacred music such as motets and mass settings were polyphonically composed. Some polyphony is set in strict imitation: one or more identical musical lines follows the first musical line to the end. The formal term for this is **canon**, but it is also known informally as a **round**. "Row, Row, Row Your Boat" is an example of a round that children still sing.

Form

Musical form refers to the organization of musical works. An aesthetic combination of unity and variety is achieved through repeating or contrasting sections in a musical work. This balance of the familiar with the unusual can result in powerful expressions for listeners by keeping our interest as we travel on an audible journey toward a sonic "home." Structures are often expressed in letters so that they can be seen at a glance; for instance, two contrasting musical sections can be expressed as AB or a three-part organization in which the first and last sections are the same with a contrasting middle section can be expressed as ABA.

Song Form in American Popular and Stage Music

The most typical structure for popular songs is **strophic form**, which repeats the music with each verse, or stanza, of text. A **verse** refers here to a group of lines that form a unit within a poem. The simplest type of strophic form would be expressed in letters as AAA …, or a simple repeat of the same music with each new verse. Participants can learn songs in strophic form much more easily than songs that don't repeat the melody so predictably. Other types of strophic form are more complex, such as forms that feature both repeating and nonrepeating sections.

In the Tin Pan Alley and show tunes songs described in Chapter 2, American Music for Stage and Screen, the verse text and music usually does not repeat, but the **chorus,** also known as the **refrain,** is a line or group of lines in a poem or song that repeats both text and music. Verse-chorus musical form can be expressed as ABAB …, or verse, chorus, verse, chorus, etc. During the early-twentieth-century development of Tin Pan Alley songwriting, the chorus became the most important component of the song, and eventually the verses dwindled to only one after the piano introduction and sometimes none at all. The most common song structure became one with repeated choruses, expressed as AABA: the chorus (A) is repeated three times with a contrasting bridge section (B) between the last two choruses. AABA, an especially common song form in musical theater and in popular music, has become known as the "standard" form. Other common chorus/bridge patterns include ABAC and AABC, where "C" is a new contrasting section. All of the sections described here—verse, chorus, and bridge—are meant to contrast each other in various musical elements, such as melody, harmony and rhythm. Irving Berlin's "Blue Skies" exemplifies this verse-AABA form, and also demonstrates the career of a versatile hit Tin Pan Alley Song in a number of shows, all with different plots. Written in 1926 for a less than successful musical, it was used in the film *The Jazz Singer* the following year (see "Film Music" in Chapter 2), and eventually sung by Bing Crosby in the 1946 film named after the song itself: Blue Skies.

Example of an AABA song

Instrumental Form in Western Art Music

Music throughout history and across cultures incorporates formal schemes, but eighteenth-century Europeans were particularly focused on form. This was at least, in part, because extended multimovement instrumental works, such as sonatas, string quartets, and symphonies, were especially popular. Many of these compositions had no narrative or pictorial reference outside the music itself; this is known as **absolute music**. Clear, compelling structures are crucial in order to maintain the listeners' interest: in other words, the form tells—and *is*—the story.

A **theme**, which is a basic building block of form in Western music, is a melody or motive that recurs and has structural relevance throughout the work or movement. In the various forms listed below, themes can appear in different keys or with varied musical elements such as rhythm or timbre. They are often modified and fragmented. The purpose of a theme is to trigger our musical memory and remind us of where the music began—our sonic "home." When you whistle or hum a familiar song, that melody is probably the theme. Multimovement instrumental works in the classic era are long and complex enough to have several themes.

Sonata form

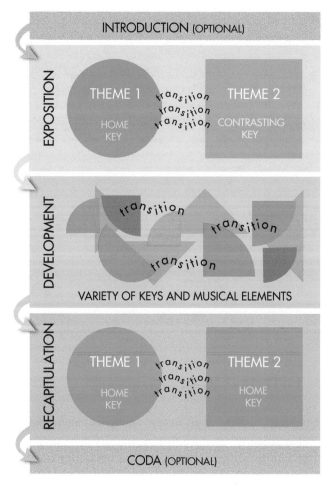

Multimovement works in the classic era typically employ **sonata form** in the first movement. This form can be thought of as having three distinct sections, with an optional introduction and conclusion. The **exposition** introduces the main themes. It begins, sometimes after a brief introduction, with a theme in the home key (the opening key of the movement), followed by a transitional passage toward another key in which a contrasting theme is stated. This section often includes thematic groups rather than a single theme, depending on the complexity of the music. The exposition is usually repeated, giving the listener a chance to become familiar with the main themes of the composition.

The **development**, or second section, uses those themes from the exposition in all sorts of ways to intensify the drama and tension. The themes are stated by different instruments in the orchestra in various ways: loudly or softly, in complex or simple textures; fragmented or in whole phrases; and often traveling to different keys. When the development reaches its most dramatic point, we have the last section in the form, which we call the **recapitulation**, or "recap," for short. This section restates the first themes, sometimes exactly as we heard it at the very beginning, only this time—and this is the difference between the exposition and the recap—all the themes stay in the home key: the tonal center that began the movement. Finally, a **coda** usually ends the movement. Coda, from the word "tail" in Latin, signifies the very end of the movement with additional material after the recap has restated all the opening themes in the home key.

The second movement of a multimovement work is often in **ternary form**, also referred to as "three-part form" or "ABA form." It is usually slower than the first movement in order to provide a contrast in tempo. The opening section gives way to a contrasting middle section and returns to the opening theme or themes in the third and final section.

The **minuet and trio** usually defines the third movement. It is also in three parts overall, but each of the three sections are two-part dances. The movement begins with the distinctive themes of the minuet, followed by the contrasting themes of the trio, and ends with the repetition of the minuet. The entire movement is typically in triple meter. The second and third movement forms were often reversed during the classic era, with the minuet and trio appearing as the second movement instead. Later, the "scherzo," which often retained the minuet and trio ABA scheme and triple meter but expressed a more mercurial, emotional affect, was more common in the nineteenth century.

Theme and variations form is another option for one of the movements in a multimovement work. The theme is stated at the beginning and then repeated a number of times with variations in different musical elements, such as melody, rhythm, harmony, and instrumentation.

The final movement is often in **rondo form**, or **sonata rondo form**. The "A" theme keeps recurring in a rondo form, in alternation with a B theme, and often with other themes as well: ABABA, ABACABA, ABACADA are a few of the many possible rondo schemes. The sonata rondo form combines rondo with sonata-allegro form by including a development section somewhere in between the first and final A sections and often by keeping the final A, which acts as the recapitulation, in the original key. The final movement in a multimovement work is often lively and exciting.

Interpretation

Interpretation in musical performance refers to the expressive choices by composers and performers that can create magical moments for the audience out of a musical work. These decisions have mainly to do with **tempo**, **dynamics**, **articulation**, and rhythmic flexibility. Most interpretation terms are in Italian, after the dominant musical culture around the time composers began to routinely mark their musical scores with interpretive directions for performers.

The speed of a musical work (not to be confused with rhythm, which refers to the relative duration of individual notes) is known as **tempo**. Movements of works—and, in some cases, entire works—are often entitled with a tempo term as can be seen on concert programs. The following tempos are common in Western art music:

Grave	extremely slow
Adagio	very slow
Andante	at a walking pace, moderately slow
Moderato	moderate
Allegro	fast
Vivace	very fast
Presto	extremely fast

The level of volume in music is known as **dynamics**. The following terms—and their abbreviations as notated in music—are the most common dynamic markings:

Pianissimo (pp)	**very soft**
Piano (p)	**soft**
Mezzo piano (mp)	**moderately soft**
Mezzo forte (mf)	**moderately loud**
Forte (f)	**loud**
Fortissimo (ff)	**very loud**
Crescendo (<)	**gradually growing louder**
Decrescendo (>)	**gradually growing softer**

Articulation refers to the quality of distinction between separate notes—whether the notes flow smoothly or more detached—in musical performance. This clarity, or the lack thereof, can mean all the difference between a calm or an edgy musical expression of the same melody: articulation can be as powerful an interpretive device as tempo or dynamics. Idiomatic qualities of musical instruments and their performance techniques necessarily help determine the characteristic articulation. The following terms are particularly associated with bowed stringed instruments, but all except *pizzicato* can apply to almost all pitched musical instruments and to vocalists.

Legato notes flow smoothly from one to the next, without space in between. Notes that are sharply detached from each other are considered **staccato** style articulation. **Pizzicato** notes on bowed stringed instruments are plucked rather than bowed, which results in a detached style. **Vibrato** style is a rapid variation in pitch that is sometimes obvious but other times can be almost imperceptible. A wide range of vibrato styles exists among vocalists due to differences in both anatomy and training. The text in vocal music necessitates articulation on yet another level: **diction** in musical performance refers to the style and clarity of the singer's enunciation of the words.

Rubato, which refers to rhythm rather than articulation or tempo, is the rhythmic flexibility performers use for the sake of expression. Chopin's music is notably characterized by a great deal of *rubato* in performance, but most music performed by humans includes some degree of rhythmic flexibility.

ENDNOTES

[1] These roman numerals indicate which step of any given seven-note scale is used as the root of the chord; therefore, from this list, we can infer the exact chords in the 12-bar blues progression in any key.

Appendix:
Musical Instruments

Fig MI-1 *The Enraged Musician* by William Hogarth (1697–1764)

Human Voice

Physiological differences and vocal technique determine the range of a person's singing voice. In Western musical tradition, these ranges are roughly broken down into the following four most basic categories (often abbreviated as "SATB"):

Soprano range is the highest of the four, and **alto** range is the next highest. Women and children singers most commonly fall into these categories, which are often referred to as female voices.

The third highest is the **tenor**, and the lowest of the four is the **bass** (pronounced "base"). These are most commonly male voices and are sometimes referred to as such.

Exceptions are common, however, regarding vocal range and gender; some women can easily sing in ranges lower than alto, and many men can sing in higher ranges than tenor.

In Western tradition, a vocal ensemble is known as a **choir** or a **chorus.** These terms denote similar ensembles and are sometimes used interchangeably, but a choir can imply a smaller group than a chorus, and "choir" can also suggest a focus on religious music more so than a chorus. In either type of ensemble, vocalists are typically grouped by range. Sometimes a choir member stands in the front and performs a "solo," a special musical part that no one else performs. (Note the second definition of "chorus" in the glossary which refers to structure rather than ensemble.)

Fig MI-2 *Choir Concert* by Max Scholz München

Fig MI-3 Student Chorus: Boston University Tanglewood Institute Young Artist Vocal Program in performance, 2011.

Aerophones

Musical instruments which produce sound by vibrating air.

Fig MI-4 Accordion: Brazilian forró accordionist Dominguinhos.

The **accordion** is a free-reed aerophone with keyboard and folded bellows that are held and controlled by the player's arms.

Fig MI-5 Aulos: Youth playing the aulos, detail of a banquet scene on an Attic cup, c460–450 BCE.

An ancient reed aerophone with two pipes, the **aulos** was used in Greek tragic drama and associated with the worship of Dionysis.

Fig MI-6 Bamboo pipe band, Solomon Islands.

Bamboo Bands are Melanesian ensembles that became popular in the 1920s; sets of variously sized bamboo tube aerophones tied together are end blown or struck, often in ensemble with panpipes, guitar, and voice, with rhythms and melodies that are influenced by popular music. Bamboo bands are still popular today, especially in the Solomon Islands.

Fig MI-7 Bandoneón: Matìas Rubino, bandoneon tango player. Buenos Aires, Argentina, 2006.

The **bandoneón**, also known as a **concertina**, is a type of **button accordion** popular in Argentina that is played by pushing or pulling the bellows with both hands while pressing buttons, which determine pitch. It is associated with the tango.

Fig MI-8 Bassoon: Bassoonist with Seattle band Edmund Wayne plays in Boise Idaho, 2013.

A long wooden tube folded in on itself, the **bassoon** is played by blowing through a mouthpiece with a double reed. Bassoon music is usually in the bass and tenor ranges.

Fig MI-9 Brass Instruments: The United States Army Brass Quintet, 2010. Instruments from left: trumpet, French horn, tuba, trombone, and trumpet.

Aerophones that use vibrating lips for tone production are known in Western orchestral tradition as **brass instruments**. Most brass instruments use valves or slides to change pitches. Usually made of metal, brass instruments are especially loud and often symbolize hunting, battle, and heroism in music. Brass instruments include the French horn, trombone, trumpet, and tuba.

Fig MI-10 Clarinet: Pete Fountain at the New Orleans Jazz & Heritage Festival, 2006.

The **clarinet** is played by blowing through a mouthpiece with a single reed. Clarinets are usually made of wood, and the most common type of clarinet is in the alto range.

Fig MI-11 Conch shell trumpet: Conch shell is blown to signal start of annual training exercise, Hawaii National Guard Regional Training Institute, Waimanalo, Hawaii, 2012.

Conch shell trumpets, which are the most widespread type of aerophones in Polynesia, are often used in signaling. Air is blown through a hole in the side or tip.

Fig MI-12 Didjeridu: Didjeridu player, with electric guitar player in background.

The Australian **didjeridu (didgeridoo, didjeridoo, didj)** is a large aerophone, 3–7 feet long and about 1–3 inches in diameter, made out of eucalyptus wood hollowed out by termites. Performers use a technique called circular breathing in which the player inhales through the nose and blows air out into the instrument at the same time, so the sound is continuous. Traditional performers often imitate nature and animal sounds through airflow punctuated with vocalizations such as hums or growls. This instrument is traditionally taboo for female instrumentalists, but, recently, women have begun to perform it outside of traditional ceremonies. Although the didjeridu likely originated in some cultures specific to northern Australia, it has come to represent all Australian aboriginal cultures as a pan-Aboriginal cultural symbol.

Fig MI-13 Dung chen: Monks in Lhasa, tibet, playing the dung chen in 1938.

Bundesarchiv, Bild 135-KA07-089
Foto: o.Ang. | 1938/1939

Low-range metal trumpet aerophones of Tibet, known as **dung chen**, are frequently played in pairs and are said to imitate the sound of elephants trumpeting.

Fig MI-14 English horn: drawing of an English horn player.

An alto range wooden instrument positioned vertically, the **English horn** is played by blowing through a mouthpiece with a double reed.

Fig MI-15 Flute: Hans-Martin Müller performing in Cologne, Germany, 2014.

Originally made of wood, today's **flutes** are usually metal. Flutes are soprano instruments that are played by blowing across the sound-hole while the player holds the instrument almost horizontally.

The tubing of the **French horn**, often called simply the **horn**, is coiled around itself, culminating in a widely flared bell. Horns also usually employ valves to control pitch. The range of the horn is in between that of the trumpet and the trombone. (See photo under "brass instruments," above.)

Fig MI-16 Hichiriki: Image of a Hichiriki.

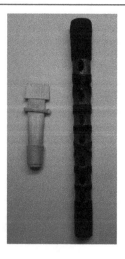

The **hichiriki** is a small double reed bamboo pipe of Japan used in gagaku and other traditional Japanese genres.

Fig MI-17 Ney: Ney performer Javid Yahyazadeh, 2012.

This rim-blown flute aerophone, known as the **ney**, has been prominent in Middle Eastern and Central Asian regions since ancient Egyptian cultures. Finger holes determine pitches.

Fig MI-18 Oboe: Oboe player reading music.

Oboes are "double-reed" instruments: they are wooden instruments that are played by blowing through a mouthpiece with two reeds while the instrument is positioned vertically.

Fig MI-19 Ocarina: A pre-Columbian ocarina, c1300–1500, Tairona people, Sierra Nevada de Santa Marta, Colombia.

A small, hollow aerophone with a mouthpiece and usually with finger holes, the **ocarina** was often made of clay and shaped in the form of animals. "Ocarina" is the European name for this **vessel flute**, which has pre-Columbian origins in Latin America.

Fig MI-20 Organ: View of pipes and organist at keyboards of the Salt Lake Tabernacle organ in Salt Lake City, Utah.

The **organ** is a keyboard instrument that produces sounds when the keys and pedals, which determine pitch, are depressed, and a bellows powers air to flow through differently sized pipes (electricity is a modern alternative). The organ has been associated with sacred music for centuries, but is used for secular music, as well. Organs often have more than one **manual**, or **keyboard**.

Fig MI-21 Panpipes: Panpipe performers in Buenos Aires, Argentina, 2014.

Panpipes, or sets of end-blown flutes, can be found in many places in the world. This aerophone has several pipes of varying lengths bundled together. The Latin American panpipe has pre-Columbian origins; it is known as the *siku* in the Aymaran language, and its genre is referred to as *sikuri* **music**.

Fig MI-22 Recorder: Illustration of recorder in Jacques-Martin Hotteterre's method for flute, 1707.

Recorder: an end-blown wind instrument with finger holes and a thumb-hole to produce varied pitches. Ensembles or "consorts" of differently sized recorders were popular in Europe from medieval times through the baroque era. Since the late twentieth century, recorders have become popular again in educational settings.

Fig MI-23 Ryuteki: Ryuteki performer in Kamakura, Kanagawa, 2004.

Ryuteki: A transverse bamboo flute aerophone of Japan, common in gagaku and other traditional Japanese genres.

Fig MI-24 Sackbut: Sackbut performer with York Waits, 2006.

A brass wind instrument featuring a telescoping slide that varies pitch, the **sackbut** is essentially an early trombone. It was one of the loudest Renaissance instruments, suitable for large events and fanfares.

Fig MI-25 Saxophone: Saxophone performer Candy Dulfer.

The **saxophone**, which was invented by Aldophe Sax in the mid-nineteenth century, is a single reed woodwind instrument. It is similar to the clarinet but usually made out of brass.

Fig MI-26 Shakuhachi: Shakuhachi performer Masakazu Yoshizawa, 2007.

The **shakuhachi** is a Japanese end-blown bamboo flute with a wide range of expressive dynamics.

Fig MI-27 Sho: Sho performer in Japan, 2007.

Sho: A mouth organ aerophone of Japan made of 17 bamboo pipes with internal reeds; harmonies of up to 6 notes are sounded simultaneously with the aid of finger holes on the pipes.

Fig MI-28 Shofar: Shofar performer on Rosh Hashana, 2010.

The **shofar** is traditionally used for special occasions in Jewish liturgy, especially during the New Year holidays, Rosh Hashana and Yom Kippur. A trumpet aerophone made out of a ram's horn, this instrument necessarily exhibits a wide variety of shapes and sizes, which affects its sound quality and pitch.

Trombones are distinguished by their slides, which regulate pitch. They have a lower range than the horn and are quite loud. (See "brass instruments," above, for picture.)

The **trumpet**, which is a lip-vibrated wind instrument, has the highest range in the brass family. Most trumpets are equipped with valves to control pitch. The **cornet** is similar to the trumpet but smaller and with a slightly different timbre. (See "brass instruments," above, for picture.)

The **tuba** is the largest brass instrument with pitches in the bass range. Its tubing is coiled into an elliptical shape, culminating in a widely flared bell. Most tubas feature valves to control pitch. (See "brass instruments," above, for picture.)

Woodwinds: In Western orchestral tradition, aerophones in which the sound is produced when air vibrates through a tube; keys are stopped along the tube to change pitch. Woodwinds include the flute and the reed instruments, such as clarinet and oboe. Most woodwinds are, or originally were, made of wood. Woodwinds include the bassoon, clarinet, English horn, flute, and oboe.

Chordophones

Musical instruments which produce sound by vibrating strings.

Bowed Chordophones

Bowed stringed instruments are chordophones in which sounds are produced primarily by means of a bow rubbed across strings that are stretched tightly over a resonator box. Sound is also occasionally produced on bowed stringed instruments by plucking the strings directly. In Western orchestral tradition, bowed stringed instruments are considered the "heart" of the orchestra and include, in order of pitch range from highest to lowest, the **violin**, **viola**, **violoncello** (commonly known as "cello"), and

Fig MI-29 String quartet (Violin, Viola, and Cello): Aiana String Quartet performing in San Francisco, CA, 2010. Instruments from left: violin, violin, viola, and cello (cello is most commonly played from a seated position).

double bass (pronounced "base," and also commonly known as "bass," "string bass," or "contrabass").

Fig MI-30 Double bass: Singer and bassist Esperanza Spalding performing at Nobel Peace Prize Concert, 2009.

The **erhu** is a Chinese bowed string instrument that sounds uncannily like the human voice.

The **violin** is the smallest instrument in the bowed string family; it has the highest range of pitches and, therefore, carries the melody in most ensembles. The ability of the violin to evoke the human voice has ensured its stature as one of the most expressive instruments. The term **fiddle**, although referencing an instrument structurally identical to the violin, implies a traditional folk or bluegrass style of repertory, technique, and performance practice. (Also see "bowed stringed instruments, above.)

Fig MI-31 Erhu: Erhu performer in Hubei Province, China, 2006.

Keyboard Chordophones

Fig MI-32 Piano: Sergei Rachmaninoff, celebrated pianist and composer, at a Steinway grand piano, 1936 or before.

Piano: a keyboard instrument that is not only popular but is indispensable in many styles of music, including ragtime and jazz. Sound is produced when keys are depressed, causing hammers to strike and rebound from strings. Considered to be the "king" of the instruments, piano provides the foundation of study for music students and is one of the most popular solo and ensemble instruments in art, jazz, and popular music styles.

Fig MI-33 Harpsichord by Andreas Ruckers (Antwerp, 1646) and later remodeled by Pascal Taskin (Paris, 1780).

Harpsichord: A keyboard instrument popular in the seventeenth and eighteenth centuries, which produces sound when keys are depressed, causing jacks and attached picks to rise and pluck strings in a large sound resonator. This instrument has a particularly bright timbre. Harpsichords also often have more than one manual, or keyboard.

Plucked Chordophones

Fig MI-34 Akonting: Akonting player in Bagaya, Senegal, 2011.

Fig MI-35 Banjo: Banjo performer Will Lee, Lexington, VA, 2008.

The **akonting** is a long-necked plucked chordophone from Africa, possibly an ancestor to the American banjo. A gourd pierced with a long pole made out of a bamboo-like woody grass called *bangoe* in Manding, a West African language, this instrument's tuning and performance practice has much in common with the American banjo.

Banjo: a plucked stringed instrument, usually with four or five strings, a fretted neck, and a circular resonator. This instrument likely originated in Western African cultures where it is still used and known by a variety of names, including *akonting* and *banza*.

Biwa: A fretted 4–5 stringed lute chordophone of Japan, played with a large plectrum; used in gagaku and other traditional Japanese genres.

Fig MI-36 Biwa: Biwa performer image, Tokyo National Museum.

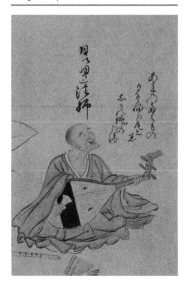

Fig MI-37 Charango: Charango performer Gabriel Moruga of Argentina.

Charango: a small, fretted chordophone with 4 or 5 single, double, or triple strings. It is most commonly performed strummed in ensemble as accompaniment to vocal and dance music.

Fig MI-38 Appalachian dulcimer: Loraine Wyman, folk song collector and dulcimer performer, is shown with Appalachian dulcimer in a 1917 issue of Vogue Magazine.

Dulcimer: a box zither chordophone family of instruments with various numbers of strings that are plucked, strummed, hammered, or bowed. Dulcimers do not have necks or keyboards. Several types are prominent in American traditional folk music.

Fig MI-39 Hammered Dulcimer: Hammered duclimer reenactor, New Salem, Illinois, 2006.

Fig MI-40 Acoustic Guitar: Patti Smith, left, and Lenny Kaye perform on acoustic guitars.

The **guitar** is a plucked stringed chordophone, usually with 6 single or double strings and with a fretted neck. The **acoustic** (nonelectric) **guitar** is a common accompaniment instrument for traditional folk music.

Fig MI-41 Baroque Guitar: *Young woman playing a guitar* by Johannes Vermeer (1632–1675).

Early (pre-nineteenth century) **guitars** were smaller than most modern guitars and were strung in four or five courses or mostly double strings. Various types were popular in the sixteenth through eighteenth centuries as both strummed and plucked instruments.

Fig MI-42 Electric Guitar: Electric guitar perfomer Carlos Santana in Barcelona Spain, 1984.

An electrified guitar which typically has 6 single strings, the **electric guitar** can be hollow-bodied, which has some acoustic resonance, or solid bodied (pictured here), which completely relies on the electrified amplification. It was first developed in the early twentieth century and originally used by blues and jazz musicians but has since become a symbol of rock music, owing to its dominant role in the rock band.

Fig MI-43 Guitarròn: Mariachi band performing in Mexico City, with guitarròn player in center, 2010.

The **guitarrón** is a large bass guitar popular in Mexico, especially in mariachi ensembles.

Fig MI-44 Steel Guitar: Fender Dual 8 Lap Steel Guitar.

The **steel guitar**, also known as the **pedal steel guitar** or, in the context of Hawaiian music, **Hawaiian guitar**, positions the guitar horizontally and changes pitches by moving a metal or glass bar over the strings rather than with permanently fixed frets as on a conventional guitar. Pedals and knee-levers change the tunings of the strings. Originally developed in

Hawaii, this instrument has become a standard member of country music bands in the US and around the world.

Fig MI-45 Harp: Armelle Gourlaouën with 3 different types of harps; from left: classical harp, Celtic harp, and "troubadour" harp.

Harp: a plucked stringed instrument with its strings positioned perpendicular to the soundboard in a triangular frame. Harps have been especially popular for vocal accompaniment throughout Europe and the British Isles ever since medieval times.

Fig MI-46 Kora: Kora performer in Dakar, Senegal, 2007.

A Western African plucked-stringed harp chordophone, made from a large gourd pierced with a wooden pole that serves as a neck, the **kora** features

19 or 21 strings that rise vertically from the gourd that acts as a bowl resonator. It is traditionally considered to be the domain of male griots and is used either as accompaniment to vocal music and in ensemble or as a solo instrument.

Fig MI-47 Koto: *Playing the Koto* by Toshikata Mizuno (1866–1908).

Koto: A 13-stringed zither chordophone of Japan, plucked by picks attached to the thumb and fingers.

Fig MI-48 Lute: *The Lute Player* by Caravaggio (1571–1610).

Lute: A plucked stringed, fretted chordophone with courses (double strings), a rounded back, and a flat top. This instrument originated in the Middle East and flourished in Europe from the late Middle Ages through the baroque era.

Fig MI-49 Lyre: Muse playing the lyre; Attic Greek vessel, 440–430 BCE.

Lyre: An ancient plucked stringed chordophone associated with the worship of Apollo.

Fig MI-50 Qanun: Azerbaijani musician Meshadi Jamil Amirov performing qanun, 1915.

Qanun: A large zither of the Middle East and parts of Asia, commonly used in Arabic classical ensemble music.

Fig MI-51 Sitar: Sitar repair shop, Varanasi Banares, India.

Sitar: a long-necked, fretted, plucked chordophone of Hindustani (northern) India with extra strings that provide melody, drone, and sympathetic resonance, creating rich sonorities. It is associated with virtuosic, cultivated music.

Fig MI-52 Tambura: Shubha Mudgal performing the tambura, 2008.

Tambura: A long-necked, unfretted drone lute chordophone of South Asia. The drone pitch provides a reference from which the vocal or instrumental soloist develops the raga.

Fig MI-53 Ud: Iranian 'Ud player, Salar Ayoubi, 2017.

The **'ud** is a lute-type chordophone with a fretless neck, used in accompaniment or soloistic functions. It is the predecessor of the European lute.

Fig MI-54 Ukulele: Jake Shimabukuro performs the ukulele, 2012.

Ukulele (Hawaiian, "jumping flea"): a small, treble, guitar-like instrument tuned with 4 strings. It was brought to the Hawaiian islands by Portuguese settlers in the 1870s.

Fig MI-55 Zheng: Vi An Diep performing on a 21-string zheng in Calgary, Alberta, Canada, in 2008.

Zheng: a Chinese board zither chordophone with numerous strings; it is associated with cultivated music.

Idiophones

Musical instruments which produce sound by vibrating the substance of the instruments themselves.

Fig MI-56 Cymbals: *Fanfara-Serenada* by Stanislaw Lentz (1861–1920) depicts musician, including a drum and cymbal player.

Fig MI-57 Triangle: A young musician from the Philadelphia Youth Orchestra plays the triangle.

Fig MI-58 Wood blocks.

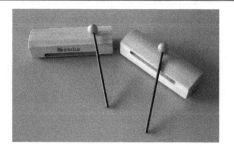

In Western orchestral tradition, percussion sections include varieties of **idiophones. Cymbals** are metal plates that are struck together. A metal bar shaped into a triangle shape and struck is known as the **triangle**. The **wood block** is usually an oblong block of wood that is struck by a stick. All of the instruments described above produce sounds of indefinite pitch, but **tubular bells** (also known as chimes) are idiophones that, like those in the **xylophone family**, do have definite pitch. They consist of sets of tuned metal tubes; the varying lengths of the tubes delineate pitch.

Fig MI-59 Tubular bells: Percussion table, with tubular bells on right.

Fig MI-60 Bones: *The Bone Player* by William Sidney Mount (1807–1868).

Bones: In American vernacular music, pair of sticks made of bones or wood that are rhythmically struck together. In Aboriginal Australian music,

clapsticks are a set of wooden sticks often used as a rhythmic accompaniment to didjeridu performance.

Fig MI-61 Finger cymbals: Close-up of a person with finger cymbals.

Finger cymbals are used by dancers to accompany themselves.

Fig MI-62 Gamelan: Most instruments in a gamelan ensemble are metal idiophones.

Gamelan instruments: Percussive metal idiophones for ensemble and music of the same name. Traditional Indonesian instruments in the **gamelan ensemble**, which is comprised mainly of metal percussive idiophones.

Fig MI-63 Mbira: Holding an mbira.

Lamellophones generate sound by the vibration of thin plates, usually made of metal or wood. Various types and sizes are widely distributed among African cultures. Performers pluck the plates with thumbs and fingers. Mbiras and kalimbas are examples of lamellophones.

Fig MI-64 Marimba: Two marimba players with a percussionist.

Marimba: a keyed idiophone from the same family as the xylophone. Keys, traditionally made of wood, produce various pitches according to the key lengths when they are struck with mallets, and the sound travels through resonators attached below the keys.

Fig MI-65 Maracas from Mexico

The **shaken idiophone**, or **rattle**, is one of the earliest known instruments. A common type of rattle is a hollow gourd filled with dried seeds (such as **maracas**), but rattles can also be made out of animal bones or other materials, and the sound-making materials can be on the outside of a gourd or strung together.

Percussion Family of instruments in which sound is produced variously by striking, shaking, and in other ways; a wide variety of instruments can be part of the orchestral percussion section, including both idiophones and membranophones.

Sistrum (plural: sistra): A U-shaped rattle idiophone popular in ancient Egypt; loose-fitting, often metallic bars intersecting the "U" slide back and forth to produce sound when the hand shakes it. Sistra are still used in the Ethiopian church, and similar instruments are used in sub-Saharan Africa.

Fig MI-66 Sistrum: Wall painting fragment shows a woman holding a sistrum, which was often played during temple ceremonies. What remains of the inscription suggests that she may have served with the temple staff of the god Amen.

Fig MI-67 Sistrum: Modern sistrum from Ethiopia.

Fig MI-68 Steel drums: Steel pan drum band at the Caribana parade, Toronto Canada, 2009.

Steel drums, or **pans**, are idiophones made from 55-gallon oil drums. The bottoms of the oil drums are shaped and tuned to distinct pitches, which are struck with rubber-tipped mallets in performance. They originated from Trinidad and Tobago and are currently popular throughout the Caribbean and especially in calypso music.

Fig MI-69 Susap: A susap performer from Papua New Guinea, Melanesia.

Susap: A bamboo mouth-harp idiophone of Melanesia.

Fig MI-70 Tambourine: Close-up of a tambourine, which is both a membranophone and an idiophone.

A small, hand-held frame drum, often with small metal disks or bells around the sides, the **tambourine** can, therefore, be both a membranophone and an idiophone. It was originally popular in Middle Eastern cultures and became an established rhythm instrument in medieval and Renaissance Europe, as well. Various types of membranophones in the Middle East include **goblet-shaped drums** and **frame drums** such as **tambourines**, which are also idiophones when encircled with metal cymbals. The **riqq** is similar to the tambourine. The **daff** is a large tambourine.

Fig MI-71 Daff: Depiction of a woman playing the daff; detail from a 17th century wall painting in Chehel-sotoon palace, Isfahan, Iran.

Fig MI-72 Vibraphone: Lionel Hampton performing on vibraphone at the Aquarium in New York City, 1946.

Fig MI-73 Xylophone: Xylophone with mallets.

Xylophone and similar instruments feature rows of bars, usually made of wood, that are struck by mallets. The different lengths of the bars determine pitch. The bars and resonators of **vibraphones** are made of metal rather than wood, creating a characteristic vibrato sound. The keys of the **marimba**, also similar to the xylophone, are traditionally made of wood, and produce various pitches according to the key lengths when they are struck with mallets; the sound travels through resonators attached below the keys.

Membranophones

Musical instruments which produce sound by vibrating stretched skins, or membranes, over a hollow resonator.

Fig MI-74 Timpani: Timpanist performs with the Philadelphia Youth Orchestra, 2014.

Fig MI-75 Snare drum: Snares on a snare drum.

Fig MI-76 Bass drum: The Revolution Drum and Bugle Corps of Texas warming up at a drum corps show, 2007.

Most membanophones are known in English generically as "drums." Some membranophones have a **definite pitch**, but others are **unpitched**, with little or no discernable pitch when they are played. In Western orchestral tradition, percussion sections feature a variety of membranophones. **Timpani** (also known as **kettledrums**) are large orchestral drums capable of defined pitch and powerful dynamics. The smaller **snare drum** features eight or more "snares" or strings stretched across the bottom, which results in a buzzing effect when the drum is struck. **Tenor drums** are similar in size to snare drums but without the snares. **Bass drums** are the largest orchestral instruments; they are unpitched. Cultures throughout Africa feature **drum ensemble** traditions rich with virtuosic, polyrhythmic styles. Dance and vocal music are usually part of the performance, and spectators are also participants.

Fig MI-77 Drumming ensemble: A group of drummers in Accra, Ghana, 2007.

Fig MI-78 Bongos: Image of Bongo drums.

Bongos (bongo drums)

A pair of small Afro-Cuban membranophones joined together.

Fig MI-79 Frame drum (double-headed): Large double-headed frame drum for powwows is played by several drummers together in a "drum circle."

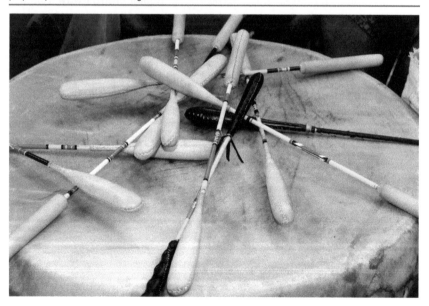

Frame Drums

Common Amerindian membranophones include the **single-headed frame drum**, which is held by one hand and struck by the other. Large **double-headed drums** used in powwows are beaten with sticks.

Fig MI-80 Frame drum (single-headed): Tibetan women in Lhasa with single-headed frame drums, 1938.

Fig MI-81 Jembe: Lenke wood jembe from Mali, 2005.

The **jembe** (or **djembe**) is an African membranophone played with both hands; it stands up to about two feet tall and is commonly played in ensemble with other membranophones of various types.

Percussion

Family of instruments in which sound is produced variously by striking, shaking, and in other ways; a wide variety of instruments can be part of the orchestral percussion section, including both idiophones and membranophones.

Fig MI-82 Slit drums: Wooden slit drums from Vanuatu, in Melanesia, on exhibit at the Bernice P. Bishop Museum, 2014.

Slit drums: Log idiophones struck rhythmically. They are hollowed out with narrow slits cut long-ways in the middle, up to about 20 feet long, often with carved semblances of animals or deities at the ends.

Fig MI-83 Tabla: Ustad Zakir Hussain performing tabla at Kornark Odisha, India, 2012.

A pair of pitched hand drums with contrasting shapes and ranges, the **tabla** is a popular membranophone in South Asia and the Middle East.

Fig MI-84 Taiko: A Taiwanese taiko drummer, 2007.

Taiko (Japanese: "drum") are large, double-sided Japanese flat membranophones that are struck with sticks, and sometimes hung on a frame.

Electrophones (or Electronophones)

Musical instruments which generate sound electronically.

Fig MI-85 Early Minimoog by R. A. Moog, c1970.

Fig MI-86 Synthesizer: Jean Michel Jarre playing an AX-Synthesizer, 2009.

Synthesizer: An electronic musical instrument that features a great variety of timbres and pitch combinations. Synthesizers are most often played by means of a piano-style keyboard, but they can be built and programmed to be played in any other manner as well.

Fig MI-87 Theremin: Lydia Kavina performing on theremin in Ekaterinburg, 2005.

Theremin: Electronic musical instrument invented by Lev Sergeyevich Termen in 1920 that the player does not touch; radio frequency oscillators sense hovering hand movements to change pitch and volume. The result is an eerie, electronic sound.

Fig MI-88 Turntablism: Set of Technics 1200 turntables with a Vestax PMC-06 Pro A mixer, used for turntablism.

Turntablism became an important, sometimes virtuosic, mode of musical expression in the late twentieth century. Reusing bits of preexisting re-corded music in a process called **sampling** is a common practice among the hip hop DJs, who also use **scratching** technique: manipulation of the vinyl recording under the needle to create pitched, percussive rhythmic sounds from the sampled music. Scratching is best accomplished with two turntables and a sound mixer.

Image Credits

- Figure MI-1: William Hogarth / Copyright in the Public Domain.

- Figure MI-2: Max Scholz München / Copyright in the Public Domain.

- Figure MI-3: Tanglewd / Copyright in the Public Domain.

- Figure MI-4: Copyright © 2003 by Victor Soares/Abr, (CC BY 3.0) at https://commons.wikimedia.org/wiki/File:Dominguinhos_de_Morais.jpg.

- Figure MI-5: Jastrow / Copyright in the Public Domain.

- Figure MI-6: Source: https://www.youtube.com/watch?v=Tj5ciY4Njic.

- Figure MI-7: Copyright © 2006 by Jorge Royan, (CC BY-SA 3.0) at https://commons.wikimedia.org/wiki/File:Buenos_Aires_-_Bandoneon_tango_player_-_7435.jpg.

- Figure MI-8: Copyright © 2013 by Kencf0618, (CC BY-SA 3.0) at https://commons.wikimedia.org/wiki/File:EdmundWayneBassoon.JPG.

- Figure MI-9: Chris Branagan / Copyright in the Public Domain.

- Figure MI-10: Copyright © 2006 by Masahiro Sumori, (CC BY-SA 3.0) at https://commons.wikimedia.org/wiki/File:PeteFountain2006.jpg.

- Figure MI-11: Anita VanderMolen / Copyright in the Public Domain.

- Figure MI-12: Copyright © 2011 by Graham Crumb, (CC BY-SA 3.0) at https://commons.wikimedia.org/wiki/File:Didgeridoo_Player_(Imagicity_1064).jpg.

- Figure MI-13: Copyright © 1938 by Bundesarchiv, (CC BY-SA 3.0) at https://commons.wikimedia.org/wiki/File:Bundesarchiv_Bild_135-KA-07-089,_Tibetexpedition,_Mönche_mit_Blasinstrumenten.jpg.

- Figure MI-14: Pearson Scott Foresman / Copyright in the Public Domain.

- Figure MI-15: Copyright © 2014 by Annamarie Ursula, (CC BY-SA 3.0) at https://commons.wikimedia.org/wiki/File:Hans-Martin_Müller_(Rhenania_140105)_(Annamarie_Ursula)_P1120356.JPG.

- Figure MI-16: Copyright © 2006 by Achim Raschka, (CC BY-SA 3.0) at https://commons.wikimedia.org/wiki/File:Hichiriki.JPG.

- Figure MI-17: Copyright © 2012 by Jean-Pierre Dalbera, (CC BY 2.0) at https://commons.wikimedia.org/wiki/File:Lensemble_Badila_(Auditorium_du_musée_Guimet)_(8255223222).jpg.

- Figure MI-18: Copyright © 2008 by Samuraijohnny, (CC BY-SA 2.0) at https://commons.wikimedia.org/wiki/File:Oboe-player.jpg.

- Figure MI-19: Source: https://commons.wikimedia.org/wiki/File:Pre-Columbian_ceramic_ocarina.jpg.

- Figure MI-20: Copyright © 2004 by Bobjgalindo, (CC BY-SA 3.0) at https://commons.wikimedia.org/wiki/File:TabernacleOrgan2.jpg.

- Figure MI-21: Copyright © 2014 by Ministerio de Cultura de la Nación Argentina, (CC BY-SA 2.0) at https://commons.wikimedia.org/wiki/File:Música_del_altiplano_en_la_estación_de_trenes_de_Constitución_(15667022841).jpg.

- Figure MI-22: Jacques-Martin Hotteterre / Copyright in the Public Domain.

- Figure MI-23: Copyright © 2004 by Ken@Okinawa, (CC BY-SA 2.0) at https://commons.wikimedia.org/wiki/File:Ryuteki_player_by_Ken@Okinawa_in_Kamakura,_Kanagawa.jpg.

- Figure MI-24: Trombone-angel / Copyright in the Public Domain.

- Figure MI-25: Copyright © 2008 by Rvb, (CC BY-SA 3.0) at https://commons.wikimedia.org/wiki/File:Candy_Dulfer_-_26724.jpg.

- Figure MI-26: Copyright © 2007 by Dmitri Shvetsov, (CC BY-SA 3.0) at https://commons.wikimedia.org/wiki/File:Masakazu_Yoshizawa_2007-02-24-16-20-34.jpg.

- Figure MI-27: Copyright © 2007 by Katorisi, (CC BY 3.0) at https://commons.wikimedia.org/wiki/File:Sho,katori-jingu-shrine,katori-city,japan.JPG.

- Figure MI-28: Copyright © 2010 by Sigckgc, (CC BY 2.0) at https://commons.wikimedia.org/wiki/File:Blowing_The_Shofar_on_Rosh_Hashanah_(4974050267).jpg.

- Figure MI-29: Copyright © 2010 by Nicky Nylon, (CC BY-SA 3.0) at https://commons.wikimedia.org/wiki/File:AianaStringQuartePlaying.jpg.

- Figure MI-30: Copyright © 2009 by Harry Wad, (CC BY-SA 3.0) at https://commons.wikimedia.org/wiki/File:Nobel_Peace_Price_Concert_2009_Esperanza_Spalding1.jpg.

- Figure MI-31: Anna Frodesiak / Copyright in the Public Domain.

- Figure MI-32: Source: https://commons.wikimedia.org/wiki/File:Rachmaninoff_playing_Steinway_grand_piano.jpg.

- Figure MI-33: Copyright © 2009 by Gérard Janot, (CC BY-SA 3.0) at https://commons.wikimedia.org/wiki/File:ClavecinRuckers%26Taskin.JPG.

- Figure MI-34: Copyright © 2011 by Geertivp, (CC BY-SA 4.0) at https://commons.wikimedia.org/wiki/File:Joueur_d%27ekonting_à_Bagaya.jpg.

- Figure MI-35: Copyright © 2008 by Artaxerxes, (CC BY-SA 3.0) at https://commons.wikimedia.org/wiki/File:Will_Lee_1.jpg.

- Figure MI-36: Source: https://commons.wikimedia.org/wiki/File:Biwa-hoshi.jpg.

- Figure MI-37: Hibby / Copyright in the Public Domain.

- Figure MI-38: Eugene Hutchinson / Copyright in the Public Domain.

- Figure MI-39: Copyright © 2006 by Robert Lawton, (CC BY-SA 2.5) at https://commons.wikimedia.org/wiki/File:Hammered_dulcimer_reenactor.JPG.

- Figure MI-40: Copyright © 2007 by CGAphoto, (CC BY 2.0) at https://commons.wikimedia.org/wiki/File:Patti_Smith_performing_at_Lollapalooza_Festival,_Grant_Park,_Chicago_(2).jpg.

- Figure MI-41: Johannes Vermeer / Copyright in the Public Domain.

- Figure MI-42: Copyright © 1984 by F. Antolín Hernandez, (CC BY 2.0) at https://commons.wikimedia.org/wiki/File:Santana_1984.jpg.

- Figure MI-43: Copyright © 2010 by Guillaume Corpart Muller, (CC BY-SA 3.0) at https://commons.wikimedia.org/wiki/File:20070810_-_Tenampa_-_078.jpg.

- Figure MI-44: Copyright © 2010 by Drew Coffman, (CC BY 2.0) at https://commons.wikimedia.org/wiki/File:Fender_Dual_8_Professional_Lap_Steel_Guitar.jpg.

- Figure MI-45: Source: https://commons.wikimedia.org/wiki/File:A-Gourlaouen01.JPG.

- Figure MI-46: Copyright © 2007 by Erica Kowal, (CC BY-SA 2.0) at https://commons.wikimedia.org/wiki/File:Dakar-KoraPlayer.jpg.

- Figure MI-47: Toshikata Mizuno / Copyright in the Public Domain.

- Figure MI-48: Caravaggio / Copyright in the Public Domain.

- Figure MI-49: Source: https://commons.wikimedia.org/wiki/File:Mousai_Helikon_Staatliche_Antikensammlungen_Schoen80_n1.jpg.

- Figure MI-50: Source: https://commons.wikimedia.org/wiki/File:Meshadi_Jamil_Amirov_playing_qanun.jpg.

- Figure MI-51: Copyright © 2005 by Jorge Royan, (CC BY-SA 3.0) at https://commons.wikimedia.org/wiki/File:India_-_Varanasi_sitar_repair_-_2898.jpg.

- Figure MI-52: Copyright © 2008 by Sajal Kayan, (CC BY 2.0) at https://commons.wikimedia.org/wiki/File:Shubha_Mudgal_in_playing_the_Tanpura_(2527339532).jpg.

- Figure MI-53: Copyright © 2017 by Iran Music 1, (CC BY-SA 4.0) at https://commons.wikimedia.org/wiki/File:Salar_Ayoubi.jpg.

- Figure MI-54: Copyright © 2012 by Joe Bielawa, (CC BY 2.0) at https://commons.wikimedia.org/wiki/File:Jake.DSC_0055-Cedar.12_(6826826238).jpg.

- Figure MI-55: Copyright © 2008 by Robert Thivierge, (CC BY-SA 3.0) at https://commons.wikimedia.org/wiki/File:Vi_An_Diep_plays_guzheng_1_(cropped).jpg.

- Figure MI-56: Stanislaw Lentz / Copyright in the Public Domain.

- Figure MI-57: Copyright © 2014 by Philadelphia Youth Orchestra, (CC BY-SA 2.0) at https://commons.wikimedia.org/wiki/File:Triangle_(13513809145).jpg.

- Figure MI-58: Copyright © 2012 by Ferbr1, (CC BY-SA 3.0) at https://commons.wikimedia.org/wiki/File:Dos_bloques.JPG.

- Figure MI-59: Copyright © 2007 by Sheila Miguez, (CC BY-SA 2.0) at https://commons.wikimedia.org/wiki/File:Percussion_table_P5210012_(510027062).jpg.

- Figure MI-60: William Sidney Mount / Copyright in the Public Domain.

- Figure MI-61: Copyright © 2015 by Gudzwabofer, (CC BY-SA 4.0) at https://commons.wikimedia.org/wiki/File:Finger_cymbals.jpg.

- Figure MI-62: Sengkang / Copyright in the Public Domain.

- Figure MI-63: Copyright © 2005 by Alex Weeks, (CC BY-SA 3.0) at https://commons.wikimedia.org/wiki/File:Holding_an_mbira_dzavadzimu.jpg.

Glossary

A

Aboriginal Regarding indigenous peoples, or earliest inhabitants of a land; used often to describe indigenous Australians (Chapter 12, Music in Oceania).

Absolute music Music without extra-musical references; see Musical Elements Appendix (Chapter 8, Classic Era Music).

A Cappella (It. "in the chapel style") Vocal music unaccompanied by musical instruments, usually in reference to Western art music. (Unit 2, Western Art Music, Introduction)

Accompanied monody A single vocal line with instrumental accompaniment (Chapter 7, Baroque Music).

Accordion A free-reed aerophone with keyboard and folded bellows that are held and controlled by the player's arms; see Musical Instruments Appendix.

Acoustics The science of sound (Chapter 6, Antiquity to 1600).

Adhan Islamic call to prayer traditionally sung from a minaret before each of five daily prayers (Chapter 14, Music in the Middle East).

Aerophones Musical instruments which produce sound by vibrating air, such as flutes, pan-pipes, and trumpets; see Musical Instruments Appendix.

Affect Emotional state; in baroque music, a common musical goal was the expression of a single affect throughout a work or movement (Chapter 7, Baroque Music).

Akonting A long-necked plucked chordophone from Africa, likely an ancestor to the American banjo. A gourd is pierced with a long pole made out of a bamboo-like woody grass called *bangoe* in Manding, a West African language. This instrument's tuning and performance practice has much in common with the American banjo; see Musical Instruments Appendix.

Alternative rock Originally, underground or experimental rock music from "indie" rather than major record producers. Despite the term's connotation of nonconformity, alternative currently enjoys wide commercial success among mainstream audiences (Chapter 5, Modern American Popular Music Part II: After 1970).

Alto The second highest of the four most basic categories of a person's singing voice range; see Musical Instruments Appendix, and also see "part song."

American minstrelsy (blackface minstrelsy) Popular nineteenth-century musical variety shows that portrayed black plantation life with actors in blackface playing stereotyped characters such as "Jim Crow." Minstrel shows became a vehicle for the dissemination of Black culture in the form of songs, dance, and the banjo. Touring minstrel productions performed throughout the US, Europe, and other parts of the world (Chapter 2, American Music for Stage and Screen).

Anthem Sacred polyphonic choral composition with English text, similar to the motet (Chapter 6. Antiquity to 1600).

Antiquity Used here to refer to classical Greek and Roman civilizations before the medieval era, c. eighth century BCE to fifth century CE (Unit 2, Western Art Music, Introduction, and Chapter 6, Antiquity to 1600).

Apartheid ("apartness" in Afrikaans) A system of racial segregation and discrimination enforced by the South African government from 1948–1991 in which the rights of non-Whites were severely curtailed. Music played a significant role in the national resistance to apartheid and in international condemnation (Chapter 13, Music in Sub-Saharan Africa).

Aria (It. "air") Lyrical, melodious song, usually with a clear meter (Chapter 7, Baroque Music).

Arpeggio (arpeggiate, v.; arpeggiation, n.) Notes of a chord sounding successively, either ascending or descending, instead of all at once (Chapter 7, Baroque Music).

Articulation Quality of distinction between separate notes—whether the notes flow smoothly or more detached—in musical performance; see Musical Elements Appendix.

Art song See "Leid" (Chapter 9, Romantic Era Music).

Ashkenazim (Adj. Ashkenazy) (From the Hebrew word for "German") Northern and Central European Jews (Chapter 14, Music in the Middle East.)

Atonality Music without tonality or total center and, thus, no distinction between dissonance and consonance (Chapter 10, Modern Art Music.)

Aulos An ancient reed instrument with two pipes, used in Greek tragic drama and associated with the worship of Dionysis; see Musical Instruments Appendix (Chapter 6, Antiquity to 1600).

Avant-garde (Fr. "Vanguard") Ultramodern, experimental art; in music associated with a wide variety of composers, especially Schoenberg and Cage (Chapter 10, Modern Art Music).

B

Ballad Typically a narrative, strophic song. "Child Ballads" refer to songs discovered by Francis James Child (1825–1896) in his research (Chapter 1, American Traditional Music).

Ballet Theatrical, formal dance tradition that originated in Europe. Ballet underwent an especially active period of development in France during the reign of Louis XIV. Dancers are held to a rigorous tradition of technical mastery in graceful, fluid movements through choreography that demand athletic prowess and stamina (Chapter 7, Baroque Music).

Bamboo Bands Melanesian ensembles that became popular in the 1920s; sets of variously sized bamboo tube aerophones tied together are end blown or struck, often in ensemble with panpipes, guitar, and voice, with rhythms that are influenced by popular music. Bamboo bands are still popular today especially in the Solomon Islands; see Musical Instruments Appendix.

Bandoneón (button accordion, concertina) A type of accordion aerophone with buttons instead of a keyboard; used in tango ensembles; see Musical Instruments Appendix.

Banjo A plucked stringed chordophone, usually with 4 or 5 strings, a fretted neck, and a circular resonator. This instrument likely originated in Western Africa (Chapter 2, American Music for Stage and Screen, and Chapter 13, Music in Sub-Saharan Africa).

Bard Originally "praise singer," an entertainer who sang, chanted, or recited poetry (Chapter 6, Antiquity to 1600).

Baroque Derived from "misshapen pearl" in Portuguese; Western European musical style c. 1600–1750; highly ornamented style (Unit 2, Western Art Music, Introduction, and Chapter 7, Baroque)

Bass The lowest of the four most basic categories of a person's singing voice range; see Musical Instruments Appendix, and also see "part song."

Basso continuo Continuous instrumental accompaniment notated in a bass line with single notes, numbers, and other symbols. Musically, the *continuo* functions much like the rhythm section in a modern rock or jazz band; it provides the foundational rhythmic and harmonic accompaniment, typically with a combination of notated music and improvisation (Chapter 7, Baroque Music).

Bassoon Woodwind double-reed aerophone, which mostly plays music in the bass and tenor ranges; see Musical Instruments Appendix.

Beat Basic unit of musical time; see Musical Elements Appendix.

Bebop (or bop) Creative, highly improvisatory, complex jazz genre, which encouraged individualism among performers in small combos that usually consisted of only four to six musicians. The music's irregular phrasing, unexpected accents, and fast pace made for high art but not dance music (Chapter 3. Jazz).

Bel canto (It. "beautiful singing") "Beautiful singing" style of Italian opera, characterized by a prominent, expressive vocal melody with subservient orchestral accompaniment (Chapter 9, Romantic Era Music).

Biwa A fretted 4–5 stringed lute chordophone of Japan, played with a large plectrum; used in gagaku and other traditional Japanese genres; see Musical Instruments Appendix.

Bluegrass music Improvisatory dance music style named after Bill Monroe and the Bluegrass Boys, rooted in rural American string bands and with influences from other genres, especially American blues and jazz. Performers typically play acoustic instruments with banjo, guitar, and fiddle most dominant (Chapter 4. Modern American Popular Music Part I: Up to 1970).

Blue notes Slightly lowered pitches on certain scale degrees in blues and jazz melodies (Chapter 3, Jazz).

Blues Popular musical style with distinctive, recognizable harmonic and melodic patterns. A pervasive and powerful influence on music throughout the world since the early twentieth century, various blues genres originated with American Black musicians (Chapter 3, Jazz).

Bones In American vernacular music, pair of stick idiophones made of bones or wood that are rhythmically struck together; see Musical Instruments Appendix and also see "clapsticks."

Bongos (bongo drums) A pair of small Afro-Cuban membranophones joined together; see Musical Instruments Appendix.

Book musical Musical theater in which the drama, rather than song, is most important; usually adapted from a book (Chapter 2, American Music for Stage and Screen).

Bossa nova A musical genre based on Afro-Brazilian samba rhythms but with a more complex pattern of syncopation. "Bossa" connotes "flair" or "ability;" this style expresses an offhand sophistication that influenced North American jazz musicians (Chapter 11, Music in the Americas).

Bowed stringed instruments Family of chordophones in which sounds are produced primarily by means of a bow rubbed across strings that are stretched tightly over a resonator box. Sound is also occasionally produced on bowed stringed instruments by plucking the strings directly. In Western orchestral tradition, bowed stringed instruments are considered the "heart" of the orchestra and include, in order of pitch range from highest to lowest, the **violin**, **viola**, **violoncello** (commonly known as "cello"), and **double bass** (pronounced "base," and also commonly known as "bass," "string bass," or "contrabass"); see Musical Instruments Appendix.

Brass instruments Aerophones that use vibrating lips for tone production; most brass instruments use valves or slides to change pitches. Usually made of metal, brass instruments are especially loud and often symbolize hunting, battle, and heroism in music. Brass instruments include the French horn, trombone, trumpet, and tuba; see Musical Instruments Appendix.

Break strain (or "dogfights") Contrasting passage of duel-like exchanges between instrument families in marching or concert band music (Chapter 10, Modern Art Music).

British Invasion Extraordinary popularity of touring British performers in the US, beginning with the Beatles in 1963; their music "invaded" the US charts and grabbed much of the market, forcing the domestic US music industry to struggle harder for their spots on the charts (Chapter 4, Modern American Popular Music Part I: Up to 1970).

Bush songs Ballads sung by nineteenth-century Australian settlers, similar in style and structure to traditional music of the British Isles. Bush songs are often sung unaccompanied and sometimes supported by instruments such as the harmonica (known as the "mouth organ" in Australia), tin whistle, button accordion, or fiddle. Collector A. B. Paterson ("Banjo Paterson," 1864–1941), who wrote the lyrics to the famous "Waltzing Matilda," published *Old Bush Songs* in 1905 (Chapter 12, Music in Oceania).

C

Cadence Conclusion or resting point at the end of a musical phrase; see Musical Elements Appendix.

Cadenza Solo virtuosic, improvisatory passage; especially common in concertos (Chapter 8, Classic Era Music).

Cajun French-speaking cultural group in southwestern Louisiana, descended from French colonists of Canada who were exiled by the British in the eighteenth century. Cajun music is drawn from a variety of cultures, including dances and folk tunes from European countries, and syncopated rhythmic styles from Africa and the Caribbean. The music is traditionally sung in French, or French and English (Chapter 1, American Traditional Music).

Call and response The alternation between leading and responding groups or individuals in music or speech; common in many cultures and often improvisatory (Chapter 1, American Traditional Music).

Calypso Afro-Caribbean dance music genre accompanied by steel bands; song texts often express sociopolitical commentary (Chapter 11, Music in the Americas).

Canon (or round) Two or more musical lines, or voices, in strict imitation throughout a musical work or a section of a musical work; see Musical Elements Appendix.

Cantata Vocal work with instrumental accompaniment. Performed by solo vocalist or choir, this genre often includes more than one movement and has either a sacred or a secular topic (Chapter 7, Baroque Music).

Cantillation Chanted recitation of religious literature in Jewish sacred music (Chapter 14, Music in the Middle East).

Carnatic (var. Karnatak) Southern Indian region and culture; the Dravidian language family is prevalent. Religious and vocal music is especially important in this devout society, with less emphasis on instruments and improvisation (Chapter 15, Music in India and Japan).

Castrato (castrati, pl.) Male singer who is castrated before puberty to preserve his high vocal register. Castrato singers were able to embody the combination of the high vocal register usually associated with women combined with male strength and stamina. Castrati often sang as leading men in the most heroic operatic roles (Chapter 7, Baroque Music).

Chamber music Music for a small instrumental ensemble, usually one player to a part (Chapter 8, Classic Era Music).

Chanson (Fr. "song") French secular vocal genre, often polyphonic, and sometimes performed with instruments (Chapter 6, Antiquity to 1600).

Character piece Descriptive, usually short instrumental work, especially popular in the romantic era (Chapter 9, Romantic Era Music).

Charango Small guitar-like fretted chordophone with 4–5 courses, popular in the Andes; see Musical Instruments Appendix.

Child Ballads See "Ballad" (Chapter 1, American Traditional Music).

Choir See "Chorus."

Chorale German strophic hymn (Chapter 6, Antiquity to 1600).

Chorale cantata Cantata based on a chorale, which includes quotations of the featured hymn tune (Chapter 7, Baroque Music).

Chord Two or more different pitches sounded together; see Musical Elements Appendix.

Chordophones Musical instruments which produce sound by vibrating strings, such as guitars, harps, and bowed stringed instruments; see Musical Instruments Appendix.

Chord progression A series of chords that uses specific combinations of pitches to set up listeners' expectations in certain ways; see Musical Elements Appendix.

Choreography The sequence of dance movements or the notated version of dance movements. Choreographers create dance sequences for stage, such as in Broadway musical and ballet performances (Chapter 2, American Music for Stage and Screen).

Chorus 1. A group of singers and a work or musical passage written for a group of singers. A "choir" is generally a smaller group of singers than a chorus; see Musical Instruments Appendix. 2. "Chorus" (or "refrain") also refers to form; for instance, in American vernacular music, a chorus is a line or group of lines in a poem or song that repeats both text and music; see Musical Elements Appendix.

Chromaticism ("chromatic," adj.) Music that uses altered pitches from the prevailing key (See "diatonicism" for the antonym.) (Chapter 8, Classic Era Music).

Circular Breathing Aboriginal Australian didjeridu technique in which the player inhales through the nose and blows air out into the instrument at the same time, so the sound is continuous; see Musical Instruments Appendix, "Didjeridoo" (Chapter 12, Music in Oceania).

Clapsticks A pair or set of wooden sticks used as idiophones to strike each other in Aboriginal Australian music-making, especially as a rhythmic accompaniment to didjeridoo performance; see Musical Instruments Appendix.

Clarinet Single-reed woodwind aerophone; see Musical Instruments Appendix.

Classic Era European music between approximately 1750–1820. "Classical music" is generally used to refer broadly to all Western Art Music, but music specifically of the classic era features aesthetic qualities inspired by classical Greek culture, such as reason, symmetry, and clarity (Unit 2, Western Art Music, Introduction, and Chapter 8, Classic Era Music).

Coda Derived from Latin for "tail," an optional final section in various forms, which presents musical material after the structural conclusion of the movement; see Musical Elements Appendix.

Coloratura (lt. "coloring") Elaborately ornamented style in vocal music, especially opera, which typically includes many notes rapidly executed. The term is also a reference to singers who specialize in this style, as in "coloratura soprano" (Chapter 9, Romantic Era music).

Concept album An album that provides thematic unity with ambitious virtuosity, depth, and, often, experimentation in the music, lyrics, and cover art; concept albums strive toward—and sometimes achieve—cultivated art. The Beatles' *Sgt. Pepper's Lonely Heart's Club Band* (1967) is the first album for which critics used the term (Chapter 4, Modern American Popular Music Part I: Up to 1970).

Concept musical Musical theater that emphasizes innovative themes, settings, and music rather than traditional, linear story lines. Some of these musicals make statements on culture, politics, religion, or some other aspect of the human condition (Chapter 2, American Music for Stage and Screen).

Concerto An instrumental work that contrasts orchestra with soloist or small ensemble, usually comprised of three movements. The **concerto grosso** emphasizes the difference between a small group of players and the entire orchestra; the **solo concerto** showcases a soloist against the entire orchestra (Chapter 7, Baroque Music).

Conch shell trumpet Traditional Oceanic aerophone, often used for signaling. Air is blown through a hole in the side or tip; see Musical Instruments Appendix.

Conjunto A small Latin American ensemble that often includes accordion and guitar, especially common in *Tejano* music in the border regions between Mexico and the US (Chapter 11, Music in the Americas).

Consonance A combination of pitches that seem to match or sound stable; see Musical Elements Appendix.

Consort A term used in England to refer to an instrumental ensemble (Chapter 6, Antiquity to 1600).

Cool jazz Sophisticated jazz genre after bebop with a more relaxed and less frenetic style. Cool jazz uses narrower melodic ranges and places more emphasis on small ensembles than on individuals. *Birth of the Cool* by Miles Davis (1926–1991) was the album that launched the style (Chapter 3, Jazz).

Corroboree Aboriginal Australian ceremonial events usually performed after sunset, which can also include storytellers and dancers decorated with body paint (Chapter 12, Music in Oceania).

Counter-Reformation The Roman Catholic response to the Reformation, which included the Council of Trent (1545–1563) and various reforms (Unit 2, Western Art Music, Introduction, and Chapter 6, Antiquity to 1600).

Creole A cultural group, especially in Louisiana, that includes people of European and Afro-Caribbean descent; this term can also refer generically to a mixture of cultures and languages (Chapter 1, American Traditional Music).

D

Dance Suite, or Suite Group of contrasting instrumental dances. Most dances have a simple two-part structure with each section repeated: AABB (Chapter 7, Baroque Music).

Development Second section of sonata form, which intensifies drama with modulation and manipulation of thematic material; see Musical Elements Appendix.

Diaspora (Greek, "scattering of seeds"): The migration or dispersion of a group of people beyond their original homeland. Music can show the effects of diaspora in a given culture and can also be a telling measure of a society's cohesiveness despite diaspora (Unit 3, World Music, Introduction).

Diatonicism ("diatonic," adj.) Music that uses unaltered pitches from the prevailing key (See "chromaticism" for the antonym.) (Chapter 8, Classic Era Music).

Diction Style and clarity of a singer's enunciation of the words in a vocal performance; see Musical Elements Appendix.

Didjeridu (didgeridoo, didjeridoo, didj) Large aerophone, 3 to 7 feet long and about 1 to 3 inches in diameter, made out of eucalyptus wood hollowed out by termites. Performers use circular breathing technique in which the player inhales through the nose and blows air out into the instrument at the same time, so the sound is continuous. Traditional performers often imitate nature and animal sounds through airflow punctuated with vocalizations such as hums or growls. Although the didjeridu likely originated in cultures specific to northern Australia, it has come to represent all Australian aboriginal cultures as a pan-Aboriginal cultural symbol; see Musical Instruments Appendix.

Diegetic music (source music) In film, music that the characters experience from inside the story; the characters hear, or might even produce, the music (Chapter 2, American Music for Stage and Screen).

Disco Dance club or dance music especially successful during the 1970s. Disco featured highly produced music with electronic beats based on funk rhythms, typically in quadruple meter. DJs, or disc jockeys, became the key personnel, and sometimes cult figures (Chapter 5, Modern American Popular Music Part II: After 1970).

Dissonance A combination of pitches that clash or sound unstable; the listener expects a resolution to follow a dissonant chord; see Musical Elements Appendix.

"Dogfights" See "Break strains" (Chapter 10, Modern Art Music).

Dreamtime Australian aboriginal spiritual belief system and concept of creation; a continuous, living spiritual force that represents many facets of aboriginal belief systems and myths. Dreamtime's power can be tapped through ritual music, dance, and journeys (Chapter 12, Music in Oceania).

Drone Sustained pitch or pitches (Chapter 15, Music in India and Japan).

Dulcimer A box zither chordophone family of instruments with various numbers of strings that are plucked, strummed, hammered, or bowed. Dulcimers do not have necks or keyboards. Several types are prominent in American traditional folk music; see Musical Instruments Appendix.

Duple meter A metric pattern in which the first of every two beats is typically accented as in ***strong,* weak** (see "meter"); see Musical Elements Appendix.

Dynamics The level of volume, or loudness and softness, in music; see Musical Elements Appendix.

E

EDM Electronic dance music after the disco era. Popular genres of EDM include Chicago's "house" music; Detroit's more futuristic "techno" music; "trance," which is similar to techno but with more emphasis on the melodic line; and "dubstep," a Jamaican-influenced type from the UK, which has a strong, pronounced bass line with a syncopated rhythm (Chapter 5, Modern American Popular Music Part II: After 1970).

Electronophones Musical instruments which generate sound electronically, such as synthesizers (Unit 3, World Music, Introduction, and see Musical Instruments Appendix).

Empfindsam* (Ger. "sensitive" or "sentimental") style,** or ***Empfindsamkeit A classic era musical style which uses expressive effects that include "sigh" motives, chromaticism, and unusual rhythms to evoke emotions such as melancholy or nostalgia (Chapter 8, Classic Era Music).

Enlightenment (Age of Reason) Generally considered as lasting from the late seventeenth through the end of the eighteenth centuries, this rationalist movement sought to look beyond the Bible for answers to life's mysteries in philosophy, politics, science, scholarship, and the arts. (Unit 2, Western Art Music, Introduction, and Chapter 8, Classic Era Music).

Erets-Israel ("Land of Israel") Songs Israeli folk songs in monophonic texture, set to Hebrew texts. They originated either as Hebrew translations of songs from the diaspora or as newly composed melodies set to Zionist poetry. The Israeli national anthem, *"Hatikvah"* ("The Hope"), is one example of an Erets-Israel song (Chapter 14, Music in the Middle East).

Ethnocentrism   Perception or judgment that is limited by one's own cultural point of view, often with a presumption of superiority. Our own ethnocentrism can block our interest and understanding of unfamiliar musical styles. When we listen attentively to music of other cultures, we take a step toward understanding that may seem small but is deeply significant (Unit 3, World Music, Introduction).

Ethnomusicology   The study of social and cultural contexts in music-making as well as of the music itself. The ethnomusicologist goes beyond the question, *"What* are we listening to?"* to ask contextual questions, such as *"Why*, and *when*, is this music performed?" and *"What does this music mean to the culture?,"* This is often true of the "musicologist," as well, but most musicologists focus on the Western art music traditions introduced in Unit 2, Western Art Music, whereas ethnomusicologists study and teach about music throughout the world in a wide variety of cultures.

Exoticism   Evocation of foreign cultures in the arts (Chapter 9, Romantic Era Music).

Exposition   First section of sonata form, which introduces the main themes of the movement and moves away from the home key; see Musical Elements Appendix.

Expressionism   Early-twentieth-century movement in visual arts, literature, and music, which emphasized the hidden emotions, such as anxiety and shame; likely influenced by Freudian theories of the subconscious. Schoenberg, who was also a visual artist, is the composer most associated with expressionist music (Chapter 10, Modern Art Music).

F

Fiddle   A bowed stringed chordophone, which produces sounds primarily with a bow rubbed across strings that are stretched tightly over a resonator box. Although this instrument is structurally identical to a violin, the term "fiddle" implies a traditional folk or bluegrass style of repertory, technique, and performance practice; see Musical Instruments Appendix.

Field Holler   A type of work song associated with field and levee workers, often sung by individual workers as a way of communicating across a distance with other workers and passersby. Field hollers have been described as long shouts, or cries (Chapter 1. American Traditional Music).

Film score   See "Soundtrack" (Chapter 2, American Music for Stage and Screen).

Fin' amor **(Occitan: "refined love")**   Popular theme in early modern European literature of idealized love, which expressed the pain of unrequited love, devotion to the beloved, and the refinement of the lover through a lifetime of suffering and service (Chapter 6, Antiquity to 1600).

Floating rhythm   Ambiguous rhythm and meter (Chapter 10, Modern Art Music).

Fuging tunes   Genre of early American imitative part-songs that feature sections with staggered entrances. Although these tunes usually begin with voices together, the songs feature successive, imitative entrances of musical lines just as they are in musical rounds such as the familiar nursery song, "Row, Row, Row Your Boat." Unlike rounds (which continue in strict imitation throughout the entire melody), the musical lines of fuging tunes depart from strict imitation at some point before they end (Chapter 1, American Traditional Music, and Chapter 7, Baroque Music).

Fugue Polyphonic composition in which a **subject**, or theme, is imitated successively in several musical lines. The second statement of the subject immediately following in another musical line, or voice, is known as the **answer**, and the **countersubject** is the musical material of the original voice after the subject is finished, set against the answer in a new voice (Chapter 7, Baroque Music).

Funk Dance music that uses soul, blues, jazz, and rock idioms. Its defining characteristic is a bass-heavy, polyrhythmic, syncopated dance rhythm, often referred to as a "groove" (Chapter 5, Modern American Popular Music Part II: After 1970).

Fusion A blend of blend of jazz and rock musical styles or, more generally, blends of jazz with other styles such as other types of popular music and non-Western music, especially South Asian music (Chapter 3, Jazz).

G

Gagaku ("elegant music") A traditional Japanese musical genre that emphasizes preservation over change in every aspect of style, technique, and performance practice (Chapter 15, Music in India and Japan).

Galant Classic era musical style characterized by sparse texture, short phrases, and simple, attractive melodies (Chapter 8, Classic Era Music).

Grand Ole Opry Radio show broadcasting from WSM in Nashville, 1925 to present. The Grand Ole Opry is one of several popular radio shows from the early twentieth century, which gathered country music performers from different regions to broadcast variety shows. On stage together, the musicians influenced one another and developed the hybrid foundation of country music in the US. The name and institution "Grand Ole Opry" has become almost synonymous with "country music" (Chapter 4, Modern American Popular Music Part I: Up to 1970).

Griot (alt. jeliya or jelilu) A hereditary class of oral historians who carry on the musical and literary traditions of the culture in Western Africa. Their role can include any combination of musician, storyteller, poet, historian, and praise singer. The term, g*riot,* is French, and is used by Westerners as an umbrella term for several different subtypes throughout West Africa (Chapter 13, Music in Sub-Saharan Africa).

Guitar A plucked stringed chordophone, usually with 6 single or double strings, and with a fretted neck. The acoustic (nonelectric) guitar is a common accompaniment instrument for traditional folk music; see Musical Instruments Appendix (Chapter 1, American Traditional Music).

Guitarrón Large bass guitar popular in Mexico, especially in mariachi ensembles; see Musical Instruments Appendix.

H

Haka A war dance and chant, which has become an iconic Maori display of spirit and courage. From wide, battle-ready stances, performers stamp their feet rhythmically and aggressively. They begin the dance with quivering motions that are thought to connect the dancer's body and mind, bringing the dance to life. Arm and hand gestures throughout the dance convey information. Facial expressions are fearsome, with wide-open eyes and protruding tongues. The text is chanted and shouted rather than sung. The haka includes many subtypes and individual compositions. Although it is clearly warlike, it can also be performed for celebration, commemoration, or political comment (Chapter 12, Music in Oceania).

Harlem Renaissance Originally known as the "New Negro Movement," an interdisciplinary cultural movement centered in but not limited to Harlem, New York, that celebrated and fostered African American achievements in scholarship and the arts, which reached its height in the 1920s. Musicians associated with the Harlem Renaissance include Louis Armstrong, Duke Ellington, W. C. Handy, Jelly Roll Morton, William Grant Still, and many others (Chapter 3, Jazz).

Harmony The relationships and progressions between pitches that sound simultaneously in musical texture; see Musical Elements Appendix.

Harpsichord A keyboard stringed instrument popular in the in the seventeenth and eighteenth centuries; see Musical Instruments Appendix.

Hazzan Jewish cantor, who leads the congregation in cantillation. Second only to the rabbi in the moral and religious leadership of the congregation, the hazzan is expected to freely elaborate on traditional melodies (Chapter 14, Music in the Middle East).

Heavy metal Rock music that emphasizes aggressive and virtuosic electric guitar performances, vocal screams, dramatic staging with light shows, and sometimes outrageous costumes, "big" hair, and heavy makeup. Closely allied terms and styles for both US and UK bands include "hard" rock, "glam" (short for glamour) metal, "thrash metal," and others (Chapter 5, Modern American Popular Music Part II: After 1970).

Heterophony Musical texture that consists of a single musical line with simultaneous variation: while one or more voices proceed monophonically, at least one voice embellishes the monophonic line; see Musical Elements Appendix.

Hichiriki A small double reed bamboo pipe aerophone of Japan, used in gagaku and other traditional Japanese genres; see Musical Instruments Appendix.

Highlife West African early-to-mid-twentieth-century music that blended African idioms with European and American—especially Caribbean—influences. Associated with "high society" parties, the music was typically in simple duple meter with a steady tempo for the dancers. Melodies were catchy and often joyful in syncopated rhythm. The song texts—written in a West African language or in English—were most often about love, but some included sociopolitical references. Castanets, maracas, and drums dominated the rhythm section, with wind instruments and guitars on the melody. During World War II, swing music inspired highlife bandleaders such as E. T. Mensah (1919–1996), who toured West Africa with his band "The Tempos" (Chapter 13, Music in Sub-Saharan Africa).

Hillbilly music Term used in the early twentieth century to denote Southern popular music; the music industry replaced this term with "country" and later "country and western" in the mid-twentieth century (Chapter 4, Modern American Popular Music Part I: Up to 1970).

Hindustani Northern Indian region and culture; the Hindi language family is prevalent. A blend of central and South Asian influences result in a more diverse and secular society than in the Carnatic culture, with a rich tradition of improvisatory instrumental music (Chapter 15, Music in India and Japan).

Hip-Hop African American/Latino urban culture that originated in New York's South Bronx in the 1970s; rap music, scratching, and turntablism can be described as part of hip-hop culture (Chapter 5, Modern American Popular Music Part II: After 1970).

Homophony   Musical texture that features one dominant melody with subordinate chordal accompaniment; see Musical Elements Appendix.

Hornbostel-Sachs Instrument Classification System   System in which musical instruments are classified according to sound production. It was developed by early-twentieth-century musicologists Erich von Hornbostel (1877–1935) and Curt Sachs (1881–1959) and is particularly valuable for the study of musical instruments across a wide variety of cultures and historical eras (Unit 3, World Music, Introduction).

House   (See "EDM") (Chapter 5, Modern American Popular Music Part II: After 1970).

Hula   Traditional Hawaiian dance, often used with or instead of song to express mele (poetic song text) The dancer sings and, in seated dances, also plays rhythmic idiophones or membranophones. Hand, wrist, and arm movements convey the words, phrases, and rich, multilayered meanings of the mele in graceful gestures. Hula costumes can include decorative accessories such as leis (flower necklaces) (Chapter 12, Music in Oceania).

I

Idée fixe   Term associated with Berlioz, often translated as "obsession"; similar to *leitmotif*, *idée fixe* is a musical motive representing a person or idea (Chapter 9, Romantic Era Music).

Idiophones   Musical instruments which produce sound by vibrating the substance of the instruments themselves, such as castanets, rattles, and the triangle; see Musical Instruments Appendix.

Impressionism   Late-nineteenth-century French visual arts movement, featuring paintings that emphasize spontaneity and the "first impressions" of their subjects using light and color, with ambiguous boundaries. Debussy is the composer most associated with impressionism; his music features ambiguities in harmony and meter and emphasizes timbre (Chapter 10, Modern Art Music).

Improvisation   The creation of music during performance; common in many cultures and genres, it is a hallmark of American jazz (Chapter 3, Jazz).

Interlocking rhythms   Multiple layers of rhythmic lines that seem to intersect and interact with each other; the resulting sound picture creates a more complete impression than the sum of its parts (Chapter 13, Music in Sub-Saharan Africa).

Interpretation   Expressive choices by composers and performers in the performance of a musical work, mainly in regard to tempo, dynamics, articulation, and rhythmic flexibility; see Musical Elements Appendix.

Interval   The distance between two pitches. Musicians use intervals as building blocks for chords, scales, and melodies; see Musical Elements Appendix.

Inversion   In the context of serialism, melody or tone row presented inverted (upside down) (Chapter 10, Modern Art Music).

Isicathamia   (See "Mbube")

J

Jùjú   Yoruban popular dance musical genre of Nigeria. A blend of traditional Yoruban talking drum and praise-singing styles with American and South Asian popular music, jùjú uses both traditional and modern electronic instruments, with a vocal chorus of praise singers (Chapter 13, Music in Sub-Saharan Africa).

K

Key (See "Tonality," and Musical Elements Appendix.)

Klezmer (From the Hebrew words "kley" for "tool," or "instrument," and "zmer" or "to make music"): Improvisatory and highly ornamental dance music of Ashkenazi Jews, commonly featuring woodwinds, bowed strings, and accordions (Chapter 14, Music in the Middle East).

Kora A Western African plucked-string harp chordophone, made from a large gourd pierced with a wooden pole that serves as a neck, with 19 or 21 strings. It is traditionally considered to be the domain of male griots, and is used either as accompaniment to vocal and ensemble music or as a solo instrument; see Musical Instruments Appendix.

Koto A 13-stringed zither chordophone of Japan, plucked by picks attached to thumb and fingers; see Musical Instruments Appendix.

L

Legato Type of articulation in which notes flow smoothly from one to the next, without space in between; see Musical Elements Appendix.

Leitmotif (Ger. "leading motif") Term associated with Wagner and similar to *idée fixe*, *leitmotif* is a musical motive representing a person, place, object, or idea (Chapter 9, Romantic Era Music, and Chapter 2, American Music for Stage and Screen).

Libretto (It. "little book") The text, or dramatic script, of a musical work. A librettist is the author of the text (Chapter 2, American Music for Stage and Screen, and Chapter 7, Baroque Music).

Lied (Ger. "song," pl. lieder) or art song In German, song in general; specifically, nineteenth-century German solo vocal settings of poetry with piano accompaniment (Chapter 9, Romantic Era Music).

Lining out Performance practice in which the leader shouts or sings each line of a song in advance for the rest of the singers to imitate (Chapter 1, American Traditional Music).

Lute A plucked stringed, fretted chordophone with courses (double strings), a rounded back, and a flat top that flourished in Europe from the late Middle Ages through the baroque era; see Musical Instruments Appendix.

Lyre An ancient stringed instrument, which was associated with the worship of Apollo; see Musical Instruments Appendix.

M

Madrigal Secular polyphonic vocal genre in sixteenth-century Italy and England (Chapter 6, Antiquity to 1600).

Major/Minor key, or tonality In Western music since the early eighteenth century, sets of pitches and harmonies built on seven-note scales with specific patterns of whole steps and half steps. Music in minor keys, built on minor scales, is often associated with unhappy or nostalgic feelings while the brighter sounding music in major keys, built on major scales, is sometimes linked with more positive emotions; see Musical Elements Appendix.

Maori Indigenous people of Aotearoa (New Zealand) (Chapter 12, Music in Oceania).

Maqam (pl. maqamat) An Arabic mode or a type of scale, with characteristic intervals, melodies, rhythms, topics, and symbolic associations (Chapter 14, Music in the Middle East).

Marching band, concert band Ensembles composed of wind and percussion instruments and which often specialize in marching music. Marching bands march with their instruments, sometimes in choreographed patterns, as they perform in events such as parades and competitive sports. Concert bands perform on stage (Chapter 10, Modern Art Music).

Mariachi Traditional Mexican folk music that includes vocalist with trumpet or violin on melody, guitar, or harp as harmonic accompaniment, and *guitarrón* on the bass line. Songs are punctuated by high-spirited hoots and shouts. Although mariachi music originated in western Mexico, its wide popularity has made this genre emblematic of Mexican culture in general (Chapter 11, Music in the Americas).

Mashup A new electronically edited version of two or more preexisting musical works that are combined (see "remix") (Chapter 5, Modern American Popular Music Part II: After 1970).

Mass setting Mass worship service set to music (Chapter 6, Antiquity to 1600).

Mawwal A vocalist's improvisatory, melismatic interpretation of Arabic poetry (Chapter 14, Music in the Middle East).

Mbalax A fusion of Western popular music with traditional Senegalese rhythms (Chapter 13, Music in Sub-Saharan Africa).

Mbaqanga South African hybrid popular music style of the mid-twentieth century that was a fusion between local African roots and Western styles such as jazz, rock 'n' roll, and reggae. A typical band consisted of a lead vocalist or a melody instrument backed by electric guitars, drums, and sometimes accordion or violin. The lyrics of *mbaqanga* songs were mostly in English and Bantu languages, purposely avoiding Afrikaner, the official language of South Africa during apartheid years (Chapter 13, Music in Sub-Saharan Africa).

Mbube (Zulu, "lion") and isicathamia (Zulu, "to walk stealthily like a cat") A South African choir music genre in which the leader ("controller") directs the choir ("the chord") in a call and response style. Musical textures include a cappella polyphony and hymn-like homophonic four-part harmonies, performed with intricate polyrhythms, vocal sound effects, and visually arresting choreography. The genre blends traditional Zulu music and dance styles with Western musical styles, such as Christian hymns, that had been taught by missionaries since colonial times. Popular competitions brought the genre to prominence, especially with Solomon Linda (1909–1962) and the Evening Birds and Joseph Shabalala (b. 1941) with Ladysmith Black Mambazo, who pioneered the quieter, more rhythmically precise style, isicathamia (Chapter 13, Music in Sub-Saharan Africa).

Measure (bar) A unit of a fixed number of beats in music notation. Although the number of beats can vary widely, in Western music measures most often contain 2, 3, 4, or 6 beats; see Musical Elements Appendix.

Medieval Era The period of European history spanning approximately the fifth to the fifteenth centuries CE. This was a transitional period marked by the collapse of the Roman Empire, the Christianization of Europe, and the continuous development of national identities and boundaries (Unit 2, Western Art Music, Introduction, and Chapter 6, Antiquity to 1600).

Mele Traditional Hawaiian poetic song texts that can be sacred or secular, with a vast array of topics, including genealogical songs that trace lineage, name songs that honor people, love songs, and welcome songs. Mele accompanied by dance are typically in duple meter, and mele without dance are generally nonmetric chants (Chapter 12, Music in Oceania).

Melismatic text-setting style   A text setting style in which many notes per syllable are sung (Chapter 6, Antiquity to 1600).

Melodic contour   The shape of a melody, such as ascending, descending, or wavelike; see Musical Elements Appendix.

Melodic range   The distance between the lowest and highest notes of any given melody; see Musical Elements Appendix.

Melody   A succession of musical tones or pitches that has identifiable shape and meaning. Melodies can vary greatly in length and complexity, but even the simplest melodies are capable of tremendous power over our emotions and memories; see Musical Elements Appendix.

Membranophones   Musical instruments which produce sound by vibrating stretched skins, or membranes over a hollow resonator; most of these are drums; see Musical Instruments Appendix.

Meter   The pattern of accents in a series of beats. The first of every two beats is commonly accented in duple meter, and the first of every three beats is usually accented in triple meter, for example; see Musical Elements Appendix.

Micropolyphony   A term associated with Ligeti; densely textured polyphonic lines (Chapter 10, Modern Art Music).

Miniature   In music, a short, often programmatic instrumental work especially popular in the romantic era meant to be the abstract musical equivalent of a poem (Chapter 9, Romantic Era Music).

Minimalism   Musical style inspired by the mid-twentieth-century visual arts movement, characterized by repetitive or slowly changing basic musical elements and strong connections with vernacular and world musical styles (Chapter 10, Modern Art Music).

Minstrel   Itinerant musician-entertainer in medieval Europe (Chapter 6, Antiquity to 1600).

Minuet and Trio   A type of ternary form based on the minuet dance; both of the "A" sections feature the minuet, and the "B" section features a contrasting trio; see Musical Elements Appendix.

Modified Strophic form   Texted vocal music that combines features of strophic and through-composed forms (Chapter 9, Romantic Era Music).

Monophony   Musical texture that consists of only a single musical line or voice. More than one instrument or singer can sound monophonically if all sound the same pitch; octaves can be considered monophonic texture; see Musical Elements Appendix.

Moteatea   Maori traditional chant, song, or sung poetry; a core musical practice meant to connect performers and listeners with their spiritual selves and remind them of the meaning of past events and their present condition. Moteatea performance, which also functions as speech, can help resolve disputes between individuals or tribes. Traditional songs are performed in unison, with melodies in a narrow range (Chapter 12, Music in Oceania).

Motet   A polyphonic vocal work. Early medieval motets are based on a preexisting musical line, with one or more additional texted musical lines, and often feature multiple texts in both Latin and French that are simultaneously performed (Chapter 6, Antiquity to 1600).

Muezzin A Muslim prayer caller, who is a trained singer; he is expected to have a virtuosic ability to ornament the melody of the adhan (Chapter 14, Music in the Middle East).

Music of the spheres Mystical concept developed by Pythagoras and his followers of "unheard music" created by the movement of heavenly bodies (Chapter 7, Antiquity to 1600).

Musical Form Organization or structure of musical works; see Musical Elements Appendix.

Musical Texture The melodic and harmonic relationship of musical lines, or voices; see musical texture and **heterophony, homophony, monophony,** and **polyphony** in Musical Elements Appendix.

N

Nationalism Used here in regard to musical style, the musical expression of national or ethnic identity (Chapter 10, Modern Art Music).

New wave A "post-punk" style that still expressed alienation and independence from the establishment but with less scandal than punk and more humor and artistry (Chapter 5, Modern American Popular Music Part II: After 1970).

Ney Middle Eastern and Central Asian flute aerophone; see Musical Instruments Appendix.

Nondiegetic music (underscoring) In film, music from outside of the story that only the film's audience can hear, which is meant to heighten the narrative and symbolically express emotions and meanings the filmmakers want the audience to experience (Chapter 2, American Music for Stage and Screen).

Nonmetric Music with little or no discernible metric pattern; see Musical Elements Appendix.

O

Opera Staged drama based on a libretto, set to continuous music, which includes soloists, ensembles, chorus, and instrumental accompaniment (Chapter 7, Baroque Music).

Opera buffa Italian comic opera (Chapter 8, Classic Era Music).

Opera seria Italian dramatic, serious opera (Chapter 8, Classic Era Music).

Oral tradition Transmission of skills and information in spoken rather than written form (Chapter 1, American Traditional Music).

Oratorio Large-scale sacred vocal drama similar to opera but not staged. An oratorio often includes a narrator and is usually based on a biblical story. Oratorio forces include chorus, vocal soloists, and orchestra (Chapter 7, Baroque Music).

Orchestra A large ensemble of instruments including strings, woodwinds, brass, and percussion instruments with a conductor as the leader. Bowed stringed instruments are considered the "heart" of the orchestra (Chapter 8, Classic Era Music).

Ostinato (It. "obstinate") A repeating musical pattern. An ostinato variation set, also known as a "ground" or "ground bass," is a set of variations built on an ostinato pattern; the variations are often improvisational (Chapter 7, Baroque Music, and Chapter 10, Modern Art Music).

Ostinato variations (ground bass) From the Italian word for "obstinate," an ostinato is a repeating harmonic, melodic, or rhythmic pattern. An ostinato variation set, also known as a "ground" or "ground bass," is a set of variations built on an ostinato pattern; the variations are often improvisational (Chapter 7, Baroque Music).

Outlaw country Country music style based in Texas that rejects established production conventions such as heavy studio accompaniment in favor of a more individualistic, authentic, and improvisatory approach, inspired by earlier honky-tonk and Western swing musical styles (Chapter 5, Modern American Popular Music Part II: After 1970).

Overture An instrumental introduction to an opera or other dramatic work (Chapter 7, Baroque Music).

P

Panpipes Sets of end-blown flute aerophones of varying lengths bundled together. The Latin American panpipe has pre-Columbian origins; see Musical Instruments Appendix.

Parlor song Song meant for amateur performance; usually strophic ballads with sentimental topics and simple musical settings (Chapter 9, Romantic Era Music).

Part-song, Part-singing Choral music, or a way of singing choral music, in which the vocal parts are divided into sections according to ranges, typically soprano (high voice), alto (medium high), tenor (medium low), and bass (low), commonly referred to as "SATB" (Chapter 1, American Traditional Music and Chapter 9, Romantic Era Music).

Pastoral Reference to rustic topics, such as nature, countryside, peasants, farmers, and shepherds (Chapter 6, Antiquity to 1600).

Patter song Vocal style in which many syllables of text are sung as quickly as possible for comic effect (Chapter 9, Romantic Era Music).

Payola From the terms, "pay" and "Victrola," the illegal use of money or other forms of bribery in the music industry to increase airplay for a song in order to make it more popular. The career of the popular DJ Alan Freed ended when he was convicted of payola practices (Chapter 4, Modern American Popular Music Part I: Up to 1970).

Pentatonic Scale Five-note scale, especially common in Native American and Asian cultures. Among these different cultures, pentatonic scales feature a multitude of intervals and nuances (Chapter 11, Music in the Americas).

Percussion Family of instruments in which sound is produced variously by striking, shaking, and in other ways; a wide variety of instruments can be part of the orchestral percussion section, including both idiophones and membranophones; see Musical Instruments Appendix.

Phrase A unit of meaning within a larger structure; see Musical Elements Appendix.

Piano Considered to be the "king" of the instruments and indispensable in many styles of music, including ragtime and jazz. Sound is produced when keys are depressed, causing hammers to strike and rebound from strings. The piano provides the foundation of study for music students and is one of the most popular solo and ensemble instruments in art, jazz, and popular music styles; see Musical Instruments Appendix.

Piano quintet A chamber ensemble of or composition for piano and four other instruments, usually string quartet (Chapter 9, Romantic Era Music).

Piano trio A chamber ensemble of or composition for piano and two other instruments, usually violin and cello; a work composed for this chamber ensemble (Chapter 9, Romantic Era Music).

Pitch The "highness" or "lowness" of a sound. High pitches have a higher frequency than lower pitches; that is, high pitches create more waves in any given time period than lower pitches; see Musical Elements Appendix.

Pizzicato Bowed string musical notes or passages which are plucked rather than bowed, resulting in a detached style; see Musical Elements Appendix.

Plainchant (Gregorian chant) Christian, monophonic sacred chant originating in medieval Christian worship traditions (Chapter 6, Antiquity to 1600).

Points of imitation Brief passages of imitation between musical lines; often at beginnings of text phrases in vocal music (Chapter 6, Antiquity to 1600).

Polyphony Musical texture that consists of two or more independent musical lines; see Musical Elements Appendix.

Polyrhythm Different rhythms or meters performed simultaneously; see Musical Elements Appendix.

Polytonality Two or more tonalities occurring simultaneously (Chapter 10, Modern Art Music).

Post-tonal music Music of the twentieth century and later that is not tonal, such as atonal or serialist music (Chapter 10, Modern Art Music).

Powwow (pow-wow) Native American social gathering for cultural activities, including music, dance, food, and crafts. Processionals and drum circles are common in these celebrations (Chapter 11, Music in the Americas).

Prepared piano Piano music in which the piano has been "prepared" with items such as bolts, clips, and rubber bands placed in the strings, affecting the timbre; especially associated with John Cage (Chapter 10. Modern Art Music).

Primitivism Late-nineteenth-century visual arts movement inspired by the idea of a primal, ancestral society close to nature and without the trappings of Western civilization. Primitivism in music uses these ideas in its themes and topics, as in Stravinsky's *Rite of Spring* ballet (Chapter 10, Modern Art Music).

Program music Instrumental music with extra-musical references, such as a story or pictorial idea (Chapter 9, Romantic Era Music).

Psalmody Most strictly, the singing of psalms; however, in this text psalmody refers to seventeenth-nineteenth century sacred vocal music in North America (Chapter 1, American Traditional Music).

Psychedelia An artistic and musical style of the mid-1960s that evoked mind-altering drug use. Bright colors and surreal images prevailed in the visual arts and fashion. Music's sonic landscape was expanded by experimentation with electronic sounds and eclectic styles (Chapter 4, Modern American Popular Music Part I: Up to 1970).

Punk Experimental and provocative rock music that furiously challenges the status quo. The music is self-consciously simple and emphasizes aggressive guitar strumming with an often confrontational, loud, and strained vocal delivery. Song lyrics protest the establishment with irony and, at times, intense bitterness (Chapter 5, Modern American Popular Music Part II: After 1970).

Q

Qanun   A large zither of the Middle East and parts of Asia, commonly used in Arabic classical ensemble music; see Musical Instruments Appendix.

Quadruple meter   A metric pattern in which every 4 beats is accented, typically with the first beat accented and the third beat secondarily accented as in **strongest**, weak, *strong*, weak; see Musical Elements Appendix.

R

Race records (or race music)   Term used in the early twentieth century to denote music recorded by Black artists for Black listeners; after World War II this term was replaced with "rhythm and blues" (Chapter 5, Modern American Popular Music Part II: After 1970).

Raga   South Asian musical system of scale patterns and melodic figures. Ragas have extra-musical associations, such as time of day, emotions, colors, and deities (Chapter 15, Music in India and Japan).

Ragtime   Syncopated musical genre popular in the late nineteenth and early twentieth centuries; the most well-known composer of this style was Scott Joplin (c. 1867–1917) (Chapter 3, Jazz).

Rap music   A musical style from hip-hop culture that includes spoken rhyme over a rhythmic background and manipulation of preexisting recordings, influenced by the reggae DJ "rappers" of the 1950s. Recognized styles include "old school," "new school," and "gangsta rap." Recently, pop-oriented and collaborative rap has increased in popularity (Chapter 5, Modern American Popular Music Part II: After 1970).

Rave   International electronic music dance party movement of the late 1980s and early 1990s; associated with the use of hallucinogenic drugs, including MDMA (ecstasy) (Chapter 5, Modern American Popular Music Part II: After 1970).

Recapitulation   Third section of sonata form, which returns to the main themes and original key; see Musical Elements Appendix.

Recital   Solo or small ensemble musical performance (Chapter 9, Romantic Era Music).

Recitative   Speech-like vocal music without strong meter that is often used to deliver plot points and dialogue in opera and other dramatic vocal works (Chapter 7, Baroque Music).

Reformation   Used here to refer to the Protestant Reformation, the sixteenth-century Christian religious movement that resulted in the establishment of Protestant churches and profound changes in Christian worship (Unit 2, Western Art Music, Introduction, and Chapter 6, Antiquity to 1600).

Refrain   See "Chorus (refrain)" in Musical Elements Appendix.

Reggae   Jamaican musical genre characterized by syncopation and social justice topics. Reggae has been enormously influential in American popular music (Chapter 11, Music in the Americas).

Remix   A new, electronically edited version of a preexisting work (see "mashup") (Chapter 5, Modern American Popular Music Part II: After 1970).

Renaissance ("Rebirth")   The period of European history from the end of the medieval era in the early fifteenth century to c. 1600, characterized by a renewed interest in classical cultures. These interests inspired what we now call the humanist movement, which sought to preserve and emulate ancient intellectual and artistic achievement. (Unit 2, Western Art Music, Introduction; Unit 1, American Vernacular Music, Introduction; and Chapter 6, Antiquity to 1600).

Retrograde In the context of serialism, melody or tone row presented backwards (Chapter 10, Modern Art Music).

Retrograde inversion In the context of serialism, melody or tone row presented both backwards and inverted (upside down) (Chapter 10, Modern Art Music).

Rhythm In general: Those aspects of music that have to do with time, including beat, meter, accent, and duration. Specifically: The duration of individual notes and pauses; see Musical Elements Appendix.

Riqq An Arabic frame drum membranophone and idiophone, similar to the tambourine; see Musical Instruments Appendix under "idiophones."

Rockabilly Early rock and roll style heavily influenced by country and blues, characterized by expressive vocal sounds and electrified instrumental accompaniment; Buddy Holly and Elvis Presley were prominent rockabilly performers (Chapter 4, Modern American Popular Music Part I; Up to 1970).

Romanticism Used here to refer to the nineteenth-century European movement characterized by a more subjective point of view than the rationalist classical era. Romantic music emphasized intense emotional expression, literary programs, and the use of large musical forces (Unit 2, Western Art Music, Introduction).

Rondo form A musical form in which the "A" theme keeps recurring in alternation with a "B" theme and often with other themes as well: ABABA, ABACABA, and ABACADA are a few of the many possible rondo schemes; see Musical Elements Appendix.

Round See "Canon" in Musical Elements Appendix.

Rubato (It. "robbed or stolen time") Rhythmic flexibility for the sake of expression; see Musical Elements Appendix.

Ryuteki A transverse bamboo flute aerophone of Japan; see Musical Instruments Appendix.

S

Sacred music Religious music (Chapter 6, Antiquity to 1600).

Salsa An amalgamation of Afro-Caribbean and North American jazz dance music with syncopated, polyrhythmic instrumental accompaniment. Instrumentation includes bongos and jazz band instruments (Chapter 11, Music in the Americas).

Sampling (See "Turntablism") (Chapter 5, Modern American Popular Music Part II: After 1970).

Sarabande Popular dance form, which originated as a lively triple meter dance in Latin America (*zarabanda*), and later came to be quite slow in baroque Europe, with a strong second beat due to its choreography (Chapter 7, Baroque Music, and Chapter 10, Modern Art Music).

Scale An ascending or descending series of pitches, arranged in a specific pattern of intervals; see Musical Elements Appendix.

Scat Improvised jazz vocalizations of nonsense syllables that are improvised, often in imitation of musical instruments (Chapter 3, Jazz).

Scratching (See "Turntablism") (Chapter 5, Modern American Popular Music Part II: After 1970).

Secular music Nonreligious music (Chapter 6, Antiquity to 1600).

Sephardim (Adj. Sephardic) (From the Hebrew word for "Spain") Descendants of Jews who left the Iberian Peninsula after the 1492 expulsion (Chapter 14, Music in the Middle East).

Serialism (See "Twelve-tone method") Twentieth-century method of composition devised by Schoenberg in which each of the twelve notes of the octave are placed in a particular order, or tone row, and are not repeated out of that order; various techniques are associated with serialism, which has been a strong influence among modern composers (Chapter 10, Modern Art Music).

Shape note tradition Notation with variously shaped note heads to help hymn singers learn to read music; especially popular in southern United States sacred music during the nineteenth century and still in use (Chapter 1, American Traditional Music).

Sheet music Unbound sheets of printed music, usually of individual songs or brief instrumental works (Chapter 2, American Music for Stage and Screen).

Sho A mouth organ aerophone of Japan made of 17 bamboo pipes with internal reeds; harmonies of up to 6 notes are sounded simultaneously with the aid of finger holes on the pipes; see Musical Instruments Appendix.

Shofar A trumpet aerophone made from an animal's horn, traditionally used in Jewish High Holy Days liturgy; see Musical Instruments Appendix.

Singsing Special performances in traditional Melanesian cultures that can last for many hours and include elaborately decorated clothing and masks. Singsings can mark community or individuals' life events, and they can also celebrate meetings between cultures (Chapter 12, Music in Oceania).

Singer-songwriter Generally, performers who write their own music and lyrics. More specifically, singer-songwriters are a category of artists who, since the mid-twentieth century, typically play their own accompaniment on acoustic instruments and whose themes offer depth and sincerity (Chapter 4, Modern American Popular Music Part I: Up to 1970).

Sistrum (plural: sistra) A U-shaped rattle idiophone popular in ancient Egypt; loose-fitting, often metallic bars intersecting the "U" slide back and forth to produce sound when the hand shakes it. Sistra are still used in the Ethiopian church, and similar instruments are used in sub-Saharan Africa; see Musical Instruments Appendix.

Sitar A long-necked, fretted lute chordophone of Hindustani (northern) India with extra strings that vibrate sympathetically, creating rich sonorities; see Musical Instruments Appendix.

Slit Drums Log idiophones struck rhythmically. They are hollowed out with narrow slits cut long-ways in the middle, up to about 20 feet long, often with carved semblances of animals or deities at the ends; see Musical Instruments Appendix.

Sonata A multimovement instrumental work for soloist or small ensemble (Chapter 8, Classic Era Music).

Sonata form Dominant musical form in Western art music since the eighteenth century, typically used in the first movement of multimovement works; see Musical Elements Appendix.

Sonata rondo form A combination of sonata and rondo forms, which includes a development section and often keeps the final "A" section, which acts as a recapitulation, in the original key; see Musical Elements Appendix.

Song cycle   A set of songs, or *lieder*, unified in some way, usually by poet and theme (Chapter 9, Romantic Era Music).

Songlines (history song, song series)   In aboriginal Australian traditions, groups of "small" songs often linked together in a series but with a wide range of functions and symbolic meanings. Songlines often transcend individual cultures to include a variety of languages and geographical areas within aboriginal Australia; in this way they are "song maps" of ancient chants that can direct journeys and evoke Dreamtime myths and ancestors. Performances occur in the context of dance or during activities such as travel, healing, and everyday tasks. The term "songlines" was popularized by British travel writer Bruce Chatwin after his book T*he Songlines* was published in 1987 (Chapter 12, Music in Oceania).

Sonic geography   Music in which geographical space and environmental sounds of nature are integral aspects of the music. Sonic geography is especially associated with John Luther Adams (Chapter 10, Modern Art Music).

Soprano   The highest of the four most basic categories of a person's singing voice range; see Musical Instruments Appendix, and also see "part song."

Sound   The auditory reception of wavelike vibrations in a medium, usually *air*; see Musical Elements Appendix.

Soundtrack (sound track, film score)   All the sound in a film, including special effects, dialogue, and music; specifically, the music in a film or, even more specifically, those excerpts that are collected and published as albums (Chapter 2, American Music for Stage and Screen).

Source music   See "Diegetic music" (Chapter 2, American Music for Stage and Screen).

Spectral music   Music in which the acoustic properties of sound (sound spectra) are used as the conceptual basis of musical compositions, instead of traditional concepts of musical elements such as rhythm and melody (Chapter 10, Modern Art Music).

Sprechstimme (Ger. "speaking voice")   Speech-like vocal technique characterized by melodramatic or eerie effect; especially associated with Schoenberg (Chapter 10, Modern Art Music).

Sprezzatura   Rhythmic, harmonic, and melodic freedom in order to more dramatically express the meaning of the words in vocal music (Chapter 7, Baroque Music).

Staccato   Type of articulation in which notes are sharply detached from one another; see Musical Elements Appendix.

Steel drums (pans)   Caribbean tuned drum (or pan) idiophones, originally made from 55-gallon oil drums, and played with mallets. Steel bands, or ensembles made up of steel drums, are especially popular in calypso music; see Musical Instruments Appendix.

Steel guitar (pedal steel guitar, Hawaiian guitar)   Chordophone which is positioned horizontally and changes pitches by moving a metal or glass bar over the strings rather than with permanently fixed frets as on a conventional guitar. Pedals and knee-levers change the tunings of the strings. Originally developed in Hawaii, this instrument has become a standard component of country music bands in the US and around the world; see Musical Instruments Appendix.

String quartet   A chamber ensemble made up of two violins, viola, and cello; music written for this ensemble, usually in four movements (Chapter 8, Classic Era Music).

Strophic form   Song structure in which the music is repeated for each stanza of text; see Musical Elements Appendix.

***Sturm und Drang* (Ger. "storm and stress")**   An especially emotional style of music that was inspired by the eighteenth-century German literary movement. The music is characterized by sudden, extreme changes in volume and vigorous rhythms (Chapter 8, Classic Era Music).

Susap   A bamboo mouth-harp idiophone of Melanesia (Chapter 12, Music in Oceania).

Suzuki Method   A musical education method created by Shin'ichi Suzuki (1898–1998) in which students are taught a variety of musical instruments with emphases on listening, repetition, group lessons and performances, and parental involvement. The ultimate goal is character development rather than professional music-making (Chapter 15, Music in India and Japan).

Swing   The characteristic lilting rhythm of jazz; an improvisational melodic and rhythmic expression of music that engages listeners physically, emotionally, and intellectually. Swing dance music ranges from sweet (simple, danceable) to hot (sophisticated, sometimes complex) styles (Chapter 3, Jazz).

Syllabic text-setting style   See "Text-setting styles" (Chapter 6, Antiquity to 1600).

Symphonic poem (also orchestral poem, tone poem)   Single movement programmatic orchestral work (Chapter 9, Romantic Era Music).

Symphony   Multimovement work for orchestra; music written for this ensemble, usually in four movements (Chapter 8, Classic Era Music).

Syncopation   Shift of metric accent from the expected pattern to the unexpected. For instance, duple meter typically expresses the ***strong* weak** metric pattern, but a syncopation of duple meter can include a **weak *strong*** metric pattern instead; see Musical Elements Appendix.

T

tabla   A pair of hand-played membranophones (drums) with contrasting shapes and pitch ranges from the Middle East and South Asia; see Musical Instruments Appendix.

Taiko (Japanese: "drum")   A large, double-sided flat drum, hung on a frame; see Musical Instruments Appendix.

Tala   Metric and rhythmic structure in South Asian music; one specific rhythmic cycle. Rhythmic cycles can be extremely long and complex when compared to common Western meters and rhythmic patterns (Chapter 15, Music in India and Japan, and Chapter 10, Modern Art Music).

Talking Instruments   Western African musical instruments that are used to create speech-like sounds such as inflection, rhythm, and accent. Talking instruments include drums, trumpets, flutes, whistles, and stringed instruments. Style varies according to spoken and musical dialect, individual musicians' styles, and instrumental idioms. Musicians can elaborate on words and phrases melodically, rhythmically, or in other ways (Chapter 13, Music in Sub-Saharan Africa).

Tambourine   Small frame drum membranophone, which can also be an idiophone when the frame includes metal cymbals; See Musical Instruments Appendix (Chapter 2, American Music for Stage and Screen).

Tambura   A long-necked, unfretted drone lute chordophone of South Asia. The drone pitch provides a reference from which the vocal or instrumental soloist develops the raga; see Musical Instruments Appendix.

Tango Argentine dance genre with African, Iberian, Caribbean, and Eastern European roots, characterized by striking dance choreography. Instrumentation includes the bandoneón (Chapter 1, Music in the Americas).

Taqsim An introductory, improvisatory instrumental solo in Arabic music (Chapter 14, Music in the Middle East).

Tarab An ecstatic musical experience in Arabic music (Chapter 14, Music in the Middle East).

Techno (See "EDM") (Chapter 5, Modern American Popular Music Part II: After 1970).

Teen idol A charismatic vocalist with a non-threatening image who sings highly marketable music usually written by others. Teen idols are usually young, and their performances are marketed for teens and preteens (Chapter 4, Modern American Popular Music Part I; Up to 1970).

Tejano (Tex-Mex) music Mexican popular musical style along the border with Texas, performed by a *conjunto,* a small ensemble that includes accordion and guitar (Chapter 11, Music in the Americas.

Tempo The speed of a musical work; see Musical Elements Appendix.

Tenor The third highest of the four most basic categories of a person's singing voice range; see Musical Instruments Appendix, and also see "part song."

Ternary form ("three-part form" or "ABA form") A form in which the opening section is followed by a contrasting middle section, then returns to the opening theme or themes in the third and final section; see Musical Elements Appendix.

Terraced descent Gradually descending melodic contour in which each successive phrase takes place in a progressively lower pitch range (Chapter 11, Music in the Americas.

Text-setting styles Ways of fitting texts to melodies; **syllabic** text-setting matches one note to each syllable of text, and **melismatic** text-setting features many notes for each syllable of text (Chapter 6, Antiquity to 1600).

Texture See "Musical texture" in Glossary and in Musical Elements Appendix.

Thematic development The continuous alteration and expansion of a theme throughout a musical work or movement, utilizing a variety of musical elements and styles (Chapter 8, Classic Era Music).

Theme Melody or motive that recurs and has structural relevance throughout the work or movement; see Musical Elements Appendix.

Theme and variations form A form in which a theme is repeated with variations in different musical elements, such as melody, rhythm, harmony, and instrumentation; see Musical Elements Appendix.

Theremin Electronic musical instrument invented by Lev Sergeyevich Termen in 1920 that the player does not touch; radio frequency oscillators sense hovering hand movements to change pitch and volume. The result is an eerie, electronic sound; see Musical Instruments Appendix.

Through composed Music without repeating sections; each stanza is musically distinct (Chapter 9, Romantic Era Music).

Timbre The characteristic tone quality or tone color of sound; for instance, a trumpet and a violin may produce the same pitch, but the two sound sources have distinctly different timbres; see Musical Elements Appendix.

Tin Pan Alley Early-twentieth-century song-writing and sheet music industry; district where several music publishers conducted business in close proximity in New York City on West 28th St. between Fifth and Sixth Avenues in Manhattan during the late 1890s; style of songwriting that became known as the "standard" form: AABA or repeating choruses with a contrasting bridge section between the last two choruses (Chapter 2, American Music for Stage and Screen).

Tombeau (tombeaux, pl.) A musical commemoration or lament on someone's death; typically characterized by a slow tempo with musical depictions of mourning such as descending lines or sounds that recall tolling bells (Chapter 7, Baroque Music).

Tonality (key) The organization of pitches and harmonies in hierarchical systems. Major and minor tonalities are the most common types in Western music; see Musical Elements Appendix.

Tonal language Language in which inflection and accent help determine the meaning of a word, so musical elements such as pitch and accent are already important aspects of speech. Many African and East Asian languages are tonal, but English and most other European languages are not (Chapter 13, Music in Sub-Saharan Africa).

Tone cluster A group of adjacent notes that sound simultaneously; the result is extreme dissonance (Chapter 10, Modern Art Music).

Tone row Particular arrangement of all 12 pitches of the octave in serialist compositions. In the context of various techniques, the pitches are not to be repeated out of order (Chapter 10, Modern Art Music).

Total serialism Compositional method popular among some composers in the mid-twentieth century in which twelve-tone technique is applied to musical elements other than pitch (Chapter 10, Modern Art Music).

Trance See "EDM" (Chapter 5, Modern American Popular Music Part II: After 1970).

Triple meter A metric pattern of 3 beats, typically with the first beat accented as in *strong*, weak, weak; see Musical Elements Appendix.

Tropicalia movement An artistic movement launched by the 1960s Brazilian band Tropicalia, which favored international influences rather than a return to native authenticity. Controversy over this issue led to the incarceration of two of Tropicalia's band members. The original band's musical style was an amalgam of styles popular in the late 1960s, ranging from Brazilian and Caribbean popular genres to psychedelic rock and jazz (Chapter 11, Music in the Americas).

Troubadours and trouvéres French aristocratic "inventors of song" or poet-musicians whose songs often expressed the *fin' amor* tradition (Chapter 6, Antiquity to 1600).

Turntablism The DJ's use of a two-turntable and mixer console as a musical instrument, especially in hip hop, disco, and EDM music. Important techniques include sampling, in which bits of preexisting recorded music are reused, and scratching, which is the manipulation of the vinyl recording under the needle to create pitched, percussive rhythmic sounds from the sampled music; see Musical Instruments Appendix.

Twelve-bar blues form In the context of American blues music, a chord progression over which a melody is varied. The types of chords as well as the number of chords in a blues progression can vary, but the basic twelve-bar blues chord sequence has become powerfully iconic in many musical genres; see Musical Elements Appendix.

Twelve-tone method, or serialism Twentieth-century method of composition devised by Schoenberg in which each of the 12 notes of the octave are placed in a particular order, or tone row, and are not repeated out of that order. Various techniques are associated with serialism, which has been a strong influence among modern composers (Chapter 10, Modern Art Music).

U

'Ud Plucked stringed Middle Eastern chordophone; the predecessor of the European lute; see Musical Instruments Appendix.

Ukulele, uke (Hawaiian, "jumping flea") A small, four-stringed folk guitar chordophone introduced to Hawaii by Portuguese settlers in the 1870s; see Musical Instruments Appendix.

Underscoring See "nondiegetic music" (Chapter 2, American Music for Stage and Screen).

V

Vaudeville (Fr. "city voices") Light variety show that can include music, dance, comedic skits, and acrobatics (Chapter, American Music for Stage and Screen).

Verismo **(It. "realism")** Realistic style in Italian operatic topics, which include vivid and often controversial portrayals of social hardship, cultural bias, and violence (Chapter 9, Romantic Era Music).

Vernacular music The music that is most accessible, or familiar, to most people in a given culture (Unit 1, American Vernacular Music, Introduction, and Chapter 6, Antiquity to 1600).

Verse A group of lines that form a unit within a poem. In American vernacular music, the verse text does not usually repeat; see Musical Elements Appendix.

Vibrato A rapid variation in pitch, especially associated with vocalists and with bowed stringed instruments; see Musical Elements Appendix.

Villancico A Hispanic sacred or secular vocal work for choir, which sometimes includes soloists and continuo; strummed and plucked harp and guitar are often prominent in the accompaniment (Chapter 7, Baroque Music).

Vocable In music, vocal sound without literal meaning (Chapter 11, Music in the Americas).

Voëlvry (Afrikaans "free as a bird" or "outlawed") Afrikaner youth protest movement of the 1980s, promoted by the South African record label Shifty Records and their signed artists, including the Gereformeerde ("Reformed") Blues Band led by Ralph Rabie (1960–2002), and singer-songwriter Roger Lucey (b. 1954). *Voëlvry* recalled earlier American antiwar and civil rights activism, in part, because Afrikaner youth rejected their government's policy to draft Whites into military service for deployment in Black townships and in border wars (Chapter 13, Music in Sub-Saharan Africa).

W

Wall of sound Phil Spector's influential production technique in popular music of the 1960s, characterized by large background ensembles blended together to accompany vocal soloists and groups (Chapter 4, Modern American Popular Music Part I: Up to 1970).

Woodwinds In Western orchestral tradition, aerophones in which the sound is produced when air vibrates through a tube; keys are stopped along the tube to change pitch. Woodwinds include the bassoon, clarinet, English horn, flute, and oboe. Most woodwinds are, or originally were, made of wood; see Musical Instruments Appendix.

Word-painting Musical expression of the text (Chapter 6, Antiquity to 1600).

Work song Music to accompany work-related tasks. Work songs typically use call and response when performed in groups and can be memorized, improvised, or a combination of both (Chapter 1, American Traditional Music).

Z

Zarzuela Light musical drama typically on a mythological topic; this Hispanic genre includes sung and spoken dialogue with plucked string and continuo accompaniment (Chapter 7, Baroque Music).

Zydeco music A blend of African American, Caribbean, and Cajun styles. Common instrumentation includes fiddle, accordion, electric guitar, brass instruments, and washboard. The music is improvisatory and traditionally sung in French, or French and English (Chapter 1, American Traditional Music).

Unit 1
Sources

Alexander, J. Heywood, ed. *To Stretch Our Ears: A Documentary History of American's Music.* New York, London: W. W. Norton, 2002.

Ancelet, Barry Jean. *Cajun Music: Its Origins and Development.* Lafayette, LA: Published by The Center for Louisiana Studies, Lafayette: University of Southwestern Louisiana, 1989.

_____, and Elemore Morgan Jr. *Cajun and Creole Music Makers.* Jackson: University Press of Mississippi, 1999.

Baumann, Max Peter. "Yodel." In *Grove Music Online. Oxford Music Online,* accessed April 14, 2012, http://www.oxfordmusiconline.com/subscriber/article/grove/music/52555.

Bowman, Durrell. "Zimmer, Hans Florian." *Grove Music Online. Oxford Music Online.* Oxford University Press, accessed December 23, 2013, http://www.oxfordmusiconline.com/subscriber/article/grove/music/A2103654.

Bracket, David. *The Pop, Rock, and Soul Reader*, 2nd ed. New York and Oxford: Oxford University Press, 2009.

Buhler, James, David Neumeyer, and Rob Deemer. *Hearing the Movies: Music and Sound in Film History.* New York and Oxford: Oxford University Press, 2010.

Burnim, Mellonee V., and Portia K. Maultsby. *African American Music: An Introduction.* New York: Routledge, 2006.

Clarke, Donald. *The Rise and Fall of Popular Music.* New York: St. Martin's Griffin, 1995.

Cohen, Norman. *Folk Music: A Regional Exploration*. Westport, CT: Greenwood Press, 2005.

_____. "Tin Pan Alley's Contribution to Folk Music." *Western Folklore*, Vol. 29, No. 1, published by Western States Folklore Society, Jan. 1970, pp. 9–20.

Collier, James Lincoln. "Jazz (i)." *The New Grove Dictionary of Jazz*, 2nd ed. *Grove Music Online. Oxford Music Online*. Oxford University Press, accessed December 30, 2013, http://www.oxfordmusiconline.com/subscriber/article/grove/music/J22380.

Cooke, Mervyn. *A History of Film Music*. New York: Cambridge University Press, 2008.

Covach, John. *History of Rock*, parts one and two. Coursera online course, University of Rochester, May–August 2013.

Crawford, Richard. *An Introduction to America's Music*. New York: W.W. Norton, 2001.

Dettmar, Kevin J. H. *Think Rock*. Boston: Pearson, 2011.

Eagle, Bob. "Directory of African-Appalachian Musicians." *Black Music Research Journal*, Vol. 24, No. 1 (Spring, 2004), pp. 7–71, published by Center for Black Music Research—Columbia College Chicago and University of Illinois Press. Article Stable URL: http://www.jstor.org/stable/4145499.

Epstein, Dena J. "Black Spirituals: Their Emergence into Public Knowledge." *Black Music Research Journal*, Vol. 10, No. 1, Spring 1990, published by Center for Black Music Research—Columbia College Chicago and University of Illinois Press, pp. 58–64.

Epstein, Dena J., and Rosita M. Sands; Mellonee V. Burnim and Portia K. Maultsby, eds., "Secular Folk Music," *African-American Music: An Introduction*, pp. 35–50. New York: Taylor & Francis Group LLC, 2006.

Ferris, Jean. *America's Musical Landscape*, 6th ed. New York: McGraw Hill, 2010.

Fink, Michael. *Inside the Music Industry: Creativity, Process, and Business*, 2nd ed. New York: Schirmer Books, 1996.

Garafalo, Reebee. *Rockin' Out: Popular Music in the U.S.A.*, 5th ed. Toronto: Pearson, 2011.

Goldmark, Daniel, Lawrence Kramer, and Richard D. Leppert. *Beyond the Soundtrack: Representing Music in Cinema. Berkeley:* University of California Press, 2007.

Guthrie, Woody. *Bound For Glory*. New York: Dutton, 1943/1968.

Henderson, Clayton W. "Minstrelsy, American." In *Grove Music Online. Oxford Music Online*, accessed July 18, 2012, http://www.oxfordmusiconline.com/subscriber/article/grove/music/18749.

Hoy, Jim, and Tom Isern. "Tales Out of School October 2003 Home on the Range—A Lesson on Our State Song." Emporia State University, accessed 12/5/16, http://www.emporia.edu/cgps/tales/nov2003.html.

Jackson, George Pullen. *White and Negro Spirituals: Their Life Span and Kinship; Tracing 200 Years of Untrammeled Song Making and Sing among Our Country Folk with 116 Songs as Sung by Both Races*. New York: J. J. Augustin, 1943.

Joyner, David Lee. *American Popular Music*, 3rd ed. Boston: McGraw Hill, 2009.

Koster, Rick. *Louisiana Music*. Cambridge, MA: Da Capo Press, 2002.

Kroeger, Karl. "Billings, William." In *Grove Music Online. Oxford Music Online*, accessed April 14, 2012, http://www.oxfordmusiconline.com/subscriber/article/grove/music/03082.

Lambert, Frank. "'I Saw The Book Talk': Slave Readings of the First Great Awakening." *Journal of African American History*, Vol. 87, The Past Before Us, Winter, 2002, pp 12–25.

Lomax, Alan, and Ronald D. Cohen, eds. *Alan Lomax: Selected Writings 1934–1997*. New York: Routledge, 2003.

Malone, Bill C. *Country Music, USA*, 2nd revised ed. Austin: University of Texas Press, 2002.

_____, and David Stricklin. *Southern Music/American Music*, revised edition. Lexington: University Press of Kentucky, 2003.

Mark, Rebecca, and Rob Vaughan. "Ethnicity," in Credo Reference, accessed on 9/3/12, http://www.credoreference.com.jproxy.lib.ecu.edu/entry/abcarcsouth/ethnicity#s000103b.

Maultsby, Portia. "Rhythm and Blues," in *African American Music: An Introduction*, ed. by Mellonee V. Burnim and Portia K. Maultsby. New York: Routledge, 2006.

Monson, Ingrid. "Jazz: Chronological Overview." *African American Music*. New York: Taylor & Francis Group LLC, 2006.

Morton, Jelly Roll, and Alan Lomax. *The Complete Library of Congress Recordings*. Cambridge, MA: Rounder Records, 2006.

Negus, Keith. *Music Genres and Corporate Cultures*. London and New York: Routledge, 1999.

Norfleet, Dawn M. "Hip-Hop and Rap," in *African American Music: An Introduction*, ed. by Mellonee V. Burnim and Portia K. Maultsby. New York: Routledge, 2006.

Oliver, Paul. "Dorsey, Thomas A." In *Grove Music Online. Oxford Music Online*, accessed September 21, 2012, http://www.oxfordmusiconline.com/subscriber/article/grove/music/08044.

_____. "Field holler." In *Grove Music Online. Oxford Music Online*, accessed September 22, 2012, http://www.oxfordmusiconline.com/subscriber/article/grove/music/49331).

Pegg, Carole. "Folk music." In *Grove Music Online. Oxford Music Online*, accessed April 14, 2012, http://www.oxfordmusiconline.com/subscriber/article/grove/music/09933.

Peel, Ian. "Scratching." In *Grove Music Online. Oxford Music Online*, accessed August 3, 2012, http://www.oxfordmusiconline.com/subscriber/article/grove/music/47225.

Plantenga, Bart. *Yodel-Ay-Ee-Oooo: The Secret History of Yodeling Around the World*. New York: Routledge, 2004.

Pleasants, Henry, and Horace Clarence Boyer. "Jackson, Mahalia." In *Grove Music Online. Oxford Music Online*, accessed September 22, 2012, http://www.oxfordmusiconline.com/subscriber/article/grove/music/14028.

Porterfield, Nolan, and Darius L. Thieme. "Lomax." In *Grove Music Online. Oxford Music Online*, accessed April 14, 2012, http://www.oxfordmusiconline.com/subscriber/article/grove/music/48410.

Schmid, Will. *A Tribute to Woody Guthrie and Leadbelly*. Virginia: Music Educators National Conference in cooperation with The Smithsonian Institution, Office of Folklife Programs, 1991.

Schwandt, Erich, et al. "Burlesque." In *Grove Music Online. Oxford Music Online*, accessed July 19, 2012, http://www.oxfordmusiconline.com/subscriber/article/grove/music/04381.

Shearon, Stephen, and Harry Eskew, et al. "Gospel music." In *Grove Music Online. Oxford Music Online*, accessed September 22, 2012, http://www.oxfordmusiconline.com/subscriber/article/grove/music/A2224388.

Simonot, Colette. ""Disco." *Grove Music Online. Oxford Music Online*. Oxford University Press, accessed May 21, 2014, http://www.oxfordmusiconline.com/subscriber/article/grove/music/A2249311.

Stempel, Larry. *Showtime: A History of the Broadway Musical Theater*. New York: W.W. Norton, 2010.

Stone, John A. *Put's Golden Songster*. San Francisco: D. E. Appleton & Co., 1858, accessed 12/8/16, https://archive.org/stream/putsgoldensongst00ston#page/52/mode/2up.

Stuessy, Joe, and Scott Lipscomb. *Rock and Roll: Its History and Stylistic Development*, 7th ed. Boston: Pearson: 2013.

Sykes, Charles. "Profiles of Record Labels," in *African American Music: An Introduction*, ed. by Mellonee V. Burnim and Portia K. Maultsby. London: Routledge, 2006.

Szatmary, David P. *Rockin' Time: A Social History of Rock–and-Roll*, Boston: 8th ed. Pearson, 2014.

Tanner, Paul, David W. Megill, and Maruice Gerow. *Jazz,* 11th ed. Boston: McGraw Hill, 2009.

Thorp, N. Howard ("Jack"). *Songs of the Cowboys*. Boston: Houghton Mifflin Company, 1921.

Toll, Robert C. *Blacking Up: The Minstrel Show in Nineteenth-Century America*. New York: Oxford University Press, 1974.

Toop, David. "Hip hop." *Grove Music Online. Oxford Music Online*, accessed August 3, 2012, http://www.oxfordmusiconline.com/subscriber/article/grove/music/46869.

––––––––. "Rap." *Grove Music Online. Oxford Music Online*, accessed August 3, 2012, http://www.oxfordmusiconline.com/subscriber/article/grove/music/46867.

Walser, Robert. "Rock and roll." *Grove Music Online. Oxford Music Online*, accessed August 2, 2012, http://www.oxfordmusiconline.com/subscriber/article/grove/music/49136.

Wilton, Peter. "Soul." In *The Oxford Companion to Music*, edited by Alison Latham. *Oxford Music Online*, accessed August 2, 2012, http://www.oxfordmusiconline.com/subscriber/article/opr/t114/e6358.

Wright, Josephine. "Songs of Remembrance." *Journal of African American History*, Vol. 91, No. 4, P. Sterling Stuckey: In Praise of an Intellectual Legacy (Autumn, 2006), published by Association for the Study of African-American Life and History, Inc., pp. 413–424.

Unit 2
Sources

Amadeus. DVD. Directed by Milos Forman, screenplay and original play by Peter Shaffer. 1984; Burbank, CA: Orion Pictures/Warner Brothers, 2002.

Anderson, Julian. "Spectral music." In *Grove Music Online. Oxford Music Online*. Oxford University Press, accessed February 13, 2017, http://www.oxfordmusiconline.com/subscriber/article/grove/music/50982.

Arlt, Wulf. "Machaut, Guillaume de." In *Grove Music Online. Oxford Music Online*, accessed January 3, 2012, http://www.oxfordmusiconline.com/subscriber/article/grove/music/51865.

Avins, Styra. *Johannes Brahms: Life and Letters*. Oxford and New York, Oxford University Press, 1997.

Bierley, Paul E., and H. Wiley Hitchcock. "Sousa, John Philip." In *Grove Music Online. Oxford Music Online*. Oxford University Press, accessed February 4, 2017, http://www.oxfordmusiconline.com/subscriber/article/grove/music/A2259047.

Böker-Heil, Norbert, et al. "Lied." In *Grove Music Online. Oxford Music Online*. Oxford University Press, accessed December 18, 2016, http://www.oxfordmusiconline.com/subscriber/article/grove/music/16611.

Brett, Philip et al. "Britten, Benjamin." In *Grove Music Online. Oxford Music Online*. Oxford University Press, accessed January 8, 2017, http://www.oxfordmusiconline.com/subscriber/article/grove/music/46435.

Britannica Academic, s.v. "Yijing," accessed January 5, 2017, http://academic.eb.com.jproxy.lib.ecu.edu/levels/collegiate/article/41854.

Britten, Benjamin. War Requiem, op. 66. Boosey & Hawkes.

Brown, Rae Linda. "Price, Florence Bea." In *Grove Music Online. Oxford Music Online*. Oxford University Press, accessed February 13, 2017, http://www.oxfordmusiconline.com/subscriber/article/grove/music/48286.

Burkholder, J. Peter, Donald Jay Grout, and Claude V. Palisca. *A History of Western Music*, 9th ed. New York: W. W. Norton, 2014.

Burkholder, J. Peter, et al. "Ives, Charles." In *Grove Music Online. Oxford Music Online*. Oxford University Press, accessed February 5, 2017, http://www.oxfordmusiconline.com/subscriber/article/grove/music/A2252967.

Cessac, Catherine. "Jacquet de La Guerre, Elisabeth." In *Grove Music Online. Oxford Music Online*, accessed May 18, 2012, http://www.oxfordmusiconline.com/subscriber/article/grove/music/14084.

Comstock, Sarah. "Early American Drama," *The North American Review*, published by University of Northern Iowa, Vol. 225, No. 842, April 1928, pp. 469–475.

Crossley-Holland, Peter, et al. "Bard." In *Grove Music Online. Oxford Music Online*, accessed January 9, 2012, http://www.oxfordmusiconline.com/subscriber/article/grove/music/02026.

David, Hans T., and Arthur Mendel, eds. *The Bach Reader: A Life of Johann Sebastian Bach in Letters and Documents*, rev. ed. New York: W.W. Norton, 1972.

Eisen, Cliff, et al. "Mozart." In *Grove Music Online. Oxford Music Online*, accessed January 16, 2012, http://www.oxfordmusiconline.com/subscriber/article/grove/music/40258pg3.

Esses, Maurice. *Dance and Instrumental Diferencias in Spain during the 17th and Early 18th Centuries*. Hillsdale, NJ: Pendragon Press, 1993.

Feisst, Sabine. "Adams, John Luther." In *Grove Music Online. Oxford Music Online*. Oxford University Press, accessed February 13, 2017, http://www.oxfordmusiconline.com/subscriber/article/grove/music/A2247990.

Forney, Kristine, and Joseph Machlis. *The Enjoyment of Music: an Introduction to Perceptive Listening*, 10th ed. New York: W. W. Norton, 2007.

Fuller, David, et al. "Couperin." In *Grove Music Online. Oxford Music Online*, accessed May 21, 2012, http://www.oxfordmusiconline.com/subscriber/article/grove/music/40182pg4.

Gillies, Malcolm. "Bartók, Béla." In *Grove Music Online. Oxford Music Online*. Oxford University Press, accessed February 10, 2017, http://www.oxfordmusiconline.com/subscriber/article/grove/music/40686pg7.

Godt, Irving. "The International Reputation of Marianna Martines (1744–1812)," *Journal of Musicology*, Vol. 13, No. 4 (Autumn, 1995), pp. 538–561.

_____. "Marianna in Vienna: A Martines Chronology," *Journal of Musicology*, Vol. 16, No. 1 (Winter, 1998), pp 136–158.

Griffiths, Paul. "Messiaen, Olivier." In *Grove Music Online. Oxford Music Online*. Oxford University Press, accessed February 4, 2017, http://www.oxfordmusiconline.com/subscriber/article/grove/music/18497.

Hanning, Barbara Russano. *Concise History of Western Music*, 4th ed. New York: W.W. Norton, 2010.

Heartz, Daniel. *Music in European Capitals: The Galant Style, 1720–1780*. New York: W.W. Norton, 2003.

Hill, John Walter. *Baroque Music: Music in Western Europe, 1580–1750*. New York: W.W. Norton, 2005.

Hudson, Barton. "Cabanilles, Juan Bautista José." In *Grove Music Online. Oxford Music Online*, accessed May 17, 2012, http://www.oxfordmusiconline.com/subscriber/article/grove/music/04504.

Hudson, Richard, and Meredith Ellis Little. "Sarabande." In *Grove Music Online*. *Oxford Music Online*, accessed May 17, 2012, http://www.oxfordmusiconline.com/subscriber/article/grove/music/24574.

Kerman, Joseph, et al. "Beethoven, Ludwig van." In *Grove Music Online*. *Oxford Music Online*, accessed January 16, 2012, http://www.oxfordmusiconline.com/subscriber/article/grove/music/40026.

Kmetz, John, et al. "Germany." In *Grove Music Online*. *Oxford Music Online*, accessed May 24, 2012, http://www.oxfordmusiconline.com/subscriber/article/grove/music/40055.

La Gorce, Jérôme de. "Lully." In *Grove Music Online*. *Oxford Music Online*, accessed May 18, 2012, http://www.oxfordmusiconline.com/subscriber/article/grove/music/42477pg1.

Latham, Alison. "Cantigas de Santa Maria." In *The Oxford Companion to Music*, edited by Alison Latham. *Oxford Music Online*, accessed January 12, 2012, http://www.oxfordmusiconline.com/subscriber/article/opr/t114/e1132.

Lesure, François, et al. "France." In *Grove Music Online*. *Oxford Music Online*, accessed May 18, 2012, http://www.oxfordmusiconline.com/subscriber/article/grove/music/40051.

Lockwood, Lewis. "Renaissance." In *Grove Music Online*. *Oxford Music Online*, accessed January 30, 2012, http://www.oxfordmusiconline.com/subscriber/article/grove/music/23192.

Lowens, Irving, and S. Frederick Starr. "Gottschalk, Louis Moreau." In *Grove Music Online*. *Oxford Music Online*. Oxford University Press, accessed January 29, 2017, http://www.oxfordmusiconline.com/subscriber/article/grove/music/11530.

Macdonald, Hugh. "Symphonic poem." In *Grove Music Online*. *Oxford Music Online*. Oxford University Press, accessed December 27, 2016, http://www.oxfordmusiconline.com/subscriber/article/grove/music/27250.

Mathiesen, Thomas J., et al. "Greece." In *Grove Music Online*. *Oxford Music Online*, accessed April 21, 2012, http://www.oxfordmusiconline.com/subscriber/article/grove/music/11694pg1.

Michałowski, Kornel, and Jim Samson. "Chopin, Fryderyk Franciszek." In *Grove Music Online*. *Oxford Music Online*. Oxford University Press, accessed December 25, 2016, http://www.oxfordmusiconline.com/subscriber/article/grove/music/51099.

Nettl, Bruno. "Music." In *Grove Music Online*. *Oxford Music Online*, accessed April 21, 2012, http://www.oxfordmusiconline.com/subscriber/article/grove/music/40476.

Neville, Don. "Metastasio, Pietro." In *Grove Music Online*. *Oxford Music Online*, accessed January 16, 2012, http://www.oxfordmusiconline.com/subscriber/article/grove/music/53181.

Palisca, Claude V. "Camerata." In *Grove Music Online*. *Oxford Music Online*, accessed April 6, 2012, http://www.oxfordmusiconline.com/subscriber/article/grove/music/04652.

_____. "Mei, Girolamo." In *Grove Music Online*. *Oxford Music Online*, accessed April 6, 2012, http://www.oxfordmusiconline.com/subscriber/article/grove/music/18271.

Pritchett, James, et al. "Cage, John." In *Grove Music Online*. *Oxford Music Online*. Oxford University Press, accessed January 5, 2017, http://www.oxfordmusiconline.com/subscriber/article/grove/music/A2223954.

Reich, Nancy B. *Clara Schumann: The Artist and the Woman*. Ithica and London: Cornell University Press, 2001.

_____. "Schumann, Clara." In *Grove Music Online. Oxford Music Online*. Oxford University Press, accessed December 26, 2016, http://www.oxfordmusiconline.com/subscriber/article/grove/music/25152.

Reilly, Edward R., et al. "Weiss." In *Grove Music Online. Oxford Music Online*, accessed May 28, 2012, http://www.oxfordmusiconline.com/subscriber/article/grove/music/30065pg2.

Rollin, Monique. "Gaultier, Denis." In *Grove Music Online. Oxford Music Online*, accessed May 21, 2012, http://www.oxfordmusiconline.com/subscriber/article/grove/music/10745.

Rosselli, John. "Castrato." In *Grove Music Online. Oxford Music Online*, accessed May 12, 2012, http://www.oxfordmusiconline.com/subscriber/article/grove/music/05146.

Russell, Craig H.. "Murcia, Santiago de." In *Grove Music Online. Oxford Music Online*, accessed May 14, 2012, http://www.oxfordmusiconline.com/subscriber/article/grove/music/41508.

Samson, Jim. "Romanticism." In *Grove Music Online. Oxford Music Online*. Oxford University Press, accessed January 14, 2017, http://www.oxfordmusiconline.com/subscriber/article/grove/music/23751.

Schulenberg, David. *Music of the Baroque*. New York: Oxford University Press, 2001.

Silbiger, Alexander. "Chaconne." In *Grove Music Online. Oxford Music Online*, accessed May 17, 2012, http://www.oxfordmusiconline.com/subscriber/article/grove/music/05354.

Smith, Bethany Jo. "'Song to the Dark Virgin': Race and Gender in Five Art Songs of Florence B. Price." Unpublished Master's thesis, University of Cincinnati, 2007.

Southern, Eileen. *The Music of Black Americans: A History*, 3rd ed. New York: W.W. Norton, 1997.

Stein, Louise K. "Hidalgo, Juan, (i)." In *Grove Music Online. Oxford Music Online*, accessed May 14, 2012, http://www.oxfordmusiconline.com/subscriber/article/grove/music/12991.

Stevens, John, et al. "Troubadours, trouvères." *Grove Music Online. Oxford Music Online*, accessed January 14, 2012, http://www.oxfordmusiconline.com/subscriber/article/grove/music/28468.

Stevenson, Robert. "Juana Inés de la Cruz, Sor." In *Grove Music Online. Oxford Music Online*, accessed May 14, 2012, http://www.oxfordmusiconline.com/subscriber/article/grove/music/43201.

Strizich, Robert. "Sanz, Gaspar." In *Grove Music Online. Oxford Music Online*, accessed May 14, 2012, http://www.oxfordmusiconline.com/subscriber/article/grove/music/24565.

Taruskin, Richard, and Christopher H. Gibbs. *The Oxford History of Western Music: College Edition*. Oxford: Oxford University Press, 2013.

Tilmouth, Michael, and David Ledbetter. "Tombeau (i)." In *Grove Music Online. Oxford Music Online*, accessed May 21, 2012, http://www.oxfordmusiconline.com/subscriber/article/grove/music/28084.

Walker, Alan, et al. "Liszt, Franz." In *Grove Music Online. Oxford Music Online*. Oxford University Press, accessed December 25, 2016, http://www.oxford-musiconline.com/subscriber/article/grove/music/48265pg9.

Webster, James, and Georg Feder. "Haydn, Joseph." In *Grove Music Online. Oxford Music Online*, accessed January 16, 2012, http://www.oxfordmusiconline.com/subscriber/article/grove/music/44593.

Wessely, Helene, and Irving Godt. "Martínez, Marianne von." In *Grove Music Online. Oxford Music Online*, accessed January 16, 2012, http://www.oxfordmusiconline.com/subscriber/article/grove/music/17913.

Whenham, John. "Orfeo (i)." In *The New Grove Dictionary of Opera*, edited by Stanley Sadie. *Grove Music Online. Oxford Music Online*, accessed May 12, 2012, http://www.oxfordmusiconline.com/subscriber/article/grove/music/O005849.

Wilhoite, Meg. "Shaw, Caroline." In *Grove Music Online. Oxford Music Online*. Oxford University Press, accessed February 13, 2017, http://www.oxfordmusiconline.com/subscriber/article/grove/music/2277536.

Wilson, Blake, et al. "Rhetoric and music." In *Grove Music Online. Oxford Music Online*, accessed April 5, 2012, http://www.oxfordmusiconline.com/subscriber/article/grove/music/43166.

Wolff, Christoph, et al. "Bach." In *Grove Music Online. Oxford Music Online*, accessed May 28, 2012, http://www.oxfordmusiconline.com/subscriber/article/grove/music/40023pg10.

Tignor, Robert, Jeremy Adelman, Stephe Aron, Stephen Kotkin, Suzanne Marchand, Gyan Prakash, and Michael Tsin. *Worlds Together, Worlds Apart*, 4th ed. Vol, 2. New York: W.W. Norton, 2014.

Unit 3
Sources

The author owes special thanks to Dr. Mario Rey, PhD, East Carolina School of Music, who guided the preparation of Chapter 11 in great detail.

Allen, Lara. "Mbaqanga." In *Grove Music Online. Oxford Music Online.* Oxford University Press, accessed June 22, 2016, http://www.oxfordmusiconline .com/subscriber/article/grove/music/51740.

_____. "Commerce, Politics, and Musical Hybridity: Vocalizing Urban Black South African Identity during the 1950s." *Ethnomusicology*, Vol. 47, No. 2, Spring–Summer, 2003, pp. 228–249. Published by University of Illinois Press on behalf of Society for Ethnomusicology.

Anderson, Robert, et al. "Egypt." In *Grove Music Online. Oxford Music Online.* Oxford University Press, accessed July 19, 2016, http://www.oxfordmusiconline.com/ subscriber/article/grove/music/08621.

Anku, Willie. "Principles of Rhythm Integration in African Drumming." *Black Music Research Journal*, Vol. 17, No. 2 (Autumn, 1997), pp. 211–238. Published by Center for Black Music Research, Columbia College Chicago and University of Illinois Press.

Arnold, Alison, et al. *South Asia: The Indian Subcontinent.* Garland Encyclopedia of World Music, Volume 5, accessed August 16, 2016, http://search.alexander-street.com/view/work/326926.

Bachmann, Werner, and Belkis Dinçol. "Anatolia." In *Grove Music Online. Oxford Music Online.* Oxford University Press, accessed July 9, 2016, http://www .oxfordmusiconline.com/subscriber/article/grove/music/00840.

Bakan, Michael B. *World Music: Traditions and Transformations*. New York: McGraw-Hill, 2007.

Béhague, Gerard. "Bossa nova." In *Grove Music Online. Oxford Music Online*, accessed May 1, 2012, http://www.oxfordmusiconline.com/subscriber/article/grove/music/03663.

_____. "Tango." In *Grove Music Online. Oxford Music Online*, accessed May 1, 2012, http://www.oxfordmusiconline.com/subscriber/article/grove/music/27473.

Bellman, Jonathan. "Indian Resonances in the British Invasion, 1965–1968." *Journal of Musicology*, Vol. 15, No. 1, Winter, 1997, University of California Press, pp. 116–136.

Bohlman, Philip V. "Middle East." In *Grove Music Online. Oxford Music Online*, accessed June 19, 2012, http://www.oxfordmusiconline.com/subscriber/article/grove/music/19659.

Britannica Academic, s.v. "Asia," accessed October 1, 2016, http://academic.eb.com.jproxy.lib.ecu.edu/levels/collegiate/article/110518.

Britannica Academic, s.v. "Central Africa," accessed June 2, 2016, http://academic.eb.com/EBchecked/topic/102127/central-Africa.

Britannica Academic, s.v. "Egypt," accessed July 20, 2016, http://academic.eb.com.jproxy.lib.ecu.edu/levels/collegiate/article/106015#261333.toc.

Britannica Academic, s.v. "India," accessed October 1, 2016, http://academic.eb.com.jproxy.lib.ecu.edu/levels/collegiate/article/111197#214184.toc.

Britannica Academic, s.v. "Israel," accessed July 15, 2016, http://academic.eb.com.jproxy.lib.ecu.edu/levels/collegiate/article/106444#23111.toc.

Britannica Academic, s.v. "Japan," accessed September 11, 2016, http://academic.eb.com.jproxy.lib.ecu.edu/levels/collegiate/article/106451#.

Britannica Academic, s.v. "Middle East," accessed July 07, 2016, http://academic.eb.com/EBchecked/topic/381192/Middle-East.

Britannica Academic, s.v. "Nelson Mandela," accessed June 25, 2016, http://academic.eb.com/EBchecked/topic/361645/Nelson-Mandela.

Britannica Academic, s.v. "Saint Theophilus of Alexandria," accessed July 21, 2016, http://academic.eb.com.jproxy.lib.ecu.edu/levels/collegiate/article/72040.

Burkholder, Peter J., Donald Jay Grout, and Claude V. Palisca: *A History of Western Music*, 9th Ed. New York: W. W. Norton, 2014.

Campbell, Kay Hardy, and Ellen Koskoff et al., eds., "Women's Music of the Arabian Peninsula," *The Concise Garland Encyclopedia of World Music*, pp. 839–843. New York, London: Taylor and Francis Group LLC, 2008.

Chamorro, Arturo. "Mariachi." In *Grove Music Online. Oxford Music Online*, accessed May 1, 2012, http://www.oxfordmusiconline.com/subscriber/article/grove/music/46539.

Charry, Eric. "Griot." In *Grove Music Online. Oxford Music Online*. Oxford University Press, accessed May 27, 2016, http://www.oxfordmusiconline.com/subscriber/article/grove/music/42012.

_____. "Plucked Lutes in West Africa: An Historical Overview." *The Galpin Society Journal*, Vol. 49, March 1996, pp. 3–37. Published by Galpin Society.

Chatwin, Bruce. *The Songlines*. New York: Viking Penguin, 1987.

Coester, Markus. "Localising African Popular Music Transnationally: 'Highlife-Travellers' in Britain in the 1950s and 1960s." *Journal of African Cultural Studies*, Vol. 20, No. 2, December 2008, pp. 133–144. Published by Taylor & Francis, Ltd.

Collins, John. "The Early History of West African Highlife Music." *Popular Music*, Vol. 8, No. 3, African Music, October 1989, pp. 221–230. Published by Cambridge University Press.

Commonwealth of Australia. "Documenting a Democracy: Timeline." *Museum of Australian Democracy*. 2011, accessed Winter 2016, http://foundingdocs.gov.au/timeline.html.

Conway, Cecelia. "Black Banjo Songsters in Appalachia." *Black Music Research Journal*, Vol. 23, no. 1/2 (Spring–Autumn 2003), pp. 149–166. Pub Center for Black Music Research—Columbia College Chicago and University of Illinois Press.

Conyers, Claude. "Salsa." In *Grove Music Online. Oxford Music Online*, accessed May 1, 2012, http://www.oxfordmusiconline.com/subscriber/article/grove/music/A2092687.

DAM website, accessed August 9, 2016, http://www.damrap.com/album/whos-terrorist-ارهابي-مين/116.

Danielson, Virginia. *A Voice Like Egypt*. Documentary film. Directed by Michael Goldman. Egypt: Arab Film Distribution, 1996.

_____. *The Voice of Egypt: Umm Kulthum, Arabic Song, and Egyptian Society in the Twentieth Century*. Chicago: University of Chicago Press, American University in Cairo Press, 1997.

_____, Scott Marcus, and Dwight Reynolds, eds. *Garland Encyclopedia of World Music*. Volume 6: *The Middle East*. Routledge, Array, accessed July 15, 2016, http://search.alexanderstreet.com/view/work/326926.

Davis, Stephen. "Reggae." In *Grove Music Online. Oxford Music Online*, accessed May 1, 2012, http://www.oxfordmusiconline.com/subscriber/article/grove/music/23065.

Densmore, Francis. *Teton Siuox Music*. Smithsonian Institution Bureau of American Ethnology, Washington, DC: Government Printing Office, 1918.

Diabate, Toumani. "Maitre de Kora," accessed July 5, 2016, http://www.toumani-diabate.com/index.html.

Dje Dje, Jacqueline Codgell. "West Africa: An Introduction," from Garland Encyclopedia of World Music, Vol. 1, *Africa*. London, New York: Routledge, pp.442–470.

Doubleday, Veronica. "Rūmī, Jalāl al-Dīn." *Grove Music Online. Oxford Music Online*, accessed June 20, 2012, http://www.oxfordmusiconline.com/subscriber/article/grove/music/51738.

Drewett, Michael. "The Road from Crisis to Catharsis in the Songs of Roger Lucey." *International Review of the Aesthetics and Sociology of Music*, Vol. 42, No 2, December 2011, pp. 379–396.

Duran, Lucy. "Key to N'Dour: Roots of the Senegalese Star." *Popular Music*, vol 8, no. 3, African Music (October 1989), pp. 275–284. Published by Cambridge University Press.

Electronic Text Corpus of Sumerian Literature (ETCSL): Oxford University, http://etcsl.orinst.ox.ac.uk/edition2/general.php.

Electronic Text Corpus of Sumerian Literature (ETCSL) project, Faculty of Oriental Studies, University of Oxford, accessed August 11, 2016, http://etcsl.orinst.ox.ac.uk/cgi-bin/etcsl.cgi?text=t.2.4.2.02# and http://etcsl.orinst.ox.ac.uk/edition2/general.php specific lines and hymns. A Praise Poem, t.2.4.2.02 358–373; 154–174.

Esses, Maurice. *Dance and instrumental diferencias in Spain during the 17th and early 18th centuries*. Stuyvesant, NY: Pendragon Press, 1992–1994.

Fairley, Jan. "Calypso." In *Grove Music Online. Oxford Music Online*, accessed May 1, 2012, http://www.oxfordmusiconline.com/subscriber/article/grove/music/04624.

Fleck, Béla. *Throw Down Your Heart*, DVD, Directed by Sascha Paladino, released by Docudrama in 2008.

Freemuse, website, http://freemuse.org. The World Forum on Music and Censorship; an independent international membership organization advocating and defining freedom of expression for musicians and composers worldwide.

Gilbert, Shirli. "Singing against Apartheid: ANC Cultural Groups and the International Anti-Apartheid Struggle." *Journal of Southern African Studies*, Vol. 33, No. 2, June 2007, pp. 421–441. Published by Taylor & Francis, Ltd.

Global Slavery Index. "Global Findings," accessed June 1, 2016, http://www.globalslaveryindex.org/findings/.

Glowczewski, Barbara. "Dynamic Cosmologies and Aboriginal Heritage." *Anthropology Today*, Vol. 15, No. 1, February 1999, pp. 3–9. Published by Royal Anthropological Institute of Great Britain and Ireland.

Grundlingh, Albert. "'Rocking the Boat' in South Africa? Voëlvry Music and Afrikaans Anti-Apartheid Social Protest in the 1980s." *The International Journal of African Historical Studies*, Vol. 37, No. 3, 2004, pp. 483–514. Published by Boston University African Studies Center.

Halachmi, Anat, producer and director. *Arotzim Shel Za'am ("Channels of Rage")*, DVD. NOGA Communications Channel 8, produced by Anat Halachmi, supported by Israeli Film Counsel, Ministry of Education and Culture and Sport, 2003.

Hendricks, Karen S. "The Philosophy of Shinichi Suzuki: 'Music Education as Love Education.'" *Philosophy of Music Education Review*, Vol. 19, No. 2 (Fall 2011), pp. 136–154. Published by Indiana University Press.

Hirsch, Lee. *Amandla! A Revolution in Four-Part Harmony*. DVD, documentary. South Africa and USA: Artisan Entertainment, 2002.

Hirshberg, Jehoash et al. "Israel." *Grove Music Online. Oxford Music Online*. Oxford University Press, accessed August 4, 2016, http://www.oxfordmusiconline.com/subscriber/article/grove/music/41316.

Hood, Mantle. "Musical Ornamentation as History: The Hawaiian Steel Guitar." *Yearbook for Traditional Music*, Vol. 15, *East Asian Musics* (1983), pp. 141–148.

Howe, Sondra Wieland. "Sources of the Folk Songs in the Violin and Piano Books of Shinichi Suzuki." *The Bulletin of Historical Research in Music Education*, Vol. 16, No. 3 (May, 1995), pp. 177–193. Published by Sage Publications, Inc.

Hudson, Richard. *The Folia, the Saraband, the Passacaglia, and the Chaconne: The Historical Evolution of Four Forms That Originated in Music for the Five-Course Spanish Guitar*. Rome: American Institute of Musicology, 1982.

Iamblichus. *Life of Pythagoras*. Translated by Thomas Taylor. London: J. M. Watkins, 1818, Chapter 4, p. 9, accessed August 13, 2016, http://platonicphilosophy.com/files/Iamblichus%20-%20The%20Pythagorean%20Life.pdf.

Imada, Adria L. "Hula Circuits through the American Empire." *American Quarterly*, Vol. 56, no. 1 (March 2004), pp. 111–149.

Impey, Angela. "Popular Music in Africa." *The Garland Encyclopedia of World Music*, Ed. Ruth Stone. New York and London: Garland Publishing, 1998, pp. 415–437.

International Labour Organization Report, 103rd Session, 2014: "Supplementing the Forced Labour Convertion, 1930 (No. 29), to address implementation gaps to advance prevention, protection and compensation measures, to effectively achieve the elimination of forced labour," accessed May 31, 2016, http://www.ilo.org/ilc/ILCSessions/103/on-the-agenda/forced-labour/lang--en/index.htm.

Jacobs, Elizabeth D., and William R. Seaburg, eds. *The Nehalem Tillamook: An Ethnography*. Corvallis: Oregon State University Press, 2003.

Jagfors, Ulf. "The African Akonting and the Origin of the Banjo." *The Old-Time Herald, A Magazine Dedicated to Old-Time Music*, Winter 2003–04, Vol. 9/2, pp. 26–33.

Jules-Rosette, Benneta, and David B. Coplan. "'Nkosi Sikelel' iAfrika': From Independent Spirit to Political Mobilization." *Cahiers d'Études Africaines*, Vol. 44, Cahier 173/174, Réparations, restitutions, réconciliations: Entre Afriques, Europe et Amériques, 2004, pp. 343–367. Published by EHESS.

Kaeppler, Adrienne L., and J. W. Love, eds. "Australia and the Pacific Islands." *The Garland Encyclopedia of World Music*. New York and London: Garland Publishing, 1998.

_____. "The Music and Dance of Polynesia." *The Garland Encyclopedia of World Music*. New York: Routledge, 2013, Vol. 9, *Australia and the Pacific Islands*, pp. 768–770.

_____, Te Ahukaramu Charles Royal, Te Puoho Katene, Jennifer Shennan, et al. "East Polynesia." *The Garland Encyclopedia of World Music*. New York: Routledge, 2013, Vol. 9, *Australia and the Pacific Islands*, pp. 865–955

Kaminski, Joseph S. "Threshold to Asante Sacred Experience through Music." *International Review of the Aesthetics and Sociology of Music*, Vol. 45, No. 2 (December 2014), pp. 345–371. Published by Croatian Musicological Society.

_____. "Surrogate Speech of the Asante Ivory Trumpeters of Ghana." *Yearbook for Traditional Music*, Vol. 40 (2008), pp. 117–135. Published by International Council for Traditional Music.

Kapstein, Ethan B. "The New Global Slave Trade." *Foreign Affairs*, Vol. 85, No. 6 (Nov.–Dec. 2006), pp. 103–115.

Keita, Salif. *La Différence*. EmArcy B002SBV0QW, 2010. CD.

Kilmer, Anne, and Sam Mirelman. "Mesopotamia." In *Grove Music Online. Oxford Music Online*. Oxford University Press, accessed July 15, 2014, http://www.oxfordmusiconline.com/subscriber/article/grove/music/18485.

Kishibe, Shigeo et al. "Japan." *Grove Music Online. Oxford Music Online*. Oxford University Press, accessed September 5, 2016, http://www.oxfordmusiconline.com/subscriber/article/grove/music/43335pg1.

Knopoff, Steven. "Didjeridu." In *Grove Music Online. Oxford Music Online*, accessed June 5, 2012, http://www.oxfordmusiconline.com/subscriber/article/grove/music/07750.

Koskoff, Ellen. "Music and Dance of Micronesia." *The Concise Garland Encyclopedia of World Music*. New York: Routledge, 2008, Vol. 1 Africa, pp. 697–707.

_____. "The Music and Dance of Polynesia." *The Concise Garland Encyclopedia of World Music*. New York: Routledge, 2008, Vol. 1 Africa, pp. 711–713.

Koskoff, Ellen, ed. *The Garland Encyclopedia of World Music: Vol. 3, The United States and Canada*. New York and London: Garland Publishing, 2001.

Kualapai, Lydia. "The Queen Writes Back: Lili'uokalani's Hawaii's Story by Hawaii's Queen." *Studies in American Indian Literatures*, Series 2, Vol. 17, No. 2, Honoring A. Lavonne Brown Ruoff, Summer 2005, pp. 32–62. Published by University of Nebraska Press.

Kubik, Gerhard. "Africa." In *Grove Music Online. Oxford Music Online*, accessed June 12, 2012, http://www.oxfordmusiconline.com/subscriber/article/grove/music/00268.

Kubik, Gerhard. "Kwela." In *Grove Music Online. Oxford Music Online*. Oxford University Press, accessed June 22, 2016, http://www.oxfordmusiconline.com/subscriber/article/grove/music/15727.

Ku'uleialoha Stillman, Amy. "Not All Hula Songs Are Created Equal: Reading the Historical Nature of Repertoire in Polynesia." *Yearbook for Traditional Music*, Vol. 27, 1995, pp. 1–12.

Linda, Solomon. "Mbube." Recorded by Gallo Records, 1939.

Linford, Scott V. "Historical Narratives of the Akonting and Banjo," in the online Ethnomusicology Review, history submitted July 27, 2014, accessed July 5, 2016, http://ethnomusicologyreview.ucla.edu/content/akonting history.

Makeba, Miriam, with James Hall. *Makeba: My Story*. Markham, Ontario: Penguin Books Canada LTD, 1987.

Mandela, Nelson. *Long Walk to Freedom*. Randburg, South Africa: Macdonald Purnell, 1994.

Marett, Allan et al. "Australia." *Grove Music Online. Oxford Music Online*, accessed June 5, 2012, http://www.oxfordmusiconline.com/subscriber/article/grove/music/40021.

Mattshikiza, Todd, Pat Williams, and Harry Bloom. *King Kong*. African jazz opera, West End Productions, 1959.

McDonald, David A. *My Voice is My Weapon: Music, Nationalism, and the Poetics of Palestinian Resistance*. Durham and London, NC: Duke University Press, 2013.

McDonald, Simon. *Traditional Singers and Musicians in Victoria*. Wattle LP, 1962.

McKinnon, James W., and Robert Anderson. "Sistrum." In *Grove Music Online. Oxford Music Online*. Oxford University Press, accessed July 11, 2016, http://www.oxfordmusiconline.com/subscriber/article/grove/music/25899.

McLean, Mervyn. *Weavers of Song: Polynesian Music & Dance*. Honolulu: University of Hawaii Press, 1999.

Mensah, Atta, and Gregory F. Barz. "Highlife." In *Grove Music Online. Oxford Music Online*. Oxford University Press, accessed May 24, 2016, http://www.oxfordmusiconline.com/subscriber/article/grove/music/13000.

Miller, Terry E., and Andrew Shahriari. *World Music: A Global Journey*, 2nd ed. New York: Routledge, 2009.

Mirelman, Sam. "New Developments in the Social History of Music and Musicians in Ancient Iraq, Syria, and Turkey," *Yearbook for Traditional Music*, Vol. 41 (2009), pp. 12–22.

Mitchell, Doug. *Stopping the Music: A Story of Censorship in Apartheid South Africa*. A Cutting Grooves Production, 2002.

Montagu, Jeremy. "Shofar." In *Grove Music Online. Oxford Music Online*. Oxford University Press, accessed August 1, 2016, http://www.oxfordmusiconline.com/subscriber/article/grove/music/25658.

Morley, Iain. *The Prehistory of Music: Human Evolution, Archaeology, and the Origins of Musicality*. Oxford: Oxford University Press, 2013.

Moyle, Alice M., and Stephen A. Wild. "Corroboree." In *Grove Music Online. Oxford Music Online*, accessed June 6, 2012, http://www.oxfordmusiconline.com/subscriber/article/grove/music/06567.

Muller, Carol. "A Guide to African Music: A Music of Encounters." *South African Music: A Century of Traditions in Transformation*, pp. 247–252. Santa Barbara, CA: ABC-CLIO, 2004.

_____. *Listening to World Music*, Coursera course, August, 2012, https://www.coursera.org.

Nagatomo, Shigenori, "Japanese Zen Buddhist Philosophy." In *The Stanford Encyclopedia of Philosophy* (Spring 2016 Edition), Edward N. Zalta (ed.), http://plato.stanford.edu/archives/spr2016/entries/japanese-zen/.

N'Dour, Youssou. *Egypt*. Nonesuch. Audio CD. 2004.

Nettl, Bruno, Charles Capwell, Isabel K. F. Wong, Thomas Turino, Philip V. Bohlman, and Timothy Rommen. *Excursions in World Music*, 5th ed. Englewood Cliffs, NJ: Pearson Prentice Hall, 2008.

Nettl, Bruno et al. "Amerindian music." In *Grove Music Online. Oxford Music Online*, accessed April 29, 2012, http://www.oxfordmusiconline.com/subscriber/article/grove/music/45405.

_____ *Folk and Traditional Music of the Western Continents*. Englewood Cliffs, NJ: Prentice Hall, 1965.

_____ *Music in Primitive Culture*. Cambridge, MA: Harvard University Press, 1956.

Nettl, Bruno, Charles Capwell, Isabel K. F. Wong, Thomas Turino, Philip V. Bohlman, and Timothy Rommen. *Excursions in World Music*, 5th ed. New Jersey: Pearson Prentice Hall, 2008.

Neubauer, Eckhard, and Veronica Doubleday. "Islamic religious music." In *Grove Music Online. Oxford Music Online*, accessed June 20, 2012, http://www.oxfordmusiconline.com/subscriber/article/grove/music/52787.

Ngema, Mbongeni. *Sarafina!* South African musical; premiered in Johannesburg, South Africa, in 1987 and on Broadway in 1988.

Nidel, Richard. "Australia and the South Pacific." *World Music*. New York: Taylor & Francis Group LLC, 2005, pp. 351–360.

Odell, Jay Scott. "Banjo." In *Grove Music Online. Oxford Music Online*. Oxford University Press, accessed May 22, 2016, http://www.oxfordmusiconline.com/subscriber/article/grove/music/A2256043.

O'Loughlin, Marjorie. "Listening, Heeding, and Respecting the Ground at One's Feet: Knowledge and the Arts Across Cultures." *Philosophy of Music Education Review*, Vol. 5, No. 1, Spring 1997, pp. 14–24. Published by Indiana University Press.

Peña, Manuel. "Música Fronteriza/Border Music" from *Aztlán: A Journal of Chicano Studies*, vol. 21, nos. 1–2, pp. 191–225, UCLA Chicano Studies Research Center.

Perseus Digital Library, Gregory R. Crane, Editor-in-chief, Tufts University, accessed August 13, 2016, http://www.perseus.tufts.edu/hopper/text?doc=Perseus%3Atext%3A1999.01.0166%3Abook%3D2%3Apage%3D657.

Poché, Christian. "'Ūd." *Grove Music Online. Oxford Music Online*. Oxford University Press, accessed August 15, 2016, http://www.oxfordmusiconline.com/subscriber/article/grove/music/28694.

Provine, Robert C., Yosihiko Tokumaru, and J. Lawrence Witzleben. *Garland Encyclopedia of World Music* Volume 7—East Asia: China, Japan, and Korea: Part 4 Japan: Section 1 Issues and Processes in Japanese Music, Taylor & Francis Group. New York: Routledge, 2001).

Reck, David R. "Beatles Orientalis: Influences from Asia in a Popular Song Tradition." *Asian Music*, University of Texas Press, Vol. 16, No. 1. 1985, pp. 83–149.

Roberts, Janet. "Enheduanna, Daughter of King Sargon: Princess, Poet, Priestess (2300 B.C.)." *Journale de Estudios Orientales*, transoxiana 8—Junio 2004, http://www.transoxiana.org/0108/index08.html.

Robertson, Carolina, and Gerard Béhague. "Latin America." *Grove Music Online. Oxford Music Online*, accessed April 30, 2012, http://www.oxfordmusiconline.com/subscriber/article/grove/music/16072.

Rogosin, Lionel. *Come Back, Africa*. Documentary DVD. Milestone Films, 1959.

Romero, Brenda Mae. "The Matachines Music and Dance in San Juan Pueblo and Alcalde, New Mexico: Contexts and Meanings." PhD Dissertation, University of California, Los Angeles, 1993.

Salloum, Jacqueline, producer and director. *Slingshot Hip-Hop*, DVD. 2005.

Schaffer, Matt. "The Mandinka Legacy in the New World." *History in Africa*, Vol 32. Cambridge University Press, 2005, pp. 321–369.

Seroussi, Edwin et al. "Jewish Music." *Grove Music Online. Oxford Music Online*. Oxford University Press, accessed August 1, 2016, http://www.oxfordmusiconline.com/subscriber/article/grove/music/41322pg3.

Shahriari, Andrew. "Afropop." *Exploring Popular World Music*, Chapter 7. Pearson, 2011, pp. 128–149.

Shain, Richard M. "The Re(Public) of Salsa: Afro-Cuban Music in Fin-De-Siècle Dakar." *Africa: Journal of the International African Institute*, Vol. 79, No. 2, 2009, pp. 186–206. Published by Cambridge University Press on behalf of the International African Institute.

_____. "Roots in Reverse: Cubanismo in Twentieth-Century Senegalese Music." *The International Journal of African Historical Studies*, Vol 35, No. 1, Special Issue: Leisure in African History (2002), pp. 83–101. Published by Boston University African Studies Center.

Shankar, Ravi. *My Music, My Life*. San Rafael, CA: Mandala Publishing, 1968, 2007.

Shelemay, Kay Kaufman. *Soundscapes: Exploring Music in a Changing World*, 1st ed. New York, London: W. W. Norton & Co., 2001.

Shibata, Minao, and Masakata Kanazawa. "Suzuki, Shin'ichi." *Grove Music Online. Oxford Music Online*. Oxford University Press, accessed September 11, 2016, http://www.oxfordmusiconline.com/subscriber/article/grove/music/27166.

Shoup, John. "Pop Music and Resistance in Apartheid South Africa." Alif: *Journal of Comparative Poetics*, No. 17, Literature and Anthropology in Africa, 1997, pp. 73–92. Published by Department of English and Comparative Literature, American University in Cairo and American University in Cairo Press.

Slawek, Stephen. "Shankar, Ravi." *Grove Music Online. Oxford Music Online*. Oxford University Press, accessed September 2, 2016, http://www.oxfordmusiconline.com/subscriber/article/grove/music/25580.

Smith, Barbara B. et al. "Polynesia." *Grove Music Online. Oxford Music Online*, accessed June 8, 2012, http://www.oxfordmusiconline.com/subscriber/article/grove/music/41191.

South African Government, website, accessed June 29, 2016, http://www.gov.za/about-sa/national-symbols/national-anthem.

Stone, Ruth M., ed. "Africa." *The Garland Encyclopedia of World Music*. New York and London: Garland Publishing, Inc., 1998.

_____, ed. "Popular Music in South Africa." *Garland Encyclopedia of World Music*, Volume 1: Africa. New York: Routledge, 2002, pp. 775–96, accessed March 26, 2016, http://search.alexanderstreet.com/view/work/1000224740.

Strehlow, T. G. H. "Australian Aboriginal Songs. *Journal of the International Folk Music Council*, Vol. 7, 1955, pp. 37–40.

Strom, Yale. *The Book of Klezmer: The History, the Music, the Folklore*. Chicago: Chicago Review Press, Inc., 2002.

Suzuki Association of the Americas, website, https://suzukiassociation.org.

Suzuki, Shinichi. *Nurtured By Love: A New Approach to Education*. Translated by Waltraud Suzuki. New York: Exposition Press, 1969.

Tang, Patricia. ""Rhythmic Transformations in Senegalese Sabar." *Ethnomusicology*, Vol. 52, No. 1, Winter, 2008, pp. 85–97. Published by University of Illinois Press on behalf of Society for Ethnomusicology.

Thomas, David. "A Wise Man Keeps on Singing." *The Telegraph*, June 27, 2002. Published by the Telegraph Media Group.

Tignor, Robert, Jeremy Adelman, Peter Brown, Benjamin Elman, Xinru Liu, Holly Pittman, and Brent Shaw. *Worlds Together, Worlds Apart: A History of the World: From the beginnings of Humankind to the Present,* 3rd ed. New York: W. W. Norton, 2010.

Tokens, The. "The Lion Sleeps Tonight." Recorded by RCA Records, 1961.

Touma, Habib Hassan. *The Music of the Arabs.* Portland, Oregon: Hal Leonard Corporation, 2003.

Vasarhelyi, Elizabeth Chai. *Youssour N'Dour: I Bring What I Love.* Groovy Griot in Association with 57th & Irving Productions, 2008. Documentary film.

Verster, François. *A Lion's Trail.* PBS documentary, 2002.

Vetter, Roger. *Rhythms of Life, Songs of Wisdom.* CD Booklet. Smithsonian Folkways SF CD 40463, 1996.

Walt Disney Company, The. *The Lion King,* animated feature film, 1994.

Waterman, Christopher A. "Jùjú." *Grove Music Online. Oxford Music Online.* Oxford University Press, accessed May 26, 2016, http://www.oxfordmusiconline.com/subscriber/article/grove/music/40959.

Weavers, The. "Wimoweh." Possibly recorded by Decca, 1951.

Yarshater, Ehsan. *Encyclopedia Iranica.* New York City: London: Columbia University, accessed October 15, 2016, http://www.iranicaonline.org/articles/music-history-i-pre-islamic-iran.

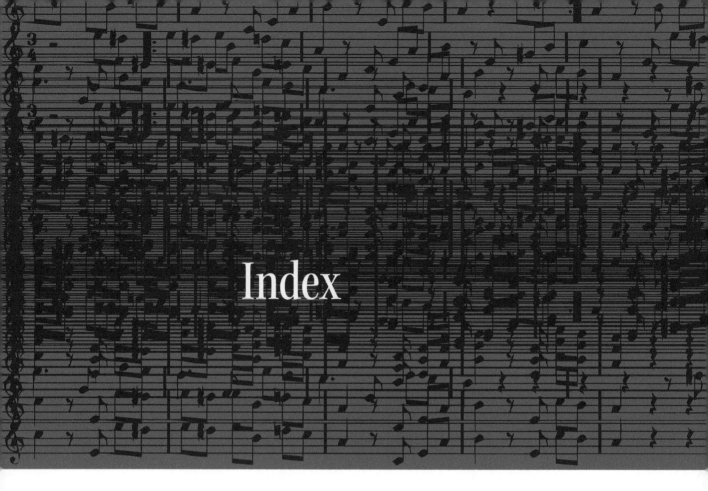

Index

C